DEEPLY DIVIDED

DEEPLY DIVIDED

RACIAL POLITICS AND
SOCIAL MOVEMENTS
IN POSTWAR AMERICA

DOUG McADAM
KARINA KLOOS

OXFORD
UNIVERSITY PRESS

OXFORD
UNIVERSITY PRESS

Oxford University Press is a department of the
University of Oxford. It furthers the University's objective
of excellence in research, scholarship, and education
by publishing worldwide.

Oxford   New York

Auckland   Cape Town   Dar es Salaam   Hong Kong   Karachi
Kuala Lumpur   Madrid   Melbourne   Mexico City   Nairobi
New Delhi   Shanghai   Taipei   Toronto

With offices in

Argentina   Austria   Brazil   Chile   Czech Republic   France   Greece
Guatemala   Hungary   Italy   Japan   Poland   Portugal   Singapore
South Korea   Switzerland   Thailand   Turkey   Ukraine   Vietnam

Published in the United States of America by
Oxford University Press
198 Madison Avenue, New York, NY 10016

© Oxford University Press 2014

Library of Congress Cataloging-in-Publication Data
McAdam, Doug.
Deeply divided : racial politics and social movements
in Postwar America / Doug McAdam and Karina Kloos.
pages cm
Includes bibliographical references and index.
ISBN 978-0-19-993785-1 (hardcover : alk. paper)
1. Democracy—United States.   2. Equality—United States.   3. United States—Politics and
government.   4. United States—Social conditions.   5. Political parties—United States.
6. Divided government—United States.   I. Kloos, Karina.   II. Title.
JK1726.M397 2014
320.973—dc23
2014000094

3 5 7 9 8 6 4 2

Printed in the United States of America
on acid-free paper

CONTENTS

ACKNOWLEDGMENTS

By the time the author of any book collapses across the finish line and sends their manuscript off to the publisher, they are bound to feel a lot like Blanche DuBois and to be fully mindful of how much they have come to "depend on the kindness of strangers" to produce the book in question.

This is even truer in our case, given the breadth of scholarship we have sought to synthesize in the book. Our research has taken us far afield from our home discipline of sociology and obliged us to engage with bodies of work in political science, history, and economics, to name just the three most important "other" disciplines that have shaped our understanding of the period and the change processes that are the focus of the book. Given the synthetic nature of the project, perhaps the greatest debt we owe is to the many "strangers" in these other fields who have been so generous with their time, their expertise, and in some cases, their data. It would, in particular, be hard to overstate the importance of the help and advice we have received from a veritable who's who of political scientists in the area of American politics. These include: Larry Bartels, Robert Erikson, Mo Fiorina, Shigeo Hirano, David Mayhew, Nolan McCarty, Josh Pasek, Keith Poole, Howard Rosenthal, Dorian Warren, and John Zaller.

But we're just getting started. A host of scholars from other disciplines and fields of study helped shape the book as well. These would include: Thomas Piketty, who, before becoming the most famous social scientist on the planet, generously shared with us the time series data on income inequality that he and Emmanuel Saez had painstakingly compiled over the last decade or so; David Grusky, Sean Reardon, and Don Barr, who gave us invaluable advice and feedback on our extended discussion of the trends in inequality in the United States over the past 3–4 decades; Barry Eidlin, who deepened our understanding of the comparative decline of unions in the United States and Canada since 1970; Adam Bonica, who generously shared data and the latest findings from his innovative research on the partisan impact of the 2010 midterm elections; Andrew Cherlin, who educated us on the key economic dynamics of the postwar period; Abby Scher, who alerted us to the literature on right wing activism—especially women's activism—in the postwar period; Monica Prasad, who shared her deep knowledge of the Reagan presidency and especially the substantive influences that shaped the president's tax and fiscal policies during his first year in office; and finally Sid Tarrow, who was kind enough to read and comment on the entire manuscript for us.

Then there were groups of scholars who gave us critical feedback on parts of the manuscript, at two especially important junctures in the life of the project. The first was the Political Sociology Workshop at Stanford which read very early drafts of the first two chapters of the book and whose feedback helped to shape the manuscript at that formative stage of the project. To the members of that seminar—including Susan Olzak, Andy Walder, Gi-wook Shin, Priya Fielding-Singh, Jennifer Hill, Rachel Wright, Rachel Gong, Marion Coddou, Brian Cook, Ryan Leupp, John Munoz, Nandini Roy, and Jeffrey Sheng—we offer our sincere thanks.

The second group intervened at the other end of the creative process, after the first author had taken up residence at Russell Sage in New York and was struggling to revise the last two chapters of the book. Fortunately, he was able to prevail upon some of his extraordinary "classmates" at Russell Sage to read and talk through the revisions of these especially tricky chapters with him. For their especially timely intervention and feedback, we are grateful to: Robert Erikson, Cybelle Fox, Lee Ann Fujii, Shigeo Hirano, Belinda Robnett, and Caitlin Zaloom.

Our debt to the Russell Sage Foundation, however, goes far beyond the intellectual input we received from the aforementioned group of scholars. Quite simply, it would be hard to imagine a more stimulating, more facilitative, more encouraging, setting in which to bring a book project to a close. While we are deeply grateful to the entire staff for all they did to make the first author's year at the Foundation so productive and enjoyable, we want to single out a few staff for special thanks. We are especially beholden to: Claire Gabriel and the rest of the staff of Information Services, for the extraordinary support they gave us with various aspects of the research process; to Galo Falchettore and Kunwal Nasrullah for their superb technical help in the production of some of the figures used in the book; and, most importantly, to the Foundation's new president, Sheldon Danziger, for running the overall show with his unique combination of administrative efficiency, personal charm, and intellectual incisiveness.

It would also be hard to imagine a more supportive staff at a publishing house. Peter Worger orchestrated the entire production process with exemplary speed and efficiency. But it was the extraordinary attention and support accorded the book by our editor, James Cook, that is especially noteworthy. Not only was James a source of sage advice on the project from beginning to end, but he also read and commented on every page of the manuscript. In the current era of academic publishing, we doubt many other authors could make the same claim.

We close on a more personal note. Books, as all authors know, depend not just on the "kindness of strangers" but also the forbearance of those special others whose lives are impacted by the crazy hours, wild mood swings, and other demands of the book process. Accordingly, to our families and close friends, we offer our deepest thanks for your patience, support, and yes, forbearance, throughout the four-year process that birthed the book. Finally, a special thanks to Mary Noble for early stages of editing, and to Jason Yeatman for technical expertise, to say nothing of ongoing moral support and lots of shared celebrations.

DEEPLY
DIVIDED

I

How Did We Get into This Mess?

WHEN BARACK OBAMA CAPTURED THE WHITE HOUSE IN 2008, many heralded his victory as marking the long overdue onset of color-blind politics in America. As National Public Radio (NPR) reported, "*The Economist* called it a post-racial triumph... [and] the *New Yorker* wrote of a post-racial generation."[1] Even John McCain, just after his presidential loss to Obama, declared that "America today is a world away from the cruel and prideful bigotry of [a century ago]. There is no better evidence of this than the election of an African American to the presidency of the United States."[2] Sadly, the widely advertised post-racial society never quite materialized. Indeed, a growing body of evidence suggests that, if anything, the influence of what Tesler calls "old fashioned racism" has grown considerably since Obama took office.[3]

Furthermore, those hoping that Obama's presidency would begin to moderate the extreme partisan tensions of the Bill Clinton and George W. Bush years and perhaps even bring about greater economic equality have been disappointed. The harsh reality is that for all its historic significance, Obama's presidency has done little to reduce the country's underlying racial, political, and economic divisions. America's racial politics—its history no less than its contemporary manifestations—will come in for a great deal of attention in this book. We begin, however, by considering these other two central features, the extreme economic inequality and unprecedented partisan polarization that mark contemporary America. The country is now more starkly divided in political terms than at any time since the end of Reconstruction and more unequal in material terms than roughly a century ago and greater, even, than on the eve of the Great Depression.

In Figure 1.1 we use research by two economists, Thomas Pikkety and Emmanuel Saez, on income inequality to map fluctuations in the economic gap between America's haves and have nots since 1913, which is as far back as the data go. Figure 1.2 shifts the focus from economics to politics. For better than 30 years, political scientists Keith Poole and Howard Rosenthal have refined the analysis of congressional voting into something of an art. Using their spatial model of voting, they have been able for the entire history of Congress to map the left/right oscillations in both the House and Senate and to assess just how ideologically close or far apart the two parties have been at any point in our history. Using the Poole and Rosenthal data, Figure 1.2 maps partisan polarization in Congress since 1879.

Figure 1.2 confirms the deep political divisions that characterize the present-day United States. In truth, we probably didn't need the Poole-Rosenthal data to know just how divided we now are. The events of the past six years—serial budget crises, government shutdown, willful sabotage of presidential appointments, and so on—have told us all we

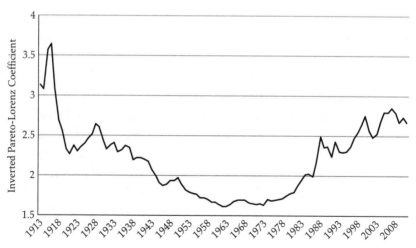

Figure 1.1 Income Inequality, 1913–2012
Source: The World Top Incomes Database, Piketty and Saez (2007)

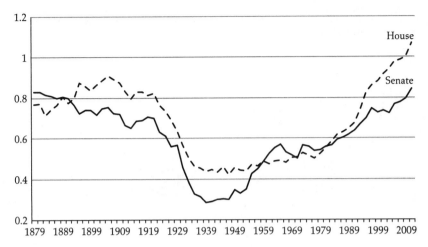

Figure 1.2 Political Polarization, 1879–2012
Source: Polarized America / voteview.com

need to know about escalating paralysis and government dysfunction. Just how bad has it gotten? Consider that as of October 2013, one in three Americans identified government dysfunction as the "most important problem" confronting the country.[4] While the percentage of subjects concurring in this judgment had increased steadily over the course of the Obama presidency, never before had a plurality of respondents identified "government/Congress, politicians" as the country's most pressing problem. This finding coupled with a close examination of the last few years of the Poole-Rosenthal time series highlight the sad reality: far from waning, partisan polarization has escalated sharply since Obama took office. The same is true for economic inequality. A growing body of studies now confirms that income inequality has also increased significantly on Obama's watch.[5]

There is another important point to be made as well. The two trend lines closely mirror each other. If it looks like the two trends are related, it's because, as shown in Figure 1.3, they are.[6] The growing partisan divide has, we will argue, been one of the principal engines of rising economic inequality over the past three to four decades.

We will devote a great deal of attention to these two defining features—political division and economic inequality—of the contemporary American political economy, documenting both and assessing the links between them. As the title of the chapter suggests, however, the central

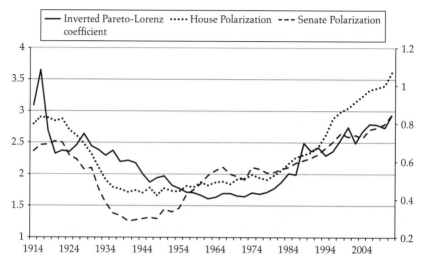

Figure 1.3 Income Inequality and Political Partisanship, 1913–2012
Sources: The World Top Incomes Database, Piketty and Saez (2007); Polarized America/ voteview

question that motivates the book is about *origins* and the complex history of American politics since roughly the onset of World War II. How did we go from the striking bipartisan cooperation and relative economic equality of the war years and postwar period—clearly reflected in the figures shown previously—to the extreme inequality and savage partisan divisions of today? We offer a stylized answer to that question in this first chapter, devoting the balance of the book to a detailed historical narrative designed to document and elaborate the broad brushstroke account offered here.

On Parties, Movements, and the Rise and Fall of the Median Voter

In recent years, a growing chorus of political commentators has lamented the absence of anything resembling a bipartisan "middle" in American politics. What a difference a few decades make. While it is now commonplace for political analysts and observers to celebrate the strong, bipartisan consensus that prevailed in the postwar period, there were those at the time who saw the dominance of moderates in both parties as a kind of tyranny of the middle. In 1950, the American Political Science Association issued a report entitled "Toward a More

Responsible Two-Party System" that identified the ideological sameness of the two parties as the central problem of American democracy.[7] More colorfully, George Wallace explained his third party challenge to Nixon and Humphrey in 1968 in very similar terms. Said Wallace: "there is not a dime's worth of difference between the Democrat and Republican parties!"

Whatever one's normative take on the centrist tendencies of the era, the received wisdom among contemporary scholars was that the two party, winner-take-all structure of the American system virtually compelled candidates—especially presidential nominees—to hue to the center if they hoped to be elected. In his influential 1957 book, *An Economic Theory of Democracy*, Anthony Downs argued that in a two-party system candidates could be expected to "rapidly converge" on the center of the ideological spectrum "so that parties closely resemble one another." Introduced a year later, Duncan Black's Median Voter Theorem represented a highly compatible, if more formalized, version of Downs's "convergence" theory. For several decades thereafter this general model of voting was thought of as akin to a natural law when it came to US politics, especially in elections involving large numbers of voters. Since the ideological preferences of voters were assumed to be distributed normally around a moderate midpoint, any candidate adopting a comparatively extreme position on the liberal to conservative continuum would seem to be easy prey for a more centrist candidate. Not only was the theory appealingly parsimonious, but it also seemed to accord with the available real-world "data." When Downs and Black offered their versions of the theory, Eisenhower—the quintessential moderate Republican—was in office. Both candidates in the 1960 race—Kennedy and Nixon—were moderates within their respective parties. The same was true in 1968, when, as Wallace complained, the general ideological positions of the nominees of the two major parties seemed largely indistinguishable. But perhaps the most powerful affirmations of the theory came in 1964 and 1972 when the decidedly conservative and liberal candidates, Barry Goldwater and George McGovern, respectively, were soundly trounced by their more moderate opponents (Lyndon Johnson in 1964 and Nixon in 1972). In short, the theory seemed pretty nigh incontrovertible: the median voter could be counted on to punish any candidate crazy enough to assume an extreme partisan position. Or to use Cox's useful distinction, "centripetal" pressures seemed to be far more influential to the workings of the US electoral system than "centrifugal."[8]

Reagan's victory in 1980, however, was much harder to square with this view, as was the growing body of empirical evidence attesting to increasing polarization between party elites and activists during the 1980s and even more so, the 1990s. By the mid- to late 1990s, campaign strategists and political journalists were routinely acknowledging the brave new world of extreme partisan politics.[9] Consider the following representative comments of election analysts in advance of the 1998 midterm elections:

> As they gear up for the election, Republicans and Democrats are operating on the premise that turnout will be low and the outcome will be determined by partisan activists. Consequently, GOP leaders intent on revving up the party's conservative base are about to serve up as much red meat as a Kansas City steak house.[10]

> Even if there is a backlash against [Paul] Starr, Republicans don't really care. They are not focused on swing voters or fence-sitters. Their strategy for the fall is clear and calculating: appeal to the hard-core Republican base. Get them as outraged as possible. Make sure they give money and vote heavily.[11]

Scholars too acknowledged just how far we had come from the reassuring centrist logic of the "median voter theorem." Fiorina captured the emerging consensus when he asked:

> Whatever happened to the median voter? Rather than attempt to move her "off the fence" or "swing" her from one party to another, today's campaigners seem to be ignoring her. Instead, they see their task as making sure that strong partisans and ideologues don't pout and stay home. Why has a model of centrist politics that seemed like an appropriate description of American politics in the 1950s and even the 1960s become an inappropriate model by the 1990s?[12]

The central puzzle for us is how did we get from the seeming "natural law" of the median voter theorem to the decisive power wielded by ideological extremists, as exemplified by today's Republican Party? There is now a substantial literature—rooted in scholarship, but much of it written for a popular audience—that purports to answer this question. The problem is that the literature focuses almost all of its attention on the shifting fortunes of the two major parties and the vagaries of electoral politics. Its main storylines include the loss of the white South by the Democrats in the 1960s, Nixon's success in wooing disaffected Dixiecrats in 1968 via his "southern strategy," and the thunder on the right of the Reagan Revolution of the 1980s. These are critically important parts of the broader story and, as such, will come in for a great deal of attention in later chapters. The lacuna is not what the literature focuses on but what it almost always omits. The omission reflects a long-standing, if unfortunate, disciplinary division of labor when it comes to the analysis of American politics. In general, the otherwise impressive literature on the development of today's distinctive US political economy has been impoverished by its almost total neglect of social movement dynamics. Yes, the electoral realignment of the South occasioned a tectonic shift in American politics and moved both parties substantially off center politically. And yes, Reagan's two-term presidency not only deepened partisan divisions but also accelerated the economic trends that have left us so fundamentally unequal today. But to represent these features of the present-day political economy as byproducts of party politics alone—which is what most scholarly accounts tend to do—is to badly distort the more complicated origins of the mess in which we find ourselves. All of these features of contemporary US politics have been—and continue to be—powerfully shaped by the interaction of movements, parties, and governmental institutions. The best scholarly work on contemporary American politics continues to be done by political scientists, but reflecting the aforementioned disciplinary divide, political scientists tend to focus their attention exclusively on political parties and institutions and leave the study of social movements or other forms of noninstitutionalized politics to sociologists.[13] This means that the crucial role played by social movements in the evolution of the American political economy since the 1960s has been almost completely neglected in even the best work on the topic.[14] This book is our attempt to at least partially redress this glaring omission. Besides fashioning a fuller account of the origins of today's divided America, we also hope this perspective will aid in explaining the challenges we will need to confront if we are to overcome these divisions.

We begin with a stark theoretical claim: the convergence perspective of Downs and Black (among others) only holds under conditions of general social movement quiescence. If we are right in this claim, it carries with it important empirical implications for an understanding of the extent of bipartisan consensus in the postwar period as well as the collapse of that consensus and the increasing polarization that has followed. Owing in large part to the "chilling effect" of the Cold War and McCarthyism, the immediate postwar period was uniquely devoid of significant social movement activity. This spared the two parties the centrifugal pressures that *can* follow when mobilized movement elements seek to occupy their ideological flanks. We have highlighted the word "can" in the previous sentence to call attention to an important caveat. In arguing that social movements *can* push parties off center, we are certainly not saying they will. The vast majority of social movements exert little or no effect on parties. In truth, most movements have no interest in engaging with parties or national politics more generally. And the great majority of those that do fail to achieve the kind of standing or sustained presence on the national scene necessary to exercise influence over either or both of the two major parties. But there are movements that do, and when they do, they greatly complicate the relatively straightforward strategic calculus articulated by the likes of Downs and Black. The Tea Party movement affords a clear contemporary example of the phenomenon. Much as Mitt Romney and his advisers might have wanted to hew to the moderate center of the ideological distribution during the 2012 presidential race, the threat of the mobilized Tea Party wing of the GOP (Republican Party)—coupled with the low voter turnout characteristic of the current primary system—effectively denied them this option. When challenged by sustained, national movements attuned to electoral politics, "playing to the base" can come to be seen as more important strategically than courting the "median voter."

By revitalizing and legitimating the social movement form, the civil rights movement of the early 1960s reintroduced these centrifugal pressures to American politics. Or more accurately, it was one movement— civil rights—and one powerful *countermovement*—white resistance or as we prefer, "white backlash"—that began to force the parties to weigh the costs and benefits of appealing to the median voter against the strategic imperative of responding to mobilized movement elements at their ideological margins. Owing in part to the tight control they exercised over national conventions and the selection of presidential candidates, the parties were able to manage these pressures for a while, but this became increasingly more difficult with the convention and primary reforms of the early 1970s. To fully appreciate the difficulties the two parties have had in managing these pressures is to begin to understand just how we got from the centripetal pressure of the medium voter to the centrifugal force of today's extreme partisanship. A full accounting of that story is the task we set for ourselves in the book. We begin, however, with an extended aside regarding the relatively narrow face of polarization in the contemporary United States. Quite simply, as we document in the next section, the deep partisan divide that characterizes today's Congress, party activists, and other political elites is typically *not* mirrored in the general public. Quite the opposite: the general public has remained largely centrist in its views, while the parties—especially the GOP—and their candidates have been pushed off center. It is the dynamic interaction of movements and parties, in our view, that has been doing the "pushing."

The Narrow Face of Partisan Polarization

Scholars first began to report evidence of growing political polarization in the United States in the 1980s. This research, however, focused overwhelmingly on growing divisions among political elites and party activists. So, for example, in 1984 Poole and Rosenthal offered compelling evidence of increasing partisan polarization in both houses of Congress. Around the same time, scholars began to take note of the more extreme ideological character of party activists compared to the general public and primary voters relative to all registered voters.[15] Systematic empirical work on the topic of *mass* polarization, however, took much longer to appear. And when it did, it offered a stark contrast to the work on elite polarization. Given the preoccupation of political scientists with political institutions, it is perhaps not surprising that sociologists were the first to call attention to the disconnect between elite and mass trends in this regard. Writing in 1996, sociologists Paul DiMaggio, John Evans, and Bethany Bryson sought to answer the stark question posed in the title of their article: "Have Americans' Social Attitudes Become More Polarized?" Based on exhaustive analyses of General Social Survey (GSS) and American National Election Studies (ANES) data, their conclusion was unequivocal: "we find no support for the proposition that the United States has experienced a dramatic polarization in public opinion on social issues since the 1970s."[16] Seven years later, Evans extended the analysis using the 2002 GSS and ANES data, and reached the same general conclusion. Even after the divisive and controversial 2000 election that brought George W. Bush to power, Evans found little evidence of increasing *mass* polarization in the United States.

If political scientists were slow to research the topic, they have made up for lost time in the last decade or so.[17] Morris Fiorina was among the first to take up the issue and, from our assessment of the empirical evidence, has produced—with several colleagues—perhaps the most substantial body of work on the topic.[18] In their 2008 review, Fiorina and Abrams summarize the various strands of empirical evidence that have been adduced regarding the matter. Regardless of whether one looks at changes over time in the response of the general public to particular issues or more global ideological positions, the conclusion remains the same. As Fiorina and Abrams put it: "the most direct evidence. . . . shows little or no indication of increased mass polarization over the past two or three decades."[19] We turn now to a brief review of research on these topics.

Issue Polarization—Abramowitz documents remarkable stability in public opinion on six issues about which the ANES has regularly questioned survey respondents since 1984: health insurance, government spending, aid to blacks, defense spending, jobs/standard of living, and abortion.[20] Three aspects of his results are worth highlighting. First, regardless of the issue, ANES respondents have consistently favored moderate, centrist positions over more extreme responses (e.g., liberal or conservative). Second, there has been remarkably little change in the aggregate positions of the respondents on all six issues over time. And third, the ideological direction of what little change has occurred has not been consistent. Of the four issues that show any directionality, two—government spending and health insurance—have shifted leftward, while two others—aid to blacks and defense spending—show slightly more conservative responses over time. It is worth noting that the six issues included in the analysis have been among the most divisive in American public life over the past few decades. In short, the absence of over time polarization cannot be attributed to any lack of controversy when it comes to the issues included in the analysis.

The time series data on the abortion issue affords perhaps the most surprising and, as such, powerful refutation of the idea that the American public has become dramatically more polarized over the last few decades. Figure 1.4 shows the aggregate trend in public opinion on the issue from 1975 to 2013.

No issue has generated anywhere near the vitriol and strong passions as abortion since the *Roe v. Wade* decision was issued in 1973. And yet, despite the strong emotions, notwithstanding the rising tide of violence directed at abortion providers and clinics and the trend toward ever more restrictive state and local legislation, the aggregate views of the American public on the issue have remained essentially unchanged for 30 years. What's more, as the figure shows, the clear modal response to the issue has remained the moderate one; that is, "legal under some circumstances," with somewhere between 50 and 60 percent of survey

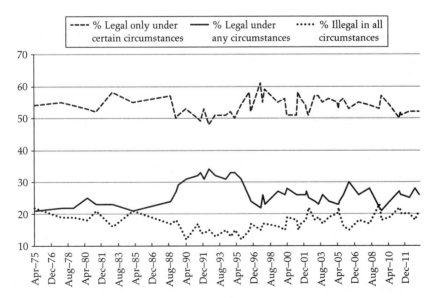

Figure 1.4 Public Opinion on Abortion, 1975–2013
Source: Gallup

respondents favoring this option. The two more extreme, or polarized, positions—legal or illegal "in all circumstances"—have typically been favored by no more than a quarter of all respondents.

Changes in Ideological Orientation—So much for single issues; it could be argued, though, that the better way to look at the issue of polarization is with time series data on changes in the general ideological orientation of the American public. That, after all, is essentially how McCarty, Poole, and Rosenthal have sought to document increasing polarization among members of Congress.[21] Rather than look at any single issue, they have used each member's overall voting record to locate him or her along a single left to right ideological continuum. ANES has measured the overall distribution of ideological orientations in the general public since the early 1970s. The scale runs from "extremely liberal" at one end of the continuum to "extremely conservative" on the other. Using the ANES data, Figure 1.5 maps the aggregate change in ideological identification since the early 1970s.

Needless to say, the results reported here stand in stark contrast to the trend toward increasing polarization among political elites. Indeed, the data are remarkable for the evidence they offer of no trend at all. In two key respects, these data mirror the time series data on abortion reported

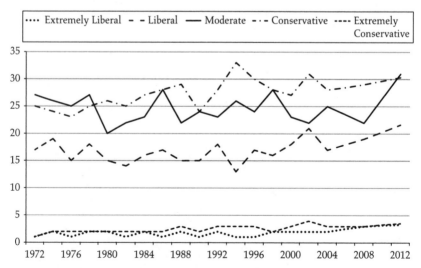

Figure 1.5 Political Identification, 1972–2012
Source: American National Election Studies
*Data for 2006 and 2010 are interpolated

in Figure 1.4. That is, the overall distribution of views has changed very little over the past 40 years, and the majority of Americans continue to embrace the moderate, centrist position when questioned about political matters. Bottom line: regardless of how one measures mass polarization, there is little evidence that it is occurring or at least not at anything like the rate it has been taking place among political elites and activists. Most Americans have remained remarkably consistent and generally moderate in their social and political views even as the partisan divide among political elites and party activists has widened dramatically.

There is, however, one broad category of survey items that *does* show significant change in the political views of the American public over the past three to four decades. We refer to the sharp increase in recent years in public distrust of, and lack of confidence in, elected officials and specific governmental institutions. Figure 1.6 reports the results of yet another item that is fully consistent with the overall master trend.

Figure 1.6 shows just how much public "trust in the federal government" has declined since the early 1960s. In 1964, better than three quarters of those surveyed reported that that they trusted the government to "do the right thing," "just about always," or "most of the time." The comparable percentage for 2012 was just 24 percent.

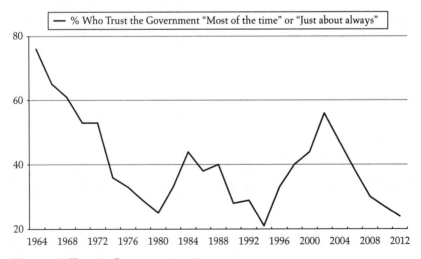

Figure 1.6 Trust in Government, 1964–2012
Source: American National Election Studies
* In 1958, 73% reported high trust in the government; survey not conducted in 1960, 1962, 2006 and 2010; data for 2006 and 2010 are interpolated

It seems entirely reasonable to us to see the growing public distrust of—indeed, disgust with—political elites and governmental institutions as driven, in large measure, by popular opposition to extreme partisanship and the toll it continues to take on effective, responsive governance. That is certainly how we interpret the Gallup "most important problem" survey finding reported earlier. Administered in early October 2013, at the height of the government shutdown, the poll results serve as a stark public rebuke to the crisis and the partisan politics that brought it about. The finding is just the latest in a series of opinion polls documenting the growing disconnect between political elites, elected officials, and the general public. None of these results are perhaps as telling as the time series data amassed by Gallup on the congressional approval rating since Obama took office in January of 2009. Each month Gallup asks its respondents whether they "approve or disapprove of the way Congress is handling its job." The results of these repeated inquiries are shown in Figure 1.7.

Perhaps reflecting the generalized optimism that accompanied Obama's earliest days in office, or the legislative momentum that came with a unified Democratic Congress, nearly 40 percent of those surveyed in early 2009 "approved" of the way Congress was discharging its responsibilities. The numbers dropped quickly, however, as the partisan reality in Congress set in and declined even further after 2010 as

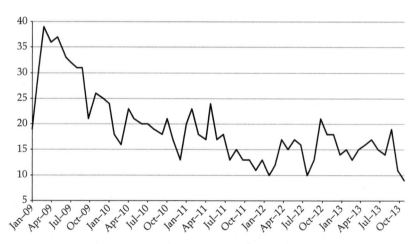

Figure 1.7 Congressional Approval, 2009–2013
Source: Gallup

the GOP's capture of the House made legislative gridlock the norm in Washington. The nadir came on the heels of the government shutdown when just 9 percent of respondents gave Congress a passing grade, a historic low. From a 39 to a 9 percent approval rating in less than five years: is it any wonder that Americans now regard the dysfunction in Washington as the nation's number one problem?

Solving the "Convergence" Puzzle: The Rise of Movement Politics and the Marginalization of the Medium Voter

The data reviewed in the previous section presents a serious puzzle, at least when viewed from the traditional convergence perspective. If the general public does not share the extreme partisan views of the political elites and party activists and, more to the point, is increasingly dismayed and disgusted by the resulting polarization and institutional paralysis that have followed from those views, how has the GOP managed to move so far to the right without being punished by the voters? Our answer—already telegraphed above—is that over the past half century social movements have increasingly challenged, and occasionally supplanted, parties as the dominant mobilizing logic and organizing vehicle of American politics. This is especially true today on the right, where the Republican Party and the policies of its House delegation largely reflect the views of its mobilized movement wing. In short, as movement politics has increasingly challenged the traditional pragmatic, centrist logic of electoral politics, the GOP has come to fear the Party's movement base much more than the increasingly irrelevant "median voter." Indeed, another way to interpret the survey evidence of growing public distrust of government officials and institutions is as an expression of the feelings of anger and frustration that come from being ignored.

The question we take up in the balance of the book is this: how did we get here? How did certain sustained national movements come to successfully challenge the monopolistic influence that parties had exercised over electoral politics in the postwar period? We begin with a brief sketch of the story we take up in earnest in the next chapter. Before we do so, however, we want to make clear that in arguing that movements have emerged in recent decades as a powerful, and sometimes decisive, force in American politics, we are not for a minute suggesting that this is a new development. It may appear this way, but only because we are comparing recent decades to the party-dominated postwar period. It is the postwar era, however, that is the anomaly. Sustained, national movements have interacted with parties (and other actors) to powerfully shape politics throughout US history. The list of significant cases is far too long to take up here. A few examples will have to suffice. None is more important than the case of the abolition movement and the founding of the Republican Party. Though opposed by radical abolitionists, the decision by moderates to pursue their anti-slavery agenda by electoral means led eventually to Lincoln's victory and the single most convulsive event—the Civil War—in the nation's history. It is worth noting that secession was also simultaneously a movement and a party.

Many other significant examples come to mind as well. The GOP is not the only major party with movement roots. The modern Democratic Party was born of the populist ferment of what would come to be known as Jacksonian Democracy. The movements of the Progressive Era powerfully shaped electoral politics at all levels, but perhaps none so much as in cities, where mostly Republican reformers sought to replace Democratic political machines with crusading mayors and/or progressive city managers. In the 1920s, a resurgent Ku Klux Klan developed into a powerful electoral force all over the country, shaping politics and policy, not just in the South but in such unlikely locales as Detroit, Dayton, and Oakland, California.[22] Finally, if Franklin Roosevelt's policies helped to empower organized labor, the labor movement, in turn, quickly emerged as among the key components of the New Deal electoral coalition. In this sense, the New Deal Democrats and the labor movement were mutually constitutive. Indeed, in all of these cases, it distorts reality to represent movements and parties as distinct. Organized labor has been stitched into the fabric of the Democratic Party establishment since the New Deal. Labor leaders functioned simultaneously as movement activists and as key allies of Franklin Delano Roosevelt (FDR) and subsequent Democratic presidents. In these, and many other examples, the line between movements, parties, and governmental institutions blurs, as is the case with today's GOP and the Tea Party movement.

What was so unusual about the immediate postwar period was the relative absence of this normal dynamic synergism between movements, parties, and elected officials. Labor certainly remained central to the Democratic Party in the 1940s and '50s, but it functioned much less like a movement than a pillar of the establishment during this period. Some of this had to do with the sustained prosperity of the era, which served to greatly mute the traditional enmity between capital and labor. But labor's relative quiescence during these years wasn't simply a function of being "bought off;" of apathy born of material comfort. We would do well to remember that the Labor Management Act of 1947—better known as Taft Hartley—powerfully constrained the ability of labor to act as a social movement during the postwar period.

What about other progressive political forces? It is true that the first major campaign of the modern civil rights movement—the Montgomery Bus Boycott—took place during the mid-1950s, but after the initial triumph in Montgomery, the movement lapsed into comparative inactivity in the late 1950s. In any case, as a grass-roots struggle, the movement was very much confined to a handful of southern communities during the decade and not at all the force in national politics it was to become in the early 1960s.

For its part, the Republican Party was also largely devoid of a *significant* movement wing during the postwar period. We need to be careful here. As a number of scholars have noted, there *were* a number of strands of right-wing activism during these years. In her superb 2001 book, *Suburban Warriors*, Lisa McGirr documents the social and regional basis of grass-roots conservative politics in the post-World War II United States. Abby Scher, in her dissertation, focuses specifically on the mobilization of conservative women during the McCarthy era. And Phillips-Fein chronicles the rise of a business counteroffensive to the New Deal that emerged during the 1950s.[23] Relative to the major movements of the 1960s and beyond, however, none of these strands of right wing activism were very large, nor did they deploy the kinds of disruptive tactics that many of the later movements would. Finally, and most importantly, these various manifestations of conservative activism were largely disconnected from the Republican Party.

There is a similar story to be told about conservatism *within* the postwar GOP. Just as there were forms of grass-roots, right-wing activism during these years, there was also no shortage of strident conservatives in the GOP during the era. Indeed, the efforts of GOP conservatives to secure the presidential nomination for their nominal leader, Ohio senator Robert Taft, exposed deep divisions within the party at its conventions in 1940, 1948, and 1952. There was, however, virtually no grass-roots or true *movement* manifestation of conservative Republicanism during these years. The same was true for McCarthyism in the early 1950s. With his sensational charges of communist infiltration of many institutions in American life, at the peak of his power, Joe McCarthy (R-Minnesota) certainly exercised great influence in American politics, but his was a power born of personal ambition and institutional position, not grass-roots movement backing.

Our claim then is not that there was no social movement activity in this period—after all every era boasts some level of activism—but about the relative magnitude of that activity and, more importantly, the extent to which it was manifest to any great degree within the two major parties. It is in this sense that we would be hard pressed to think of another extended period in US history that saw as little significant movement activity as the middle decades of the 20th century. Under these unusual circumstances, parties were largely spared the grass-roots movement pressures so typical of US history and so salient in today's politics. It was the absence of these pressures, we believe, that "enabled" the electoral dynamics accurately depicted by Downs and Black in their respective theories. With no significant centrifugal movement pressures to push them off center, parties were free to hue to the middle and court the "median voter." The absence of significant movement wings probably also helps to explain the healthy ideological overlap in the two parties in the postwar period. Spared the need to move to the right or left to accommodate an extreme movement base, the two parties logically framed their policies to appeal to the moderate center of the ideological continuum, creating all sorts of possibilities for bipartisan cooperation in the process.

This unusual arrangement held for roughly two decades, from 1940 to 1960. The absence of significant movement activity during the war years was attributable, both to the pressure for national unity typical of any wartime emergency, and to the fact that the ideological inspiration for most of the activism of the 1930s—Soviet communism—was now effectively joined to the patriotic war effort by virtue of the alliance between the United States, Great Britain, and the Soviet Union. If our alliance with the USSR helped to mute movement activity during the war, it was the Soviet threat and the chilling effect of McCarthyism that did much to constrain domestic dissent and activism during the immediate postwar era.

It took the revitalized civil rights struggle to restore the normal party-movement dynamism to American politics. And here is where we begin our story. We do so through a stylized recounting of three key "moments" between 1960 and 1972 that simultaneously speak to the return of the movement form *and* its decisive influence on some of the major political changes of the period—changes that are almost always represented in narrowly institutional terms as the work of parties and political elites. Instead, these "moments" speak to the return of the normal tug of war between movements and parties, between grass-roots insurgents and established elites that remain such a central feature of politics in contemporary America.

Besides the tug of war between parties and electorally attuned movements, our story turns centrally on the sustained significance and powerful structuring effect of race and region on American politics. More accurately, it is the *interaction* of these three forces—race, region, and movements—that have overwhelmingly shaped the evolution of American politics from 1960 to the present. We begin with race. Virtually all of the major movements that will take their turn center stage in our narrative—civil rights, white backlash, New Left, Tax Revolt, Christian Right, Tea Party—bear the very strong, if variable, imprint of race. So it is the shifting vagaries of American *racial* politics—channeled and expressed through a series of electorally attuned movements—that will propel much of our narrative forward.

Then there is the matter of region or, more specifically, the disproportionate political and electoral significance of the "solid South" throughout most of the 20th century. But here again, it is the interaction of these factors, not their independent effects, that is the key to our story. Region and race, after all, have long been inextricably linked in the structuring of American politics. Or put another way, it is race that has long accounted for the "solidity" of the South's political/electoral loyalties. It was the white South's hatred of the Republican Party—the despised "party of Lincoln"—that bound the region to the Democrats for nearly a century following the close of Reconstruction. And it was white southern anger at the Democratic Party's embrace of civil rights reform that set in motion the slow but steady process of regional realignment that by the 1990s had made the South the geographic foundation of today's GOP and, importantly, its Tea Party movement wing. In short, the complex interplay between region, race, and movement-party dynamics will continually inform and structure the story we have to tell. To illustrate these themes, we offer brief sketches of the first three "moments" in our story.

Moment 1: *The Revitalized Civil Rights Struggle and the Collapse of the New Deal Coalition*

The standard textbook account of the civil rights struggle holds that it was "born" of Rosa Parks's refusal to give up her seat on that bus in Montgomery in December of 1955 and effectively "died" with the assassination of Martin Luther King Jr. in 1968. Never mind that the Cold War renationalized the "Negro question" well before Montgomery, that northern cities experienced considerable civil rights activity in the 1940s and early 1950s, or that the black power phase of the struggle remained a powerful political and cultural force throughout the 1970s and beyond.[24] There is another fundamental problem with the canonical narrative other than its truncated beginning and ending dates. That is the implicit image of the movement as a powerful, sustained force from Montgomery through at least the late 1960s. It wasn't. Following the high water mark of Montgomery, the movement largely collapsed in the late 1950s under the relentless assault of the segregationist counter-movement that developed in the South in response to the twin threats posed by Montgomery and the Supreme Court decision in *Brown v. Board of Education*. As the 1960s dawned, the movement was largely moribund. It was the 1960 sit-ins that revitalized the struggle and marked the beginning of the movement's heyday—nearly a decade of unrelenting pressure on all of America's institutions, but none so important to us as its legal and two-party electoral systems. Squarely in the crosshairs in this regard was the Democratic Party, which not only controlled Congress and the White House during most of this period but which also had to try to balance the interests of the two exceedingly strange and antagonistic bedfellows—southern segregationists and African Americans—which claimed the party as their home.

The textbook account also errs in typically depicting the Democrats as the movement's staunch ally. What is missed in this account is the lengths to which all Democratic presidents—at least from Roosevelt to Kennedy—went to placate the white South and accommodate the party's Dixiecrat wing. And indeed, prior to the resurgence of the movement in the early 1960s, the Democrats had been largely successful in this. While Congress did pass a weak Civil Rights Act in 1957, the measure relied much more on Republican than Democratic support. It was the confluence of the Cold War and the sustained pressure of the resurgent civil rights struggle that made the Democrats' grudging, cautious stance on the issue ultimately untenable. Occupying the White House during the first half of the 1960s, it was the Democrats who confronted the resurgent civil rights movement during an especially hot phase of the Cold War (think only of the Berlin Wall, the Bay of Pigs, and the Cuban Missile Crisis). Locked into an intense ideological struggle with the Soviet Union for influence around the globe, America's racial "troubles" posed an enormous liability to its foreign policy aims during this period. It was the movement and its savvy ability to exploit this liability by provoking highly publicized instances of segregationist violence—via the Freedom Rides, Birmingham, Selma—that finally forced the Democrats to move decisively to the left in the early to mid-1960s and unambiguously embrace not just civil rights reform but also a broad array of progressive social programs. And it was this leftward shift that eventually cost the party its southern wing and fractured the New Deal coalition that had kept the White House and Congress overwhelmingly in Democratic hands since 1932.

Moment 2: Courting Segregationists—The GOP and Its Southern Strategy

The threat posed by the revitalized civil rights struggle occasioned a dramatic upsurge in countermovement activity by segregationists in the South. Some of this activity took extra-legal form, with a resurgent Klan active in the Deep South, and countless instances of violence directed at civil rights workers throughout the region. But the countermovement had an electoral component as well. After he stood "in the school house door" in June of 1963 to block the admission of the first black students at the University of Alabama, Governor George Wallace became the leading symbol of resistance to integration in the United States. While hailed as a hero by the white South, Wallace was reviled by opinion leaders and "responsible" politicians elsewhere in the country. So when he announced he would contend for the Democratic presidential nomination in the spring of 1964—against a popular sitting president from his own party—his candidacy was met with widespread disbelief and derision. The laughter, however, proved short-lived. Wallace shocked political pundits by capturing a third of the votes cast in the April Wisconsin Democratic primary. Wallace went on to claim 30 percent of the vote in Indiana, despite a concerted effort by the national Democratic establishment to stop him in the state, and then narrowly lost in Maryland, lamenting that "if it hadn't been for the nigger bloc vote, we would have won it all!"[25]

These were the only three primaries Wallace entered, though heading into the convention, he also controlled slates of uncommitted delegates in both Mississippi and Alabama. Although there was never any question about who the nominee would be—at the time Lyndon Johnson's (LBJ) approval ratings were among the highest in presidential history—Wallace's surprising showing sent shock waves through both parties. For its part, the Democratic establishment resolved to do what it could to mollify its southern wing in advance of the election. Meanwhile, some Republicans—including Barry Goldwater, the party's surprise nominee in 1964—began to openly call for a shift to the right to capture the Wallace vote and make inroads in the no longer "solid South."[26]

In the end, LBJ's popularity and the association of his candidacy with the memory of his martyred predecessor, John F. Kennedy, resulted in a landslide victory for the Democrats. Not lost on political strategists in both parties, however, was the fact that the GOP carried the Deep South for the first time in history. Among those taking note of the seismic shift in the electoral landscape was Richard Nixon who would emerge, four years later, as the Republican standard bearer. He would run on what he termed his "southern strategy," betting that anger over the civil rights policies of the Democrats made the region ripe for the taking. But Wallace was back in 1968 too, this time running as a third party candidate. Wallace didn't expect to win, of course, but he hoped to deny the victory to the two major candidates—Hubert Humphrey was the Democratic standard bearer—thereby forcing the House of Representatives to resolve the deadlocked contest. By carrying the Deep South (save for South Carolina), Wallace almost pulled it off. In the end, though, Nixon claimed the rest of the South (except Texas) and emerged with one of the narrowest victories in the annals of presidential politics, edging Humphrey in the popular vote by just 43.4 to 42.7 percent.

The significance of Wallace's third party movement for the future electoral prospects of both Republicans and Democrats was clear on the face of the 1968 election returns. With the two parties evenly dividing 86 percent of the vote, the remaining 14 percent who supported Wallace clearly emerged as the balance of power looking to 1972. Much to the consternation of the GOP's once dominant liberal-moderate establishment, Nixon's narrow victory clearly suggested that the party's future lay not in the 43 percent of the popular vote he received, but in the 57 percent he shared with Wallace. Republican strategists believed that this total represented a dominant conservative majority that, if successfully tapped, would ensure the electoral success of the party for years to come. "It suggested," Goldman noted at the time, "a course of strategy that could keep the Presidency Republican for a generation—precisely by isolating the Democrats as a party of the blacks and building the rickety Nixon coalition of 1968 into a true majority of the white center."[27] As we document in Chapter 3, Nixon would spend much of his first term in office fashioning a conservative politics of racial reaction with the goal of cutting more deeply into Wallace's support heading into the 1972 race. So even as civil rights forces and the broader New Left were pushing the Democrats sharply to the left in the 1960s and early 1970s, the GOP was shifting to the right in response to the Wallace movement and the broader nationwide "white backlash."

Moment 3: Barbarians inside the Gate and the Primary Reforms of 1970–72

So as the 1970s dawned, both parties were shifting to accommodate the mobilized movement wings at their respective margins. The Democrats were contending with the increasingly radical movements of the New Left, while the GOP moved right to court racial conservatives and other disaffected elements of the former New Deal coalition. Still, control over party matters—and especially the all-important issue of selecting a presidential nominee—remained firmly under the control of party elites and other insiders. Within the Democratic Party, however, grass-roots movement pressure had been building through two divisive national conventions to take control of the nominating process away from party bosses and, in the parlance of the New Left, "let the people decide."

In 1964 the pressure came from the upstart Mississippi Freedom Democratic Party (MFDP), which sent an interracial delegation to Atlantic City to challenge the seating of the lily-white party regulars from that state. Fearing the erosion of southern support, the Johnson forces were determined to do whatever was necessary to ensure that the regular Mississippi delegation was not seated:

> In the end, the pressure worked. Support for the challenge evaporated in the Credentials Committee and the MFDP forces were left to consider a rather weak compromise proposal: two at-large convention seats and a promise that the whole matter of racial exclusion would be reviewed prior to the 1968 convention. . . . The delegates overwhelmingly rejected the compromise. [The head of the delegation] Fanny Lou Hamer summed up the feeling of most when she said, "we didn't come all this way for no two seats!"[28] That was not quite the end of it though. Using credentials borrowed from sympathetic delegates from other states, a contingent of MFDP members gained access to the convention floor and staged a sit-in in the Mississippi section. The sight of black Mississippians being carried from the convention floor by uniformed, white security officers was but the ultimate ironic denouement to [the convention].[29]

For all the drama in Atlantic City, however, 1964 would pale in comparison to the violence and mayhem that marked the 1968 convention in Chicago. The New Left was at its peak in 1968 and movement forces were active inside and outside the convention hall. What everyone remembers about Chicago in 1968 were the pitched battles in the streets of Chicago between the police and anti-war demonstrators. Inside the hall, however, another ultimately much more consequential, if invisible, battle was being waged by New Left reformers and party regulars. We devote a lot of attention to this confrontation in Chapter 4. Here we content ourselves with a brief summary of the controversy, the process it set in motion, and the critically important changes that resulted from that process.

The dispute centered on the arcane details of delegate selection. The bigger issue was control over the system by which the party nominated its presidential candidate. What the battles in the street had in common with the reform efforts inside the convention was Vietnam. Johnson had been forced to withdraw from the race as a result of the popular support granted to the anti-war candidacy of Democratic senator Eugene McCarthy. After Johnson's withdrawal from the race, Bobby Kennedy—also running as an anti-war candidate—threw his hat in the ring, gradually establishing himself as the front runner in the race. His assassination in June of that year dealt the anti-war forces—and the country as a whole—a huge blow, but McCarthy remained in the race. What both of these candidates—McCarthy and Kennedy—had demonstrated was the depths of opposition to the war within the Democratic Party. And yet because of his support among the party establishment, Hubert Humphrey arrived in Chicago as the Democrat's presumptive nominee, even though he had not contested a single primary during the run-up to the convention. Motivated by their anger over Vietnam and the injustice of a nominating process that allowed a candidate to claim the nomination without regard to the popular will of party regulars, the reformers inside the hall sought to democratize the nominating process. In the end, they failed to do so, at least at the convention itself. But they came away from the convention with something far more valuable than the reforms they had sought in Chicago. In a confused, chaotic, little remembered, voice vote toward the end of the convention, the Party committed itself to creating a commission to review the nominating process and recommend needed reforms in advance of the 1972 confab.

The main outlines of the story are as clear as they are critically important to an understanding of the close connection between movement and electoral politics in contemporary America. The New Left reformers seized control of the commission and, over roughly a two-year period, fashioned and implemented a sweeping set of institutional changes that effectively democratized delegate selection and the broader nomination process. Interestingly, while the proposed reforms did *not* specifically mandate the establishment of primaries as the principal vehicle of state delegate selection, the ultimate outcome of the reform process was the creation of our current system of binding popular primaries and caucuses. The numbers tell the story. In 1968, the Democrats held 17 nonbinding primaries in advance of the convention. By 1980 that number had doubled. More surprising still, with no significant internal party demand for such reforms, the Republicans nonetheless adopted the same general institutional innovations as the Democrats. Indeed, the rate of increase in GOP primaries exceeded that of the Democrats, rising from just 15 in 1968 to 35 in 1980.

So what? The preeminent scholar of the reform process, Byron Shafer, minces no words in arguing for the significance of the resulting changes. Calling them "the greatest systematically planned...shift in the institutions of delegate selection in all of American history," Shafer gets to the real heart of the matter when he notes that as a result of the reforms "the official party had been *erased* from what was still nominally the party's nomination system."[30] But if parties—or more accurately, party elites—were no longer able to control the nominating process as they once had, where did control now reside? Answer: with those members of the party who choose to participate in the new primary (or caucus) process. What we have learned since the implementation of the new nominating system, however, is that only a small percentage of registered voters—and a much smaller fraction of all age eligible— actually take part in the primaries. *And* that this small minority tend to be more ideologically extreme in their views than the typical member of the party.[31] In short, while reformers had sought to democratize the nominating process, the resulting system has proven to be the perfect vehicle for empowering the movement wings of the two parties. Whether or not this is the same as democratizing the process we leave for you to decide. For now, we mean only to underscore the cumulative significance of the three "moments" reviewed in this chapter. By the time of the 1972 election, both parties—but especially the Democrats—had moved sharply off center, relative to their ideological positions in 1960, to accommodate racially inflected movements on their margins, movements whose influence was greatly enhanced by that year's primary reforms.

With those reforms, the tug of war between movements and parties in American politics would become that much more intense.

Plan for the Book

Everything that has come before can be thought of as a teaser. We have outlined the basic argument at the heart of the book and offered a stylized sketch of the beginnings of a very complicated story, stretching over many decades, about the growing influence of social movements in American politics. The balance of the book is given over to a very detailed retelling of that story, with chapters proceeding in chronological order. Chapter 2 focuses on the period from 1940 to 1960, when the absence of significant movement activity elevated the "median voter" to preeminent status and allowed for the development of the substantial bipartisan convergence and relative material equality that we remember as such distinctive features of the era. In Chapter 3 we take up the crucial period of the 1960s, revisiting—in much more detail—the first two critical "moments" touched on earlier. Chapter 4 concerns the exceedingly strange but highly consequential 1970s, with special emphasis on the way the reforms associated with the third "moment" reviewed here marginalized party elites and granted movement activists a decisive role in the nomination of presidential candidates. We go on to detail the clear impact that movements had in both the 1972 and 1976 presidential contests. Our focus in Chapters 5 and 6 is on the Reagan presidency and the striking contrast between Reagan's rather modest achievements in office (Chapter 5) and the much more consequential "slow release" Reagan Revolution that unfolds *after* he leaves the White House (Chapter 6). The "revolution" had the effect of decisively redefining the legitimate parameters of federal policy making and transforming Reagan from the somewhat sad and spent political force of his last year in office into the iconic touchstone figure he is today. In Chapter 7 we take up the Obama years and the deepening partisan divisions, growing governmental crises, and emerging warfare within the GOP occasioned by the rise of the Tea Party. Finally, Chapter 8 is given over to a discussion of the badly frayed state of American democracy and a normative consideration of the current mess and what it would take to reverse the political and economic trends of the past 30–40 years.

2

Postwar America

Bipartisan Consensus, the Median Voter, and the Absence of Social Movements

AMONG THE TWO RICHEST VEINS that science fiction writers continue to mine are those that center on time travel and the idea of alternative worlds or parallel universes. And within the alternative worlds category, one specific and especially rich variant of the "other worlds" theme involves worlds "turned upside down"—that is, realities that are the exact opposite or inverse of our own. Were we able to travel back in time to the United States in the years immediately following World War II, we would encounter a world that, at least in its overarching political economy, would come very close to being the "world turned upside down" so beloved of science fiction writers and fans.

We opened Chapter 1 with two figures, one showing annual income inequality scores for roughly the past 100 years; the other reporting changes in the partisan polarization of the House and Senate since 1879. We led with these two figures to document the extreme inequality and yawning partisan gap that characterize the contemporary United States. But these figures—reproduced here (Figures 2.1 and 2.2)—are just as useful for calling attention to the broad contours of the "inverse" political economy that prevailed in America in the middle decades of the previous century.

If the last annual value in each of the two figures represents the peak—or near peak—in the overall time series, the values for the quarter

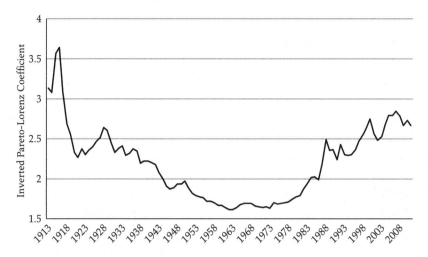

Figure 2.1 Income Inequality, 1913–2012
Source: The World Top Incomes Database, Piketty and Saez (2007)

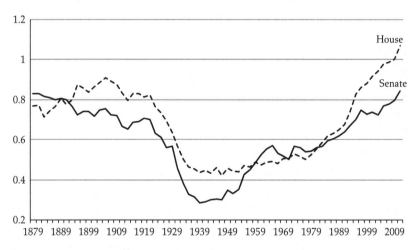

Figure 2.2 Political Polarization, 1879–2012
Source: Polarized America/voteview.com

century from 1940 to 1965 represent the clear valley in both distribu-
tions. In the aggregate, Congress was as ideologically "close" then as it is
deeply divided now. And as economically unequal as we are now, we
were as comparatively equal then as we have ever been or at least since
we have had the data on which to make the comparison. To these two
trends, we now add a third, also unique to this particular era: the almost
total absence of social movement activity in the 1940s and 1950s.

Our focus in this chapter is squarely on these three features of the postwar period and on the relations between them. We begin with a summary of the central argument on offer in the chapter. The relative material equality enjoyed by Americans during the postwar period resulted from a number of factors. Any list of such factors would have to start with such economic influences as the sustained prosperity enjoyed by the United States following the war and the unprecedented bargaining power exercised by unions for much of this period. There was, however, an important political-policy basis to the comparative equality as well. A strong bipartisan consensus developed in these years in support of progressive tax policies and the gradual extension or elaboration of the kinds of social programs first enacted in the New Deal. This consensus, in turn, was rooted in the unprecedented overlap in the ideological preferences of the two major parties. For one of the few, if only, times in US history, moderate centrists were clearly dominant in both parties for an extended period of time.

We are careful not to exaggerate the extent of this overlap or the bipartisan consensus it enabled. There were, in fact, significant divisions and ideologically extreme elements in both parties in these years. The GOP featured a strident conservative wing, defined domestically by its opposition to New Deal style programs and in foreign policy by its noninterventionist stance in the 1930s and early 1940s and later embrace of an extreme form of anti-communism. The nominal head of this wing was Senator Robert Taft of Ohio, who mounted strong bids to be the party's presidential nominee in 1940, 1948, and 1952.[1] If anything, the divisions within the Democratic Party were even more pronounced, with moderate to conservative southern segregationists coexisting uneasily with a coalition of labor and civil rights forces that first coalesced in the late 1930s and grew ever larger and more restive as the postwar period unfolded.[2] Still, despite the presence of these significant liberal and conservative wings, the moderate centrists remained firmly in control in both parties. Tellingly, Taft was never able to break through and secure the GOP presidential nomination, and despite the growing size and significance of the liberal civil rights wing, the Democratic establishment remained committed, we contend, to accommodating the policy prerogatives of the Dixiecrats until well into the 1960s. The critical overlap, then, was defined by the inter-section of the policy preferences of the centrist elements in both parties.

That leaves one final piece of the puzzle. The overwhelming centrism of the two parties was importantly "enabled" in this period by the con-spicuous absence of mobilized social movement wings in either party. Absent significant grass-roots activity in both the 1940s and 1950s, the parties were spared the centrifugal pressures that almost always accompany mass movements of the left or right. This in turn, allowed the parties to successfully manage—marginalize, if you will—the more extreme elements at their ideological margins. But this is just the barest of sketches; we will use the balance of the chapter to develop the argument more fully. We first take up the significant ideological conver-gence that characterized the dominant wings of the two parties in the 1940s, '50s, and much of the '60s.

The Triumph of the Center

Given the extraordinary depth of the current partisan divide, it is hard to fathom a time when location along the standard left/right axis told you so little about the ideological composition of the congressional delegations of the two major parties. But that was certainly the case in the "opposite world" of politics that prevailed in the United States from roughly 1940 to 1965. In this period, there were countless Republican members of Congress whose voting records were more liberal than their Democratic counterparts. In the aggregate, Democrats *were* more liberal in their policy preferences than Republicans, but not by all that much. Consider the sharp contrast with the most recent period: when Obama took office in 2008, there was *no* ideological overlap whatsoever between Democrats and Republicans in either the House or Senate.[3] That is, the most conservative Democratic senator, Ben Nelson of Nebraska, was still further to the left than his most liberal Republican counterpart, Olympia Snowe of Vermont. The same was true in the House; and this was *before* the 2010 midterm elections brought several dozen Tea Party–backed movement conservatives into that venerable body! Much of the book is devoted to understanding where this deep partisan chasm came from. Here, however, we are concerned with its opposite, the substance and origins of the operative bipartisan consensus that developed during the 1930s and lasted well into the 1960s.

The Emerging Consensus

As with so many features of American life in the mid- to late 20th century, the extent of partisan polarization in Congress bears the clear imprint of the Great Depression and the political fallout that followed from it. As shown in Figure 2.2, polarization remained consistently high between 1880 and 1920. It moderated somewhat in the '20s, but the two congressional delegations remained highly distinct ideologically at the time of the stock market crash in 1929. The electoral fallout from the crash began almost immediately and accelerated as the economic crisis intensified. With Hoover in the White House and the Republicans in control for most of the 1920s, popular anger over the Depression was directed at the GOP, with disastrous consequences for the party. By 1937, Democrats outnumbered Republicans in the Senate by a staggering 76 to 16 margin. In the House the Democratic majority was 334 to 88. "Never before or after this time were the Democratic and Republican parties so imbalanced in Congress during peacetime."[4] But the crisis also had the effect of slowly narrowing the *aggregate* ideological distance between the two parties.

At least two processes appear to have been at work here. While traditional Republicans regarded Roosevelt with deep suspicion when he took office in 1933, his immense popularity forced the dwindling GOP congressional delegation to at least somewhat moderate their views to accommodate the new reality. If FDR's landslide victory in 1932 wasn't enough to convince Republicans of the wisdom of some adjustment, his even more impressive win four years later likely did the trick. After capturing 57 percent of the popular vote and 89 percent of the electoral vote in 1932, Roosevelt upped those percentages in 1936 to 61 and 98 percent, respectively. Not to take at least some account of the will of the electorate was to court electoral suicide. No doubt many of the record number of Republican incumbents turned out in these years were too stubborn or too slow to moderate their views, while at least some of the lucky few who survived did so. The more important mechanism at work here, however, was replacement. While the modal Republican in

Congress circa 1930 was doomed to be replaced by a Democratic challenger, a smaller number were replaced during this period by a fellow Republican. This happened for a variety of reasons, most commonly through a successful primary challenge, but occasionally also through retirement or death in office. In these cases, the incoming Republican was almost always more liberal in his views than the senator or House member he was replacing.[5] Taken together, these processes had the effect of slowly shifting the mean of the Republican Party in the Democratic direction. As we saw in Figure 2.2, both houses of Congress experienced a steady decline in partisan polarization throughout the 1930s.

Besides the electoral dynamics set in motion by the Depression, the attack on Pearl Harbor in 1941 and the ensuing wartime emergency also served to damp down partisan division as the nation came together behind the war effort. Given this combination of factors, it is perhaps not surprising that, as Figure 2.2 shows, the level of party polarization was at or near all-time lows during the war years. Finally, just as the war was starting to wind down, a second period of liberal Republican replacement strengthened the centripetal trend evident since the onset of the Depression. As Poole and Rosenthal document, starting in 1944, GOP newcomers to Congress are typically more ideologically liberal than their exiting party peers.[6] Moreover this pattern holds until 1964. These are the years that mark the entrance of such centrist stalwarts as Gerald Ford, William Scranton, George Romney, Charles Percy, and Nelson Rockefeller into the GOP, thus solidifying the brand of moderate Republicanism that will serve as the party's center of gravity through at least the 1970s. It is also an ideological stance that harmonizes well with the dominant centrist stance of the Democrats in the postwar period.

There is, however, one other very general cultural influence that develops in the immediate aftermath of the war that also serves to unify the nation and, by extension, its elected officials. It is a much more amorphous influence than the specific sources of ideological convergence noted earlier; nonetheless, it is critically important to an understanding of not just the striking bipartisanship of the era but also the high levels of trust and confidence in government that suffuse the postwar period. Emerging triumphant from the war and blessed with a booming economy, most Americans felt a sense of national pride and unity perhaps unmatched in the nation's history. There was more than a bit of a "chosen people" quality to the narrative. We were a "can do" country that accomplished whatever we set out to. We had pulled ourselves out of the Depression, beat back the forces of fascism in World War II, and rebuilt Europe after the war. In the American ideology, we were not simply the most powerful and richest nation on Earth; we were morally the "best" as well. In short, a sense of moral superiority and national mission pervaded the postwar years.

What was the nature of this "national mission?" It is hard to specify with any real precision. In truth, it meant different things to different people. Here, though, we want to highlight one component of the national narrative that seems, in retrospect, to have been especially resonant in the postwar period and critical to the emerging moral and political sensibilities of a majority of elected officials—Republican no less than Democrat—who came of age during the era. Without for a minute denying the often grudging, contested nature of the struggle, we now have sufficient historical perspective to appreciate the commitment to social and political inclusion that characterized the United States in the post–World War II period. In truth, at least some of the hard-won foundation underlying this commitment had been laid during the 1930s. For example, the decisive shift in the legal philosophy of the Supreme Court after, say, 1937–38; the willingness of many Americans to celebrate the achievements of African American sports and cultural figures, such as Jesse Owens, Marian Anderson, and Joe Louis—all of these changes speak to a far more inclusive vision of American society at the end of the 1930s than the one that prevailed at the outset of the decade.[7]

If the cultural foundations were present before the war, however, the official embrace of the ideal and the pace of actual policy efforts to promote various forms of inclusion accelerated sharply in the postwar period. Having just waged a war against the "master race" ideology of the Nazis and spearheaded the founding of the United Nations—with its ringing declaration of human rights and the rights of national self-determination—policymakers across a broad array of institutional arenas took seriously the need to broaden access to the American dream. More than anything, it was the burgeoning Cold War and the ensuing political and ideological struggle with the Soviet Union that accelerated the push for various forms of inclusion in the postwar United States.

Perhaps the best way to underscore the stark link between these two issues is to quote from a 1952 brief filed by the US attorney general in support of a then little known school desegregation case—*Brown v. Topeka Board of Education*—just coming before the Supreme Court. The brief speaks eloquently to the close connection that the Truman administration saw between the Soviet threat and the newfound federal enthusiasm for civil rights. In part the brief read:

> It is in the context of the present world struggle between freedom and tyranny that the problem of racial discrimination must be viewed.... Racial discrimination furnishes grist for the Communist propaganda mills, and it raises doubts even among friendly nations as to the intensity of our commitment to the democratic faith.[8]

But even if some of the motives underlying the push were less than pure, the commitment to social and political inclusion has to be counted as one of the central features of life in the postwar United States. Nor was race the only subtext for the push. After all, these were also the years

- when "quotas" on Jewish admissions to many colleges and universities were relaxed or removed;
- of Levittown and the dream of home ownership for segments of the population who had never imagined such a thing possible;
- when the GI Bill helped to lift countless servicemen from modest backgrounds squarely into the middle class;[9]
- when labor unions secured unprecedented material benefits for working men and women;
- of Jackie Robinson and a more general integration of American sports;
- when Americans did the previously unthinkable and elected a Catholic president;
- of a rock and roll revolution that integrated American popular music;
- when the civil rights stirrings of other groups—women, gays, lesbians, Hispanic Americans, among others—began in earnest;

- and, of course, of *Brown v. Board*, Little Rock, and the full flowering of the African American freedom struggle.

It is easy to dismiss these trends as forms of tokenism that did little to change the reality of class and racial privilege in the United States. There is certainly some truth to this view. Yet substantively and symbolically, there is no gainsaying the significance of these trends, especially to those whose life chances were enhanced by them.

We are still careful, however, not to overstate the extent of equality in this period. After all, Jim Crow remained the overriding social and political reality in the South until well into the 1960s. While teaching at the University of Arizona, the first author learned from a Japanese-American colleague that a cross had been burned on his lawn when he and his white wife moved to Tucson in the early 1960s. Restrictive covenants were the norm in the real estate business throughout the United States during the era. Whatever measure of inclusion had been achieved was grudging and hard-won. There were also plenty of Americans—most notably southern segregationists—who were having none of it. But it won't do to deny the generalized idealism and inclusive spirit of the period. As much as anything else, it was this *zeitgeist* that shaped the moral compass of those who would don the mantle of the New Left in the sixties—as well as the pervasive bipartisan sensibilities of most of the major figures in both parties who came of age after the war. We also see the period's high moral tone and emphasis on inclusion clearly reflected in the three key policy domains that dominated politics in the postwar period. These were, in order of importance, the threat of communism, civil rights, and the extension of the American welfare state. We take up each in turn, beginning with the mother of all postwar policy issues.

Communism

With the exception of slavery (and its aftermath), perhaps no issue in US history dominated federal policymaking for as long a period of time as did the threat of communism, in both its international and domestic guises. With something of a hiatus in the 1970s, keyed by Nixon's overture to China and his policy of détente with the Soviet Union, the threat of communism and the resultant Cold War was the paramount policy concern of the United States from the close of World War II until the collapse of the Soviet Union some 45 years later. Even before the war ended, US officials were fearful of Soviet intentions, but by effectively occupying Eastern Europe in 1945–1947, the USSR transformed those fears into an increasingly hard-line policy of Soviet "containment." With the events of 1948–50, however, the Cold War entered an even more dangerous and confrontational phase. These events included a wave of communist inflected nationalist revolts in Southeast Asia in 1948–49; the first successful Soviet test of an atomic device in 1949; the fall of China to the communists in that same year; and the onset of the Korean War in 1950. Coming so closely on the heels of each other, these events shocked the foreign policy establishment and led to fears that communist influence was spreading, domino-style, around the globe.

These fears found powerful domestic expression with the creation of the House Un-American Activities Committee (HUAC) in 1947 and even more so in February 1950 when the heretofore obscure Republican senator from Wisconsin, Joe McCarthy, claimed in a speech that he possessed a list of "known Communists" then employed in the State Department. He was never able to prove this or any of the other equally sensational charges he made over the next few years, but this did not stop him from dominating the headlines through 1954 and, in the process, catalyzing a nationwide obsession with, and purge of, communists in all walks of life. His bullying behavior at the 1954 Army-McCarthy hearings finally turned public opinion against him, and his formal censure by the Senate in December of that same year marked the effective end of his political career. Still the issue of communism and communist infiltration remained a powerful force in domestic politics for many years thereafter.

The point for us here is the partisan stance toward the issue by the two major parties. Reflecting the singular salience of the concern about communists during these years, we find little meaningful difference between Democrats and Republicans on the issue. From the onset of World War II until the late 1960s, one would have been hard pressed to discern any significant difference in the policy preferences of the two parties on this dominant issue. While entrenched isolationist sentiment—combined, in fact, with some admiration for the Nazis—within the

Depression-era GOP frustrated Roosevelt's efforts to mobilize the country against the growing threat of fascism in the late 1930s, the attack on Pearl Harbor decisively altered the political landscape, making opposition to the war a serious electoral liability for Republicans no less than Democrats. Notwithstanding occasional interparty sniping, the partisan divisions that had characterized FDR's early years in the White House gave way in the early 1940s to an unprecedented degree of party unity on the prosecution of the war and foreign policy more generally. To a great extent, this bipartisan consensus carried over to the central defining issue of the Soviet threat and the waging of the Cold War. It may be that the most celebrated anti-communists in Congress during the early Cold War period were Republicans—think only of Joe McCarthy and Richard Nixon—but a more systematic analysis of congressional roll call votes on military spending and domestic security issues, shows only minor partisan differences on matters of Cold War policy. As Fredik Logevall puts it in his exceptional history of American involvement in Vietnam, the late 1940s "marked the beginning of an anti-Communist crusade inside the United States... [and] an undifferentiated anti-Communism [that] became the required posture of all aspiring politicians, whether Republican or Democrat."[10]

The convergent pattern we see reflected in congressional voting is evident at the presidential level as well, where the moderate Democratic president, Harry Truman, and his centrist Republican successor, Dwight Eisenhower, came under attack for their alleged "softness" on communism. We would, in fact, be hard pressed to assay any major policy differences between the four presidents—Truman, Eisenhower, Kennedy, and Johnson—charged with countering the Soviet threat at the height of the Cold War. Indeed, a good case could be made that a Democrat, Lyndon Johnson, was the most zealous cold warrior, and Eisenhower—the lone Republican—the most cautious. However one comes down on the matter, one thing should be clear: the now conventional claim that Democrats are weak on defense and Republicans strong had little standing in the period, 1940–1965. Given the singular policy salience of the Soviet threat in these years, neither party could afford to be outflanked on the issue, at least not until domestic dissent over Vietnam split the Democratic Party in the late 1960s.

Civil Rights

Civil rights comprises the second key policy area in the postwar era. As we previously noted, however, the matter bears a strong connection to the overarching issue of the Cold War. Reflecting the ongoing salience of the unspoken "understanding" between the federal government and the southern states that had been in force since the end of Reconstruction, race remained, in policy terms, a matter of regional "custom" through the war years; this in spite of increasing attention to the issue in the late 1930s by the emerging labor-civil rights wing of the Democratic Party. All of this changes as a result of World War II, and more important, the onset of the Cold War. Quite simply, the Cold War effectively renationalizes "the Negro question." Writing with great prescience in 1944, Gunnar Myrdal explains why the United States would, in the future, no longer be able to cede control over matters of race to southern segregationists. To quote Myrdal:

> The Negro problem ... has also acquired tremendous international implications, and this is another reason why the white North is prevented from compromising with the white South regarding the Negro. ... Statesmen will have to take cognizance of the changed geopolitical situation of the nation and carry out important adaptations of the American way of life to new necessities. A main adaptation is bound to be a redefinition of the Negro's status in American democracy.[11]

The "changed geopolitical situation" to which Myrdal is referring is the Cold War; the "main adaptation" that the nation will need to carry out is civil rights reform. In order to credibly confront Soviet charges of American racism in the battle for global influence—especially among "peoples of color" in emerging Third World nations—the United States would be forced to put its own racial house in order.

As we noted in the previous section, no issue had greater salience in the postwar period than the Soviet threat, in all its foreign and domestic guises. Accordingly, it is hard not to attribute a great deal of the bipartisanship characteristic of the era to the singular importance that policymakers—on both sides of the aisle—came to attach to the issue. To the extent that civil rights came to be seen as inextricably linked to the superpower competition, it may also help to explain why such a strong aggregate consensus developed around the issue of race after so many years of neglect. We are careful, however, not to push the parallel between the two issues too far. While both issues enjoyed broad bipartisan support during this period, the nature of that support looks very different across the two policy areas.

Voting on defense bills shows a simple pattern of party convergence in the postwar period; the partisan distribution of civil rights votes, however, entails a more complicated dynamic. It will help to put the matter in broader historical perspective. With the withdrawal of federal troops from the South in 1877, race as an issue is effectively organized out of federal policymaking. That said, what few roll call votes are taken on racial matters continue to reflect the traditional divide between a generally more racially liberal GOP and the more racially conservative Democrats. This division, however, ceases to be terribly important, given the federal "hands off" policy with respect to the issue.

With the renationalization of the issue following the war, all of this changes. Legislative attention to racial matters accelerates rapidly from the late 1930s through the 1940s, '50s and '60s. With this increased attention, the traditional partisan split between Republicans and Democrats on the issue evolves into something more akin to a "three party system" in Congress. For one of the very few times in US history, congressional voting on a major policy issue betrays much greater *within* than *between* party variation. While the votes of northern and southern Democrats diverge sharply during this period—essentially defining the extreme liberal and conservative positions on the issue— the majority of Republicans, especially those who comprise the party's dominant "Eastern Establishment" wing, embrace positions that are only slightly less progressive than those of northern Democrats.[12] The result is an unusual period of broad aggregate consensus between centrist Republicans and northern Democrats on the need for civil rights reform, coupled with an intense dissent on the issue by "third party" southern Dixiecrats.

It is this dissent that irreversibly divides the two wings of the Democratic Party and improbably—given the region's long-standing hatred of the Party of Lincoln—sets in motion a decisive and highly consequential, if prolonged, process of electoral realignment that will occupy much of our attention in the next chapter as well as other points in the book. One immediate effect of the realignment was to bring the "three party" pattern of voting to a close, with the Republicans, now joined by southern Democrats, shifting decisively to the right on the issue, and the Democrats, now free of their strange southern "bedfellows," tacking equally sharply to the left. By the late 1960s, the aggregate two-party consensus responsible for the landmark civil rights legislation of the early to mid-'60s has given way to the more conventional partisan divide that we recognize today; with Republicans increasingly conservative on racial matters and Democrats generally more liberal. Anyone looking to understand the deep divisions that characterize the present day United States will need to take full account of this sea change in American racial politics. Nothing, we will argue, marks the onset of the long process that has brought us to the deeply divided present more than the shifting racial geography of American politics in the mid- to late 1960s. So important is this process that we devote the next chapter to its explication.

In bringing this section to a close, however, it is important that we stress the theme of consensus rather than division. Quite simply, race has been the single most divisive, polarizing issue in American history. That was true at the nation's founding when the thirteen states of the fledgling country waged a bitter fight over if and how much to count slaves in apportioning seats in the population-based "lower" house of Congress. It remained central in the 19th century when the fundamental incompatibility between Republican and Democratic views on the issue led to the Civil War, Reconstruction, and the long simmering hatred of the party of Lincoln by the white South. It remains true today, though now it's the Democrats who hold liberal racial views and Republicans who embrace a politics of racial reaction. What marks the postwar years as so unique, relative to these extended periods of racial division, is the aggregate bipartisan support for reform that characterized the era and was responsible for the major legislative breakthroughs so critical to the "civil rights revolution." The 1964 Civil Rights Act will serve as a case in point. In that year, 27 Republican senators joined 44 Democratic colleagues to pass the act. In the House, the winning coalition included 152 Democratic and 138 Republican representatives. Never before and never since this period has there been anything like this kind of bipartisan congressional support for progressive racial legislation.

The American Welfare State

The third major policy issue of the postwar period was the future of the American welfare state. Initially conceived as a set of emergency measures to deal with the extraordinary social and economic dislocations occasioned by the Depression, one might have imagined that the sustained postwar economic boom would have prompted lawmakers to discontinue or roll back some of the New Deal programs. Instead, the three decades immediately following the war saw broad bipartisan support for a gradual extension and elaboration of government programs designed to mitigate various forms of disadvantage. Yes, the Taft wing of the GOP mounted a vigorous, sustained dissent from this position; nonetheless, the modal view of Republican lawmakers in this period was in support of the consensus. In view of traditional Republican opposition to big government and the party's initial hostility to Roosevelt and his programs, the emerging postwar consensus on this issue requires explanation. We see four primary factors encouraging a more liberal/centrist view by GOP lawmakers on the matter. Three of the four will already be familiar. First, the extreme popularity of many of the New Deal programs—with Social Security as the clear exemplar—made it politically risky for Republican congressional candidates in the postwar years to adopt the stark anti-government stance of the 1920s GOP. But it isn't simply a matter of naked political calculus forcing the party to the center/left on the issue. Earlier we noted a very clear pattern of liberal "replacement" of Republican senators and representatives that runs from at least 1944 to 1964. That is, beginning with the 1944 elections, entering GOP lawmakers hold positions that are consistently to the left of, or identical to, those of exiting party incumbents.[13] Our interpretation of this pattern is straightforward and emphasizes consent rather than coercion. These incoming GOP cohorts—whose political sensibilities were shaped in the middle decades of the 20th century—are simply products of an era in which the idea of government intervention has achieved widespread legitimacy. Accordingly, they accept this general notion, even if they differ in their views on the specifics and ideal size of government programs.

We also cannot overestimate the role the emerging postwar consensus on civil rights played in reconciling Republican lawmakers to the more general notion of an expanding government presence in the economy and other institutional arenas. It is important to remember, in this regard, that from roughly the end of World War II until the early to mid-60s, the Republican congressional delegation was, *in the aggregate*, more moderate to liberal on civil rights matters than its Democratic counterpart. In short, the party's generally progressive racial views also encouraged GOP support in these years for a gradual expansion of the American welfare state.

Finally, the war itself almost certainly encouraged the broad legitimacy and support that attached to the federal government in the postwar period and, by extension, to its efforts to mitigate disadvantage and promote inclusion in American society. Several points are worth making here. What was World War II but a massive federal initiative designed to safeguard and advance the interests of the American people? The popularity of the war greatly enhanced public confidence in the federal government and in the general proposition that government intervention was a good and legitimate thing. The fact that the postwar national narrative also tended to represent the end of the Depression as another triumph of government intervention only reinforced the broad legitimacy of the federal establishment in the immediate postwar period.

Earlier we called attention to the clear stress—cultural no less than political—on "inclusion" in the postwar United States. The war had everything to do with this emphasis. As noted, it was waged on the basis of a stirring, anti-"master race" ideology. Notwithstanding the obvious hypocrisy inherent in this framing, the United States sought to contrast racial progress at home with the extreme racism reflected in both Nazi anti-Semitism and the Japanese treatment of its Chinese and Korean neighbors. Among other things, victory in the war was celebrated as a triumph of human rights and self-determination over racism and enslavement. The United Nations was founded to ensure that these principles would help to structure the postwar world. Having waged the war and structured the peace on the basis of these principles, the United States (and its Western European allies) was under pressure not only to put its racial house in order but also to more fully realize the promise of inclusion for all its people. It would be hard to see how the nation could have embraced this goal in the absence of a commitment to government efforts to level the playing field for previously disadvantaged groups. This commitment obviously informed federal civil rights efforts but would find expression in a host of other postwar programs designed to advance the interests of other groups as well (e.g., returning veterans, Native Americans, women, the disabled).

Whatever the mix of influences encouraging the emerging bipartisan consensus on the issue, it's clear that the period saw a rapid expansion in the size of the federal government and its spending on social programs to promote inclusion and mitigate disadvantage. Moreover, both trends were in evidence long before the heyday of Democratic liberalism in the 1960s. More to the point, they were just as evident during Republican Dwight Eisenhower's eight years in office as they were during the Democratic administrations that preceded and followed him. In particular, we call your attention to the pace of expansion in the Social Security system under Democratic and the lone Republican administration during this period. As far and away the largest and symbolically most important entitlement program to come out of the New Deal, the fate of the Social Security program under GOP and Democratic presidents is a good way to assess the extent to which the two parties were aligned on the issue of the role of government during the postwar period. The Social Security system expanded steadily in these years, but the rate of growth was especially marked during Eisenhower's time in office. Outlays in support of the system increased a whopping 41 percent per annum on Eisenhower's watch, compared to just 7.8 and 13.7 under Kennedy and Johnson, respectively. Only Truman, of the postwar presidents exceeded Eisenhower's rate of increase. Tynes nicely captures Eisenhower's wholehearted embrace of Social Security:

> Social Security was no longer the favorite child of just the Democrats.... Eisenhower [was not about to] wreck Social Security's progress and throughout his term in office, he worked with Congress to extend coverage to an additional 10 million Americans. Indeed, the 1952 election in many ways clinched the bipartisan nature of the program.... The gains made by Social Security during this Republican

administration were significant. In Congress, normal party-line distinctions were blurred in creating Social Security legislation, making consensus and expansion more likely.... The Eisenhower administration indeed boasted of its achievements in this field. Increases in benefits and rates were made with a minimum of opposition. Never before had a national political party.... [operated] so completely outside its traditional philosophical boundaries.[14]

Underscoring just how popular Social Security had become with both parties, major legislation to expand the system was passed in *every* election year—general and midterm—during the 1950s. Clearly both parties had come to view support of the system as a major priority. This broad bipartisan support, not only for Social Security but also for government intervention to mitigate disadvantage was key to a second distinctive feature of the postwar period.

Toward a More Inclusive and Egalitarian Society

Having documented and discussed the dynamics underlying the substantial convergence in policy preferences, we turn our attention now to the comparative equality that characterized the era and the ways in which the emerging bipartisan consensus critically shaped this second trend.

There has always been a substantial gap between the richest and poorest Americans. Relative to the full span of US history, however, the middle decades of the 20th century stand out as a period of striking equality (see Figure 2.1). Looking more closely still, the most equal period within these years corresponds almost perfectly to the quarter century immediately following World War II. Lacking comparable data for the 18th and 19th centuries, we can't say for sure that this was the most egalitarian period in US history, but it certainly represents the apogee of the last 100 years. In this section, we identify and discuss the factors that account for this second distinctive feature of the postwar period. We pay special attention to the ways in which the substantial policy convergence of the two parties in these years helped promote gains in equality across a wide array of institutional arenas in American life.

We begin, however, before the war, with the convulsive impact of the Great Depression. If Figure 2.1 highlights the comparative equality of the postwar period, it also captures the yawning economic chasm that marked the lives of the richest and poorest Americans at the time of the 1929 stock market crash. This stark economic disparity can be traced to events and policies in the 1920s, a period that resembles nothing so much as the United States in the first decade of the new millennium. Like the 2000s, the 1920s was an era marked by conservative Republican rule, little or no regulation of the economy, rampant speculation, profligate spending, and exceptionally low tax rates. It was the proverbial "roaring '20s," and the roar one heard was nothing so much as the full-throated cry of unrestrained greed and avarice. Just as the 2000s begat the economic meltdown of 2008, the roaring '20s came to a screeching halt with the crash of 1929.

In the immediate aftermath of the crash, inequality actually jumped to even higher levels, as the unemployment rate topped 20 percent in the early to mid-1930s. But things were about to change, first and foremost politically. In the previous section we briefly described the political fallout catalyzed by the Depression. As the crisis intensified, so did voter anger, directed primarily at a Republican Party seen as responsible for the collapse. The GOP incumbent, Herbert Hoover, was swept aside by FDR in the 1932 race, but it was the House and Senate races of the early 1930s that perhaps best capture the sea change in politics unleashed by the Depression. The 71st Congress was the last elected before the effects of the Depression had really kicked in. The distribution of House seats in the 71st Congress favored Republicans by a decisive 267 to 163 margin. In the Senate, Republicans outnumbered Democrats 56 to 39. By the time Roosevelt and the 73rd Congress took office in 1933, the counts had completely flipped, with Democrats outnumbering Republicans in the Senate 59 to 36 and in the House, by a staggering 313 to 117. But this wasn't even the high watermark of the period. When Roosevelt cruised to his second term victory in 1936, his coattails proved long enough to carry a record number of Democratic lawmakers into office with him. The resulting margins were the record-setting totals reported in the previous section: 75 to 17 in the Senate and 333 to 89 in the House. In a scant eight years, the GOP had lost an almost unimaginable 178 House and 39 Senate seats.

The canonical account of the New Deal grants almost exclusive credit to Roosevelt for the string of innovative policies enacted during his first few years in office. None of this would have been possible, however, without the extraordinary Democratic majorities noted previously. Acting in concert, Roosevelt and the Democratic Congress engaged in an unprecedented legislative blitz aimed at blunting the crisis and coming to the rescue of the hardest hit segments of society. They largely failed in the first of these goals, while enjoying considerable success in the second. While the self-congratulatory national narrative of the postwar era credited us with pulling ourselves out of the Depression, it was, in fact, the economic mobilization occasioned by World War II that did the trick. Consider the facts: as late as 1939 unemployment remained at a stubborn 16 percent, while the gross domestic product (GDP) continued to lag 12 percent *below* the comparable figure for 1929.

If New Deal programs and policies were only marginally effective in mitigating the aggregate effects of the Depression, they nonetheless worked to steadily reduce economic disparities in the United States. Indeed, Figure 2.1 shows inequality peaking the year before Roosevelt takes office and declining steadily over the course of the decade. It is, of course, impossible to disentangle the effects of any particular program or policy, but we want to call attention to two that we see as especially important in the phalanx of initiatives that make up the New Deal. The first is simply the stark philosophic shift in tax policy under FDR and the Democratic Congress. This change can be seen clearly in Figure 2.3, which plots the top federal income tax rate from 1913 to 2013.

We noted earlier that tax rates had been exceptionally low during the wild and crazy twenties. Beginning in the mid-'20s, the effective rate hovered around 25 percent or roughly a third of what it had been at the beginning of the decade. Despite the onset of the crisis, tax rates remained at historically low levels well into the Depression. By the early 1930s, however, the rate had jumped to 63 percent (1932) and then 79 percent (1936) on its way to the all-time high of 94 percent in 1944 and 1945. It may well be that nothing in the New Deal arsenal had more of a sustained, long-term impact on economic inequality than this sharp and sustained reversal in tax policy.

The other New Deal initiative that we want to highlight was the 1935 National Labor Relations Act, more commonly referred to as the Wagner Act, after New York senator Robert Wagner, the bill's principal

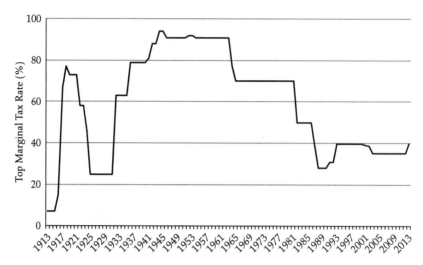

Figure 2.3 Top Federal Income Tax Rates, 1913–2013
Source: Tax Foundation

sponsor. The act effectively reversed 60 years of federal hostility or neglect of organized labor, for the first time granting working men and women rights that their European counterparts had enjoyed for decades. These included the right to form unions, to engage in collective bargaining, and to participate in strikes. The immediate effect of this labor "bill of rights" can be seen in Figure 2.4, which reports the unionized percentage of the US labor force from 1910 through 1980.

Having hovered well below 10 percent for the better part of 25 years, the rate of unionized labor increased dramatically following passage of the act. Even with stubbornly high unemployment rates acting as a serious headwind, the union share of the workforce increased by 150 percent in just five years. By 1944, fully a quarter of all working men and women belonged to a union; low perhaps by European standards, but nothing less than a revolution in the context of America's historic enmity toward labor. Armed with these new rights, organized labor was now in a much better position to secure contracts that eroded long-standing class disparities in income and benefits. When we overlay the income inequality time series on Figure 2.4, the close connection between growth in union membership and declining inequality can be seen all the more clearly (Figure 2.5).

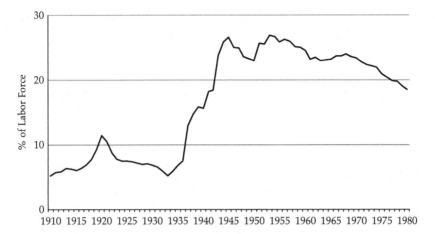

Figure 2.4 Union Membership Rates, 1910–1980
Source: Bureau of Labor Statistics, Directory of National Unions and Employee Associations
* Data are adjusted to compare calculations from differing periods

Figure 2.5 Union Membership Rates and Income Inequality, 1910–1980
Comparable income inequality data are not available from the Top World Incomes Database until 1913
Sources: Bureau of Labor Statistics; The World Top Incomes Database, Piketty and Saez (2007)

So much for the Depression decade and the war years; but the postwar period saw steady gains in income equality as well. Indeed, the lowest level of income inequality wasn't recorded until 1969. In bringing our discussion of this second feature of the postwar period to a close, we consider the somewhat different mix of factors that were at work in these years compared to those operating during the Depression era. In particular, we stress the importance of four factors. Only one of them— union membership—figured in our account of the narrowing of the economic gap in the 1930s. If anything, this first factor would seem to have been more important in promoting economic equality in the postwar period—and especially the 1940s and 1950s—than it was during the Depression, when the persistence of high unemployment rates served to undercut labor's bargaining power. Taken together, the low unemployment rates of the postwar years and record union membership combined to demarcate the pinnacle of labor's power, prestige, and bargaining leverage in the United States.

The postwar years also marked the peak of the so-called great migration, that massive exodus of poor black agricultural workers out of the South to the great industrial centers of the North and West. The migration is typically presented as having taken place over the 50-year period from 1910 to 1960. But the scale of the movement during and immediately after the war far outpaced anything that had come before. Between 1910 and 1940, some 1.8 million African Americans escaped the grinding poverty and brutality of the Jim Crow South. That figure was almost matched during the single decade of the 1940s, with only a slight slowing in the pace of the exodus in the 1950s. All told, better than 3 million blacks left the region in these two decades alone. Elsewhere the first author has discussed the political impact of the migration.[15] The economic implications of the move were hardly less important. With the cotton economy in steady decline and northern industries operating at or near full employment in these years, the net effect of the migration was to transfer millions of African Americans from the poorest region in the country to the most prosperous, and from a declining sector—cotton farming—to another—manufacturing—that was in rapid ascendance. Given the magnitude of the population shift and the stark difference in the economic health of the sending and receiving states, the migration couldn't help but elevate the aggregate economic fortunes of African Americans and contribute to narrowing the gap between the richest and poorest Americans.

To this point, our focus has been squarely on those domestic factors responsible for reducing economic disparities in the postwar United States. We would be remiss, however, if we did not also point to the extraordinarily privileged economic position the country found itself in at the close of the war vis-à-vis its would-be international competitors. While the war left much of the industrial infrastructure of our wartime enemies, Germany and Japan, and allies, Great Britain and the USSR, in ruins, we emerged from the conflict unscathed and fully operational, owing to the significant expansion in our manufacturing capacity occasioned by the war. This gave us something close to a monopoly for a period of years in a host of manufacturing sectors, but a serious leg up that lasted much longer than that. Coupled with the increased demand for all goods and services triggered by the baby boom, our advantageous international position fueled a sustained period of prosperity the likes of which the country has not seen before or since. At a time when GDP growth in the 2–3 percent range is cause for celebration, it is hard to fathom that mean GDP growth *averaged* 6.3 percent in the first two decades following the war. By holding down unemployment and enhancing the bargaining power of labor unions, this sustained prosperity also helped to lift all boats and promote generalized economic equality.

This brings us to the fourth and final factor promoting a leveling of economic circumstance. Absent the strong bipartisan consensus of the postwar period, the continuing gains in economic equality would not have been possible. With the restoration of serious party competition toward the end of the war, Democrats were no longer in a position to impose policies by fiat the way they had during the Depression. As we have seen, the egalitarian policies and programs that comprised the New Deal were leveraged by overwhelming Democratic majorities in both the House and Senate. Notwithstanding the popularity of those policies and the president who proposed them, the unprecedented numeric advantage enjoyed by the Democrats during the Depression did not survive the war years. The tide began to shift as early as the 1938 congressional elections, and by the time the 78th Congress took office in February 1943, the Democratic advantage in the House had shrunk to just 13 seats, down from a high of 244 only six years earlier. And in the first midterm elections held after the war, the GOP reclaimed both houses of Congress by significant margins. They would lose those majorities in the 1948 general election, but that hardly negates the fundamental reality of postwar politics. In stark contrast to the Depression years, the 1940s and '50s marked a serious return to competitive party politics. The implication is clear: had the Republicans been deeply opposed to the broadly egalitarian tax policies and social programs favored by Democrats, we would not have seen the steady reductions in income inequality reported in Figure 2.1. Consider the following fact: the GOP was in control of at least one of the following—the House, Senate, or White House—in 10 of the 20 years following the war. Simply put, the GOP wielded too much power during the period for Democrats to have realized their policy aims without significant Republican agreement.

This is where the GOP's dominant centrist stance in the postwar period comes into play. As Figure 2.2 makes clear, the ideological distance between the two parties was quite small well into the 1960s, and especially between 1940 and 1960. It is especially interesting to compare the policies pursued by the two parties during this era. As suggested earlier, the presidential administrations under both Democrats and Republicans expanded Social Security and oversaw relatively similar increases in the federal budget.

A comparison of the tax policies in place during the two administrations yields very similar results. Indeed, as Figure 2.3 shows, the tax rate on top income earners was essentially unchanged during the 15 years Truman and Eisenhower were in office. With the exception of one brief dip in the early 1950s, the rate was at or above 90 percent from 1945 until the early '60s. In sharp contrast to the rabidly regressive philosophy of today's Republican Party, the postwar GOP embraced essentially the same progressive tax policies first put in place by the Depression era Democrats. As much as anything else, it was the substantial ideological overlap in the two parties that was responsible for the additional gains in income (and other forms of) equality characteristic of the postwar period.

The Absence of Postwar Dissent

This brings us to the third and final trend noted at the beginning of the chapter: the relative absence of popular unrest and significant social movement activity in the immediate postwar period. This final feature of the era was not as long-lived as the other two, spanning just the decades of the 1940s and 1950s, but with significant consequences for party and electoral politics nonetheless. We contend that the comparative absence of mobilized grass-roots movements at the ideological margins of the two parties was critical to the sustained bipartisanship of the postwar period. The lack of significant social movement activity spared both parties the centrifugal pressures that have pushed parties to the left and right throughout American history. Freed from these pressures, the parties were able to hew close to the moderate center of the ideological distribution, enabling years of bipartisan cooperation on the major issues of the day.

All well and good, but to this point we have only asserted the relative lack of social movement activity in this period. Unfortunately, documenting the claim is not as straightforward a proposition as one might think. Despite the popularity of "protest event" research within the field of social movement studies, there are no systematic time series data on US movement activity covering the immediate postwar period. The most comprehensive data set on "public protest" in the country only begins in 1960 and extends through 1995.[16] There are, however, unpublished data available that allow us to construct a crude measure of movement activity for a significant part of the crucial postwar period by coding movement event counts reported in the *New York Times*.[17] The annual counts of "movement actions" from 1953 to 1980 include each of the following six movements: civil rights, environment/conservation, peace/anti-war, student, consumer, and women's. Figure 2.6 shows the annual number of "movement actions" for each of these six movements for the 18 years in question and, perhaps most important, the combined annual count of "movement actions" for all six movements listed.

Figure 2.6 supports three important points. First, consistent with the argument advanced earlier, relative to the 1960s and beyond, the 1950s saw precious little movement activity. Consider the following stark contrast: of the 10,664 movement actions represented in the figures, barely 5 percent—or 580—took place between 1953 and 1960. Second, the sheer volume of activity in the 1960s supports a second key point stressed in Chapter 1: the decade marked the reintroduction of movements as a significant force in American politics. We will have much

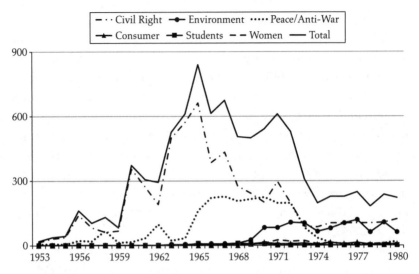

Figure 2.6 Social Movement Actions, 1953–1980
Source: New York Times

more to say about the critical importance of this latter trend in the next chapter. Here though we should say a bit more about the paucity of movement activity in the immediate postwar period and especially about the quality of the evidence supporting that conclusion.

There are obvious problems with the data presented earlier. For starters, the time series omits the 1940s entirely along with the first three years of the following decade. Even if one concedes the almost total absence of domestic dissent during the war years, is it possible that we are missing a significant uptick in movement activity following the close of World War II? We feel confident that the answer is no. We offer one final figure in support of this conclusion.

Figure 2.7 shows the annual count of civil rights "movement activity" from 1948 to 1976.[18] The five years of additional time-series data on the civil rights movement doesn't fully address the temporal lacunae noted, but it certainly helps support the claim that the volume of movement activity was, if anything, lower in the late 1940s than it was in the 1950s.

Besides the matter of missing years, however, there is also the potential issue of missing movements. After all, the actions depicted in Figure 2.6 are drawn from only six movements. Is it possible that the figures inadvertently omit other significant sources of movement

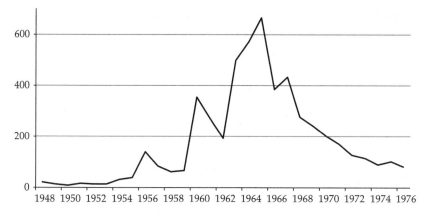

Figure 2.7 Civil Rights Movement Actions, 1948–1976
Source: New York Times

activity from the 1950s? Not if you believe the scholarly literature on the period. Besides the civil rights struggle, the only other (quasi) mass movement that merits even passing mention in accounts of the period is the effort to pressure the United States and the Soviet Union to ban the testing of nuclear weapons. Growing concern over the nuclear threat and specifically the testing of nuclear warheads by the super-powers spawned the "test ban" movement in the late 1950s.[19] In point of fact, however, as Figure 2.6 shows, the movement actually peaked in 1962, the year before the two countries and England signed a limited "test ban" treaty. Claims to legitimate movement status during this period by other progressive groups are simply not credible.

The 1950s did see the creation of the first organizations—the Mattachine Society and the Daughters of Bilitis—to advocate greater civil rights and acceptance for gay men and lesbians, respectively, but protest activity by either group was still a generation off. Other groups who would figure prominently in the New Left protest wave of the 1960s—including women, Native Americans, Hispanics, the disabled, environmentalists—were also generally quiescent in the 1940s and 1950s.

But what about the right? There were, as we noted in Chapter 1, various strands of conservative activism during the 1940s and 50s.[20] Relative to what is to come in the 1960s, however, these movements remain exceedingly small, strategically tame, and with virtually no presence in the Republican Party. There is, of course, McCarthyism, but for all its undeniable power as a political and cultural force in the early 1950s, McCarthyism lacked any real grass roots movement component. The only significant right-wing movement organization to emerge during the period was the John Birch Society, but consistent with our argument, it was actually founded in 1958–59 making it much more of a force in the 1960s than the 1950s.

Campuses were quiet as well, with a host of critics complaining of the docility and conformity of college students in that era. Sociologist Richard Flacks, who went to college during the 1950s, remembers it as "a time of almost total political apathy.... I remember not only the apathy of the fifties, but the virtual miasma of blandness that engulfed student life during those years....And underneath the apathy and the blandness was the sense that everyone was trying to 'make it'—into a secure, 'privatized,' corporate and suburban niche."[21] In his book *The Movement and the Sixties,* Terry Anderson cites a 1960 survey of American college students that provides general support for this view as well. As quoted by Anderson, the authors of a report summarizing the results of the survey stress two central findings: "a remarkable absence of any intense or consuming political beliefs, interests and convictions" and "extreme political and economic conservatism."[22] If we sometimes exaggerate the extent of college student activism in the United States in the 1960s, it would be hard to overstate the paucity of student interest and involvement in politics throughout the 1950s.

In a country born of popular struggle and powerfully shaped, throughout its history, by grass-roots movements, how do we account for the almost total absence of grass-roots activism in the 1940s and 1950s? We see two very broad factors at work here, one positive, the other more ominous. Together they amount to something of a good cop–bad cop story. The bad cop of the story is McCarthyism. In its narrowest form, McCarthyism refers to the four-year crusade (1950–54) by McCarthy and his allies to root out and expose communists in various branches of government and other institutions of American life. There was, however, a broader, more pervasive form of McCarthyism which lived on long after "Tail Gunner" Joe had been discredited and stripped of power. In this broader manifestation, paranoia regarding domestic communism morphed into a generalized fear of dissent and suspicion of those who engaged in it. This generalized opposition to dissent preceded McCarthy and indeed makes his improbable rise to power more understandable. Absent the more pervasive fears of the Cold War period, it is hard to imagine such an undistinguished thug wielding so much power for so long.

In both its broad and narrow forms, McCarthyism had a powerful chilling effect on dissent and protest in the postwar period. This was especially true on the left, which was the target not only of McCarthy's crusade, but, more significantly, the great majority of the hearings conducted by the House Un-American Activities Committee (HUAC) during its 28-year history. Established by the House in 1947, just as the issue of domestic communism was heating up, HUAC went on to hold scores of hearings in the '40s, '50s, and '60s, with the aim of rooting out "un-American" activity in all walks of American life. In the parlance of Cold War America, however, "un-American" was not much more than a synonym for "communist," "socialist," or "fellow-traveler." When it came to HUAC, McCarthy's committee, or virtually any of the other investigative bodies that popped up during this period, it was the American left that found itself squarely in the crosshairs.

It would be hard to overstate the devastating effect that the witch-hunts and other repressive activities of the period had on the American left. It is worth remembering that just 10 to 15 years earlier, during the halcyon days of the mid- to late '30s, the left was probably as strong and politically influential as it has ever been in US history. It was also the ideological inspiration and organizational source for much of the activism that took place in the 1930s.[23] While we don't have comparable "protest event" data from the 1930s, it is clear from the historiography of the period that the volume of movement activity was very high during the decade. While we tend to equate the era with strikes and other forms of disruptive and often violent labor activism in the indus-trial North, the period featured highly transgressive forms of interracial organizing by agricultural workers in the South as well. Add to that the flowering of a wide range of socialist and communist student organiza-tions on American college campuses and the various progressive cultural movements spawned by the Work Projects Administration and other New Deal initiatives, and you begin to understand just how conten-tious and turbulent the era was.

By 1950, however, all of this had changed. In truth, the war years had already taken a severe toll on the left. If, in the 1930s, the Soviet Union remained, for many, a generally positive symbol of an alternative to the rapacious capitalism that had caused the Great Depression, the nonaggression pact that Stalin signed with Hitler in 1939 sent shockwaves through the American left. Even the collapse of that pact and the forging of a wartime alliance between the United States and the USSR proved confusing to many leftists, invested, as they were, in the distinction between the humane socialism of the latter and the evil capitalism of the former. As details of the Stalinist purges of the 1930s began to emerge in the mid-'40s, the sense of crisis on the left became that much more acute. By the end of the war, many former communists and socialists had, in fact, renounced their earlier beliefs. But many had not, leaving the Old Left diminished but still somewhat organizationally intact. The strident anti-communism and witch-hunts of the postwar period saw to that. In the paranoid atmosphere of these years, the threat of being labeled a communist served as a potent deterrent to any leftist—or even liberal—association. Activism of any sort was risky, associated in the public mind with shadowy figures engaged in disreputable and vaguely traitorous goings-on. If the number of leftists formally charged under any of the new "anti-American" statutes or subjected to informal purges by unions, universities, or other institutions was relatively small, the human and organizational toll the repression exacted on the left was enormous. Under the threat of repression, former comrades turned on each other, naming names and decimating leftist organizations and networks in the process. It was the loss of this infrastructure, as much as the repression itself, that crippled progressive activism throughout this period.

So what is the good cop of the story? In fact, we have already touched on it at several points in the chapter. We refer to the overwhelmingly positive national narrative that informed public discourse and permeated political culture in the immediate postwar period. As we noted, most Americans viewed the United States, not simply as the most powerful, or richest nation on earth, but as morally superior as well. "Our" triumph in World War II as well as our struggle with the Soviet Union was seen in moral terms: as good prevailing over evil. Notwithstanding the nation's idealistic embrace of greater inclusion, these were conservative years in the United States, informed by a strident patriotism that equated America with might and right. In this highly charged, borderline jingoistic atmosphere, oppositional ideologies and movements didn't stand much of a chance. Let us revisit one of the time-series figures introduced in the previous chapter. Figure 2.8 shows change over time in the percentage of the American public reporting that they trust the government to do what is right "just about always" or "most of the time."

Given the deep political divisions that characterize contemporary America, the record low levels of trust shown in Figure 2.8 in the most recent surveys is probably not terribly surprising. What may be surprising, however, are the exceptionally high levels of expressed trust in government that prevailed in the earliest years in the series. More than three quarters of those surveyed in 1958 and 1964—the first two times the question was asked—reported high levels of trust in the government. By 2012, that percentage had shrunk to just 24 percent. While data are not available before 1958, there is every reason to believe that the underlying levels of trust in government were broadly comparable throughout the 1940s and 1950s to the figures reported in 1958 and 1964. Our point is a pretty basic one: to the extent that social move-

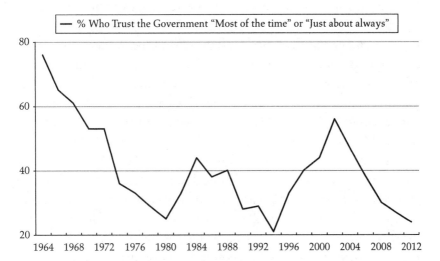

Figure 2.8 Trust in Government, 1964–2012
Source: American National Election Studies
* In 1958, 73% reported high trust in the government; survey not conducted in 1960, 1962, 2006, and 2010; data for 2006 and 2010 are interpolated

ments typically reflect some level of distrust of government, the extraordinarily high levels of popular trust that prevailed in the postwar period would have made the job of movement organizers much more difficult. We attribute the quiescence of the period as much to the generalized trust and pro-American views of the general public as to the "chilling effects" of postwar repression. Whatever the precise mix of factors, however, the empirical reality seems clear enough. It may well be that no extended period in US history was marked by as little grass-roots social movement activity as the 1940s and 1950s.

Summing Up

The postwar period looms large in the collective memory of many Americans, especially those who came of age during the era and even more so those old enough to have experienced those years after the trauma and privations of World War II and the Great Depression. Ronald Reagan is only the best example of a politician who came to office by essentially promising a return to the peace and prosperity of those years. In this sense, the period remains a kind of normative touchstone for many. The more we gain historical perspective on the period, however, the more it appears anomalous relative to what came before and after. Consider the time-series figures introduced in this and the previous chapter; in all of them, it is the postwar period that appears the exception to some more general rule. The comparative income equality of the postwar period rests between extended periods of extreme inequality on either side. The striking ideological convergence of the two parties in the middle decades of the 20th century is preceded and followed by even longer periods of political polarization. In the case of movement activity and trust in government, we lack the comparative data to know exactly what came before, but it is almost certain that here again the postwar years were the exception. We know, for example, that the 1930s were an exceptionally turbulent period, with labor and other forms of unrest spreading apace of the Depression. And while Roosevelt may have slowly restored trust in government over the course of his four-term presidency, we have little doubt that the crash and subsequent economic crisis would have initially undermined public confidence in government. So here again, we strongly suspect that the absence of movement activity and high levels of expressed trust in government are sandwiched between periods of considerable popular dissent and relative distrust of, and lack of confidence in, the federal government. Finally, the sustained prosperity of the period stands in stark contrast to both the extreme privations of the Depression 1930s and the "stagflation" of the 1970s.

If, however, the postwar period was as anomalous as it appears, the question becomes, how did we get there? How did the United States come to be characterized by so many trends that were antithetical to what had come before and would follow afterward? We close with a stylized summary of our answer to this question. That answer begins with the "Big Bang" of the Depression and the political and economic dislocations that accompanied it. Politically, the crisis left the Republican Party in tatters and the Democrats with a stranglehold on federal power. In the meantime, the economic crisis sparked widespread and oftentimes violent unrest and generated considerable sympathy for communist and other socialist alternatives to the capitalism widely blamed for the Depression. The popular unrest pushed the Democrats further to the left politically than they had ever been before while their unprecedented numeric advantage in Congress allowed them to translate this leftward shift into the myriad policies and programs we know as the New Deal. If the aggregate effects of the Depression proved more resistant to these policy responses than Democrats had hoped, they did have the effect of significantly reducing economic disparities in the country. The policies also restored considerable trust in government and proved popular with the general public. They also had a decisive effect on a new generation of GOP lawmakers who, in accepting the broad contours of the emerging welfare state, moved the party decisively closer to the Democrats and set the stage for a return to competitive party politics by the 1940s.

In turn, the impulse to bipartisan cooperation was powerfully reinforced by the wartime emergency and in its immediate aftermath, by the singular threat of communism, in both its international and domestic guises. By renationalizing the "Negro question," the Cold War creates one final basis for significant bipartisan agreement on the need for meaningful civil rights reform (with vigorous dissent from the "third party" Dixiecrats). Together these three issues—the threat of communism, civil rights, and the status of the welfare state—provide a basis for considerable bipartisan cooperation on the major issues of the day. The booming economy certainly didn't hurt matters either, serving to reinforce the general sense of social order and well-being that suffused the period. Finally, the absence of significant popular dissent by either the left or right enables this consensus, by freeing the parties from the need to accommodate mobilized movement wings at their ideological margins. Spared these additional centrifugal pressures, centrist Republicans and Democrats are able to manage the restive right and left wings of their respective parties and hew closely to the political center throughout the postwar period. The result was two decades of sustained prosperity, unprecedented bipartisan cooperation, precious little domestic unrest, and broad public trust and confidence in government. When and why did this all start to unravel? We take up this question in the next chapter.

3

The Center Will Not Hold

The 1960s and the Shifting Racial Geography of American Politics

IT IS HARDLY NEWS THAT THE YEARS 1960 TO 1972 marked a sea change in American culture and politics. At the beginning of the period, the distinctive postwar status quo, detailed in the previous chapter, seemed as strong as ever. Politically centrist coalitions remained dominant in both major parties, allowing for considerable bipartisan cooperation on most issues. Facing off in the first presidential contest of the 1960s were two pragmatic moderates, John F. Kennedy (JFK) for the Democrats and the GOP nominee, Richard Nixon. Both men were more attuned to foreign than domestic affairs, but in fact, their views on the three major policy issues of the day—communism, civil rights, and the role of government—were similar, as were the broader party platforms on which their campaigns were nominally based. Both parties advocated civil rights reform, aggressive action to counter Soviet threats wherever they appeared in the world, and a continued active role for the federal government in countering disadvantage and inequities through various programs and policies. As we noted in the previous chapter, public trust in government was at the highest levels observed for that particular survey question.

By the end of the period, things looked very different. The year 1972 marked another presidential contest, but this time the candidates and their parties offered a stark ideological choice. The Democratic candidate, George McGovern, was running on the most liberal platform in party history. It called for an immediate end to the Vietnam War and generally downplayed the Soviet threat. It also called for more concerted federal action to counter the effects not only of racial discrimination but also of other forms of disadvantage, with specific attention to the plight of Hispanics, Native Americans, the disabled, and women, among others. By contrast, the GOP platform, called for "peace with honor" in Vietnam, while excoriating (Democratic) anti-war demonstrators for dishonoring American troops by giving aid and comfort to the enemy. While touting President Nixon's diplomatic overtures to both China and the Soviet Union, the platform also warned against complacency when it came to the continuing communist threat. Finally, the platform embraced a much more conservative stance not only on the issue of race—arguing against forced busing to achieve educational desegregation—but on government action to address social ills more generally. Reflecting the general turbulence and deep divisions of the late 1960s and early 1970s, public trust and confidence in government was down sharply from the beginning of the period. While more than three quarters of those polled in both 1958 and 1964 indicated they trusted the federal government to do the right thing "just about always" or "most of the time," by 1972 that percentage was down to just slightly more than half of all respondents.[1]

How are we to understand these changes? More to the point, why had the two parties moved so sharply away from each other? What had become of the sustained bipartisan consensus that prevailed in the United States from roughly 1940 until well into the 1960s? The temptation, of course, is simply to blame the collapse of the consensus on the generalized turbulence occasioned by "the Sixties." The Sixties is, in fact, invoked in just this way in countless popular narrative histories with the blame for all manner of contemporary ills laid to the general unrest and chaos of those years. In some cases, the attribution may be justified. When it comes to the considerable partisan overlap of the postwar period, however, the account is far too crude to serve as a satisfactory answer to the question. Two points are worth making here. First, in strictly chronological terms, the Sixties is really a misnomer. While we tend to think of the entire decade as an undifferentiated, rebellious whole, most Americans did not experience it that way.

Instead the early years of the decade—up through, say, 1964—were really more aligned with the staid, conformist '50s than the stereotypic Sixties. Conversely, much of the political upheaval and countercultural experimentation we associate with the Sixties were actually more in evidence in the 1970s than in the prior decade. It is, for example, commonplace to include feminism, environmentalism, and gay liberation in the long, undifferentiated list of "'60s movements," even though these struggles really only emerged or took off in the 1970s. Similarly, if we track the incidence of virtually any alleged Sixties countercultural practice—drug usage or cohabitation outside marriage, for example—we typically see that the real escalation in the behavior took place in the 1970s rather than in the previous decade.[2] In this sense, the most intense period of generalized political and cultural ferment is a span of years bridging the 1960s and '70s. We might nominate 1967–1973 for this honor, but the precise time period matters less than the general point. The temporal heart of the "'60s phenomenon" comes later in time than most popular narrative histories suggest.

Our second point is related to the first but assumes a substantive, rather than temporal, focus. Over the years, the first author has taught many courses on the Sixties. He has always opened those classes by asking the students to offer up images of the period in question. These images are always the same; with more stress on the counterculture than politics and with images invariably drawn from the late '60s/early '70s rather than the very early 1960s. To oversimplify, the images tend to focus on the "sex, drugs, and rock and roll" dimension of the Sixties, with a few images of anti-war protests and/or women's lib "bra burners" thrown in as a reminder that politics played some part in the period too. This is, to put the matter bluntly, a decidedly white, middle-class perspective on the Sixties, probably filtered through the students' parents backward-looking, simplified, positive or negative view of the era. Once in a great while, a student—typically of color—may throw in an image of Martin Luther King Jr. (MLK) or police dogs and fire hoses from Birmingham, but this is the exception.

So what does this aside have to do with the question posed earlier regarding the collapse of the postwar consensus? Answer: while the generalized rebellion and turbulence of the late 1960s and early 1970s exacerbated partisan divisions within the two parties, the decisive break occurred much earlier, with the seeds sown in the first few years of the decade. Our stereotypic rendering of the substantive issues that catalyzed the Sixties is as badly distorted as our temporal map of the period. To wit: the collapse of the postwar consensus had everything to do with race and much less to do with the issues—Vietnam, sexism, cultural liberation—that defined the later years of the period. To be clear, these later issues—especially Vietnam—clearly magnified partisan divisions, but they were not the root cause of them. That honor, as with the origin of the convulsive Sixties more generally, goes to the African-American freedom struggle and the enduring changes it brought to the structure of American politics.

This is really the story of the return of social movements to American politics after the relative quiescence of the postwar period. More accurately, it is the story of not one, but *two* parallel movements, the revitalized civil rights movement of the early 1960s and the powerful segregationist countermovement, that quickly developed in response to the black freedom struggle. Our claim is that these two struggles did much more than simply bring the movement form back to American politics; more important, over a fairly short span of time in the early to mid-'60s, the two movements decisively altered the partisan geography of the United States and in the process pushed the national Democratic and Republican parties sharply to the left and right, respectively, undermining the centrist policy convergence of the postwar period and setting the parties on the divisive course they remain on today. Our concern in the chapter is not the present but the seismic shifts that took place roughly a half-century ago. We take up the two movements in turn, being sure to note the dynamic connections between them as we go. We begin, appropriately, with the "borning struggle" of the civil rights movement.

The Civil Rights Revolution

As one of the handful of most significant movements in US history, the civil rights struggle is routinely credited with any number of specific effects, ranging from the restoration of voting rights in the South to the collapse of the constitutional underpinnings of "separate but equal," and just for fun, the rise of blue jeans as the ultimate fashion fad of the

1960s.[3] Arguably the most important legacy of the movement, however, is one whose significance is only now starting to be recognized. In setting in motion a fundamental transformation of the racial geography of American politics, the movement brought to a close the most sustained period of progressive policymaking in federal history (1932–1968) and ushered in the era of rising inequality and political polarization in which we remain mired.

The pivot point of this transformation comes, as we will show, in the early to mid-1960s, as a result of the relentless pressure that civil rights forces brought to bear on the American state and the Democratic administrations that were serving at the time as its stewards. However, to really grasp the decisive effect the movement had on the Democratic Party, the New Deal coalition, and American politics more generally, it will be necessary to go back even further in time and describe in some detail the distinctive racial geography that structured politics in this country from the close of the Civil War to the onset of the 1960s. Only by putting the events of that pivotal decade, the '60s, in broader historical context can one appreciate the seismic shift in the political landscape set in motion by the civil rights revolution.

The Solid South, the Party of Lincoln, and the Geography of Race, 1876–1960

The standard narrative account of the relationship between the civil rights movement and the Democratic Party tends to depict the two as staunch allies in the struggle. To be sure, the celebrated legislative achievements that marked the struggle—the Civil Rights Act of 1964 and the 1965 Voting Rights Act—could not have been achieved without the contributions of both parties. But to see the movement and the party as allies is to ignore the enduring and deep antipathy that marked the relationship between civil rights forces and the Democratic Party until well into the 1930s. More accurately, the relationship evolved through three distinct phases. The first lasts from the close of the Civil War until Roosevelt's election in 1932. This is the period of intense, sustained enmity between the Democratic Party and civil rights forces who, in truth, are a small and beleaguered group during this, the heyday of Jim Crow. The antagonism is rooted in history. It is hard to overstate the lasting hatred that southern whites felt toward a Republican Party (the despised Party of Lincoln), which, from their point of view, had inflicted the "War of Northern Aggression" on the region. With most southern blacks stripped of the franchise during this period, white voters transform the region into a one-party racial autocracy—the "solid South"—which will serve as the electoral foundation of the national Democratic Party from the end of Reconstruction until well into the 1960s.

Figure 3.1 shows the electoral map of Herbert Hoover's victory in the 1928 presidential contest and clearly underscores the dependence of the Democratic Party on the votes of southern segregationists. Of the scant 87 electoral votes captured by the Democratic candidate, Al Smith, in that year's race, 64 came by way of southern states. This was altogether typical of the results in the early decades of the 20th century, during which the Party was uniquely beholden to its southern, segregationist wing.

Roosevelt's election in 1932 marked the onset of a second, much more complicated, contradictory—one might even say "schizophrenic"—period in the relationship between the Democratic Party and

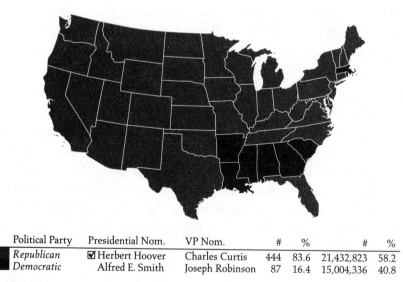

Political Party	Presidential Nom.	VP Nom.	#	%	#	%
■ Republican	☑ Herbert Hoover	Charles Curtis	444	83.6	21,432,823	58.2
Democratic	Alfred E. Smith	Joseph Robinson	87	16.4	15,004,336	40.8

Figure 3.1 1928 Presidential Election
Source: UCSB American Presidency Project

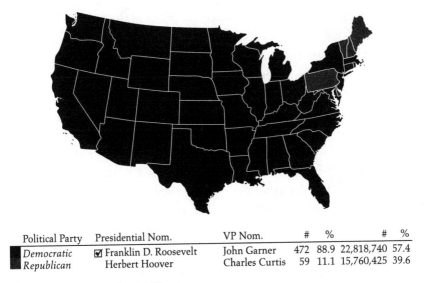

Political Party	Presidential Nom.	VP Nom.	#	%	#	%
Democratic	☑ Franklin D. Roosevelt	John Garner	472	88.9	22,818,740	57.4
Republican	Herbert Hoover	Charles Curtis	59	11.1	15,760,425	39.6

Figure 3.2 1932 Presidential Election
Source: UCSB American Presidency Project

civil rights forces. Besides reclaiming the White House after a 12-year hiatus, FDR's victory also served to fundamentally transform the party. The electoral map of the 1932 contest tells the story (see figure 3.2).

While the South remained solidly Democratic in 1932, Roosevelt's resounding victory essentially marked the birth of the modern Democratic Party and the northern, liberal labor wing that would, in time, come to be the dominant force in the party. By the late 1930s, the most progressive elements in this wing had allied themselves with civil rights forces and racial liberals in the GOP to introduce anti-lynching bills in Congress. By the mid-'40s, these same labor/civil rights Democrats had supplanted liberal Republicans as the cutting edge of the civil rights struggle in Congress.[4] Finally, in the 1960s, this wing would succeed in allying the broader party with the civil rights movement, ushering in the third and final period in that evolving relationship. During this second period from 1932 until the early '60s, however, the party remained fundamentally divided on the issue of race, though by default committed to accommodating the regional "sensibilities" of the Dixiecrats. No one was more adept at this accommodation than FDR during his long tenure in office. Given his patrician background, his clear liberal views, and the even more radical sensibilities of some of his key advisers, especially those of his wife, Eleanor, you would have thought that southern whites would have abandoned the party in droves during the Roosevelt years. To the contrary, Roosevelt was wildly popular in the South, carrying every single state of the former Confederacy in all four of his presidential races.

Some of this popularity was due to the fact that, unlike today, social programs had considerable appeal in the South, the nation's poorest region, struggling as it was under the added burden of the Great Depression. But make no mistake about it; had Roosevelt openly espoused pro–civil rights views, his stance on any other issue would have mattered little to the white South. In truth, FDR took great care during his 13 years in office to give the white South—and especially the region's powerful congressional delegations—no reason to doubt his commitment to the long-standing federal-southern "understanding" with respect to race.

With the close of Reconstruction in 1877, federal involvement in racial matters came to an abrupt end. Control over racial issues reverted to the states. Roosevelt was not about to violate this tacit "hands off" policy. Even on as morally a compelling issue as lynching "Roosevelt remained silent on racial matters throughout his four-term presidency, refusing to come out in favor of anti-lynching legislation on the numerous occasions such bills were brought before Congress."[5] But FDR's accommodation of the policy prerogatives of the southern wing of his party went far beyond his refusal to publicly advocate for black civil rights. It informed, as Ira Katznelson has so brilliantly documented, the discriminatory implementation of virtually all of the key New Deal programs enacted on his watch. Even as he advocated a fair deal for all, Roosevelt was perfectly willing to deny to blacks various forms of relief in exchange for crucial southern support for his legislative agenda. FDR also catered to the Dixiecrats in his choice of running mates. Of the three vice-presidents who served under Roosevelt, two, John Nance Garner of Texas and Harry Truman from Missouri, came from former slaveholding states or territories. Needing the electoral votes of the "solid South" and the legislative cooperation of the region's senior senators and House members, Roosevelt was only too happy to use the implementation of New Deal programs and his powers of appointment to reassure the South of his sensitivity to their distinctive regional "traditions." Translation: the "southern way of life" will be safe on my watch.[6] Nor was this all just cynical calculus on Roosevelt's part. As William Leuchtenburg makes clear in his 2005 book, *The White House Looks South*, FDR enjoyed a special relationship with the South, nurtured in large part by his 21-year residence in Warm Springs, Georgia. Roosevelt first went to the small spa town when he contracted polio in 1924 but fell in love with the place and the warmth of the local residents and maintained a second home there until his death in 1945.

The important point is that as long as the progressive racial views of northern liberal Democrats were held in check and tacit support for Jim Crow remained the guiding—if unofficial—policy of the party, the South remained solidly and reliably in the Democratic column. In turn, the need to accommodate the views of the Dixiecrats had a moderating effect on the party's policy preferences, most notably with respect to race. So even in the face of the gradual ascendance of the party's liberal labor wing after 1932, the Democrats remained, *in the aggregate*, moderately centrist in their policies. And with moderate to liberal Republicans consistently replacing their more conservative predecessors after 1944, the GOP, as we have seen, also moved steadily to the ideological center during the postwar period. These trends set the stage for the unprecedented period of sustained bipartisanship documented in the previous chapter. But even as the postwar period was getting under way, the seeds of change in the two-party system were being sown.

The Cold War and the Renationalization of Race

In the preceding section, we devoted considerable attention to Roosevelt's strategic silence on matters of race and his unwavering efforts to accommodate the Dixiecrat wing of his party. By contrast, within a year of FDR's death in office in 1945, his successor, Harry Truman, violated the tacit federal "hands off" policy with respect to race when he created a national Committee on Civil Rights and charged it with investigating "the current state of civil rights in the country and recommending appropriate legislative remedies for deficiencies uncovered."[7] Two years later, in 1948, Truman went even further, issuing two landmark Executive Orders, the first establishing a fair employment board within the Civil Service Commission, and the second calling for the gradual desegregation of the armed forces. Why did Truman act when Roosevelt had not? Comparing the domestic political environments in which FDR and Truman found themselves only deepens the puzzle. While Roosevelt's electoral margins left him politically secure, Truman's status as an unelected incumbent made him uniquely vulnerable to challenge as he headed into the 1948 presidential campaign. Moreover, with black voters now returning solid Democratic majorities, Truman had seemingly little to gain and everything to lose by alienating the Dixiecrat wing of his party. And that, of course, is exactly what his open advocacy of civil rights reform did. Angered by his proactive support for civil rights, the Dixiecrats broke with the party in 1948 and ran their own candidate, Strom Thurmond, for president on the States Rights Party ticket. The electoral votes of the once "solid South" were now in peril. Given Truman's own roots in the South and early racial attitudes,[8] to say nothing of the general conservatism of the Cold War period, one could hardly think of a less likely candidate and less propitious time to be advocating politically and socially progressive causes.

The otherwise puzzling contrast between Truman's aggressive actions and Roosevelt's resolute inaction on the issue becomes entirely comprehensible, however, when placed in the very different international contexts in which they occurred. The postwar world that confronted Truman exposed the United States to two unprecedented sources of pressure regarding its treatment of African Americans. One, ironically, was the anti-racist ideology the allies had espoused in waging war against the Axis powers, and which, following the termination of hostilities, was explicitly encoded in the founding language of the United Nations. While all of the allies had long been identified with egalitarian principles in the abstract, the war effort and the boost it gave to the postwar stress on global human rights forced France, Great Britain, and the United States to more scrupulously conform to these principles. For France and Britain this meant decolonization; for the United States, civil rights reform.

The second, and far more significant, source of pressure came courtesy of the Cold War. The onset of the Cold War effectively ruled out any possibility of a return to the isolationist foreign policy that had, since the First World War, shaped America's relationship to the rest of the world. With both France and Great Britain decisively weakened by World War II and in no position to counter the emerging Soviet threat, it fell to the United States to assume the role of global "policeman for Democracy." As a consequence of this role, federal policymakers—first and foremost the president—found themselves exposed to international political pressures and considerations their predecessors had been spared. Extensive research has greatly enhanced our understanding of this period by documenting the rising tide of international criticism directed at the United States—by allies and nonaligned countries as well as the Soviet bloc—during the Cold War period.[9] Locked in an increasingly intense ideological struggle with the USSR for influence around the world—and especially with emerging Third World nations—American racism suddenly took on great international signif- icance as an effective propaganda weapon of the Soviets. Viewed in this light, Truman's civil rights initiatives should be seen for what they were: not so much domestic reform efforts as a critical component of his Cold War foreign policy.[10] In short, after a 70-year hiatus, the onset of the Cold War renationalized the issue of race. But if the pressures that had occasioned this renationalization were primarily international, the domestic political consequences that followed from it were to be signif- icant and long lasting. As a harbinger of what was to come in the 1960s, the 1948 Dixiecrat revolt, merits a bit more attention.

The Dixiecrat Revolt

We pick up the story with the 1948 election. The question is what became of that year's Dixiecrat revolt within the Democratic Party? Leading up to the election, it looked for all the world as if the third party candidacy of the Dixiecrat's standard bearer, Strom Thurmond, was going to cost Truman the election. As most everyone knows, it did not turn out that way. The photo of Truman celebrating his victory while displaying a copy of the *Chicago Tribune* headline proclaiming "Dewey Defeats Truman" is one of the iconic shots in the annals of the American presidency. Although the 1948 electoral map (see Figure 3.3) shows Thurmond carrying the Deep South (except Georgia), the revolt failed to spread far enough to deprive Truman of his narrow victory over the Republican nominee, Thomas Dewey.

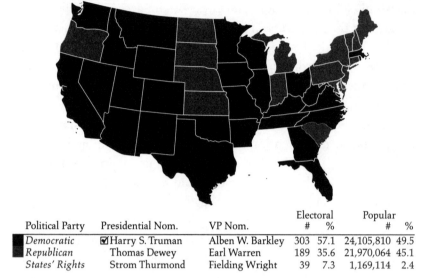

Political Party	Presidential Nom.	VP Nom.	Electoral #	%	Popular #	%
Democratic	☑Harry S. Truman	Alben W. Barkley	303	57.1	24,105,810	49.5
Republican	Thomas Dewey	Earl Warren	189	35.6	21,970,064	45.1
States' Rights	Strom Thurmond	Fielding Wright	39	7.3	1,169,114	2.4

Figure 3.3 1948 Presidential Election
Source: UCSB American Presidency Project

So what became of the South's anger toward Truman and the national Democratic Party for its "betrayal" of the region? Certainly Truman did nothing in his second term in office to assuage the Dixiecrats. On the contrary, his Cold War–motivated advocacy of civil rights reform continued throughout his remaining four years in office. He closed out his term by directing his attorney general to file an amicus brief in support of a school desegregation case, *Brown v. Topeka Board of Education*, at that time before the US Supreme Court. The link between the imperatives of the Cold War and the administration's open embrace of civil rights reform were clearly spelled out in the brief, which read in part: "It is in the context of the present world struggle between freedom and tyranny that the problem of racial discrimination must be viewed.... Racial discrimination furnishes grist for the Communist propaganda mills, and it raises doubt even among friendly nations as the intensity of our devotion to the democratic faith."[11]

Given Truman's sustained, if mostly symbolic, advocacy of civil rights, one might have expected a repeat in the 1952 election of what happened four years earlier; that is, another third party challenge by the white South under the banner of "state's rights." But no such challenge was mounted, nor apparently contemplated. The reasons for this are not so hard to discern. For starters, the target of the Dixiecrats' wrath four years earlier—Truman—was not on the ballot in 1952. Nor did the 1952 Democratic platform feature civil rights reform anywhere near as prominently as it had in 1948. What's more, the Republican platform was virtually indistinguishable on the issue from that of the Democrats. Most importantly, with the Korean conflict still raging and Joe McCarthy at or near the peak of his power, the issue of race received very little attention in the run-up to the election. Instead, the Cold War—in various guises—dominated debate within and between the two parties in '52. In the end, Eisenhower's popularity rendered the issue moot in any case. As the electoral map for that year shows (see Figure 3.4), only the return of the South to the Democratic fold prevented Ike from a clean sweep of the country. The Dixiecrat revolt appeared to be a thing of the past.

Eisenhower's two terms in office only reinforced the sense that the traditional sectional loyalties had been restored. The South's traditional enmity toward the GOP was rekindled in these years now that it was a Republican president responding to the new Cold War realities with the same kind of advocacy of civil rights seen under Truman.[12] Reflecting the

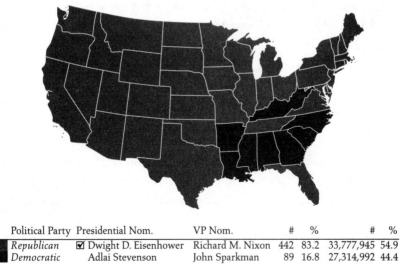

Political Party	Presidential Nom.	VP Nom.	#	%	#	%
Republican	☑ Dwight D. Eisenhower	Richard M. Nixon	442	83.2	33,777,945	54.9
Democratic	Adlai Stevenson	John Sparkman	89	16.8	27,314,992	44.4

Figure 3.4 1952 Presidential Election
Source: UCSB American Presidency Project

prevailing bipartisan consensus on the issue, Eisenhower's actions in this area essentially mimicked those of his predecessor. "During his first term, Eisenhower continued the trend established by Truman. Through executive action he accelerated the desegregation of the armed services and pressed for the integration of facilities throughout the District of Columbia."[13] Eisenhower also continued Truman's practice of directing his attorney general to file amicus briefs in support of civil rights cases reaching the Supreme Court. It was also on his watch that the Court issued its unanimous, landmark decision in the *Brown* case. And while Eisenhower famously cautioned that court cases and legislation alone could not change racial attitudes, he was steadfast in calling on all Americans to abide by the Court's decisions in this area. Eisenhower's time in office also coincided with the first piece of federal civil rights legislation—the 1957 Civil Rights Act—since Reconstruction. All of this angered the white South, but nothing prompted more regional vitriol than Eisenhower's decision to send federal troops to Arkansas in the fall of 1957 to enforce the desegregation of Little Rock's Central High School. Nothing Truman had done provoked anything like the backlash that followed Eisenhower's decisive stand on the matter. Editorials throughout the region inveighed against Eisenhower's action, invariably describing it as akin to another "War of Northern Aggression" or the onset of a second "Reconstruction."

Eisenhower's personal ambivalence regarding the appropriate role for the federal government in matters of race was clearly lost on the white South. By the time he left office, southern anger over the federal government's "assault" on state's rights (read: segregation) was once again primarily directed at the Party of Lincoln. There is a more general, and critically important, point to be made here. As the 1960s dawned, the Democratic Party remained deeply divided on the issue of race and, in the *aggregate*, much more opposed to civil rights reform than the Republicans. We offer two significant "data points" from the late 1950s in support of this characterization. We briefly alluded earlier to the 1957 Civil Rights Act. Notwithstanding its substantive weakness, the bill's status as the first piece of federal civil rights legislation since Reconstruction made it symbolically very significant. How did the two parties vote on the bill? Table 3.1 provides the answer to that question.

For those conditioned by today's stark partisan divisions to think of Republicans as extreme racial conservatives relative to Democrats, the

Table 3.1 Congressional Voting on 1957 Civil Rights Act

House Democrats: 118 Yes; 107 No
House Republicans: 167 Yes; 19 No
Senate Democrats: 29 Yes; 18 No
Senate Republicans: 43 Yes; 0 No

Source: govtrack.us

results of the 1957 vote will come as a revelation. While all 43 Senate Republicans backed the bill, 18 of their 47 Democratic colleagues opposed it. In the House, a stunning 90 percent of GOP representatives cast their votes in favor of the act (167–19), while Democrats essentially split on the measure (118 to 107 in favor of). Quite simply, this important piece of breakthrough legislation was primarily the work of Republican, not Democratic, lawmakers.

The second piece of evidence mirrors the first. In their 1989 book, *Issue Evolution,* Carmines and Stimson report the partisan distribution of racial "liberals" and "conservatives" in the Senate during the 85th Congress, which served from 1957 to 1959. The party difference in this regard is striking. Based on their voting records, 42 of the 46 Republican senators scored as racial "liberals." By contrast, notwithstanding the cutting-edge, civil rights views of many in the northern wing of the party, 27 of 48 Democratic senators were racial "conservatives." Taken together, these data points support two conclusions. First, as the Sixties dawned, the Democrats remained decidedly schizophrenic on the issue of race, with most northern Democrats deeply committed to reform and virtually all Dixicrats just as intransigent as ever on the matter. Second, even if the most committed racial liberals were Democrats, the GOP was, in the aggregate, far and away more progressive on civil rights issues. All of this would change—irrevocably—as both parties scrambled to respond to the dramatic rebirth and escalating turmoil of the civil rights revolution.

Kennedy, the Revitalized Movement, and the Dixiecrat Revolt Revisited

The Kennedy-Nixon presidential contest in 1960 remains one of the tightest in US history. Out of more than 68 million ballots cast, Kennedy won by only 112,000 votes. Kennedy's share of the popular vote was 49.7 percent to Nixon's 49.6 percent. The demography of Kennedy's win, however, had disquieting implications for the future of his party. Reflecting the strategic dilemma that would roil the Democrats in the decade to come, the votes of both African Americans and southern whites had proven to be crucial to JFK's razor-thin victory. In his 1976 book, *Black Ballots*, Stephen Lawson underscores the critical importance of the "black vote" to Kennedy's election. "An analysis of the returns demonstrated that Negro ballots were enough to give the Democratic contender a winning margin in New Jersey, Michigan, Illinois, Texas and South Carolina, all states that had supported Eisenhower in 1956. Had the Republican-Democratic division in the black districts of these states broken down in the same way as four years earlier, Richard Nixon would have become the thirty-fifth President."[14] At the same time, there is no gainsaying the decisive importance of the "solid South" to Kennedy's victory. As the 1960 electoral map shows (see Figure 3.5), no region of the country went as decisively for JFK as did the South. Had the Deep South abandoned the Democratic candidate as it did in 1948, Nixon would have won handily.

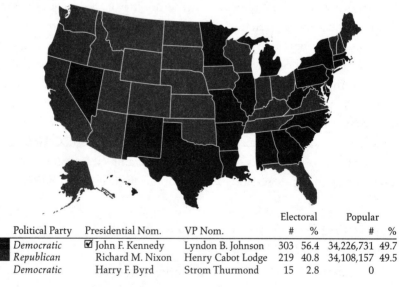

Political Party	Presidential Nom.	VP Nom.	Electoral #	Electoral %	Popular #	Popular %
Democratic	☑ John F. Kennedy	Lyndon B. Johnson	303	56.4	34,226,731	49.7
Republican	Richard M. Nixon	Henry Cabot Lodge	219	40.8	34,108,157	49.5
Democratic	Harry F. Byrd	Strom Thurmond	15	2.8	0	

Figure 3.5 1960 Presidential Election
Source: UCSB American Presidency Project

These electoral cross pressures meant that the new president began his term in a serious strategic straitjacket. If he eschewed his predecessors' civil rights agenda, he risked alienating the large and strategically positioned black vote so key to his victory over Nixon. If, on the other hand, he sought to solidify black support by aggressively promoting additional civil rights measures, he faced the specter of another Dixiecrat revolt. As bad as this strategic dilemma was, two developments in the early 1960s were to make it even worse. The first was the onset of the heyday of the modern civil rights movement. As we noted in Chapter 2, the canonical account of the civil rights struggle turns on a significant temporal distortion. The account has the movement marching inexorably forward from its "birth" in Montgomery in 1955–56 until its "death" in the late 1960s or early 1970s. This stylized account obscures, in at least two ways, a far more complicated story. First, as recent scholarship on the "long civil rights movement" reminds us the struggle began much earlier than 1955 and extended well beyond the alleged "death" of the movement circa 1970.[15] But even were we to accept the standard 1955–70 time frame, there is another lie encoded in the popular narrative. The movement hardly resembled an inexorable upward march between 1955 and 1970. Reproduced below in Figure 3.6 is the same time series of annual "civil rights movement actions" reported in the previous chapter.

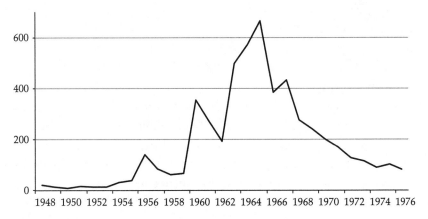

Figure 3.6 Civil Rights Movement Events, 1948–1976
Source: New York Times

In truth, after the triumph of Montgomery, the movement struggled to find its footing, and, confronted with the white South's campaign of "massive resistance" in the late 1950s, it found itself largely moribund as the new decade dawned. It was, as the figure shows, the 1960 sit-in campaign that revived the struggle and ushered in the true heyday of the movement between 1960 and 1965. The important implication of this is that neither Eisenhower nor Truman had had to contend with the intense bottom-up pressure of the fully mobilized civil rights movement. Kennedy, on the other hand, did. His were the years of the Freedom Rides, of fire hoses and police dogs in Birmingham, and King's "I Have a Dream Speech" at the epochal 1963 March on Washington. Not since the Civil War had America been challenged so intensely to put its racial house in order. And this time, courtesy of the Cold War, it had to do so with the whole world watching and the global battle for geopolitical supremacy hanging in the balance.

This brings us to the second dilemma: Kennedy had to contend with the intense bottom-up pressure of the civil rights movement during an especially "hot" phase of the Cold War. In his celebrated 1,000 days in office, Kennedy confronted no less than four major Cold War crises: the erection of the Berlin Wall by East German authorities; the collapse of the Diem regime in South Vietnam; the disastrous Bay of Pigs invasion of Cuba; and the single most dangerous confrontation with the Soviet Union in the history of the superpower competition: the Cuban missile crisis in October of 1962.

Nor, as we have tried to make clear, should these two dilemmas be regarded as separate sources of pressure on the administration. Instead, there was a close connection between the two. For their part, the Soviets monitored racial tensions and conflict in the United States very closely, launching major propaganda attacks in the wake of every celebrated attack or atrocity. And central to movement strategy during this period was a savvy understanding of just how vulnerable the United States was to criticism on racial grounds, as a result of the Cold War. Publicized instances of American-style racism constituted an enormous liability when it came to countering Soviet influence in the world, especially among "peoples of color" in the emerging nations of Asia and Africa. The central tactical dynamic at the heart of the movement during these years reflects this understanding. "Lacking sufficient power to defeat the segregationists at the state or local level [in the South], movement forces sought to broaden the conflict by inducing opponents to disrupt public order to the point where sympathetic media coverage and broad public support—international no less than domestic—for the movement could be mobilized. In turn, the media coverage and public [outrage] virtually compelled federal officials to intervene in ways supportive of the movement."[16]

The picture is of the Kennedy administration and, by extension, the Democratic Party being inexorably pushed off center by the centrifugal force of a national movement operating at the peak of its extraordinary mobilizing powers. No single episode during Kennedy's abbreviated tenure in office speaks to the force of these pressures better than the evolution of the 1964 Civil Rights Act and the final partisan breakdown of votes on the measure. To underscore the intensity of the pressure brought to bear on the president by civil rights forces during this period, we show in Figure 3.7 the number of "movement actions" reported in the *New York Times* for each month between January 1961 and Kennedy's death in November 1963.

The peak of movement activity during this period corresponds to the high drama of Martin Luther King Jr.'s Birmingham campaign in April

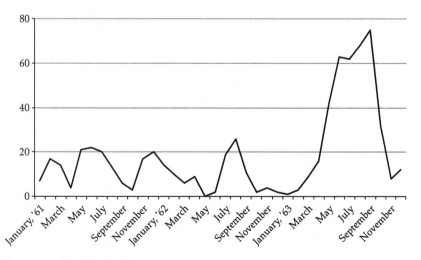

Figure 3.7 Civil Rights Movement Activity, 1961–1963
Source: New York Times

and May of 1963. To understand the intensity of the events in Birmingham and how well they fit the general strategic dynamic described, it will help to contrast the episode with the major campaign that preceded it. That episode took place in Albany, Georgia, beginning in November of 1961 and extending through the summer of the following year. In intent and scale, Albany closely resembled the later Birmingham campaign. In both cases, King and his supporters sought to bring the city to a standstill by launching a community-wide campaign of nonviolent civil disobedience to call attention to the continued denial of black civil and political rights in Albany and, by extension, throughout the Deep South. Reflecting the campaign, Figure 3.7 shows a modest increase in movement activity in late 1961 and early to mid-1962, but nothing on the scale of what would come later in Birmingham. This is entirely consistent with narrative accounts of the campaign. Those accounts stress the firm control exercised by police chief Laurie Pritchett over events in Albany. While systematically denying demonstrators their rights, Pritchett nonetheless did so in such a way as to prevent the major breakdown of public order that would have compelled federal intervention. Or, as another chronicler of the events in Albany put it, "the reason.... [the movement] failed in Albany was that Chief Pritchett used force rather than violence in controlling the situation."[17] Even in defeat, then, the strategic dynamic described earlier was evident in Albany. Failing to provoke the public violence necessary to prompt federal intervention, insurgents lacked sufficient leverage to achieve anything more than a standoff with the local supremacist forces in Albany. The setback in Albany was not without value, however, as the following revealing quote from King suggests:

> There were weaknesses in Albany, and a share of the responsibility belongs to each of us who participated. However, none of us was so immodest as to feel himself master of the new theory. Each of us expected that setbacks would be a part of the ongoing effort. There is no tactical theory so neat that a revolutionary struggle for a share of power can be won merely by pressing a row of buttons. Humanbeings with all their faults and strengths constitute the mechanism of a social movement. They must make mistakes and learn from them, make more mistakes and learn anew.... Time and action are the

teachers. When we planned our strategy for Birmingham months later we spent hours assessing Albany and trying to learn from our errors.[18]

The important implication of King's statement is that a fuller understanding of the dynamic on offer here was born of events in Albany. No doubt a part of that "fuller understanding" was a growing awareness of the importance of white violence as a catalyst of the kind of media attention that compelled federal intervention. As Hubbard argues, this awareness appears to have figured in King's choice of Birmingham as the site of his next major protest campaign. "King's Birmingham innovation was pre-eminently strategic. Its essence was not merely more refined tactics, but the selection of a target city which had as its Commissioner of Public Safety 'Bull' Connor, a notoriously racist and hothead who could be depended on *not* to respond nonviolently."[19]

The timing of the events in Birmingham strongly supports Hubbard's contention that there was strategic calculus involved in the selection of the city as the site for King's next major protest campaign. The significant fact here is that Connor was a lame-duck official at the time of the campaign, having been defeated in his bid for reelection in early April of 1963. Given this and his reputation for racist violence, why, it seems reasonable to ask, didn't King and the Southern Christian Leadership Conference (SCLC) wait until Connor was out of office to launch the campaign? Pat Watters, one of the most astute observers of the civil rights struggle, provides the logical answer to the question when he writes that "the supposition has to be that...SCLC, in a shrewd...stratagem, knew a good enemy when they saw him...one that could be counted on in stupidity and natural viciousness to play into their hands for full exploitation *in the press* as archfiend and villain."[20]

The sharp spike in "movement actions" in Figure 3.7 corresponding to the Birmingham campaign attests to the strategic savvy underlying the choice of protest site. After a few days of uncharacteristic restraint, Connor unleashed the police dogs and fire hoses featured in the iconic images that made headlines around the world and brought the weight of international and national pressure to bear on the White House. Predictably, the administration was forced to intervene and not simply to restore some measure of public order in Birmingham. More significant was Kennedy's reversal of an earlier decision to not bring civil rights legislation to Congress in '63. "The ultimate result [of Birmingham]...was administration sponsorship of a civil rights bill that, even in a much weaker form, had earlier been described as politically inopportune by administration spokesmen. Under [sustained] pressure by insurgents, the bill was ultimately signed into law a year later as the Civil Rights Act of 1964."[21]

Like Truman and Roosevelt before him, Kennedy had taken office determined to accommodate the southern wing of his party, without whom he knew he would never be returned to office in 1964. Ultimately, however, the pressure brought to bear on him by the movement—compounded by the Cold War dynamic described earlier—forced him and his party to move sharply left in policy terms. In Table 3.1 we reported the distribution of Republican and Democratic votes on the 1957 Civil Rights Act in both the House and Senate. Table 3.2 compares the 1957 votes to those cast for and against the 1964 bill. The comparison makes it clear that in shifting sharply left on civil rights, Kennedy was simply mirroring the broader trend within his party. Whereas Democratic House members had virtually split on the 1957 bill, nearly two thirds favored the much stronger 1964 measure. A similar increase in support was also evident among Democratic senators between 1957 and 1964.

There was, of course, a price to be paid for so direct a challenge to the southern wing of Kennedy's own party. As much as he had hoped,

Table 3.2 Congressional Voting on 1957 and 1964 Civil Rights Acts

---

1957 Civil Rights Act

House Democrats: 118 Yes; 107 No

House Republicans: 167 Yes; 19 No

Senate Democrats: 29 Yes; 18 No

Senate Republicans: 43 Yes; 0 No

1964 Civil Rights Act

House Democrats: 153 Yes; 91 No

House Republicans: 136 Yes; 35 No

Senate Democrats: 46 Yes; 21 No

Senate Republicans: 27 Yes; 6 No

Source: govtrack.us

at the time of his election, to be able to balance the demands of Dixiecrats and civil rights forces, by the time of his death, Kennedy was clearly perceived as siding with the movement. While doing fieldwork in Mississippi more than 20 years after JFK's assassination, it was not uncommon for the first author to find framed pictures of Kennedy and Martin Luther King Jr. on the walls of the homes of black interview subjects. JFK remained a revered figure to many in the black community, especially those old enough to have memories of his presidency.[22] On the other side of the political ledger, it seems clear that many Dixiecrats, outraged by what they saw as federal complicity in the attack on "the southern way of life," were poised to abandon Kennedy and the Democrats in 1964. In the end, though, his death meant that the revolt, if it were to come, would be on someone else's watch. That someone would be native Southerner, Lyndon Baines Johnson.

Freedom Summer and the Convention Challenge

In the immediate aftermath of Kennedy's death, the prospects for anything other than a resounding Democratic victory in 1964 seemed remote. The outpouring of grief and sympathy for the martyred president was like nothing the country had ever seen before.[23] Other sitting presidents had been assassinated, of course, but none of the earlier tragedies had touched the national psyche in quite the same way as that day in Dallas. Whatever the reasons for this unprecedented response— Kennedy's charisma, the idealism and innocence of the era, the tender ages of his orphaned children, the popularity of his widowed First Lady, the fact that the country had watched the events unfold on live television—the immediate political fallout from the tragedy seemed clear on its face. Whatever differences of opinion people had had of him in life seemed to vanish amid the outpouring of grief aroused by his death.

Correctly divining the mood of the country, Lyndon Baines Johnson (LBJ) hitched his own electoral prospects to the fallen president, in essence dedicating the balance of his term to the realization of Kennedy's legislative program. The most immediate, high-profile manifestation of this stance was Johnson's sustained and effective advocacy of what would become the Civil Rights Act of 1964. In his own words, "No memorial oration or eulogy could more eloquently honor President

Kennedy's memory than the earliest possible passage of the civil rights bill for which he fought so long." Johnson's embrace of his predecessor's civil rights agenda did not, however, mean that he was blind to the serious political risks posed by this stance. Indeed, as both a white Southerner and one of the consummate majority leaders in the history of the Senate, LBJ understood the contradictions inherent in his party better than almost anyone. As he headed into the election year of 1964, he was determined to manage those contradictions and do what he could to retain the loyalties of both civil rights forces and his fellow Dixiecrats. Johnson assumed—rightly in the end—that his support for the afore-mentioned bill would mollify those civil rights leaders who were ini-tially deeply skeptical of his commitment to the cause. The bigger trick, he knew, would be avoiding another rebellion by the southern wing of his party. The bill was bad enough. The threat of more Birminghams, with armies of civil rights protestors descending on southern cities, was worse still. Johnson did what he could to avert this threat, indirectly calling on civil rights leaders to effectively suspend disruptive demon-strations in the run-up to the fall election.[24]

With the Republican presidential candidate, Barry Goldwater, voicing strong opposition to the civil rights bill, Johnson argued that additional demonstrations would only further alienate the white South and drive Dixiecrats into the GOP fold in November. In the end, vir-tually all of the major civil rights groups acceded to Johnson's call for a suspension of direct action during this period. The Student Nonviolent Coordinating Committee (SNCC), however, did not, setting in motion one of the most dramatic chapters in the civil rights struggle and a pivotal moment in the long and consequential history of racial politics in the United States. It marks the point at which, after more than a century of intense enmity, the electoral loyalties of the white South aligned for the first time with the GOP, the despised Party of Lincoln. The politics of contemporary America, we will argue, continues to bear the clear imprint of this moment. Accordingly, the story of SNCC's summer project—or Freedom Summer as it has come to be known—bears repeating.

It is important at the outset to call attention to the fundamental con-tradiction between SNCC's plans for the summer and Johnson's call for a "cooling off" period in the movement. While Johnson had hoped to insulate the 1964 election from the divisive influence of the movement, SNCC planned to do the exact opposite—that is, to infect the election with its unique brand of confrontational politics. The inspiration for the project had come from the Freedom Vote campaign that SNCC had carried out in Mississippi the previous fall. With the state's black residents effectively denied the right to participate in the fall gubernatorial election, SNCC had organized 80,000 black Mississippians to cast "freedom votes" to protest their exclusion from the political process. To augment its relatively meager staff resources, SNCC had recruited 100 white college students—almost all from Yale and Stanford—to help with the effort.

Buoyed by the success of the campaign, SNCC was now proposing to do for the general election what it had done the previous fall in the governor's race. The difference would be in the scale of the two projects. While the Freedom Vote campaign had been a two-week affair, the new project, as the name indicated, was to last all summer. And while the fall effort had involved 100 white volunteers, the summer project would bring ten times that number to the state. Finally, while the Freedom Vote campaign had been centered in Jackson, Mississippi, the new project was to consist of some 44 projects scattered throughout the state (and a corner of Louisiana). The sheer size of the effort, to say nothing of the presence of so many white volunteers, guaranteed significant media attention from the outset. Indeed, that was one of the rationales for recruiting white students from elite institutions in the first place. In the three years SNCC had been working in the state, its field secretaries had endured countless beatings, arson attacks, and arrests. In that same span of time, at least five black Mississippians had given their lives in service to the movement.[25] And yet through it all white Mississippi remained defiant and unrepentant in its embrace of Jim Crow. Conceding stalemate, SNCC had come to see outside intervention as the key to breaking the impasse in the state. From this perspective, the fundamental goal of the project was to focus national and international attention on Mississippi—something the organization had not yet been able to do—as a means of compelling federal intervention in the state. For the Freedom Summer campaign to be successful, then, it had to attract outside media attention. What better way to do so than by recruiting the sons and daughters of upper-middle-class white America to join the effort? Their experiences during the Freedom Vote campaign had convinced the SNCC high command that nothing attracted the media quite like the scenes of idealistic white college kids helping the "downtrodden Negroes of Mississippi." The SNCC veterans had also learned that the presence of well-heeled white students ensured the conspicuous presence of federal law enforcement officials. Describing the Freedom Vote effort, veteran field-secretary, Lawrence Guyot, said: "Wherever those white volunteers went FBI agents followed. It was really a problem to count the number of FBI agents who were there to protect the [Yale and Stanford] students. It was just that gross. So then we said, 'Well, now, why don't we invite lots of whites . . . to come and serve as volunteers in the state of Mississippi?' "[26]

In a 1964 interview with the *Saturday Evening Post*, Bob Moses, the principal architect of the summer project, put the matter a bit more diplomatically when he remarked that "these students bring the rest of the country with them. They're from good schools and their parents are influential. The interest of the country is awakened and when that happens, the government responds to that issue."[27] Or as James Forman, SNCC's executive director at the time of the summer project explained some years later, "we made a conscious attempt . . . to recruit from some of the Ivy League schools. . . . [Y]ou know, a lot of us knew . . . what we were up against. So that we were, in fact, trying to consciously recruit a counter power-elite."[28] It bears repeating that the strategic logic so evident in these statements represented Lyndon Johnson's worst nightmare: a direct and highly public challenge to the entrenched political power of the very wing of his party whose support he hoped to retain in the upcoming election. Worse still, project organizers hoped to orchestrate a confrontation with Mississippi's white power structure that would compel supportive intervention by the movement's liberal northern allies, which of course included LBJ himself.

While the summer project was to have a number of components, including efforts to identify and dialogue with moderate elements in the white community and an ambitious "freedom schools" program, the centerpiece was to be an aggressive effort to register black voters in advance of the November election. Early on, however, it became clear that the state's white registrars were prepared to use every means at their disposal to block this effort. Thus stymied, project organizers engaged in a bit of strategic jujitsu, turning the registrars' intransigence against them. If white Mississippi was not going to allow its black residents to participate in the official electoral process, SNCC would organize a parallel process complete with "freedom registration forms," a new party—the Mississippi Freedom Democratic Party (MFDP)—open to all residents of the state, and the selection of an alternative delegation to challenge the seating of the regular, lily-white, party regulars at the Democratic National Convention scheduled for August in Atlantic City.

Initially, the intent behind this parallel political process was almost entirely symbolic. Much like the Freedom Vote campaign the previous fall, Mississippi's delegate selection process afforded the SNCC brain trust another opportunity to demonstrate the willingness and desire of Mississippi's black population to participate in the state's political process. A week into the summer, however, three project participants— James Chaney, Andrew Goodman, and Mickey Schwerner—went to investigate the suspicious burning of a black church near Philadelphia, Mississippi. They never made it back. Instead, after visiting the arson site, they were arrested on a trumped up traffic charge, held until after midnight, and released into the Mississippi night. It was the last time they were seen alive, except of course, by their abductors. Their burned out station wagon was found near Bogue Chitto swamp the next day, but it would be August before their bodies, bearing unmistakable signs of torture—were uncovered beneath a makeshift earthen dam near Philadelphia, Mississippi.

With the media already focused on events in Mississippi, the disappearance of the three workers and the subsequent search for their bodies, guaranteed that the project would be front page news all summer long. Predictably, the kidnapping and presumed murder of Chaney, Goodman, and Schwerner also generated outrage and support for the project throughout the country. As the summer wore on and the MFDP effort gained momentum, the possibility of unseating the regular Mississippi delegation began to be taken more seriously. Expressions of support from as many as 25 Democratic members of Congress and nine state party delegations served to raise expectations as the date of the convention drew near.[29] Still on the eve of the convention, the SNCC leadership knew its best chance of unseating the regular Mississippi delegation was likely to come from bringing the issue to the full convention rather than through any action of the Credentials Committee. As the official body charged with reviewing the credentials of all state and territorial delegations, the Committee was home to a good many party regulars whose interest lay in seeing that the proceedings went smoothly. Therefore, they were not likely to countenance the divisive challenge of some ragtag band of movement activists from Mississippi. For the MFDP, the problem was that even a floor fight over the issue required a minority report from members of the Credentials Committee. This prompted the MFDP forces to adopt a dual strategy in Atlantic City. First, they sought the support of state delegations through an intensive lobbying campaign. Second, they made a strong and emotionally powerful appearance before the Credentials Committee. The highlight of the appearance was Fannie Lou Hamer's riveting account of being savagely beaten in jail following her attempt to register to vote in Ruleville, Mississippi. At one point, she recounted how her jailers had forced several black "trustees"—longtime black prisoners—to beat her:

> The first Negro began to beat, and I was beat until he was exhausted....After the first Negro...was exhausted, the State Highway Patrolman began to beat....I began to scream, and one white man got up and began to beat me on the head and tell me to "hush." One white man—my dress had worked up high—he walked over and pulled my dress down and he [then] pulled my dress back up, way up ....All of this is on account we want to register, to become first-class citizens, and if the Freedom Democratic Party is not seated now, I question America.[30]

Hamer's electrifying testimony moved even the hardened party regulars on the Committee, as well as a national television audience, which responded with a flood of telegrams in support of the challenge. It began to look as if the moral force of the challenge might actually prevail. Almost unbelievably, the MFDP was poised to play David to the Goliath of the state's long-standing white political establishment.

What the MFDP leadership had underestimated was the lengths to which that ultimate backroom politician, Lyndon Johnson, and his supporters would go to block the challenge. Hoping to prevent a full-scale Dixiecrat revolt, the Johnson forces were prepared to do whatever was necessary to ensure that the regular Mississippi delegation was seated. Toward that end, Johnson ordered the FBI to place the SNCC/MFDP convention forces under surveillance. FBI Director J. Edgar Hoover responded by tapping the phones in SNCC's Atlantic City office. The White House let it be known that the seating of the MFDP delegation would damage the vice-presidential prospects of veteran civil rights stalwart, Hubert Humphrey. The move was probably directed at Joseph Rauh, the MFDP's chief counsel and longtime Humphrey supporter. In turn, Humphrey's staff pressured Rauh to urge moderation and compromise on the MFDP delegation. Walter Reuther, Rauh's immediate superior and the president of the United Auto Workers (UAW) union, flew in for a bit of backstage arm twisting of his own. He threatened to pull all the UAW's money out of the Mississippi movement should the MFDP persist in its challenge.[31] According to Rauh, Johnson's supporters even threatened individual members of the Credentials Committee. Later he told an interviewer that one black supporter was informed "that her husband wouldn't get a judgeship if she didn't leave us, and the Secretary of the Army told the guy from the Canal Zone that he would lose his job if he didn't leave us."[32]

In the end, the pressure proved to be too much. Support for the challenge evaporated on the Credentials Committee and the MFDP forces were left to consider a rather weak compromise proposal: two at-large convention seats and a promise that the matter of racial exclusion would be reviewed prior to the 1968 convention. When moderate civil rights leaders such as Martin Luther King Jr. and Bayard Rustin joined the chorus of those calling for acceptance of the compromise, the MFDP delegates' sense of betrayal and isolation was complete. The challenge delegation rejected the compromise. Speaking for the group, Fannie Lou Hamer summed up the feelings of most when she said, "We didn't come all this way for no two seats!"[33] That was not quite the end of it, though. Using credentials borrowed from sympathetic delegates from other states, a contingent of MFDP members gained access to the convention floor and staged a sit-in in the Mississippi section. The sight of black Mississippians being carried from the hall by uniformed, white security officers was but the ultimate dramatic denouement to Freedom Summer.

For all the public spectacle of Atlantic City, however, the significant fallout from the convention challenge played out elsewhere and largely in private. Any chance of an actual physical showdown between the two delegations evaporated early on when the lily-white party regulars packed up and headed home, incensed at the support enjoyed by the MFDP within the party. Notwithstanding his mastery of back-room politics, Johnson's efforts to hold his fractious party together came to naught. After returning to the fold following the abortive States Rights challenge of 1948, the South was in open revolt once again. But this time, instead of supporting a third party candidate, disaffected white Southerners did the unthinkable and cast their votes for the once despised Republican Party. The 1964 electoral map—shown in Figure 3.8— reveals that Louisiana, Mississippi, Alabama, Georgia, and South Carolina joined Goldwater's home state of Arizona as the only states to buck Johnson's landslide triumph in November.

The more telling visual, however, comes from comparing Figures 3.8 and 3.9, the latter showing Eisenhower's equally lopsided win in that year. In 1956 the "solid South" holds true to its historic allegiance to the Democratic Party, even in the face of Eisenhower's sweep of the rest of

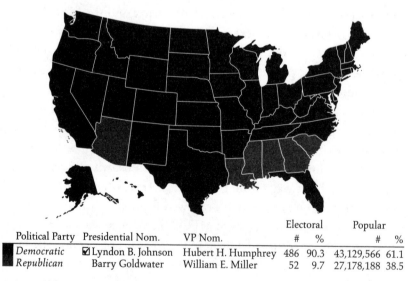

Political Party	Presidential Nom.	VP Nom.	Electoral #	%	Popular #	%
Democratic	☑ Lyndon B. Johnson	Hubert H. Humphrey	486	90.3	43,129,566	61.1
Republican	Barry Goldwater	William E. Miller	52	9.7	27,178,188	38.5

Figure 3.8 1964 Presidential Election
Source: UCSB American Presidency Project

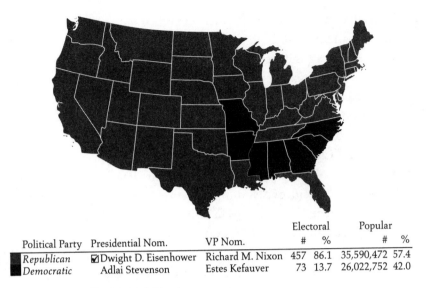

Political Party	Presidential Nom.	VP Nom.	Electoral #	Electoral %	Popular #	Popular %
Republican	☑ Dwight D. Eisenhower	Richard M. Nixon	457	86.1	35,590,472	57.4
Democratic	Adlai Stevenson	Estes Kefauver	73	13.7	26,022,752	42.0

Figure 3.9 1956 Presidential Election
Source: UCSB American Presidency Project

the country. Eight years later, the South remains out of step with the nation, but in a way that no one could have imagined in 1956. The votes of the Deep South now belong to the Republican Party and more tellingly to its conservative, anti–civil rights candidate, Barry Goldwater. The magnitude of LBJ's stunning triumph in 1964 may have obscured the revolution for most Americans, but the full implications of the electoral realignment hinted at in the 1964 returns were not lost on everyone. This brings us to the second story we promised earlier. It turns out the Democrats weren't the only party moving decisively away from the ideological middle in the mid-60s.

The GOP Looks South and Moves Right

Even as the Democratic Party was being pushed sharply left by the civil rights movement, the GOP was moving in the opposite direction. Numerous commentators have, in fact, noted the significance of the Republican shift, attributing it largely to Nixon's aggressive courtship of the white South in his successful 1968 bid for the White House.[34] We too assign great importance to the 1968 race and to the politics of racial reaction that marked Nixon's first term in office and accordingly, devote significant attention to both episodes in the next chapter. Our analysis of the Republican shift to the right, however, differs from the previous accounts in two crucial respects. First, we argue that the shift was under way much earlier than the standard account suggests. Second, we see the same movement-party dynamic at work in the Republican shift that we emphasized in our analysis of the leftward movement of the Democrats. That is, the GOP also shifts its ideological center of gravity in response to the force of social movement activity, this time on the right. The principal movement occasioning the shift is the "white resistance" countermovement that develops in response to the civil rights struggle, first in the South, but evolving into a nationwide "white backlash" as the decade progresses. Of great importance in helping to link and diffuse white resistance from south to north are the presidential challenges mounted by Alabama governor George Wallace in 1964 and 1968. These challenges will come in for special attention in our account of the Republican shift to the right during the decade.

Even if it is more amorphous and less self-consciously a movement than civil rights, we see the national "white resistance" countermovement having much the same impact on the GOP as the freedom struggle does on the Democrats. Locked in a contentious embrace throughout the decade (and beyond), these two linked struggles push the major parties steadily off center. In short, nothing serves to undermine the long-standing dominance of moderate centrists in both parties more than the centrifugal force of racial contention over the course of the 1960s. There was, however, a second grass-roots movement that aided and abetted the rightward shift of the GOP. Indeed, this second movement preceded the onset of the nationwide "white backlash" and probably helped to condition its rise. We would be remiss if, before devoting the balance of the chapter to a detailed account of "white backlash," we failed to acknowledge the significance of this earlier grass-roots effort.

Thunder on the Right: The Draft Goldwater Movement

At the time, Goldwater's sound thrashing at the hands of Johnson in 1964 seemed to affirm the resolve of the medium voter to punish any presidential candidate who dared to stray too far from the middle of the ideological continuum of US politics. A half-century of historical perspective, however, would seem to support a very different interpretation of that year's race and the movement that preceded it. It now seems clear that Goldwater's candidacy represents an important early source of centrifugal pressure that helps to set in motion the ideological makeover so evident in today's Republican Party. Moreover, consistent with the overall argument advanced here, it is pressure that reflects not so much conventional party politics as the return of social movements to American political and social life.

As recounted by Theodore White, the foremost historian of the 1964 presidential contest, Goldwater's 1964 bid for the White House was born in the run-up to the 1960 general election and with virtually no input from the candidate himself. Instead, a specific incident in the race for the 1960 GOP nomination so angered conservatives as to trigger the beginnings of what would become the draft Goldwater movement. Dubbed the Compact of 5th Avenue, the triggering incident involved a meeting in New York between the presumptive Republican nominee, Richard Nixon, and his chief challenger, liberal GOP stalwart, Nelson Rockefeller. The meeting was born of Rockefeller's threat to mount a floor fight at the convention in opposition to what he saw as the overly conservative substance of the preliminary draft of that year's party platform. Fearing what that would do to party unity, Nixon flew to New York and worked with Rockefeller to substantially modify and mute the conservative tenor of the platform, especially on the critical issue of race.

Furious at the back room nature of the Nixon/Rockefeller "deal," at the convention just days later, conservatives importuned Goldwater to challenge the Nixon nomination. In the end, the lateness of the hour doomed the effort, but not before the seeds of the later draft Goldwater movement had been sown. Cohen et al. pick up the story from there: "The principal agent of this movement was a former [Republican presidential candidate Thomas] Dewey operative named F. Clinton White. White worked loyally for Eisenhower in 1952 and Nixon in 1960, but became disgusted by the 'me-too Republicanism' of those leaders."[35] It was White who resolved to build a grass-roots movement to remake the ideological character of the GOP, or as he announced at the first national gathering of his group: "We're going to take over the Republican Party...and make it the conservative instrument of American politics."[36] If this sounds eerily similar to the goal of today's Tea Party adherents, the comparison is strictly intentional. The point is, while retrospective accounts of Goldwater's '64 presidential bid tend to focus almost exclusively on the candidate, it was the movement that largely made the candidate, rather than the other way around. Working tirelessly from 1961 to 1964, White built a grass-roots movement of conservative activists who shared his vision of a transformed Republican Party and the hope of drafting Goldwater to serve as the movement's standard bearer in '64. In the end, they were able to overcome Goldwater's initial coolness to the idea, with him signing on to the campaign in late 1963. Quoting approvingly from White's obituary in the *New York Times*, Cohen et al. reject the conventional wisdom that Goldwater's was a "candidate-centered" campaign, seeing it instead as very much a grass-roots movement-based effort.[37] As the *New York Times* reported: "The Goldwater movement germinated in 1961, when Mr. White gathered a cadre of conservatives for a private meeting in a Chicago motel. They decided to seek ideological control of the party and chose Senator Goldwater of Arizona as their nominee, although he initially spurned the idea."[38]

Notwithstanding Johnson's landslide win that November, the Goldwater movement had the effect of moving the party significantly to the right. It did so in at least four important ways. For starters, the movement brought countless new conservative recruits into the GOP. Second, it left behind a loose network of conservative groups and individual activists that simply hadn't been there before, making later mobilizing efforts by the right easier to mount. Third, the movement gave powerful voice to those frustrated by what they saw as the failure of the party to articulate an ideology distinctive from the dominant Democratic liberalism of the era. Finally, in his stark opposition to the Civil Rights Act of 1964 and general critique of federal "meddling" in this area, Goldwater sent a powerful message to racial conservatives, not only in the South, but the nation as a whole, encouraging the shift from regional "resistance" to national "backlash." Before we take up this critically important second movement, we first document the magnitude and early onset of the GOP shift to the right on racial matters.

The Shift Begins

It is now commonplace to lament the lack of a moderate, centrist wing of the Republican Party. Forget moderates, we wager that most readers would be shocked to learn that not so long ago the great majority of card-carrying racial liberals in Congress were Republicans. Earlier in the chapter we reported that Carmine and Stimson found that only four of the 46 Republican senators in the 85th Congress (1957–59) had conservative voting records on civil rights matters. Or to put it another way, exactly two thirds of the 63 senators coded as racial *liberals* by Carmine and Stimson were Republicans.[39] The popular understanding that decisive federal enactment of civil rights reform in this era was a Democratic accomplishment is simply wrong. Yes, a host of liberal Democrats contributed mightily to the key legislative victories of the period. At the same time, it was the determined opposition of conservative, segregationist Democrats that delayed meaningful reform for decades. Republicans, by contrast, were consistently more pro–civil rights in the immediate postwar period. The question remains: how, when, and why did this begin to change?

In this very brief accounting of the contributions of the two parties to the civil rights revolution, there is a hint of one of the early precipitants of the conservative turn in the Republican Party. We note that Democrats were every bit as central to resistance to early efforts at racial reform as they were later to civil rights gains. The point is, before any breakthrough on the issue could occur, the power and influence the Dixiecrats exercised over the party had to be broken. And this required a strengthening of the northern, liberal labor wing of the party. This came via the election of strong cohorts of liberal Democrats in the late 1950s and early 1960s. Ironically, the losers in the great majority of these cases were Republicans, racially *liberal* Republicans. Consider the highly consequential example of the 1958 Senate races, which were to dramatically alter the previously discussed partisan distribution of "racial liberals" in that chamber. Carmines and Stimson explain the aggregate significance of that year's races:

> eleven Republicans were replaced by Democrats; ten were racial liberals, each in turn replaced by a liberal Democrat. The forty-two Republicans to twenty-one Democrats found in the liberal ranks

of the Eighty-fifth Senate became thirty-two to thirty-one in the Eighty-sixth Senate purely by virtue of interparty electoral change.... That single election ended the pattern of greater Republican liberalism on race.... Liberal Republicans were never again the dominant force in the civil rights coalition.[40]

Nor was this election a one-time aberration. Instead the replacement of moderate-liberal Republican senators by more liberal Democratic challengers continued until at least 1966. This prompts us to underscore a very important point. The dramatic transformation of the partisan landscape of racial politics at issue here was the product of significant compositional changes in *both* parties. We begin with the Democrats. Reflecting the high watermark of postwar liberalism and the party's sharp shift leftward after 1960, waves of newly minted liberal Democrats entered the House and Senate from 1958 through the end of the 1960s. As we saw in 1958, in a good many cases, these liberal Democrats replaced liberal to moderate Republicans; in others they claimed spots held previously by more moderate Democrats. Either way, the net effect was to strengthen the northern liberal wing of the party and further marginalize the Dixiecrats.

The transformative dynamics within the GOP were a bit more complicated. Obviously, the loss of liberal Republican House and Senate seats to the Democrats had significant compositional implications for the GOP as well, thinning the congressional ranks of racially liberal Republicans, even as it increased their numbers among Democrats. But that is not the whole story. The number of liberal Republican senators dropped from 42 to just 10 between the 85th and 89th Congresses. There is probably no single factor responsible for the party's early shift to the right, though as we previously argued, the Goldwater campaign has to be accounted a major influence on the process. And while it is true that Goldwater's brand of conservatism was roundly rejected by the nation's voters in 1964, it still says something about the centrifugal movement pressures developing within the GOP that he secured the nomination in the first place.

As improbable as it sounds, Goldwater's defeat in '64 may even have reinforced the strategic wisdom of a general shift to the right, even in the face of Johnson's landslide victory. How could that be? Two points are worth making; one familiar, one not. The familiar point has to do with the powerful symbolism and strategic implications that attached to the Democrats' loss of the "solid South" in 1964. Even if the significance of the defection wasn't apparent to the electorate, it certainly wasn't lost on strategists in both parties. The second, less familiar, point is perhaps even more important. With liberal Democrats routinely capturing liberal to moderate Republican seats and Johnson claiming a still-record 94 percent of the black vote in 1964, it must have occurred to some in the GOP that tacking leftward was suicidal. Quite simply, by the early 1960s the Republicans had no comparative advantage when it came to courting liberal or black voters. Better to move to the right, especially in light of the white South's growing disaffection with the Democratic Party. Nor was this impulse to move right just a matter of strategic calculus. Ideological opposition to what had become known as "me-too Republicanism"—that is, the tendency of postwar Republicans to mirror the central policy preferences of centrist Democrats—was very much on the rise among at least some grass-roots Republicans in the early 1960s. Indeed, as noted previously, nothing fueled the rise of the draft Goldwater movement more than this anger at the failure of the GOP to differentiate its policies from those of its Democratic opponents.

The speed with which these complex dynamics transformed the two parties is captured in Table 3.3, which compares the balance of racial liberals and conservatives in the two parties in the 85th (1957–59) and 89th (1965–67) Senates.

The number of racial liberals among the Democratic senators more than doubled between the 85th and 89th sessions of Congress. Over the same period of time, the number of Republican senators with conservative voting records on civil rights measures increased more than fivefold: from 4 to 22. While racial liberals made up nearly 90 percent of all Republicans in the Senate in 1957–59, their proportion had dwindled to just 30 percent a scant eight years later. Bottom line: for all the significance attributed to Nixon's "breakthrough" election in 1968, a discernible rightward shift was evident in the party's congressional delegation earlier in the decade.

The impact of the ascendant conservatism within the GOP was clearly evident in 1966 when Lyndon Johnson sought congressional

Table 3.3 Racial Liberalism of the 85th (1957–1959) and 89th (1965–1967) Congresses

85th Congress
Liberal Democrats: 21
Liberal Republicans: 42
Conservative Democrats: 27
Conservative Republicans: 4
89th Congress
Liberal Democrats: 45
Liberal Republicans: 10
Conservative Democrats: 21
Conservative Republicans: 22

Source: Adapted from Carmines and Stimson, 1989, Table 3.3 (p. 69) and Table 3.4 (p. 72)

Table 3.4 Congressional Voting in the House on 1964 and 1966 Civil Rights Bills

1964 Civil Rights Act
House Democrats: 153 Yes; 91 No
House Republicans: 136 Yes; 35 No
1966 Fair Housing Bill
House Democrats: 183 Yes; 95 No
House Republicans: 76 Yes; 62 No

Source: govtrack.us

support for a third major civil rights bill, this one focused on the issue of fair housing. In Table 3.4 we compare partisan voting in the House on the 1964 Civil Rights Act with the outcome two years later on the failed fair housing bill.

While House Democrats remain overwhelmingly committed to civil rights reform in both years, the change in the disposition of the Republican delegation is striking. The share of House Democrats voting for the legislation is actually greater in 1966 than in 1964, but only slightly more than half of their Republican counterparts vote for the bill in 1966, compared to better than 80 percent two years earlier. The bigger—and more consequential—change, however,

Table 3.5 Congressional Voting in the Senate on 1964 and 1966
Civil Rights Bills

1964 Civil Rights Act

Senate Democrats: 46 Yes; 21 No

Senate Republicans: 27 Yes; 6 No

1966 Cloture Motion on Fair Housing Bill

Senate Democrats: 42 Yes; 21 No

Senate Republicans: 12 Yes; 21 No

Source: govtrack.us

takes place in the Senate. Table 3.5 compares partisan voting in the Senate on the 1964 Civil Rights Act with the vote taken in 1966 on a cloture motion that would have ended debate on the aforementioned fair housing bill and allowed the legislation to come to the floor for a vote.

In 1964, 27 of 33 Republican senators voted for the Civil Rights Act, paving the way for passage of the landmark bill by a decisive 73–27 margin. Two years later, 21 of 33 GOP Senators voted *against* the cloture motion, effectively killing the measure, which the House had already approved by a whopping 102 vote margin (259–157). This outcome marked a distinctive new dynamic in congressional voting on racial matters. Prior to 1957, the power of southern Democrats—in both the party and Congress—all but ruled out any hope of meaningful legislation on racial matters. But in 1957 enough Democrats had joined with Republicans to finally break the stranglehold of the Dixiecrats and pass that year's symbolically important Civil Rights Act. This ushered in a period of sustained congressional action in the area, with four major bills signed into law in a scant eight years. Just to be clear on the partisan dynamics in all of this, Republican support for civil rights reform had been something of a constant from the late 1930s to the mid-1960s. It was southern Democratic intransigence on the "Negro question" that had blocked reform until the 1957 breakthrough. With the death of the 1966 bill, however, the role of the two parties had been reversed. Going forward, the two parties would once again be at loggerheads on the issue; now, however, it would be congressional *Republicans* who typically opposed progressive action in the area.

"White Backlash"

If some of the shift to the right by the GOP in this period was an inadvertent result of the capture of moderate-liberal Republican seats by more liberal Democratic candidates, there was a far more important, strategic dynamic emerging as well. And it too precedes Nixon's breakthrough victory in 1968. Indeed, Nixon's much ballyhooed "southern strategy" in that year's race is more accurately seen as a reflection of the emerging dynamic than a bold new direction on his part. What factors, events, or persons shaped this developing strategic orientation? To us, no influence is as important in this regard as the racially conservative white countermovement, or "white resistance movement" that develops—first in the South in the early 1960s, but spreading to the rest of the country in the mid- to late 1960s—in opposition to the African American freedom struggle in both its traditional civil rights and increasingly threatening "black power" incarnations.

Given its intensity at the time and, more important, its significant long-term political and electoral consequences, it is remarkable to us that this movement is largely forgotten today and certainly not invoked as an important factor by those seeking to understand the political economy of the contemporary United States. We hope to remedy that neglect here. In our view, if it was the civil rights struggle that largely pushed the Democrats left in the early to mid-1960s, then it was the mobilized force of this amorphous "white backlash" that, more than anything, encouraged the sharp shift to the right by the Republicans in the mid- to late 1960s and beyond. Indeed, one of the central sources of continuity linking the Republican Party that emerged under Nixon in the late '60s and early '70s with the GOP of today is a sustained politics of racial reaction. We will have much more to say about this later in this and in subsequent chapters. But it is important to understand the origins of the distinctive racial conservatism that has defined the GOP for nearly half a century. Its origins, we contend, are bound up with the aforementioned white resistance movement and especially with its spread to the North in the mid- to late 1960s.

The white countermovement began, however, as a strictly southern segregationist response to the resurgent civil rights movement. The close connection between these two movements can be seen in Figure 3.10,

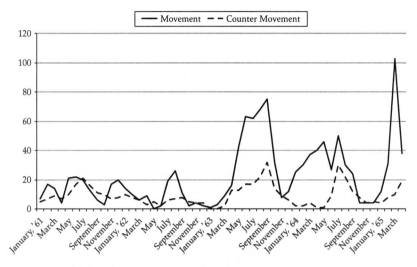

Figure 3.10 Civil Rights Movement and Countermovement Activity, 1961–1963
Source: New York Times

which shows the monthly ebb and flow of both civil rights and segregationist actions during the heyday of the struggle in the South.[41]

The actions reflected in the figure include both the iconic campaigns orchestrated by civil rights forces (e.g., the sit-ins, Selma, Birmingham, the Freedom Rides) and the infamous acts of resistance offered up by segregationists in response to the threat posed by the movement (e.g., fire hoses and police dogs in Birmingham, the burning of black churches, the murders of Evers, Chaney, Goodman, and Schwerner). What analysts have almost entirely missed, however, is the extent to which the southern segregationist countermovement morphed into and inspired the more generalized nationwide "white backlash" of the mid- to late 1960s. Make no mistake about it; these two forms of resistance were definitely linked, if not organizationally then in intent—resistance to integration—and underlying racial antipathy. And no figure was more crucial to this linkage than the South's most celebrated (and reviled) defender of "segregation now, segregation tomorrow, segregation forever," Alabama governor George Wallace.

Wallace burst on to the national scene in 1963, first by issuing the aforementioned rallying cry during his inaugural address as governor in January of that year. That was nothing, however, compared to his follow-up of June 11 when he "stood in the school house door"—actually the entrance to Foster Auditorium on the campus of the University of Alabama—to bar the admission of the first two African American students in school history. The act was, of course, futile, with the students admitted to campus with little fanfare the following day.[42] Wallace, however, had achieved his political aim: not only enhancing his popularity as governor but emerging overnight as the most potent symbol of racial resistance in the country. He showed just how "potent" when he shocked both parties and mainstream political analysts by successfully challenging the popular sitting president of his own party—LBJ—in three northern primaries in the run-up to the 1964 general election. When Wallace announced that he was entering the April Wisconsin primary, many mainstream observers saw it as something of a joke, but the laughing stopped when he captured a third of the vote there. Properly chastened by Wallace's success in Wisconsin, the Democratic establishment mobilized to stop him in Indiana, but he still polled 30 percent in the state. For his final act, he nearly upset Johnson in Maryland, publicly attributing has narrow defeat to "the nigger voting bloc." Johnson's nomination, of course, was never in danger. Still, the fact that at the height of LBJ's popularity, an unrepentant segregationist could attract the support of between 30 and 50 percent of registered Democratic voters in three northern states was nothing short of a revelation to political strategists in both parties. At least a few Democrats began to understand the electoral costs of the party's full on embrace of civil rights reform, while for their part many Republicans—including Barry Goldwater—began to openly call for a shift to the right to capture the Wallace vote and make inroads in the no longer "solid South." In the wake of Wallace's surprising showing in the North and Goldwater's capture of the Deep South in the general election, GOP calls to look south and move right were destined to grow louder and more frequent, especially as the "white backlash" took hold in the rest of the country.

White Resistance Spreads Northward

Before we continue with our chronological narrative, we would do well to pause and consider the nature of the white countermovement to the civil rights revolution as it developed in the early to mid-1960s. Some may even object to calling this diffuse resistance a "movement" at all, arguing that it lacked the organization and litany of segregationist actions evident in the South. We disagree. Most scholarly definitions of social movements read something like the following: social movements are loosely organized, sustained efforts to promote or resist change in society and which depend, at least in part, on recourse to noninstitutionalized forms of collective action. By this definition, we can certainly characterize the nationwide "white backlash" to the civil rights struggle as a movement. While it is true that the movement never spawned overarching national organizations, few movements ever do. Most are aggregations of local groups involved in local struggles over broadly similar issues. In point of fact, there were a few national organizations involved in the movement—groups like the Ku Klux Klan, the John Birch Society, and, for a brief period of time, the National Association for the Advancement of White People. More often, however, the movement spawned local groups in response to what were perceived to be threats to jobs, schools, and neighborhoods posed by civil rights "agitators," or simply appropriated existing organizations—associations of realtors, school boards, city councils, churches—in the service of the struggle.

There was also no shortage of grass-roots actions taken to advance movement aims. And let's be clear, while the overall level of white violence that characterized resistance in the north was considerably lower than that seen in the Jim Crow south, it was hardly nonexistent. Just ask the open housing marchers in Cicero, Illinois, in 1966 who were met by bricks and bottles, when Martin Luther King Jr. sought, unsuccessfully, to apply the tactics of the southern civil rights struggle to the problem of residential segregation in the North. Or ask school and law enforcement personnel about the years of riots and mass protests triggered by a 1974 court-ordered school busing plan in South Boston. In fact, there was no shortage of reactive white violence or disruptive protest in the North. More often, however, the tactics of choice involved more subtle and/or institutionalized strategies, ranging from "white flight," to legal challenges, to collusion between elected officials and union leaders. If the resulting patchwork of local groups and myriad strategies lacked the drama and narrative coherence of the pitched battles we saw in the South, it's only because the national struggle was more geographically dispersed and temporally prolonged than the far narrower segregationist resistance movement of the early 1960s. In fact, as we argue in Chapter 7, the movement is alive and well in the United States today.

Our question here, though, is when do we account the rise of the movement in the 1960s? It is hard to say exactly when the American public's broad sympathy for the civil rights struggle moved from confusion and dismay to out-and-out resistance, but Goldwater's presidential bid and Wallace's showing also in 1964 made it clear that significant opposition was already in place. But just as clearly—and with Wallace as a compelling legitimating symbol—the "backlash" accelerated in the two-year period between Johnson's triumphant victory and the midterm elections of 1966. No doubt some of the increased resistance owed to the events of the day. It seemed as if every few weeks during that span some new event, some alarming new headline tapped into white America's deep-seated and escalating fear of African Americans. A short, suggestive list of events from those years will help to make the point:

- Barely two weeks into Johnson's first full term came the violence in Selma and the largest civil rights campaign to date.
- Almost before the ink was dry on the Voting Rights Act of 1965, federal registrars began fanning out around the South, wresting control of voter registration from defiant southern officials, as the white South braced for the loss of political control they feared would follow.
- Just five days after LBJ signed the Voting Rights Act into law, the nation watched in horror as the Watts Riot exploded in Los Angeles. When it finally ran out of steam six days later, the riot had claimed 34 lives and left another 1,032 injured.
- At a rally in Greenwood, Mississippi, on June 16, 1966, Stokely Carmichael electrified many in the black community, while sowing fear in white America, by calling for the mobilization of "black power."
- At the same time Carmichael was raising the specter of "black power" in the South, Martin Luther King Jr. was heightening white fears in the North by staging open housing marches in the white suburbs of Chicago.

- On October 16, 1966, Huey Newton and Bobby Seale founded the Black Panther Party in Oakland, California.

To say that the relationship between white America and the civil rights struggle had changed between 1964 and 1966 would be a serious understatement. Whereas Johnson's public commitment to JFK's civil rights agenda had clearly aided his landslide win in 1964, Democratic candidates in 1966 now found themselves the victims of the much-heralded "white backlash." By that year's midterm elections, the degree of racial polarization in the country had grown to such an extent that for a candidate to openly court the black vote was to invite significant defections among his or her white constituents. The imprint of the backlash on the 1966 elections was unmistakable. As pollsters Brink and Harris wrote at the time: "The backlash vote of 1966 helped install sizeable numbers of conservative congressmen who threaten even the modest goals of the Great Society."[43] Much the same view was expressed by Killian: "The congressional elections of 1966 did not reveal a growing alliance between the 'have nots' ... of the United States. Instead, they reflected the existence of a backlash against the welfare programs of the Great Society."[44]

Many contests for statewide office were shaped by these same sentiments. A prime example was California's gubernatorial race, in which a liberal Democrat, Pat Brown, was defeated by conservative Republican, Ronald Reagan. And as survey results revealed, the success of the Reagan candidacy owed much to the politics of racial reaction. Specifically, on the question of whether incumbent Governor Brown had been too "soft" in his handling of the riots and racial unrest in general, California voters split roughly 50–50 on the survey. Of those who were critical of him on the issue, however, 9 of 10 voted for Reagan. In the view of the pollsters, "the California outcome could have been foretold on the single issue of race alone.... [T]he facts ... prove that three out of four people who voted for Reagan found it easier to do so because they felt they could register a protest in varying forms to the riots and racial unrest that had taken place."[45] Moreover, as the authors go on to note, the analysis of election returns from other key industrial states—notably Michigan and Illinois—showed the same general pattern evident in California.[46]

The specific electoral gains enjoyed by conservative Republicans in 1966, however, were less damaging to long-term Democratic prospects than the demographics reflected in these wins. More significant were the mass defections from the traditional New Deal coalition that had allowed Democrats to dominate presidential politics since 1932. Chief among these defectors were the white urban ethnic groups of the industrial North. By 1966 the loyalty of these groups to the Democratic Party had been rendered tenuous by the shift of racial unrest from the South to the very cities in which they lived. Worried by northern "urban disorders" and the threat of open-housing marches in their neighborhoods, these groups were no longer willing, en masse, to support a party that had come to be identified with an urban black underclass that they saw as pushing too fast for racial change. Writing in 1964, Samuel Lubell accurately forecast this trend:

> In the past, Democratic strategists have assumed that the civil rights issue helped hold together the 'big city' vote. This may have been a valid political strategy as long as the civil rights cause appeared mainly a matter of improving the treatment of Negroes in the South. But the new demands of Northern Negro militants have posed sharp conflicts with what many white voters see as their own rights. Agitation over civil rights . . . could alienate enough white voters to disrupt the Democratic majorities in the urban areas.[47]

In 1966, Lubell's prediction came true. Far from solidifying the Democratic hold on the urban vote, the racial issue tended to polarize the various components of their traditional urban coalition. While the black vote held firm, the white ethnics abandoned the party in droves. Brink and Harris recount some of the major defections: "in Illinois, the Polish and Eastern European precincts showed a precipitous drop of 17 points in the Democratic vote from two years before, and a full 22 points off the high-water mark of 75 percent registered for Kennedy six years earlier. In Ohio, Polish precincts plummeted to 44 percent Democratic in the contest for governor there, off 39 points from 1964 and 45 below JFK's showing in 1960."[48] These were significant electoral losses. As a result of these defections, a general devaluation of the black vote occurred, as political strategists of both parties came to weigh the

advantages of courting the black electorate against the costs of antago-
nizing a large and ever growing segment of the white population.

Events between 1966 and 1968 did nothing to reverse this general
trend. If anything, the increased frequency and destructiveness of the
riots in 1967 and 1968, the full flowering of the black power movement
in these years, combined on the other side with the growing use of an
inflammatory "law and order" rhetoric by white politicians, accelerated
the racial polarization already evident in the 1966 elections. As the 1968
presidential contest drew near, two candidates moved aggressively to
exploit this dramatic shift in the political landscape. Both would have
been seen as wildly improbable candidates just a few years earlier, but
their shrewd understanding of the changing nature of American racial
politics gave them a significant strategic edge heading into the 1968
contest.

The Republican nominee, Richard Nixon, was thought to have been
washed up as a serious contender when he was soundly beaten by Pat
Brown in the 1962 California gubernatorial race. And yet, here he was
six years later, running for president on what he termed his "southern
strategy." While the Democrats had lost the Deep South in 1964, Nixon
now believed that increasing racial polarization in the country rendered
the entire region up for grabs. By distancing himself from the civil
rights struggle and reminding voters of the close connection between
blacks and the Democratic Party, Nixon hoped to make big inroads in
the region while capitalizing on traditional Republican strength in the
West and Midwest.

If Nixon's candidacy was surprising, George Wallace's third party
challenge was anything but. First and foremost, there was his strong
showing in the 1964 Democratic primaries. Beyond that, however, the
deepening divisions within the country and increasing anger at urban
riots, court-ordered busing, and general lawlessness made Wallace a
more formidable candidate in '68 than he had been four years earlier.
Though still a hero to the white South, Wallace now enjoyed considerable support throughout the country and especially among the
embattled white working class of the industrial North. Like Nixon,
Wallace too had taken notice of the deepening racial divisions
nationwide, but especially the loss of the once "solid South" by the
Democrats four years earlier. As a Dixiecrat himself, Wallace aimed to

appeal to his regional base, while reaching out to disaffected whites elsewhere in the country.

Standing in the way of these two men was the Democratic nominee, Hubert Humphrey. It would be difficult, however, to think of any presidential candidate from the incumbent party in American history who went into an election burdened by more "negatives" than Humphrey in '68. For starters, it took the assassination of Robert Kennedy to open the door for Humphrey's nomination in the first place. As a result, many in Humphrey's own party saw him as an illegitimate candidate, as effectively usurping a nomination that, by rights, should have gone to Kennedy, or even the early anti-war candidate, Eugene McCarthy. More important, as Johnson's vice-president, Humphrey was tainted both by the administration's prosecution of the war in Vietnam and its increasingly unpopular social programs, including its association with the civil rights movement. Finally, as if Humphrey needed anything else to overcome, there was the almost surreal spectacle of violence and mass unrest that accompanied that year's Democratic Convention in Chicago. On the eve of the election, it seemed as if Humphrey's best chance might come from Nixon and Wallace splitting the white southern vote, allowing the Democrat to squeak by with the slimmest electoral plurality. It didn't quite work out that way. As the 1968 electoral map shown in Figure 3.11 reveals, Nixon and Wallace did indeed wind up splitting the South, with Wallace prevailing in the Deep South and Nixon capturing most of the border states.

In the end, though, the division was not enough to give Wallace the electoral votes needed to deny the outright victory to the two major parties and to force, as he had hoped, the House of Representatives to resolve the matter. Nixon edged Humphrey by the narrowest of margins, 43.4 to 42.7 percent. As both parties looked to the future, however, it wasn't the slim gap between Nixon and Humphrey on which they were focused but rather the overwhelming majority represented by the combined votes cast for Nixon and Wallace. The significance of the Wallace candidacy and the broader white resistance movement he represented for the future electoral prospects of both parties was clear on the face of the 1968 election returns. With the two major parties evenly dividing 86 percent of the popular vote, the remaining 14 percent, which had gone for Wallace, clearly loomed as

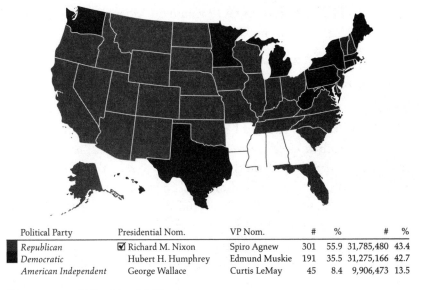

Political Party	Presidential Nom.	VP Nom.	#	%	#	%
Republican	☑ Richard M. Nixon	Spiro Agnew	301	55.9	31,785,480	43.4
Democratic	Hubert H. Humphrey	Edmund Muskie	191	35.5	31,275,166	42.7
American Independent	George Wallace	Curtis LeMay	45	8.4	9,906,473	13.5

Figure 3.11 1968 Presidential Election
Source: UCSB American Presidency Project

the balance of power in future elections. As one noted analyst wrote in the wake of the election, "it is obvious to any 'rational' politician hoping to maximize votes in 1970 or 1972 that there are several times more votes to be gained by leaning toward Wallace than by leaning toward [Eugene] McCarthy."[49]

For the Republicans, their narrow victory suggested that the party's future lay not in the 43 percent of the popular vote Nixon received but in the 57 percent he shared with Wallace. Republican strategists believed this figure represented a dominant conservative majority that, if successfully tapped, could ensure GOP control of the White House for years to come. To build this decisive majority, however, the GOP would need to attract a large number of Wallace's core southern supporters. This would not be easy. While Nixon and the Republicans had claimed the lion's share of the region's electoral votes for the first time in history, his margins had been razor thin in a number of states; less than 4 percentage points over Wallace in Tennessee, and fewer than 6 in South Carolina. If he was to improve on his overall margin of victory, Nixon would need to make even deeper inroads in the South in 1972. The centrifugal force of the Wallace candidacy and the broader white resistance movement on Nixon and the GOP would be evident within months of the latter's ascension to the White House.

Courting Racial Conservatives: Nixon's First Term in Office

As vice-president under Eisenhower and as JFK's opponent in the 1960 presidential contest, Richard Nixon had, by the Republican standards of the day, earned a reputation for being moderate to liberal on racial matters. *President* Nixon, on the other hand, was anything but, instead embracing a reactionary brand of racial conservatism almost immediately upon taking office. To understand this transformation, we need only revisit the electoral challenge confronting Nixon coming off his narrow win in 1968. Ever the savvy opportunist, Nixon clearly understood that his chances of being reelected in 1972 would depend on his ability to solidify his southern base by appealing to Wallace's supporters. And this meant finding a way to exploit racial divisions without appearing to be racist. In his 1969 book, *The Emerging Republican Majority*, Nixon adviser Kevin Phillips articulated the strategy in all its cynical brilliance. Describing the '68 Wallace movement as a "way station" for disgruntled Dixiecrats not quite ready to embrace the Republican Party, Phillips then goes on to lay out the racial politics that he is confident will drive more southern whites into the GOP. He writes: "The principal force which broke up the Democratic...coalition is the Negro socioeconomic revolution and the liberal Democratic ideological inability to cope with it. 'Great Society' programs aligned that party with many Negro demands but the party was unable to defuse the racial tension sundering the nation."[50] The "emerging Republican majority" of his title is to come from creating a home for disaffected Dixiecrats and other whites threatened by the "Negro socioeconomic revolution."

Later in the book, Phillips underscores the critical importance of defending black voting rights in the South, though not for the principled reason one might expect. As he explains: "Maintenance of Negro voting rights [in the South] is essential to the GOP. Unless Negroes continue to displace white Democratic organizations, the latter may remain viable as spokesmen for Deep Southern conservatism."[51] Translation: as long as southern blacks are free to register and take up residence in state Democratic organizations, white Southerners will continue to be driven into the welcoming arms of the GOP. But for this to happen, the national party will also need to disavow the legacy of Lincoln and accommodate the conservative racial politics of the white South. Nixon spent much of his first term in office doing just that.

Among the very first issues Nixon was called upon to deal with as president was filling the Supreme Court vacancy created by the resignation of Abe Fortas early in 1969. In quick succession, Nixon nominated two conservative southern judges, Clement Haynesworth Jr. and G. Harrold Carswell, to fill the vacancy. Both men "were burdened with controversial records on racial issues—Haynesworth with a series of votes against civil rights interests in key cases before the Fourth Circuit Court, and Carswell with his involvement in the conversion of a public golf course (under a court order to desegregate) into a private whites-only club."[52] Given their records, and with Democrats in firm control of both houses of Congress, there was very little chance of either nominee being confirmed. In the end, Nixon was forced to withdraw both nominees. It may well be, however, that Nixon anticipated this outcome and, given his long-term electoral aims, wasn't at all bothered by it. For the rebuff gave him the perfect opportunity to draw a sharp contrast between the pro-black, anti-southern, liberal Democratic Party and the conservative racial principles of the new GOP. Barely two months into his term in office, Nixon seized on the opportunity afforded him by his withdrawal of the Carswell nomination, to issue the following symbolically pregnant statement:

> I have reluctantly concluded, with the Senate presently constituted, I cannot nominate to the Supreme Court any federal appellate judge from the South who believes as I do in the strict construction of the Constitution. . . . I understand the bitter feeling of millions of Americans who live in the South about the act of regional discrimination that took place in the Senate yesterday. They have my assurances that the day will come when men like Judges Carswell and Haynesworth can and will sit on the high Court.[53]

It would be hard to imagine a more transparent signal to southern whites regarding the brave new world of racial politics ushered in by

Nixon's victory. For Dixiecrats, it was a world turned upside down, with "their" Democratic Party now in the hands of newly minted black voters and the once dreaded "Party of Lincoln" advocating the posting of "strict constructionists" (read: segregationists) to the Supreme Court. To an increasing number of southern whites, the choice was clear.

For Nixon, the dust-up over his Supreme Court nominees was just the first of several opportunities afforded him to highlight the stark difference in the evolving racial politics of the two parties. Two other issues arose early in his first term that allowed him to curry favor, not just with Dixicrats but with white voters in all regions, frightened by the rhetoric of Black Power and the threats they saw assertive blacks posing to their jobs, their neighborhoods, and especially their schools. Once in office, Nixon acted quickly to align himself with racial conservatives on the increasingly controversial issue of school integration. Less than six months into his term, Nixon's Departments of Justice and Health, Education and Welfare (HEW) jointly announced that they would no longer require school districts to comply with strict, court-ordered timetables for integration. The announcement and subsequent Justice Department motion to delay desegregation marked "the first time since the start of the modern civil rights revolution [that the Department] had placed itself on the side of the white South against black plaintiffs."[54]

As with the Haynesworth and Carswell controversies, in the end, Nixon was not able to make this particular policy change stick. In an October brief, the Supreme Court rejected the administration's motion and reinstated the order requiring immediate adoption of court-ordered desegregation plans. Once again, however, whatever substantive frustration the Court's actions may have caused him, Nixon seized on the moment to unambiguously embrace the southern segregationists' position on the matter. In the immediate aftermath of the Court ruling, Nixon warned "the many young liberal lawyers [in the Justice Department]" not to view the brief "as a carte blanche for them to run wild through the South enforcing compliance with extreme or punitive requirements...formulated in Washington."[55] No doubt the image of Nixon heroically interposing himself between an oppressive federal establishment and a defenseless region was purely intentional and designed to resonate with long-standing southern grievances stemming from the War of Northern Aggression, Reconstruction, and federal intervention during the civil rights era. Nixon's determined assault on court-ordered busing in the run-up to the 1972 election certainly burnished his reputation on the issue of school desegregation, but his fundamental position on the matter had been forcefully set in year one of his presidency. Through all of his actions in this area Nixon, as the Edsalls so perceptively note, "succeeded in defining forced desegregation as the responsibility of the courts, not of his administration, and simultaneously declared that he supported a far more slow and cautious approach to integration than did the Supreme Court—a critical step in wedding 1968 Wallace voters to Nixon's own re-election bid."[56]

On one final issue—voting rights—we see the same pattern of a conservative racial proposal by Nixon blocked at the federal level by determined liberal opposition, allowing him to further solidify his southern support by drawing a sharp contrast between the GOP position and aggressive civil rights advocacy by the Democrats. The specific issue at hand was the "preclearance" provision of the 1965 Voting Rights Act. The provision required states and local jurisdictions in the South to secure the approval of the Justice Department before implementing any changes in election laws or procedures. Given the creative penchant southern authorities had shown, since the end of Reconstruction, for devising ingenious rules to deny or limit the franchise to African Americans, the preclearance provision remained essential to the realization of the aims of the 1965 act. That is precisely why the region's white political elite sought to eliminate the provision. As black voter registration rates soared throughout the region—with especially dramatic gains in the Deep South—white politicians were increasingly drawn to legal and procedural subterfuges that would allow them to retain power in the face of declining numbers.[57] By including a proposal to eliminate the preclearance provision in a broader bill he brought to Congress in 1969, Nixon clearly aligned himself with those whites who sought to maintain political supremacy in the South. Reflecting the sea change in the racial politics of the GOP since the passage of the original Voting Rights Act, the proposal to eliminate the preclearance provision initially survived a narrow vote in the House, with nearly three quarters of all Republican House members—but only a third of all Democrats—voting in favor of the plan. The more liberal

Senate, however, opposed the measure and in conference succeeded in getting the House to reverse its position. In the end, Congress voted to extend the Voting Rights Act—including the critical "preclearance" procedure—for another five years. Once again, however, "Nixon...had realized his central goal, clearly aligning himself with the white South in a battle with the Democratic Congress, and distancing his own administration [and party] from a program of stringent federal enforcement."[58]

To say that Nixon's efforts to court southern whites were rewarded would be an understatement. The results of the 1972 election make it clear just how successful Nixon was in winning over Wallace supporters and white voters in general. Not only did he carry every southern state—the first Republican candidate to do so—but he also claimed nearly two thirds of all white voters.[59] It turns out that Nixon's much celebrated "silent majority" had a distinctly racial cast to it. This, of course, was by design. But it was Wallace's candidacy and the more amorphous white resistance movement of the mid- to late 1960s that motivated the racial politics of Nixon's first term and moved the GOP ever more decisively to the right in the early 1970s.

Summing Up

The 1960s are, of course, already remembered as a period of significant social change in the United States. In our view, however, one of the most consequential changes to mark the era has gone largely unremarked. Throughout most of American history, politics and the prospects for social change have been powerfully shaped by the interaction of social movements, parties, and governmental institutions. One of the striking features of the 1940s and 1950s was the comparative absence of grass-roots movement activity. This unusual quiescence spared the major parties the normal challenge of having to manage mobilized movements at their ideological margins, allowing both to hew close to the moderate center of the left-right continuum. The result was a sustained period of unprecedented bipartisan cooperation on the major issues of the day. This all changed in the 1960s, however, with the dramatic return of social movements as a significant force in American life and politics. The chapter presented a detailed recounting of three movements and their effects on the Democrats and Republicans, respectively. Here we revisit the two most consequential and tightly coupled of the movements.

Revitalized by the 1960 sit-in campaign, the civil rights movement roared back to life, and over the next half dozen years it put unrelenting pressure on the American state and two Democratic administrations to enact fundamental changes in the social, political, and economic status of African Americans. In the end, this pressure proved decisive in a number of important ways. Not only was it key to the major legislative and judicial victories of the period, but it also had the effect of pushing the Democratic Party decisively to the left, alienating the southern wing of the party, and ultimately breaking apart the New Deal coalition that had allowed the Democrats to effectively dominate federal policy-making since 1932.

That story and its larger social and political significance have been recognized by scholars for some time. The second story, however, has gone generally unremarked. It too was set in motion by the rebirth of the civil rights movement in 1960. We refer to the segregationist countermovement that rapidly mobilized in response to the sit-ins and grew apace of the civil rights struggle over the next few years. Overwhelmingly confined to the South in the early years of the decade, the countermovement spread northward in the mid-1960s, inspiring a more general "backlash" by racial conservatives all over the country. Aiding and abetting this process was arch-segregationist, George Wallace, whose presidential campaigns in 1964 and especially 1968 gave voice to and helped galvanize a nationwide politics of racial reaction. If the civil rights revolution had the effect of pushing the Democrats decisively leftward, something similar happened to the GOP as a result of the white resistance movement. Although the move to the right was already discernible in the early 1960s, the pace of the shift picked up markedly with the "white backlash" of the mid-1960s, and even more so following Nixon's narrow capture of the White House in '68. Simply put, the results of the election virtually compelled further movement to the right by the GOP. With Nixon and Humphrey basically splitting 86 percent of the vote, and Wallace commanding the remaining 14 percent, it was clear where the balance of power was likely to lie in 1972.

For the Republicans, the narrow victory suggested that the party's future would be best served not by trying to cut into Humphrey's

43 percent of the vote but rather by pursuing the 14 percent garnered by Wallace. Nixon and his Republican strategists believed that the 57 percent he shared with Wallace represented a racially conservative majority that, if successfully tapped, could well ensure GOP control of the White House for years to come. As Peter Goldman commented at the time, "it suggested... a strategy that could keep the Presidency Republican for a generation—precisely by isolating the Democrats as a party of the blacks and building the rickety Nixon coalition of 1968 into a true majority of the white center."[60] When Nixon captured every southern state and 65 percent of the white vote en route to a landslide win four years later, it looked, for all the world, as if this strategic vision had been realized. Alas, for the Republicans, Watergate would muddy the waters and delay the full realization of this vision for another eight years. The 1970s would, in general, prove to be a confusing, transitional period in US politics, very different in this regard from the 1960s. The decades did, however, share something very important in common. If the 1960s marked the return of social movements as a consequential force in American politics, a little-remembered institutional revolution engineered by New Left activists between 1968 and 1972 would dramatically increase the structural leverage available to future grass-roots movements. In the next chapter we take up this and other stories from the strange limbo decade of the 1970s.

4

The Strange, Consequential Seventies

WHEN THE ORIGINS OF THE DISTINCTIVE POLITICAL and economic features of the contemporary United States are discussed, two figures and two corresponding time periods tend to be stressed in particular. The first is Richard Nixon and the key role he played in the late 1960s in courting white southern voters and in pioneering the distinctive politics of racial reaction that has marked the GOP ever since. But no combination of figure and time period has received more attention in discussions of the roots of today's political economy than Ronald Reagan in the 1980s and the decisive reversal of New Deal social policy associated with his two-term presidency (1981–88). By contrast, perhaps no period since 1960 has been accorded less importance in this regard than that strange decade of the 1970s. Relative to Nixon's breakthrough election in 1968 and Reagan's ascension in 1980, the events of the '70s—Watergate, Nixon's impeachment, Ford's caretaker presidency, and the troubled administration of Jimmy Carter—seem inconsequential and without clear direction, as if the country was simply drifting between the two decades where the "real" action took place.

While conceding that there was a certain odd "limbo" quality to the period, we strongly reject the notion that the 1970s played little role in shaping the political and economic reality we confront today. On the contrary, the events of the decade served to powerfully reinforce trends that remain very much in evidence today. Most important, and central to our stress on the key role played by movements in shaping our brave new world, we argue that if the 1960s marked the return of the social movement form, various episodes in the 1970s greatly amplified the influence of movement "voice" in American life and politics. Building on this central theme, we give the balance of the chapter over to a detailed discussion of three episodes during the decade that both underscore the growing influence of movements in the United States and add to our understanding of the long-term processes that have shaped contemporary America. We begin with a little-known institutional revolution waged between 1968 and 1972. Indeed, no episode in the last half-century did more to increase the institutional leverage available to grass-roots activists than the "quiet revolution"[1] that took place in those years.

The Little Revolution That Could

Earlier in the book we lamented the disciplinary divide that has traditionally consigned the study of social movements to sociology and research on parties to political science. And throughout the book we've deployed the linguistic markers "social movement" and "political party," as if they refer to distinct phenomena, with clearly separable boundaries. This, of course, distorts the more complicated underlying reality. For while they may be conceptually distinct, the real-world boundaries between movements and parties (and even states sometimes) are often blurry. As a host of scholars reminds us, many political parties begin life as social movements.[2] The best example in US history is the Republican Party, which, in striking contrast to its current attitudes toward racial minorities, was founded in the early 1850s by moderate abolitionists determined to advance their goal of ending slavery through electoral means.

Then there are the far more numerous examples of movements that, while not establishing their own parties, seek to advance their aims by allying themselves with and shaping the policies of existing party organizations.[3] In the US context, examples of this would include the considerable influence that organized labor has wielded within the Democratic Party historically and the decisive impact the Tea Party movement has had on the policies and personnel of the contemporary GOP.[4] So successfully has the Tea Party stitched itself into the fabric of today's Republican Party that it is pointless to ask whether we should think of it as a movement *or* a political party. It clearly has elements of both, as do many movements at certain points in their history.

The "little revolution that could" involves another clear-cut instance of a movement—in this case, the anti-war movement of the 1960s—powerfully shaping the policies and practices of the Democratic Party. Indeed, it doesn't seem too far-fetched to claim that the anti-war movement—or more accurately, the congeries of movements that made up the New Left—was to the Democrats in the late '60s and early '70s what the Tea Party has been to the Republicans since 2010. In both instances, grass-roots movements came, for periods of time, to be arguably the dominant force within the two parties. We will make the case that the New Left effectively controlled the policies, practices, and ideological direction of the Democrats from after the 1968 general election through the 1972 presidential campaign. For its part, the Tea Party, as we detail in Chapter 7, has waged a spirited battle for control of the GOP, moving the party sharply rightward in the process.

In the previous chapter, we devoted a great deal of attention to the decisive impact the African American freedom struggle had in pushing an initially reluctant Democratic Party to the left, first on the issue of civil rights and then, under Johnson, on a host of social and fiscal policies. This general dynamic—that is, the centrifugal pressure on the party by progressive movement forces—did not, however, end with the gradual decline of organized civil rights activity in the late 1960s. If anything, the explosive growth of the anti-war movement in the mid- to late '60s more than compensated for the waning influence of traditional civil rights forces, especially when the force of the new movement was combined with the pressures associated with generalized campus unrest and the twin specters of black power and the "urban disorders" of the era. The combined force of these bottom-up pressures had the effect of moving the Democrats steadily leftward throughout the decade of the '60s and, as we will show, on into the '70s. This was not, however, a case where a movement was incorporated into the party establishment with little overt conflict, as had been true with the Democrats and labor in the 1930s. Even as the party was shifting left in response to the escalating pressures brought by the New Left, the "liberal" party estab-lishment was battling to limit the influence of the grass-roots activists within the party.

Much of the focus of this battle came to turn on the issue of the selection of delegates to the national convention and ultimately the related and singularly important matter of how the party selected its presidential candidate every four years. This battle was, for all intents and purposes, first joined in 1964 when the Mississippi Freedom Democratic Party (MFDP) challenged the seating of the regular all-white Mississippi delegation to the Democratic national convention in Atlantic City. Recounted in considerable detail in Chapter 3, the deal—rejected by MFDP—that "resolved" the matter in '64 included a promise by the party to review the matter of delegate selection in advance of the 1968 convention. No such review, and certainly no meaningful change in party practices, took place in the intervening four years. Left unresolved, the linked issues of delegate selection and presi-dential nominating procedures would resurface with exceptional fury when the Democrats gathered in Chicago for their 1968 confab.

For those old enough to have witnessed the events firsthand, and for those younger who have only seen grainy news footage, the sights and sounds of the '68 convention are riveting. "The Battle of Chicago" began the day before the actual convention "when 150 police broke up a demonstrators' encampment in Lincoln Park with tear gas, night-sticks, and chemical mace."[5] Protestors and police skirmished over the next three days as well, but it was the climactic spasm of violence on the last night of the convention—the night Hubert Humphrey was for-mally designated the party's presidential nominee—that everyone remembers. That night 5,000 protestors battled Chicago's finest on the Loop, with police wading into crowds and clubbing demonstrators, press, and bystanders indiscriminately. At one point, a large number of protestors were pressed up against and *through* the plate glass windows of the main restaurant at the Hilton Hotel, landing bloody in the laps of startled convention delegates dining inside. DeBenedetti captures the surreal quality of the event:

The whole Kafkaesque scene was televised to an incredulous nation. It was viewed at the convention hall, where Senator Abraham

Ribicoff of Connecticut condemned the [Chicago mayor] Daley machine for its "Gestapo" tactics. Other delegates held up signs equating Chicago with Prague, where Soviet tanks were already rolling in a crushing attack on the Czech liberalization movement. Daley had won the streets, but the cost was great. Over 1,000 people...were injured during the four days of street fighting, and 662 arrested.[6]

For all the sound and fury, however, the battle in the streets was an exercise in futility. If the immediate focus of the protestors' rage was Vietnam, the convention served as a pointed rebuke to anti-war forces. In Chicago, the party establishment brushed aside a challenge by anti-war dissidents to approve a plank supporting the war and, most egregiously, nominated Hubert Humphrey for president, despite the fact that Humphrey, as Lyndon Johnson's vice-president, was deeply implicated in the prosecution of the unpopular war. But what virtually no one knew at the time, and very few appreciate even now, is that the convention was witness to a second, much quieter, but ultimately far more consequential battle than the one in the streets that captured the headlines that long ago August. It was a battle waged by anti-war activists, but motivated by a broader issue than the war itself. Public opinion polls had been tracking support for the war since its onset in 1965. At the time of the convention, 53 percent of Americans thought the Vietnam War was a mistake.[7] And while Democratic voters were no more likely to oppose the war than their Republican counterparts, anti-war sentiment was clearly on the rise within the Democratic Party, especially among young Democrats who were overrepresented in the ranks of the anti-war movement. And yet, as noted, the rising anti-war tide within the party was given little attention by the party elite who closed ranks in Chicago to nominate Humphrey, thereby reaffirming the party's support for the war. It was this, the party's nondemocratic procedures and lack of responsiveness to the views of its rank and file that, more than anything else, animated the anti-war reformers who took advantage of the Democrat's own bureaucratic machinery to engineer a silent revolution within the convention hall while the Battle for Chicago raged without.

Prelude to Revolt

To fully understand the initial actions of these institutional activists, readers need a bit more context. If the 1960s was among the most convulsive decades in US history, 1968 was the most convulsive year in that most convulsive of decades. Much of what made it so was the confluence of a deeply unpopular war and the normal high drama and tensions attendant on a presidential race. Despite the divisiveness of Vietnam, at the beginning of the year President Johnson seemed a lock to be his party's nominee for a second term in office. But that was before the "Tet offensive" shook American confidence and trust in the war effort. On January 30, the eve of Tet, the Vietnamese lunar New Year, communist forces launched a brazen, coordinated assault on 36 of South Vietnam's 44 provincial capitals and five of its six largest cities. This included the nation's capital, Saigon, where the insurgents even managed for a time to seize the supposedly impregnable US embassy. A month-long counteroffensive by US and South Vietnamese troops succeeded in repelling the communists and inflicting massive casualties on the invaders. In conventional military terms, the United States (and its South Vietnamese allies) had won a clear-cut victory. In the process, however, it had lost the broader battle for public support of the war effort in the United States. As one analyst astutely observed, the American "people were willing, but they were not purposeful in this war. Only as long as the president could evoke the hope that his policy would yield a successful conclusion...would he have their support. [With the Tet offensive] that hope was shattered at the end of January, changing the political scene in the United States."[8] For three years the American public had been fed a steady diet of reassuring assessments—backed by lopsided casualty figures—that the war was going well and that victory was in sight. The Tet offensive exposed the lie in all these rosy assessments. The images of the offensive—US troops battling for control of the American embassy, the South Vietnamese National Police chief summarily executing a Viet Cong suspect on a street in Saigon—shattered public confidence and soured many Americans on the war. In February, for the first time ever, a plurality of survey respondents (49 to 41 percent) pronounced the war a "mistake."

Coming just weeks before the New Hampshire primary—the first of the election season—the timing of the offensive could not have been worse for Johnson's reelection chances. Although Senator Eugene McCarthy (D-Minnesota) had announced in November that he was challenging Johnson for the Democratic nomination for president, early in the year his candidacy seemed dead in the water. That all changed with the Tet offensive, with money and volunteers gravitating to the suddenly buoyant campaign. The momentum built steadily in the run-up to New Hampshire. The results turned the world of American party politics upside down, with McCarthy capturing 42.2 percent of the primary vote compared to 49.4 for the incumbent president. When Republican crossover votes and write-in ballots were counted, the contest was essentially a standoff. What just weeks before had seemed like an almost certain second term for LBJ had suddenly become a wide-open race. A series of dizzying events over the next three weeks made the contest all the more open and contentious. On March 16, just four days after the New Hampshire primary, Robert Kennedy, who had rebuffed earlier entreaties by Dump Johnson forces, entered the race. On March 31 Johnson stunned a national television audience by announcing that he was withdrawing from the contest. Then in late April, Johnson's vice-president, Hubert Humphrey threw his hat into the ring, promising to end the war without "humiliation or defeat." (Translation: if elected, Humphrey would stay the course in Vietnam.) Add to this three ring circus George Wallace's already announced third-party candidacy, and you get a sense of just how chaotic and contentious the race had become.[9]

For their part, McCarthy's supporters felt betrayed by Kennedy's entrance into the race and appalled that Humphrey would seek the nomination without contesting a single primary. For a while "Clean Gene" maintained his momentum, winning decisively in Wisconsin and Oregon. Slowly, however, the tide began to turn, with Kennedy capturing the Indiana and Nebraska contests and finally the ultimate prize, California, on June 5. Everyone knows what happened next; leaving his victory rally at the Ambassador Hotel in Los Angeles, Kennedy was shot and killed, throwing the race and the Democrats into even greater disarray. On the face of it, one would think that Kennedy's assassination would have virtually assured McCarthy of the nomination. He was the only candidate to have competed in all of the primaries, winning in Pennsylvania, Wisconsin, Oregon, Massachusetts,

New Jersey, and Illinois. In the polls he had been neck and neck with Kennedy heading into California, with Humphrey a distant third. Had the race been run under today's primary process, McCarthy would have been in the driver's seat. But this was 1968, when there were only a handful of *non-binding* primaries to be contested. As various state Democratic conventions convened in June to select their delegations for Chicago, the McCarthy camp quickly realized the fix was in. With most state party organizations dominated by establishment Democrats, hostile to the anti-war movement, the party's New Left wing found itself on the outside looking in. The immediate precipitant to the revolution came in Connecticut where despite their candidate's strong showing in the primaries and Humphrey's low poll numbers, the McCarthy forces were awarded just 9 of 44 delegates at the close of the state convention on June 23.

Let the Revolution Begin

Outraged by what they saw as a clear disparity between their candidate's considerable support in Connecticut and the meager share of delegates they had been allotted, a group of McCarthy activists gathered in West Hartford on the evening of June 23 to weigh a possible credentials challenge at the national convention. The question was the grounds on which to base the challenge since, in procedural terms, the outcome of the state convention had been strictly legal. Byron Shafer, the foremost chronicler of the revolution, explains the strategic path the group chose: "The West Hartford conferees gradually moved toward agreement on a strategic response. They proposed to establish a formally neutral investigative commission, to study the issue of fair party rules. The findings and recommendations of the commission could then become the formally disinterested support for a challenge to the Connecticut outcome."[10] It was an interesting plan, but with a scant eight weeks to go before the national convention, it must have also seemed like a bit of a pipe dream to at least some of those who were party to the scheme. Who were the plotters who gathered that evening in West Hartford? First and foremost, they were McCarthy backers, the brain-trust of his Connecticut operation. More important, they were New Left activists, with deep roots in civil rights and anti-war organizing, who had developed a deep antipathy to what they saw as the closed and anti-democratic character of the Democratic Party establishment. Geoffrey Cowan, the key point person for the effort, fit this profile perfectly. Cowan had cut his activist teeth in the civil rights movement. In fact, he had been a Freedom Summer volunteer in 1964, experiencing firsthand the exclusionary practices of the Democratic Party courtesy of that year's failed convention challenge in Atlantic City. More recently, however, he had turned his attention to the war, signing on to the McCarthy campaign as an innovative way to directly confront Johnson's Vietnam policy. Cowan arrived at the meeting in West Hartford as the McCarthy coordinator for Connecticut; he left as the executive director of the conspirators' brainchild: the Commission on the Democratic Selection of Presidential Nominees.

Cowan quickly tapped Thomas Alder, an old friend from civil rights organizing to serve as commission director and in short order they reached out to a dozen young lawyers, most with backgrounds in either civil rights and/or poverty law, to fill out the staff. Many were also supporters of McCarthy, but that was increasingly beside the point. Very quickly the initiative was evolving from a narrow strategic gambit by the McCarthy campaign in Connecticut to secure a larger number of convention delegates to a broader effort by veteran New Left activists to challenge what they saw as the anti-democratic policies and proce-dures of the Democratic Party. If it were seen in this light, however, Alder and Cowan knew the effort would almost certainly be stillborn. To have any chance of getting the initiative off the ground, they knew the commission would need to be seen as emanating as much from within the party as without. To accomplish this, Alder and Cowan simultaneously pursued an internal and external strategy. Internally, they scrambled to "appoint" commissioners who, though clearly committed to reform, represented important constituents within the party. Externally, they sought to persuade two members of both the party's Rules and Credentials Committees to call for the creation of the very "impartial" commission they had already willed into being and which they were already packing with commissioners *partial* to their reform aims. Remarkably, against long odds and extraordinary time constraints, Alder and Cowan managed to pull off this audacious sleight of hand. Dutifully, two "sponsors" on both Rules and Credentials called for the creation of the commission, even as efforts to appoint reform-minded commissioners continued apace.

One challenge remained: before the commission could get to work, Cowan and Alder had to find and persuade someone with sufficient party bona fides to serve as the titular head of the commission. After being rebuffed by several more prominent Democrats, Iowa governor Harold Hughes finally agreed to chair the commission. While Hughes did not have the national stature that Cowan and Alder had been hoping for, he was—as they would quickly learn—deeply committed to party reform. Best of all, he had said "yes." Quite remarkably, Alder and Cowan had pulled all of this off in little more than a month following the West Hartford gathering. Still, by the time the commission was fully operational, less than five weeks remained before the start of the convention. Time was running out and "[The commission still] needed fifty state reports by the end of the first week in August, a draft report for a full commission meeting at the end of the second week, and a published booklet for the convention in Chicago by the end of the third."[11] They somehow managed to accomplish all three goals. Reports on how all 50 state parties selected delegates were compiled by the first week in August. The staff used those reports to draw up a set of draft proposals comprising a sweeping blueprint for radical reform of delegate selection and, ultimately, the procedures for nominating a presidential candidate. In turn, this draft report was made available to the commissioners just hours before the group's lone meeting, on August 13 in Winnetka, Illinois. Given the radical reform sensibilities that had shaped the appointment of both staff and commissioners, the outcome of the meeting was foreordained. Working from a set of proposals prepared by staff, the commissioners, in short order, adopted a set of sweeping recommendations designed to accomplish three main aims: (1) replacement of restrictive means of delegate selection with procedures designed to ensure maximum participation by rank-and-file party members; (2) elimination of the existing, complex formula for apportioning delegates across states and using one based solely on state population; and (3) abolition of racial discrimination in delegate selection by charging states with an "affirmative obligation" to ensure that the black percentage of their delegations would match closely the African American percentage of its population.

Having secured approval of the basic blueprint for a radical, populist overhaul of the party's convention and nominating procedures, the staff set to work producing the commission report it would present in Chicago. With just four days to spare before the start of the convention, the official 80-page report, *The Democratic Choice,* was ready for distribution. Today analysts struggle to make sense of the ongoing tug of war between the Tea Party and the more establishment wing of the GOP. Nearly 50 years after it was written, *The Democratic Choice* remains a fascinating document for what it tells us about the struggle between another movement and the party it sought to remake. For if in his rendering of the commission's official recommendation, the report's author, Simon Lazurus, conformed scrupulously to the wording agreed upon in Winnetka, his framing of the overall commission effort betrayed its New Left origins and aims. Barely two paragraphs into the document, Lazurus included the following strident call for radical reform, or "purification," of the Democratic Party:

> This convention is on trial. The responsibilities of these Committees, and all delegates to this Convention are unprecedented. To an extent not matched since the turn of the century, events in 1968 have called into question the integrity of the convention system for nominating presidential candidates. Recent developments have put the future of the two-party system itself into serious jeopardy.... The crisis of the Democratic Party is a genuine crisis for democracy in America and especially for the two-party system. Racial minorities, the poor, the young... all are seriously considering transferring their allegiance away from either of the two major parties.... We recommend the following principal proposals to the Convention and its principal Committees... to *purify*—and hopefully preserve—the power exercised by future Democratic National Conventions.[12]

We can spare you a detailed recounting of the reformer's back stage maneuvers in Chicago. In any case, Shafer has already furnished such an account.[13] A few summary remarks will suffice. As an extension of the "external" strategy described, the reformers pressed their case for the overhaul of the system in both the Rules and Credentials Committees, which they had successfully enjoined to empower the commission in the first place. There was sufficient opposition in both bodies, however, that had the matter been put to a vote in either or both committees, the commission proposals would almost certainly have been rejected. In the end, however, neither side pressed for a definitive vote on the recommendations. For their part, the establishment members of the two committees were preoccupied with other, more immediate matters. Desperate to secure the nomination for Humphrey in the face of widespread anger by McCarthy and Kennedy supporters, party regulars were only too happy to throw a bone to the insurgents by supporting the idea of some kind of official party commission that would subject the matter to further study. As one of Humphrey's chief strategists later explained:

> Our objective was to get a nominee. This [the Hughes Commission report] was unimportant, except as it might have some effect on the nomination. We said to ourselves, if you're going to *study* it, you can control it. If you get the nomination, you'll have control of the DNC [Democratic National Committee]. If you have the DNC, then you'll control any *study*.[14]

Meanwhile, realizing that they did not have the votes to push through the reform proposals in either committee, the insurgents settled on a Plan B: securing full convention approval of the creation of an official party commission to study the matter further and to propose remedies for inequities uncovered. With the Credentials Committee burdened by a record 17 credentials challenges in Chicago—most brought by civil rights and other New Left forces— it would be hard, reasoned the reformers, for even the most conservative party member to deny the seriousness of the delegate selection issue. As a matter of record, the actual roll call vote that approved the creation of the commission took place just before midnight on August 27, amid total confusion concerning the substance of the resolution. Had the stakes been transparent to the voting delegates, the measure might well have been defeated. For their part, Cowan, Alder, and their allies on the floor were grateful for the chaos. With the great majority of delegates unaware of what had transpired, the Democratic Party had, by a margin of 1,350 to 1,206, committed itself to a thoroughgoing review of the process it used to select its presidential candidates.

The Commission Process

Still, this outcome hardly guaranteed that an overhaul of the nominating process was in the offing. "Whether these developments would amount to anything was unclear when the balloting ended, and unclear when the convention adjourned. . . . [M]ost analysts concluded that little of any consequence had occurred. The insurgents had indeed won a vote, but it was to be their only win. It would have no impact on the 'real business' of the convention, the nomination of a potential president."[15] And looking ahead, there was plenty of cause for pessimism regarding the likely outcome of any reform process. The old guard remained fully in control of the body—the DNC—that would presumably orchestrate whatever process ensued. Finally, even if the insurgents somehow managed to secure DNC approval of the sweeping reforms they favored, control over implementation of the changes would necessarily fall to state party organizations, which in general were also in the hands of party regulars antagonistic to the New Left.

These were, to be sure, daunting organizational barriers to reform. In the end, though the insurgents had two significant factors working in their favor. The first was the disarray and demoralization within the mainstream party that followed Humphrey's defeat in the general election. Only once in the previous 36 years had the Democrats received so meager a share of the popular vote.[16] Moreover with Nixon and the arch-conservative Wallace garnering nearly 58 percent of the ballots cast, the party's future prospects looked none too bright. The demoralizing defeat created something of a void within the party, a void the New Left wing of the party was determined to fill.

In its basic strategic contours, the situation was not unlike that which confronted the GOP in the wake of Romney's defeat in 2012. In both cases, we are looking at a party that, following a period of sustained dominance, had not only been beaten but now confronted worrisome long-term voter trends. In the case of today's GOP, it is the shrinking percentage of white voters that bodes ill for the party; in '68 it was the loss of the "solid South" that worried Democratic strategists.

In both cases, the strategic imperative seemed clear enough on the face of the returns. Since the 2012 Republican defeat, countless strategists have advised that to remain competitive, the GOP will need to broaden the party's base by reaching out to Hispanics, Asians, young people, and other demographics that broke heavily for Obama in 2012. Following Humphrey's defeat, sober analysts counseled the Democrats to move right to compete for the votes of white Southerners and the so-called northern white ethnics who had abandoned the party in droves in '68. But that's not the end of the parallels between the Republicans in 2012 and the Democrats in 1968.

Most relevant to the book's thematic focus, both parties featured ascendant movement wings at their ideological margins: the Tea Party in 2012 and New Left in 1968. And in both cases, it was these wings that, in the wake of the defeat, were best organized and energized to contest for control of their respective parties. Moreover, both movements had fashioned accounts that saw the long-term future of the party served, *not* by accommodating the electoral trends noted earlier, but by moving even more sharply to the right or left. For the Tea Party faithful, the defeat in 2012 occurred because Romney was not a "true" conservative, leaving the party's base uninspired and only partially mobilized. To succeed, according to this logic, the party only needs to be faithful to truly conservative precepts and nominate a candidate who embodies those principles. For New Left reformers in 1968, the problem with the party was its closed, anti-democratic character. If only control could be wrested from the party bosses, then the coalition of young people, racial minorities, and feminists who comprised the New Left, could remake and reenergize the party, ushering in a new era of Democratic dominance in national politics. As card-carrying members of the New Left, the dissidents who had orchestrated the convention challenge were imbued with this vision and determined to take advantage of the disarray in the mainstream party to actualize it.

They had one other thing going for them as well. If "possession is nine-tenths of the law," then control of "agenda setting" confers similar advantages to those who seek to shape policy outcomes.[17] And that is what the insurgents had enjoyed throughout the reform process. The extent and narrow basis of their control is striking. Without discounting the important contributions made by others to the effort, little more than a handful of self-conscious activists, committed to the democratization of the presidential nominating process, "owned" the reform process from the outset. Deploying lots of smoke and plenty of mirrors, this group

- conjured the "impartial" Commission on the Democratic Selection of Presidential Nominees;
- hand-picked the "commissioners" based on their commitment to the reforms the organizers favored;
- set the agenda for the commissioners by drafting reform proposals for them to consider;
- folded the official commission recommendations into an 80-page booklet, framed as a broader appeal to "purify" the Democratic Party by way of the proposed reforms;
- and, finally, used the chaos attendant to a late-night roll call vote to sneak through a resolution committing the national party to a continuation of the reform process they had launched just two months earlier.

Having successfully controlled the reform agenda through the convention, the insurgents were determined to retain this control going forward. To say they succeeded in this would be a serious understatement. This—that is, their effective control of the reform process— would prove the decisive advantage enjoyed by the insurgents. Following the convention, the revolution played out in three stages, lasting well into 1972. We briefly describe these three stages, underscoring the effective control insurgents exercised throughout the process. Other than the creation of the original "Hughes Commission," the first of these post-convention stages was the most critical to the success of the reform process.

Constituting the Commission

You will recall that during the Chicago Convention one of Humphrey's chief strategists had supported the idea of an official reform commission, arguing, in effect, that if Humphrey secured the nomination, he would then control the DNC and with it, any commission established by the DNC. With party regulars overrepresented on the DNC, this was an entirely likely scenario coming out of the convention. One could easily have imagined a determined coalition of party elite effectively cutting the reformers out of the process at this point, packing the commission with establishment types and producing a report that left the existing party structures and procedures largely intact. Needless to say, this is not at all what happened. The insurgents—who did *not* control this part of the process—had one person to thank for the somewhat unexpected conception of the commission endorsed by the DNC. That person was incoming DNC chair, Fred Harris. His immediate predecessor, Larry O' Brien, was a staunch Humphrey supporter and party traditionalist. But O'Brien was replaced before he was able to shape the ideological disposition of the commission through his powers of appointment. That task fell instead to Harris, who "had something very different in mind [from O'Brien]. He planned to install the growing 'reform wing' of the party within the commission.... Accordingly Harris labored to create a superficially indeterminate but fundamentally pro-reform majority within this Commission on Party Structure and Delegate Selection."[18]

Perhaps more important than the commissioners themselves, however, was the staff that George McGovern, chosen by Harris to chair the commission, assembled to orchestrate the commission process. Signaling his strong desire to link to what had come before, McGovern either hired or sought to retain the services of most of the key players from the original Hughes Commission. This included such stalwarts as Tom Alder, Eli Segal, Anne Wexler, and Alexander Bickel. When, in February 1969, Hughes himself was appointed as vice-chairman of the new commission, the continuity between the two bodies was strengthened all the more. Quite simply, this continuity meant that control over the reform process had once again been vested in that small group of insurgents who had launched the revolution in the first place.

The Work of the Commission

In retaining the services of a healthy subset of the original Hughes insurgents, McGovern had effectively returned agenda setting control of the revolution to the same small group who had initiated it.[19] In the following quotation, Shafer captures the influence the hand picked insurgent staff exerted on the work of the commission:

> If [the] commissioners did not arrive with specific reform suggestions of their own, that meant only that the commission remained a malleable body, dependent... on the activities of its leadership and staff for a a detailed agenda. And there, the bias toward extensive institutional change was clear and strong. It was not just that there [were] no committed defenders of the regular party and its associated interest groups among these key actors. There were not even any moderate spokesmen for the orthodox Democratic coalition.[20]

Given the composition of the staff and the fact that the commissioners had been picked, in large part, on the basis of their commitment to reform, it seems clear that the central thrust of commission recommendations had been preordained from the very beginning. And as we saw with the Hughes Commission, it was the staff that overwhelmingly shaped the outcome of the commission process. It was the staff who translated the group's general reform proclivities into specific draft recommendations that set the agenda for meetings of the full commission or its executive committee. The staff also shaped the contours of the discussions at these meetings, interpreted the substantive results of the sessions, and revised draft documents accordingly, setting the stage for the next round of commission meetings. In this way, the staff drove and owned the process throughout. As Shafer put it, the commission process "confirmed the persistence of inherent staff advantages.... It was full-time, expert, and at the center of reform communications. Moreover, staff members knew what they wanted and how they hoped to attain it. They were far more dedicated than any individual commissioner, and dedicated to one overall, desired outcome."[21]

What was the one key outcome the staff "desired?" Reflecting their movement roots, above all else staff wanted to restructure all aspects of the presidential nominating process to reflect the central New Left principle of "participatory democracy." The extent to which this central aim and overriding New Left ethos came to inform the work of the full commission is reflected in a remarkable statement made by McGovern when he opened the first meeting of the full Party Structure Commission in September of 1969. Said McGovern:

> We were created not by a faction of the party, but by a strong majority mandate of the Democratic National Convention in 1968.... We are instructed to assist the States in establishing a delegate selection system in which all Democratic voters have had full, meaningful, and timely opportunity to participate.... In blunt language, this means that the Democratic Party in national convention assembled has asked us to spell out methods for assuring that the people rather than the bosses select the presidential nominee of our party.[22]

Quite remarkable: the mantra of the New Left—"let the people decide"— was being deployed as a call to thoroughgoing institutional reform by the man destined to be the next presidential nominee of the party being transformed.

As a factual matter, the commission began its work in February of 1969 and held its last substantive sessions November 19–20 of that same year. It took the staff until April of the following year, however, to complete work on the official commission report. Even today the document makes for remarkable reading, attesting to just how much the language, ideology, and practices of the New Left had worked their way into the fabric of the ascendant movement wing of the Democratic Party. Here we simply want to call attention to the two central emphases of the report. The first was the insistence—as reflected in a host of specific recommendations—that state party organizations do everything possible to ensure popular participation in all aspects of the nominating process. Most important in this regard was the stark recommendation that three of the five existing methods of delegate selection—those that in some way restricted participation in the process—be banned in favor of the two, "candidate primaries" and "participatory conventions," that were open to all. The second, much more controversial emphasis, was on the need for "proportional representation" of explicitly identified underrepresented demographic groups. Nothing occasioned more debate and conflict within the commission than what came to be thought of as the matter of "quotas." In the end, the group stopped short of recommending fixed quotas to achieve proportional representation based on "race, color, creed, or national origin" (Guideline A-1) or "age or sex" (Guideline A-2), opting instead for language that charged the states with ensuring that the aforementioned demographic categories would be represented in their convention delegations "in reasonable relationship to the group's presence in the population of the state."[23]

Implementation

With the completion of the official commission report in April 1970, the revolution had reached its final stage. In fact, without discounting the importance of what had come before, the success of the revolution would ultimately depend on this stage of the process more than any other. The sweeping reforms called for in the final report would mean little if they were rejected by the DNC or ignored by the state party organizations responsible for carrying them out. Actually, it appears as if the key actors orchestrating the commission process—certainly Ken Bode and Eli Segal, but perhaps even McGovern—thought it very likely that the revolution would be derailed at this stage of the process. As long as the effort was confined to the internal workings of the commission, these actors remained confident of their control of the situation. The process, however, had now reached a stage where they were obliged to go public with their recommendations. It was now, they felt sure, that the imagined party establishment—powerful, well organized, and vengeful—would rise up and smite the insurgents. Nothing of the sort happened. Instead, over the next 18–24 months, the reforms were adopted by virtually all state party organizations, smoothly, steadily and with virtually no opposition from the dreaded establishment. How had this happened? Where were the reactionary forces—organized labor, Dixiecrats, traditional party bosses—in all of this?

To account for the smoothness and unalloyed success of the process, we stress two principal factors. First, and most important, in 1970–71 the dreaded establishment was nowhere near as "powerful," "organized," or even as "vengeful" as the insurgents had feared. Indeed, in the end, the very embodiment of that establishment, Larry O' Brien—former head of the DNC and longtime Johnson and Humphrey loyalist—who had been reelected as party chairman in 1970, surprised nearly everyone by working tirelessly and effectively on behalf of the reforms. He did so, the evidence suggests, because he understood just how divided the party was and, given how far along the revolution was, what kind of open warfare he would trigger if he tried to derail the process. Whatever his motives, O'Brien proved an unlikely, but effective, ally of the insurgents.

In a very real sense, however, by the time O'Brien and the DNC were called on to act on the commission recommendations, the fate of the reforms had, in our view, been largely sealed. This brings us to the second factor alluded to. Fearing what they felt sure would be the adversarial response of the DNC to the report, the commission elected to bypass the committee entirely and to simply assert their authority to communicate the reforms directly to the states and indeed, to enter into negotiations with state party officials regarding the implementation of the new rules and guidelines. As Ken Bode explained the thinking of the insurgents:

> Our theory was always that the guidelines *were* law, without being adopted by the National Committee.... O'Brien wanted the National Committee to vote, to have it legitimizing. Our feeling always was that the vote was unnecessary and irrelevant. If they wanted to read and study the guidelines, that was fine; everyone had the right to do that. But that was all they were entitled to do.[24]

Reflecting this view, the commission chose simply to release the report on its own, effectively asserting the official nature of the reforms; to send official compliance letters to all 55 state, territorial, and district party chairs; and then, sometime later, to begin the process of negotiating implementation of the reforms on a state-by-state basis. Moreover, in negotiating compliance with each separate party organization, commission staff sought to identify like-minded reformers at the state level to work with, thus greasing the reform skids all the more. Eventually the DNC did have a chance to weigh in on the commission recommendations, but by the time that happened—at a meeting on February 19, 1971—state-level negotiations had been going on for nearly a year. This put O'Brien, as chair of the DNC, in a difficult position and no doubt helps explain his decision to back the reforms. As former

DNC staff member Vick French put it: "O'Brien...saw that after the reformers had gotten as far as they did, to undo it would have instantly created open warfare. There was no other way to go, at that point. His internal party position was impossible otherwise. He was too smart and polished a pro not to know that."[25] And so the revolution ended much as it began, with a small group of committed activists engaging in another instance of strategic alchemy. If the revolution began with Cowan and Alder conjuring what became the Hughes Commission, it ended with the likes of Bode, Segal, Hughes, and McGovern simply asserting their institutional authority—independent of the DNC—to require all party organizations to comply with the new reforms. And comply they did. When it came time for the party to pick its presidential nominee for 1972, the brave new world of movement-inflected primary politics was, for all intents and purposes, in place.

Marginalizing Parties and Empowering Movements

We bring our account of the "little revolution that could" to a close by underscoring the significance of the long-term changes the reform process brought about in the relationship of movements to parties in the United States. We begin by stressing two very general points about the revolution that support our central argument that one simply cannot understand the evolution of politics and economics in the United States since 1960—or for that matter, most of American history—without paying close attention to the dynamic interaction of movements, parties, and government institutions.

The first point is straightforward: the revolution was launched, sustained, and orchestrated primarily by self-identified *movement activists* rather than *party members*. Indeed, the key actors in the process— Cowan and Alder in the beginning, Kenneth Bode and Segal later on— came out of movement backgrounds, thought of themselves as activists, and were openly hostile to the party establishment. Throughout the book we have referred to the centrifugal pressures that movements exert on parties, mindful that this language is rather amorphous, threatening to obscure as much at it reveals. Our extended discussion of the 1968– 1972 reform process affords a concrete and highly consequential example of these centrifugal forces in action. Indeed, if the major actors orchestrating the revolution lived in fear that an imagined and all-powerful party establishment would inevitably rise up and crush the revolt, with the benefit of historical perspective, the contest for control of the party in these years now looks entirely one-sided. With the establishment demoralized and in disarray after Humphrey's loss and a certain moderate element within the New Left energized and motivated to fight for control of the Democratic Party, we can now appreciate just how far left these movement forces were able to push the Democrats between the conventions in 1968 and 1972. This shift was largely the product of sustained pressure by the New Left wing of the party and the reform process detailed earlier was among the central vehicles through which the insurgents applied this pressure.

The second, and equally important, point we want to make is that the reforms implemented by the parties in 1971–72 served almost immediately to significantly reduce the power of party elites and amplify the voice of grass-roots movements in the presidential nomination process. We should not be surprised by this outcome. This, after all, had been the aim of insurgents from the beginning. All well and good, but *how* exactly did the reforms enhance the influence of grass-roots movements? The reforms empowered movement activists in two ways, each reflecting one of the two main commission aims described previously. The first of these goals bears the clear imprint of the fragmented composition of the New Left at the time of the reforms and, as a result, feels somewhat anachronistic today; the second broad empowering aim may well be more relevant and consequential today than it was in 1972.

First, the only real source of controversy and dissension among the commissioners centered on the issue of "formal proportional representation," or what came to be thought of, in shorthand, as the matter of "quotas" for specific demographic groups. In fact, the commission, as we noted, stopped short of recommending formal quotas for specific groups, instead charging party officials with the responsibility for ensuring a "reasonable relationship" between the composition of their delegations and the overall demographic proportions in their states. This requirement was very much a product of the fragmented New Left as it existed at the time the reforms were enacted. Long gone was any semblance of the broad coalitional New Left of the early to mid-1960s, replaced by a fragmented and at times fractious collection of disadvantaged minorities: blacks,

Chicanos, Native Americans, and women, to cite only the most prominent examples. In calling for proportional representation of various demographic groups, the reformers were simply betraying their sensitivity and general adherence to the separatist identity politics of the day. However anachronistic this demographic accounting may seem today, conformity to the requirement of proportional representation had the effect, in 1972, of transforming the institutional body responsible for selecting the party's presidential nominee. The immediate empowering impact of this first reform is clearly reflected in the starkly different demographics of the '68 and '72 conventions. The number of female delegates increased threefold from 13 to 40 percent between 1968 and '72. The number of black delegates also tripled, rising to 15 percent in 1972. The biggest jump, however, was in the number of delegates younger than 30 years of age. From just 3 percent in '68, the number rose to 22 percent four years later. More important than the percentage increases themselves was what they implied about the shifting balance of power between party regulars and the New Left wing of the party as of 1972. Instead of protesting their exclusion from the convention hall as they had done in 1968, large numbers of activists from the various minority movements found themselves ensconced inside the hall four years later. The New Left had effected a demographic revolution from within.

It is the reforms associated with the second major aim of the commission, however, that have had the more enduring and consequential impact on the nominating process and the political influence wielded by movement groups. More than anything else, the insurgents were intent on democratizing the nominating process and doing away with the kind of "back-room" deal making that had allowed Humphrey to secure the 1968 nomination without really contesting the few primaries held that year. Toward that end, the commission, by means of its recommendations, effectively restricted the number of legitimate vehicles for selecting delegates to just two: candidate primaries and participatory conventions. Fairly quickly, the primaries became the method of choice in most states. For the Democrats, the number increased from 17 in 1968 to 34 in 1980. The GOP trajectory was essentially the same, moving from 15 in 1968 to 35 in 1980.[26]

If the commission orchestrated a revolution that "reach[ed] into every institution of American national government and . . . alter[ed] the fabric of American national politics,"[27] no outcome of the reform process has been more critical to the revolution than the dramatic expansion of the system of binding popular primaries. This expansion was marked by two significant surprises. The first surprise was that the expansion occurred without any specific recommendation from the McGovern Commission. In point of fact, the members of the commission thought the real effect of their efforts would be the reform of state nominating conventions. Instead, perhaps reflecting the "power to the people" impulse of the growing legions of New Left reformers within the party, more and more state affiliates chose to replace their conventions with direct primaries. The bigger—*much* bigger—surprise was just how quickly Republicans followed suit in expanding their system of primaries. As noted, the GOP rate of expansion was almost identical to that of the Democrats. In view of the growing conservatism of the GOP, how are we to make sense of the state affiliates' enthusiastic embrace of the primary reforms. It is worth quoting Shafer at length on the matter:

> In part, there was a narrowly political explanation for this impact on the Republicans. In some states, where the Democrats controlled both houses of the state legislatures, party leaders simply extended their plan for delegate selection to the Republican party as well, whether leaders on the other side wanted a presidential primary or not. But in addition, many of the forces which were pushing Democratic leaders in this direction fell on Republican leaders, too. They too were sensitive to demands and arguments for "democratization" of the process; they too possessed a large—probably larger—segment of white-collar independents, for whom such reforms were especially attractive.[28]

For our purposes, however, far more important than the reasons behind the bipartisan embrace of primaries are the highly consequential effects that have followed from the expansion of the system. Quite simply, since 1972 "decision making in presidential nominations has shifted to the party's rank and file, as represented by those who participate in state and local party primaries and caucuses."[29] So what? In the context of the present discussion of the growing influence of movements, the crucial point to be made is that with relatively few people taking part in primaries and caucuses, the expansion of these institutions has served—over time—to magnify the voice of mobilized activists at the ideological margins of the parties. There is a certain irony in this. In barring the use of closed, elite-controlled methods of delegate selection, the New Left insurgents were advocating more popular, and by implication more *representative*, participation in the presidential nominating process. The irony is that in achieving the former, they may well have sacrificed the latter. That is, while many times more people now take part in the nominating process than was true under the old, party-controlled system, research on the characteristics of primary voters has generally shown that they tend to be more ideologically extreme and nonrepresentative in their views than the average party member.[30] Thus, in achieving more popular participation, the reformers unwittingly also created a system ideally suited to amplifying the "voice" of the nonrepresentative activist wings of the two parties.

When we speak of the centrifugal pressure that movements now exert on parties, primaries—congressional as well as presidential—constitute perhaps the central institutional vehicle for the exercise of this pressure. Increasingly, to emerge as a viable candidate for public office—especially on the Republican side of the ledger—those seeking office must first pass muster with the most extreme ideological elements within the party. We witnessed this with unusual force and fury in the Republican presidential primaries in 2012 during which the principal candidates vied with each other for the affections of the party's movement base by staking out ever more extreme positions on a host of policy issues. By the time he emerged battered but victorious from the primary gauntlet, Mitt Romney had positioned himself so far to the right that, try as he might, he wasn't able to tack sufficiently back to the middle to capture more independent voters. At the same time, it's also very likely that his last-minute efforts to lunge to the middle cost him the support of some movement conservatives who were wary of him to begin with.

The simple fact is that the current primary system has simultaneously empowered movement activists while rendering the once mighty median voter increasingly irrelevant. By frontloading the electoral system with a nominating process that favors small numbers of committed activists, much of the action is now taking part at the ideological edges of the system, effectively marginalizing the great majority of Americans who occupy the moderate center of the political continuum. This is the enduring, if ironic, legacy of the institutionalization of popular participation via the 1968–72 reform process. The Tea Party and its effect on the contemporary GOP is the best current example of the phenomenon, but the Democratic Party had its own Tea Party "moment" as well. It came in the early 1970s courtesy of the "little revolution that could."

The Democrat's Tea Party Moment: 1968–1972

In the myriad accounts we have read on the Tea Party and the Republican Party, we have yet to find any that draw parallels between the current situation and what we see as a similar battle waged between 1968 and 1972 by the New Left and the traditional party establishment for control of the Democratic Party. To us, the comparison is striking. In both instances, grass-roots movements born in response to wrenching national crises—Vietnam and violent racial strife in the case of the New Left and the economic meltdown of 2008 in the case of the Tea Party—birthed powerful institutional challenges to the establishments of the two major parties. The effect of these challenges was to push both parties even further toward their ideological margins. By persuading movement conservatives to run for Congress, often against "suspect" Republican incumbents, the Tea Party has sought—and continues to seek—to make the GOP over in its own image. Still, the ultimate outcome of this battle for the soul of the Republican Party remains in doubt. In the light of historical perspective, however, the fate of the New Left's battle for control of the Democratic Party is much clearer. Effectively marginalized until 1968, a growing cadre of New Left reformers—aided by a number of liberal party regulars—gradually gained control of the party in the late 1960s and early 1970s and proceeded to thoroughly dominate the nominating process and national convention in 1972. As perhaps the best example of true movement "capture" of a major party in the last 50 years, the case of the Democrats and the New Left merits further attention. It may even give us a useful comparative perspective on the current struggle between Tea Party adherents and more "moderate"—we use the term advisedly—elements within the Republican Party.

As we sought to document in the previous chapter, the Democrats had been moving steadily leftward in response to sustained pressure from two principal movements since the 1960s began. Spurred by the relentless force of the civil rights struggle, the party's grudging support for limited civil rights reform circa 1960 had given way, by mid-decade, to the major legislative victories and grand liberal vision of Johnson's Great Society. In the latter half of the decade, the anti-war movement gradually supplanted civil rights forces as the central source of centrifugal pressure on the Democratic Party. As we have seen, it was the latter movement that supplied most of the key actors who orchestrated the institutional revolution described in the previous section. But highlighting the major sources of movement pressure on the Democrats in this period doesn't tell us *how* the New Left came to "capture" the party in 1972. We see three principal factors or dynamics at work here. The first is the serious demoralization and sense of institutional crisis that developed within the party establishment in the wake of Humphrey's loss in 1968. To be sure, defeat in any general election occasions some level of depression and organizational soul searching; but the Democrats' loss in '68 was hardly a routine defeat. Consider the numbers:

- The Democrats had held the White House for 28 of the previous 36 years; Nixon was just the second Republican candidate to break through since 1932;
- The Democrats' share of the popular vote declined by almost a third between 1964—when Johnson claimed 61 percent of the vote—and 1968, when Humphrey claimed just 42.7 percent of all ballots cast;
- For the first time in history, (all but one of) the states of the "solid South" had abandoned the Democrats;
- Just as ominously for the Democrats, nearly a third of the white working class—the heart and soul of the party's northern liberal labor wing—had cast their ballots for Nixon or Wallace.

This was no generic defeat; this was nothing less than the unraveling of the vaunted New Deal coalition that had allowed the Democrats to set the national policy agenda for nearly four decades. Now with the two key components of that coalition—northern labor and white Southerners—defecting in large numbers in '68, the mainstream party found itself demoralized and in disarray as the decade wound down. This crisis afforded the New Left insurgents the perfect opportunity to vie for control of a badly weakened party establishment.

If the mainstream party emerged from the '68 election weaker than it had been at any time since the 1920s, the insurgents, on the other hand, were clearly in ascendance. More important, the institutional revolution described in the previous section would serve as the perfect vehicle for strengthening the organization and resolve of the party's movement wing. As should have been clear from our earlier account, New Left activists zealously controlled the revolution from beginning to end, affording them the opportunity, at every stage, to recruit additional adherents and to expand and strengthen reform networks through the procedural requirements of the commission process. To will into existence the Hughes Commission, Cowan and Alder had to pull together and direct the activities of a like-minded band of activist reformers. The McGovern Commission afforded a second collection of activists the opportunity to engage in an even more substantial form of mobilization extending over several years' time. And these are only the most obvious opportunities for mobilization granted the insurgents. Add in the regional hearings held during the commission process and the state-by-state efforts to identify a cadre of party activists to implement the reforms and you begin to understand how the key activists used the reform process to systematically build an insurgent movement within the institutional structure of the party. This then, was the second major factor or dynamic aiding the insurgents.

The third and final factor facilitating movement capture of the party were the reforms themselves designed, as they were, to simultaneously empower grass-roots activists and greatly reduce the power and influence of the traditional party elite. Having fashioned the reforms, the insurgents were perfectly positioned to use the resulting new rules and structures to advance the broader goal of supplanting the traditional party establishment. Shafer captures the clear connection between the emergence of the New Left wing of the party via the reform process, the advantages granted the insurgents by the new rules, and their clear desire to use the reforms to bring the "good news" of "participatory democracy" to what they saw as the closed and coercive structure of the traditional Democratic Party:

The creation of a real alternative coalition meant that as sweeping institutional change was locked into place, there was an organized coalition of [alternative] Democratic elites...in place and ready to reap the advantages which new institutions were designed to provide. Upon the success of this coalition would rest the final impact of reformed rules. A crucial precondition for that success was creation of an explicit, organized, and coordinated framework among potential members. That precondition was now met. That framework, linked by formal officeholders and buttressed by national press, was in existence. Its members were determined to claim their institutional reward.[31]

In another parallel to the Tea Party movement, the growing influence of the New Left wing of the Democratic Party revealed itself first through midterm elections. Just as the political stock of Tea Party forces rose as a result of the key role they played in helping to orchestrate the stunning GOP takeover of the House in 2010, reform activists within the Democratic Party first flexed their muscles in the midterm elections of 1970. Besides claiming a net of 12 new House seats, Democratic forces—led disproportionately by movement liberals—were victorious in 22 of that year's 35 gubernatorial contests. More to the point, the results amounted to a net gain of 12 statehouses, most of them claimed by reform Democratic candidates. These results had two immediate effects. First, the 1970 races granted insurgents that many more opportunities to mobilize reform coalitions at the state level—coalitions that would prove, in many cases, to be decisive in the implementation of the commission recommendations in 1971 and '72. Second, just as the Tea Party was largely credited with GOP gains in 2010, so too were the New Left insurgents seen as primarily responsible for the Democratic victories in 1970. In both cases, then, the midterm elections greatly enhanced the visibility and influence of the mobilized movement wings of the respective parties. Coming off these victories and, in short order, the stunning culmination of the McGovern Commission reform process, insurgents were emboldened and extraordinarily well organized heading into the 1972 presidential nominating process. And with the new participatory rules in effect, they also found themselves in the strange and unprecedented position of being institutionally advantaged vis-à-vis the traditional party elite.

At the outset of the first ever modern primary season, the consensus front runner for the Democratic nomination was Senator Edmund Muskie of Maine. In the end, however, he would suffer the same fate as Lyndon Johnson four years earlier, having his campaign derailed in the snows of New Hampshire. In Johnson's case, the effective end of his reelection bid was the result of his embarrassing showing against the anti-war candidate, Gene McCarthy. Muskie's misstep was very different but no less fatal to his presidential ambitions. Responding to a serious attack on his wife by the conservative *Manchester Union-Leader,* Muskie offered an impromptu, emotional defense of his spouse, appearing to tear up in the process. Media accounts of the incident raised questions about Muskie's emotional stability, costing him dearly in the final New Hampshire vote tally. Fair or not, Muskie's campaign was never able to gain serious traction after that.

No one benefited from Muskie's misstep more than the leading reform candidate in the field, none other than George McGovern, who as chairman of the Commission on Party Structure and Delegate Selection, had helped to orchestrate the reforms he was now perfectly positioned to exploit. And exploit them he did, capturing the delegates of 21 states to sew up the nomination in advance of the national convention. There was a certain delicious irony in McGovern's primary triumph, coming as it did at the expense of the runner-up and quintessential party insider, Hubert Humphrey. Humphrey actually outpolled McGovern across all the primaries—garnering 26 percent of the popular vote to 25 percent for McGovern—but was victorious in just five primaries to the nominee's 21. Nothing captured the "world turned upside down" quality of the new nominating system so much as McGovern's triumph over Humphrey. Humphrey had prevailed in 1968 while essentially absenting himself from the primary process. Four years later he received the most votes of any candidate, but lost, largely because McGovern's reform forces understood the new rules better and were mobilized in far more states than the Humphrey loyalists. Quite simply, had the rules remained unchanged in '72, there is little question that Humphrey would have been the party nominee again. Instead, the New Left wing had claimed the ultimate prize and now prepared to head to the national convention in Miami to continue their institutional makeover of the party and to shape the platform on which McGovern would do battle with Nixon in November.

The convention represented the high watermark of the New Left's stunning ascendance within the party. In Miami (July 10–13), the insurgents effectively completed their capture of the nation's oldest political party. Reflecting the commission's reform of delegate selection, those who assembled in Miami that year looked nothing like the delegations of years past. Women made up 40 percent of all delegates. At 15 percent, the number of black delegates exceeded their proportion in the nation's population. Young delegates—that is, younger than 30—comprised almost a quarter of those in attendance. Gone was the sea of mostly middle-aged white male faces that had dominated the proceedings of every prior convention. Invariably, media coverage of the gathering called attention to the unprecedented "rainbow" diversity of the assembled delegates.

More important than these demographic proportions were the ideological loyalties and reform aims that the army of New Left delegates brought to the business of the convention. Though the battles were now waged inside the convention hall rather than in the streets as they had been in '68, the Miami gathering proved to be far more organizationally contentious than the Chicago convention had been. The convention itself was one of the most openly combative in recent American history, with sessions beginning in the early evening and lasting until sunrise the next morning, and previously excluded groups gaining influence at the expense of elected officials and traditional core Democratic constituencies such as organized labor. Insurgents clashed with party regulars during committee meetings and on countless voice and roll call votes during full convention sessions. In the end, the activists prevailed in most of these contests. The ultimate symbol and expression of their capture of the party was the official platform adopted by the delegates. To say that it remains the most liberal in party history doesn't begin to capture its activist and oftentimes "countercultural" feel. In addition to its strong anti-war, pro-ERA, and pro-environment planks, the platform was notable for its endorsement of the "right to be different," which included the right to "maintain a cultural or ethnic heritage or lifestyle, without being forced into a compelled homogeneity."[32] The palpable New Left feel of the proceedings also leaked into the new participatory process by which names of presidential and vice-presidential candidates were placed in nomination. Among the names formally placed in nomination for vice-president were the following: César Chávez; Ralph Nader; civil rights stalwart Julian Bond; anti-war activists Ramsey Clark, Benjamin Spock, Daniel and Philip Berrigan; and the ever popular Mao Zedong.

For the New Left wing of the party, the euphoria over its dominance of convention proceedings would last only as long as the general election. The electoral map for the 1972 contest—included here as Figure 4.1—underscores the magnitude of McGovern's thrashing at the hands of Nixon.

The 37.5 percent of the popular vote accorded McGovern was the lowest in party history for a true two-party contest; the paltry 17 electoral votes that the Democratic ticket garnered by winning Massachusetts and the District of Columbia was the second lowest in Democratic history.[33] More ominous still, the white share of the popular vote awarded McGovern fell to less than a third as southern and working class whites continued to abandon their former party in droves.[34] The mushrooming Watergate scandal would soon muddy

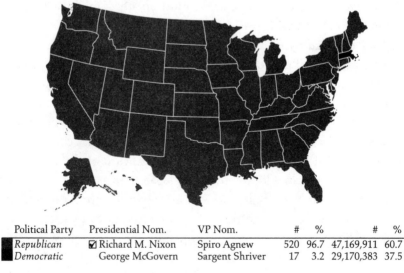

Political Party	Presidential Nom.	VP Nom.	#	%	#	%
■ Republican	☑ Richard M. Nixon	Spiro Agnew	520	96.7	47,169,911	60.7
■ Democratic	George McGovern	Sargent Shriver	17	3.2	29,170,383	37.5

Figure 4.1 1974 Presidential Election
Source: UCSB American Presidency Project

the political waters and temporarily mask the Democrats' systemic electoral woes, but the 1972 results made one thing crystal clear: the party's path back to the White House would not come by holding steady to the sharply leftward course the Democrats had been on since 1968.[35] Indeed, calls to tack back to the political center were already being voiced by members of the traditional party establishment in the immediate aftermath of the convention. And with any semblance of a broad coalitional left giving way to an increasingly fractious collection of movements as the decade wore on, the grassroots pressure needed to hold the party to the decidedly liberal stance it had embraced in 1972 waned quickly. With New Left forces in decline and little right-wing activism to be found in the early to mid-1970s, did movements cease, at least temporarily, to exert much influence on American party and electoral politics? On the contrary, the combination of Watergate and the full flowering of the movement-engineered primary reforms of 1968–72 made the 1976 election arguably *more* anti-establishment than any race in modern US history.

The "Anti-Establishment" Politics of the 1976 Election

Since 1958, the American National Election Studies has regularly asked a representative national sample of Americans about their level of trust in the federal government. In that very first survey, 73 percent of Americans said they trusted the government "to do the right thing" "most of the time" or "just about always." In 1964 the percentage peaked at 76. Even after all the turmoil and division of the late 1960s and early 1970s, a majority of Americans in 1972—53 percent to be precise—still expressed high levels of trust in the federal government. In the wake of Watergate that number plummeted to 36 percent, with just 2 percent saying the government could be trusted to do the right thing "just about always," as compared to 17 percent as late as 1966.[36] The scandal took its biggest toll, of course, on the GOP. To quote one observer: "Nixon left a shattered Republican party.... Many Republican insiders spoke of the party as going the way of the Whigs. In reality, however, the old Whig party may have enjoyed more political support in the electorate before its demise than the Republican Party did in

1974: polls revealed in 1974 that only 18 percent of voters identified themselves as Republican."[37] This remains the lowest figure ever recorded in response to this often asked survey item. But that was far from the worst of it. The Republicans paid dearly for the sharp decline in public support and identification in the midterm elections. The fallout from the scandal cost the Republicans three Senate and a whopping 48 House seats in '74. Nor did GOP fortunes improve much under Gerald Ford, who as Nixon's vice-president ascended to the White House following Nixon's resignation. Although he earned grudging respect for the equanimity he displayed under very trying circumstances, Ford was hardly free of the taint of the scandal. Instead, his pardon of Nixon on taking office produced another firestorm of protest and convinced many that Ford had cut a deal with him before Nixon resigned.

If the Republicans paid an inordinate price for the scandal, growing public distrust of government and alienation from politics touched both parties. In general, identification with both major parties was down sharply during this period compared to earlier years. Indeed, in 1973, the year the scandal broke wide open, the percentage of Americans identifying with the Democratic Party came within one percentage point of its lowest level up to that point. Bottom line: anti-Washington, anti-establishment sentiment was rampant in the run-up to the 1976 general election. And with Republicans having adopted much the same participatory primary system as the Democrats, the public would now have the opportunity to inject their anti-establishment preferences into the nominating processes of both parties. They would not disappoint.

We begin with the Republicans. No matter how he had come to office, the fact remained that Gerald Ford was a sitting Republican president. He was also a proud product of the moderate brand of Republicanism that had dominated the GOP since the late 1930s and the very embodiment of the centrist candidate that the American winner-take-all system is supposed to favor. Perhaps most important, he was a pillar of the Republican establishment. Quite simply, had the traditional, party-dominated nominating system still been in place in 1976, Gerald Ford would have breezed to the nomination. But with new participatory procedures and anti-establishment sentiment running high, Ford's path to the nomination proved tortuous.

The man who dared to challenge the sitting president of his own party was Ronald Reagan, the darling of the GOP right wing. Reagan's near mythic status in contemporary American culture and politics makes it hard for us to see him for who he was, especially in Republican establishment circles, in the early to mid-1970s. It is not too much to say, however, that he was viewed by the party's dominant centrist leaders with disdain and suspicion as an outsider and a right-wing extremist who was as unelectable as Barry Goldwater had proven to be in 1964.[38] Operating under the new rules, however, the party establishment was no longer in a position to control the nominating process. With 30 primaries scheduled that year, the balance of nominating power had clearly shifted away from the party establishment to grass-roots party activists. If the Democrats got their first taste of movement-inflected party politics with McGovern's nomination in 1972, the Republicans were introduced to the brave new world of movement-party politics via their own nomination fight four years later. The battle pitted Ford, the clear choice of the GOP establishment, against Reagan and what amounted to a grass-roots insurgency at the margins of the party. The movement "feel" of the challenge is captured in the following disparaging description of the Reagan forces offered by a Ford supporter in the heat of the campaign:

> The people coming to vote or to caucuses are unknown and have not been involved in the Republican political system before; they vote overwhelmingly for Reagan. A clear pattern is emerging; these turnouts now do not seem accidental but appear to be the result of skillful organization by extreme right wing political groups in the Reagan camp operating almost invisibly through direct mail and voter turnout efforts conducted by the organizations themselves. Particularly those groups controlled by [conservative activist] Viguerie hold a "rule or ruin" attitude toward the GOP. They are deeply interested in their particular issues, they will work to support their positions, they will turn out to vote in larger number than party regulars.[39]

Two movements in particular were key to Reagan's challenge in '76: the grass-roots effort to defeat the Equal Rights Amendment and the nascent pro-life movement, which was just beginning to gain traction four years after the cataclysmic—in the movement's view—Supreme Court decision in *Roe v. Wade*. By embracing very strong pro-life and anti-ERA positions, Reagan secured the support of the great majority of activists in both movements. For his part, Ford was dismissive of the movements and conservatives in general, seemingly "impervious to the political sea change that was occurring in American politics."[40] More specifically, Ford angered anti-ERA activists by his long-standing support for the amendment and pro-life advocates by refusing to take a strong stand on the issue of abortion.[41] As Critchlow notes: "in general, the Ford White House continued to marginalize conservatives, dismissing their threat to Ford's nomination in 1976. A few lone voices in the Ford administration...suggested reaching out to Reagan to head off a 1976 challenge, but Ford remained contemptuous of the sixty-five year old former governor of California."[42] As a product of the party-dominated, centrist politics of postwar America, the new world of movement-inflected politics was lost on Ford and his allies. In the end, though, Ford's anachronistic view of the new reality was not quite enough to confer the nomination on Reagan. Under increasing pressure from the mobilized movement wing of the party, it would be the penultimate hurrah the moderate Republican establishment would enjoy.[43] It would also be very short-lived, with the confirmed insider— Ford—humbled in the general election by arguably the biggest outsider in the history of American presidential politics, or at least the 20th century version of the same.

If Reagan's challenge to Ford was enabled by the new primary system, nothing symbolized the world turned upside down of American politics in the post–reform era so much as Jimmy Carter's presidential nomination and eventual capture of the White House. There is simply no way that Carter would have garnered the nomination under the traditional system. Carter, in fact, was much more a party outsider than McGovern, who after all had served in Congress—the ultimate insiders' club—first as a member of the House and later the Senate for 15 years before seeking the White House in '72. Carter, by contrast, was a one-term governor from the state of Georgia, just about as far removed from the federal establishment as a politician can get—something he never tired of reminding voters in the first presidential contest of the post-Watergate era. But Carter benefited from more than just the new nominating system and his outsider credentials. In the end, two other facts about Carter keyed his improbable win in the general election. The first was his status as a white Southerner, which when combined with general voter antipathy to the scandal-tainted GOP, allowed Carter to reclaim the region for the Democrats for the first and, as it turned out, *only* time since 1960. The other was his status as a "born again" Christian. Ironies abound here. Carter's very public embrace of his faith inspired many evangelicals—who had long eschewed the amoral world of secular politics—to engage politically for the first time. Indeed, as we will show, the support of many who would soon come to see themselves as part of the religious *right* would prove critical to the *liberal* Democrat's (brief) recapture of the white South. By encouraging the rise of the Christian right, however, Carter unwittingly helped galvanize a formidable new political force that would contribute mightily to his defeat in 1980, as his one-time evangelical supporters abandoned him in droves over the controversial social issues that dominated his presidency. Here we want to detail the unusual role that race, region, and religion played in Carter's unlikely triumph.

If Watergate had weakened the GOP in general in the run-up to the 1976 election, the party was probably most vulnerable in the South, the region that had keyed the GOP's resurgence in 1968. If the Democrats had hoped to exploit this vulnerability in the general election, they could not have picked a more ideal candidate to do so. As the former governor and full-time peanut farmer from Plains, Georgia, Jimmy Carter was only the second Democratic presidential candidate from the Deep South since the Civil War.[44] While the new primary process obviously militated against any kind of top-down selection of the nominee, the choice of Carter could not have been more strategically savvy had it been hatched in a confab of party insiders. Carter was well positioned to reverse Democratic fortunes in the region for several reasons. First, though many white Southerners had voted for Nixon in the previous two elections, they certainly did not do so based on any long-standing identification with the GOP. On the contrary, the region's historic loyalty to the Democratic Party made a return to the fold hardly a farfetched idea, especially since the issue—civil rights—that had occasioned the estrangement was much less salient at the time of the '76 election.

That brings us to the second, and related, factor. For some 80 years the Gallup polling organization has been asking Americans to identify the "most important problem" confronting the nation. After being regarded as the number one problem in the country during the early 1960s and remaining in the top five well into the 1970s, by 1975 "civil rights" barely registers on the list. Overall it ranks 13th, with barely 1 percent of those polled identifying it as the most important problem in the country.[45] Through his tenure in office, Nixon had worked effectively to marginalize the issue. As a result, the anger of the white South at the by now traditional Democratic embrace of the issue was muted heading into the election. Carter, to be sure, was regarded as a moderate on the issue, but by the mid-'70s this was very much the norm for elected officials in the region. Indeed, to the extent that the issue registered at all, Carter's views were seen as virtually indistinguishable from those of his Republican opponent, Gerald Ford.

That brings us to issue number three. Had Republicans passed over Ford and chosen the much more conservative Ronald Reagan as their standard-bearer, Carter's chances of reclaiming the white southern vote would have been greatly diminished. But Ford's generally liberal to moderate voting record on civil rights did little to endear him to southern white voters. And with many white Southerners feeling as if they had been burned by their support of Nixon, they were hardly disposed to look favorably on another moderate Republican whose age, background, and ideological leanings were similar to those of the disgraced former president. They were hardly alone in this regard. Consider the following telling statistic. In the same Gallup poll described earlier, a random sample of Americans was asked "which political party do you think can do a better job of handling the problem you think is most important?" Of those identifying either of the two major parties, the margin favored Democrats over Republicans 42 to 15 percent, the most lopsided split since Gallup started asking the question in 1956.[46]

But if lots of Americans were feeling estranged from the Republican Party, many white Southerners were selectively disposed to Carter's candidacy for two additional reasons. The first was simply regional pride and identification. Exactly half of the 16 presidents who had served through the Civil War had been from the South. Of the 22 in office since the "War of Northern Aggression," only one—Lyndon Johnson—had

been a Southerner. And he assumed the office only through the assassination of his predecessor. In short, since the Civil War, no region in the
country had been as politically marginal on the national stage as the
South. If part of Carter's regional appeal derived from the fact that he
seemed like "one of us" to many white Southerners, it is hard to
begrudge the felt connection.

We have saved the most interesting and, to us, most important factor
for last. Carter's candidacy resonated with another subset of Americans
who, like Southerners, had long had cause to feel politically and socially
marginal within the country. This was the vast, but largely invisible
evangelical community within the United States. There was, in point of
fact, considerable overlap between these two marginalized communities; then as now, a disproportionate number of evangelicals reside in
the states of the former Confederacy. There is, however, an important
difference between these two communities. If the South had been marginal to the national political scene, this was largely the doing of the
powers that be in the post-New Deal Democratic Party, who viewed the
Dixiecrats as a wing to be accommodated but never granted control
over the party as a whole. If, on the other hand, the evangelical community had never previously been a force in politics, it probably had as
much to do with their own aversion to the amoral, secular world of
politics than intentional exclusion by other segments of society. By the
mid-'70s, however, there were stirrings within the evangelical community. And while Carter's candidacy wasn't the only catalyst for these
stirrings, there is no question but that his status as perhaps the most
publicly religious presidential candidate in US history hastened the
political mobilization of evangelicals.

If not Carter's candidacy, to what should we attribute the embryonic
movement within the evangelical community? As with so many of the
trends discussed here, the movement had its roots in the 1960s, or more
accurately, a shared revulsion among many fundamentalist Christians
to the moral decay they saw reflected in the 1960s and 1970s. There
were other influences as well, most notably an Internal Revenue Service
(IRS) ruling in 1970 that revoked the tax-exempt status of white-only
private academies, virtually all of them in the South and many of them
affiliated with churches. But more than anything else, it was the
perceived need for a moral reawakening to combat the excesses of

the 1960s that first prompted a few brave souls to challenge the long-standing fundamentalist aversion to the "dirty" world of secular politics. No figure is more identified with the rise of the religious right than Jerry Falwell. The evolution in his thinking on the subject of political engagement is reflective of the general shift in this regard. In 1965 Falwell delivered his famous "Ministers and Marchers" sermon, excoriating clergy who marched in support of the civil rights movement, forcefully declaring that "preachers are not called to be politicians but to be soul winners."[47] But this was before the 1960s had unleashed all manner of "evil" on America. By the mid-1970s Falwell had clearly changed his tune. In a 1976 sermon, he argued that "this idea of 'religion and politics don't mix' was invented by the devil to keep Christians from running their own country."[48] The implication was clear: Christians had to mobilize to reclaim "their" country from the forces of evil—homosexuals, women's libbers, pornographers—loose in the land.

This is not to say that, by the mid-'70s, all Christians shared Falwell's views. On the contrary, his remained very much a minority opinion at the time. And certainly nothing like a coordinated movement of the Christian right was in place as the 1976 election loomed. It is in the context of this ferment, however, that Carter's candidacy takes on added significance and so much cultural resonance within the evangelical community. After all, here was a man of faith—indeed a publicly proclaimed "born-again" Christian—seeking the highest office in the land and using campaign speeches to declare that "the most important thing in my life is Jesus Christ" and "the biggest blessing we have is our belief in Christ."[49] If the rest of the country found the language strange and at times unsettling, it was powerfully affirming and inspiring for many evangelicals. In his book, *God's Own Party*, Daniel Williams explains:

> Carter's campaign excited evangelicals partly because they had been searching for a born-again candidate to carry out a "Christian" agenda, and partly because they were proud of the new respectability that Carter's candidacy gave born-again Christianity. His acceptance of the evangelical label implied that born-again Christians had finally clawed their way to the top echelons of American society and earned a right to be heard.[50]

Early on there was clearly a powerful synergy between Carter's candidacy and the political awakening of the religious right. Carter legitimated and encouraged the mobilization of evangelicals, even as his campaign was buoyed by their support. Reflecting this support, Carter swept to victory in all seven southern primaries in 1976 and wrapped up the nomination well in advance of the convention. A poll released in late September by the *New York Times* confirmed the strength of the candidate's support among southern evangelicals. It showed "that Carter was the overwhelming choice of those who described themselves as born again and that this segment of the electorate was greatest in...the South."[51]

During the fall campaign, Carter worked hard to shore up this support, agreeing among other things, to an interview on conservative evangelist—and future presidential candidate—Pat Robertson's *700 Club* television show. Helping to cement his image as a down-to-earth, political outsider from the rural South, the interview was conducted on the front porch of Carter's farm in Plains, Georgia. Keenly aware of his audience, Carter used the occasion to call for smaller government and to stress the high priority he would attach, if elected, to strengthening the American family. Indeed, he saw the two issues—size of government and the health of the family—as linked. As Carter explained: "one of the reasons that we have begun to rely much more heavily on the government to provide our needs is because of the destruction of relationships within the family or within the church."[52] This had to be music to the ears of Robertson and the millions of social conservatives watching at home. Indeed, during the interview Robertson could be heard responding to several of Carter's comments with an enthusiastic "amen."[53] While the long-standing evangelical tradition of bipartisanship ruled out an official endorsement, Robertson's enthusiastic embrace of Carter's candidacy was clear to anyone watching the show. And while his disastrous *Playboy* interview on the eve of the election no doubt cost Carter some Christian votes, the results of the actual contest, as shown in Figure 4.2, affirmed the extent of his support in both the South and among evangelicals.[54]

With the exception of Virginia, Carter swept all the states of the former Confederacy, in the process amassing more than half the 269 electoral votes needed to claim the White House. For the second

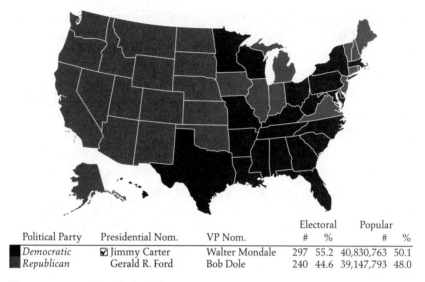

Political Party	Presidential Nom.	VP Nom.	Electoral		Popular	
			#	%	#	%
Democratic	☑ Jimmy Carter	Walter Mondale	297	55.2	40,830,763	50.1
Republican	Gerald R. Ford	Bob Dole	240	44.6	39,147,793	48.0

Figure 4.2 1976 Presidential Election
Source: UCSB American Presidency Project

time in the past three elections, the white South had effectively decided the race for president. By abandoning the Democrats in 1968, white Southerners had swung the election to Nixon. And eight years later, enough white Southerners returned to the fold to elect one of their own.

As for the burgeoning Christian right, "white fundamentalists" favored Carter over Ford by a margin of 56 to 44 percent.[55] This marked a significant shift from the previous two elections in which Nixon had outpolled his Democratic rivals Hubert Humphrey and George McGovern by 7.2 million and 10 million votes, respectively, among evangelicals. In the immediate aftermath of the election, Carter's strong showing among Christian fundamentalists was often credited with deciding what, in the end, turned out to be a very tight contest. Carter emerged with just 50.1 percent of the vote to 48 percent for Ford. Had evangelicals returned the same majorities for Ford that they had given Nixon four years earlier, the Republican candidate would have won handily. In tribute to both Carter's own faith and the growing influence of fundamentalist voters, *Newsweek*, in its October 25 issue, declared 1976 "the year of the evangelical." As we will see in the next chapter, the marriage between the two was destined to be stormy and short-lived. Before we get to that chapter, however, there is one more critically important story from the 1970s that we need to tell. It involves a set of opposing trends that began during the decade and have continued more or less unabated to the present. These trends have as much to do with today's extreme inequality and the politics that have enabled those trends as any other single factor we could point to.

The Mobilization of Capital and the Demobilization of Labor

To this point in our story, we have focused on the reintroduction and growing influence of social movements in American politics since 1960. But we mean to apply the term social movement broadly here. People normally reserve the term for emergent grass-roots efforts by traditionally *disadvantaged* societal groups. The definition offered earlier, however, makes no mention of the social and political standing of the group involved in the mobilizing effort. To reiterate, "a social movement is a loosely organized, sustained effort to promote or resist change in society." That is, the concept is neutral with respect to the power and privilege of the mobilizing group. In this sense, we can speak of the mobilization of elite groups, no less than disadvantaged segments of society. With that in mind, we want to use this final major section of the chapter to detail the self-conscious and sustained mobilization of capital in the 1970s (and beyond) as well as the waning power and influence of organized labor over the same period of time.

No two sets of actors have been more important to the ongoing, historic struggle to shape the distribution of material and other rewards in the United States than organizations representing the interests of capital and labor. As a general rule, significant gains in equality have occurred during peak periods of labor mobilization, while widening economic gaps have come about when labor is comparatively weak and capital strong. There can be little doubt as to which of these general descriptions captures the relative balance of power between these two broad forces over the past three or four decades. Capital—as reflected in both its organizational and financial commitment to politics—has clearly been ascendant over this period of time, even as labor numbers, resources, and political influence have waned. To be clear, though, we do not mean to suggest that the relative balance of power between capital and labor is somehow independent of the more narrowly political trends we have charted to this point. Clearly the power and influence wielded by either of these forces is always going to be shaped, in part, by the dynamics of electoral politics and governmental authority. In periods of Democratic dominance, labor can be expected to enjoy considerable entrée and influence; similarly, capital can count on more institutional access and receptivity when Republicans—especially conservative Republicans—are in control. Of course, the reverse is true as well; that is, the relative strength of capital and labor help to determine which party—with what specific policy emphases—tends to occupy a position of institutional authority. In short, the relationship between formal institutional politics—as embodied in elections and governance—and the mobilization of "outside" interests is complex and broadly reciprocal.

When applied to the most recent period, the implications of this perspective should be clear. As regional realignment undermined the New Deal coalition and boosted the electoral fortunes of Republicans—especially in presidential politics—it also created new opportunities for capital to exercise influence, especially as the GOP shifted to the right in the mid- to late 1970s. As big capital mobilized to take advantage of these opportunities, it became more closely aligned with, and helped to promote the sustained ascendance of the Republican right, which in turn, acted to aggressively advance tax and other fiscal policies of benefit to the upper reaches of the American class structure. Conversely, as the GOP has shifted further and further to the right and come to exercise more institutional authority, labor's access, influence, and indeed, numbers have declined accordingly.

The story of the political mobilization and increasing influence of capital on electoral politics and policymaking in the United States since roughly 1970 deserves a book of its own—indeed, several books. Here we sketch, in broad relief, two critically important facets of that story. The first is the sustained effort by the business community, beginning in the 1970s, to constitute itself as an interest group, capable of acting to shape politics and policymaking, through a set of powerful, extraordinarily well-financed organizations and lobbying operations. The second is the story of the exponential rise in individual and corporate political contributions by the very rich over the past two to three decades. The stories are not wholly separate, of course, since contributions leveraged the rise of the interest group structure, and that structure, in turn, has facilitated much of the recent epidemic in political giving by big capital. To simplify matters, however, we will treat these two stories separately.

As regards the first of the two, we turn to scholars Jacob Hacker and Paul Pierson who have already sketched the broad outlines of that story in their book, *Winner-Take-All Politics*. According to the authors, it would really be more accurate to describe the mobilization of capital in this period as a counterattack; as a response to the threat posed by the Democratic liberalism of the 1960s, and especially the sustained effort by the federal government to greatly expand "its regulatory power, introducing tough and extensive restrictions and requirements on business in areas from the environment to occupational safety to consumer protection."[56] Notwithstanding Nixon's election, the late 1960s and early 1970s was almost surely the high watermark of liberal regulatory activism in Washington. In broad relief, it was the era of Ralph Nader, Earth Day, and the creation of the Environmental Protection Agency. The liberal advocates of oversight, regulation, and protection seemed fully in control, with business interests clearly on the defensive. A fascinating memo penned in 1971 by future Supreme Court Justice Lewis Powell captures the tenor of the times and, more importantly, the political/organizational logic of the counterattack by big capital, then in its infancy. Indeed, Powell's memo was to serve as something of a blueprint for the effort. According to Powell, the "American economic system is under broad attack." If capital was going to survive the attack it would have to

learn the lesson...that political power is necessary; that such power must be assiduously cultivated; and that when necessary, it must be used aggressively and with determination—without embarrassment and without the reluctance which has been so characteristic of American business.... Strength lies in organization, in careful long-range planning and implementation, in consistency of action over an indefinite period of years, in the scale of financing available only through joint effort, and in the political power available only through united action and national organization.[57]

It is not as if capital had never sought to influence politics before. Historically, however, most of these efforts to curry favor and influence policy had been carried out by prominent businessmen interacting with politicians in informal social circles. This approach, Powell seemed to be saying, might have been effective in earlier periods when government was much smaller and far less bureaucratic. However, the extraordinary expansion of the American state in the postwar period called for a very different approach to the problem; an approach that better matched the organized, bureaucratic character of the state. Just how zealously the business community responded to Powell's call to action is reflected in some numbers reported by Hacker and Pierson:

- Between 1968 and 1978 the number of corporations with public affairs offices in Washington, DC, grew fivefold—from 100 to over 500.
- The growth in firms employing Washington lobbyists was more spectacular still. In 1971, there were just 175 such firms. Eleven years later the number had swelled to almost 2,500.
- Finally, the number of corporate PACs (political action committees) rose from some 300 in 1976 to over 1,200 a decade later.[58]

What about the second part of the story promised earlier: trends in corporate and individual political giving in the 1970s and early 1980s? Was the organizational mobilization of capital in the '70s and '80s accompanied by a significant simultaneous rise in conservative corporate and individual campaign spending and political giving? The answer should surprise no one. The surprise would have been if capital had been able to mobilize organizationally *without* the benefit of a sharp rise in ideologically motivated corporate and individual giving.

The evidence of this sharp increase in financial mobilization is clear and consistent. Given the different laws governing corporate and individual political contributions during this period, it makes sense to treat the two forms of giving separately. Conveniently, the 1971 Federal Elections Campaign Act fundamentally changed the nature of corporate political giving just as the decade of the 1970s was getting under way. Reflecting Democratic control of both houses of Congress in the early 1970s, the intent of the law was to reduce the influence of the rich in American politics. But as Val Burris notes, while the "legislation imposed limits on campaign contributions by private individuals...it also created a major loophole...by sanctioning the use of corporate funds to establish and administer political action committees."[59] For the conservative business elite, the timing could not have been better. The act afforded it a new and efficient means of channeling corporate money into the nascent mobilizing effort. The growth of corporate PACs between 1971 and the mid-1980s was breathtaking. Three years after the act was passed, the number of such PACs was still just 89, but by 1980 the number had grown to 1,206, topping out at 1,682 in 1984.[60]

More important than the meteoric rise in the absolute number of corporate PACs, however, was the evolving partisan character of the field as a whole. Scholars of campaign finance have long distinguished between two general orientations toward giving: *pragmatic* and *ideological*. Pragmatic giving reflects a desire to curry favor with whichever party and/or candidate is seen as likely to prevail in a given election. In this sense, pragmatic giving tends to transcend partisanship, with some small number of contributors actually giving to both sides to ensure that they enjoy at least some level of political access regardless of who wins the election. *Ideological* giving, on the other hand, is motivated by a desire to see conservative—or liberal—candidates elected and, specific to the right, conservative, pro-business policies enacted. Mirroring the more general partisan mobilization of capital during this period, the growth in corporate PACs—especially after the mid-'70s—was overwhelmingly ideological rather than pragmatic in character.[61] To quote Burris: "this ideological bloc grew rapidly in both size and the intensity of its partisan commitment in the years between 1976 and 1980—a trend that can be seen as an integral part of the broader right-wing political mobilization of business in that period and a key factor in explaining the electoral and legislative victories of conservatives in the early Reagan era."[62] Neustadtl and Clawson's analysis of the impact of corporate giving on the 1980 elections supports Burris's judgment. They show that by far the largest, most united segment of the business community active during the election—encompassing roughly 40 percent of the total—was motivated by its shared commitment to the ideological agenda of electing right-wing Republican challengers.[63]

Reflecting the aims of the authors of the 1971 act, rates of individual campaign contributions declined slightly during the decade of the

1970s. This does not, however, mean that individual giving was of little consequence during this period, or more to the point, that it played little role in the political mobilization of conservative capital in the 1970s and 1980s. Nothing could be further from the truth. First, even if corporate contributions rose sharply relative to individual contributions during the 1970s, the latter still accounted for a much larger percentage of total campaign contributions compared to the former. In congressional races, large individual donations typically account for 35–40 percent of all campaign donations, as compared to just 8–10 percent from corporate PACs.[64] In presidential contests the number is even higher, ranging between 70 and 90 percent of all contributions.[65] Second, the overwhelming majority of these individual contributions come from the very wealthy. Analyzing a random sample of contributors to 1996 congressional races, scholars found that of the "donors who made aggregate contributions of $8,000 or more...nearly half had annual incomes of more than $500,000 and almost all had incomes above $250,000, suggesting that top corporate officers and other capitalists were heavily represented among this elite group."[66] Finally, and most important, relative to corporate PACs, giving by individual capitalists is much more likely to reflect ideological than pragmatic motives. The most compelling evidence of this difference comes from a study by Burris of the 1980 campaign contributions of 394 large corporations and the 592 top officers of these same corporations. Relative to the corporations, the officers were much more likely to contribute to the presidential rather than congressional races (and/or to ideological or single-issue committees) and to support Republican rather than Democratic candidates.[67] Bottom line: if the "big news" in political giving in the 1970s was the rise of PACs and especially the consolidation of a large, united bloc of right-wing PACs, the huge volume and overwhelming ideological orientation of contributions by the wealthy made individual giving a crucial part of the mobilization of conservative capital during the period.

Together, the extraordinary growth of ideologically motivated PACs and the sustained tradition of conservative giving by wealthy individuals fueled the organizational mobilization of capital during this period. It is now hard to think of business as usual in Washington without conjuring up images of corporate lobbyists and the corrupting influence of unlimited contributions by big capital. We have to remind ourselves, however, that the present-day corporate culture of Washington had its roots in the business "counterattack" of the 1970s and 1980s, as chronicled by Hacker and Pierson. More important than the timing or history of the effort, however, is the contribution it made to the emerging politics of inequality as it began to take hold in the 1970s. As we document in Chapter 7, the trend toward increasing inequality in the United States begins not in the 1980s but a decade earlier. It is no coincidence that the organized effort to bring corporate influence to bear on the federal system dates to the same period.

In calling attention to the close temporal timing of these two trends, we are not advancing some kind of simple-minded conspiracy theory of how the politics of inequality gained traction. For us, the practical significance of the dramatic expansion of corporate personnel and money in Washington during this period is twofold. First, it meant that as Republicans began to shift more decisively to the right in the late 1970s and early 1980s, they were assured of finding allies aplenty in Washington's mushrooming corporate community. But more important, the expanded corporate presence simply meant that the interests and "cultural logics" of capital were much more stitched into the routine fabric of political life and policymaking in Washington than they had been in the past. In this new environment, Democratic members of Congress were, if anything, only slightly less susceptible to the influence and blandishments of the business community than Republicans. Corporate staff and lobbyists had simply become ubiquitous in Washington, establishing long-term relationships with virtually every member of the House and Senate. Given the brave new world of corporate Washington, the real surprise would have been if, starting in the late 1970s, new tax and fiscal policies *hadn't* begun to reflect the influence of big capital. But, of course, they did. Nor did it require Ronald Reagan's arrival in Washington to set the change in motion. Instead, in 1978 a "Democratic Congress overwhelmingly passed, and a Democratic president signed, a tax bill whose centerpiece was a reduction of the top rate of capital gains taxes from 48 percent to 28 percent."[68] Aided and abetted by the wildly successful mobilization of American capital, the politics of inequality had begun in earnest.

So much for capital; what was happening to organized labor as capital was mounting its sustained organizing campaign of the 1970s? We suspect you already know the answer to the question, but if not, Figure 4.3 will help fill in the basic picture.

Quite simply, since the early 1970s, unionized labor has been in free fall, as reflected not only in sharp declines in members but also in political access and influence. Let's start with the numbers. As late as 1970, one in four American workers was still unionized. By 1980, that number had dropped to fewer than one in five. Today that proportion stands at roughly one in nine. Apologists for the current state of the American political economy argue that the steep decline in unionized labor is simply a natural byproduct of changes in the structure of the US economy, brought on, or at least accelerated, by economic globalization. Without for a minute suggesting that these processes have had no effect on the political economy of the United States, we are convinced that the popular narrative of globalization exaggerates its consequences. To put it starkly, cross-national data strongly suggest that the precipitous decline in union membership in the United States after 1970 is no more "natural" than the dramatic increase in income inequality over the same period of time. As Hacker and Pierson point

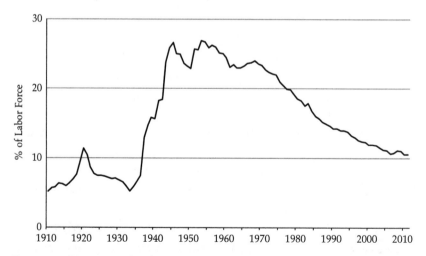

Figure 4.3 Union Membership Rates, 1910–2011
Source: Bureau of Labor Statistics, Directory of National Unions and Employee Associations
* Data are adjusted to compare calculations from differing periods

out, the fate of unionized labor in Canada over the past four or five decades bears little relationship to what we have seen in the United States.[69] In fact, it bears little relationship to the vast majority of our contemporaries, as evidenced in Table 4.1, comparing the change in union rates over time for select Organization for Economic Cooperation and Development (OECD) countries, including the United States, since 1960.

The first thing to note about the comparative data reported in Table 4.1 is that they hardly confirm the idea of a general decline in union membership across the 16 advanced capitalist economies included in the table. While 9 of the 16 experienced declining rates of unionized labor, 7 others reported gains over the full period. And of the nine that

Table 4.1   Union Membership in Comparative Perspective: Select OECD Countries, 1960–2000

	1961/1970	1971/1980	1981/1990	1991/2000
Australia	45.6	46.2	44.3	32.4
Belgium	40.6	50.8	50.6	53.1
Denmark	61.3	69.1	76.8	76.6
Germany	32.9	34.1	33.9	29.1
Finland	40.0	64.5	70.2	77.2
France	20.1	21.0	13.8	10.5
Italy	28.0	46.9	43.0	38.7
Japan	34.1	32.5	27.5	23.3
Canada	27.0	31.8	32.8	31.8
Netherlands	39.1	36.6	27.7	24.5
Norway	51.5	52.1	55.5	54.8
Austria	58.3	52.7	50.4	40.6
Sweden	66.4	73.4	81.5	85.9
Switzerland	33.5	31.1	27.9	23.2
United Kingdom	40.9	47.6	40.8	32.5
United States	26.9	22.9	18.2	14.8

Source: Adapted from Lesch, CESifo Forum 4/2004; original data come from Golden, Lange, and Wallerstein; Ebbinghaus and Visser; ILO; OECD; National Statistical Yearbook; Labour Force Surveys and Union Data; table includes all OECD countries for which data are available.

experienced declines, only France exhibits as steep a drop as the United States. In short, if the decline in union membership was simply a byproduct of structural changes in a globalizing economy, shouldn't the patterns look essentially the same across these countries, given the broad similarities in their economies? No doubt, change in the occupational structures of these former industrial economies *is* a part of the story, but the cross-national differences in union membership suggest it isn't the whole—or even the greater part—of that story. Which brings us back to politics, and in particular, to the unique politics of inequality, which has characterized the United States since the 1970s. The point is, with the exception of Great Britain under Thatcher, none of these other countries have experienced anything like the sustained assault on labor that we have seen in the United States.[70] To understand the timing and thoroughgoing nature of that assault, we need look no further than the three processes touched on earlier. These three— regional realignment, partisan polarization, and the mobilization of capital—are powerfully implicated in the sorry fate of US unions over the past four decades. Together, the first two processes moved the GOP steadily rightward during the 1970s, effectively transforming the party from its moderate, centrist postwar incarnation into the increasingly conservative, union-busting force of the Reagan years and beyond. Just as important, capital has made anti-union activities a central component of its ongoing "counterattack" since its launch in the 1970s.

The available evidence suggests that it took until the mid- to late 1970s for all of these processes to come together. But when they do, the resulting GOP-business tag team assault on labor is relentless and effective. It appears as if business was first off the mark with a significant increase in anti-labor practices in the 1970s. Hacker and Pierson note that "reported violations of the NLRA [National Labor Relations Act] skyrocketed in the late 1970s and early 1980s. Meanwhile, strike rates plummeted, and many of the strikes that did occur were acts of desperation rather than indicators of union muscle."[71] Edsall reports similar increases in charges of unfair labor practices and unlawful termination for the same general time period.[72] Motivated in large part by the rising tide of anti-union activity by employers, organized labor seized on Carter's 1976 election and the Democrats' control of Congress to press, in 1978, for the first major revision of industrial relations law since 1959. Hacker and Pierson set the stage for the ensuing legislative battle:

> The bill's target was the increasingly aggressive tactics of firms like textile manufacturer JP Stevens. Unions were convinced that the modest and long delayed penalties typically imposed by the National Labor Relations Board encouraged companies to employ any means to hold off organizing efforts. Defying the law was far cheaper than risking any prospect of unionization. The reform bill would have streamlined and accelerated NLRB decision-making and increased penalties for violators. As both labor and its opponents recognized, the stakes were far higher than the particulars of the bill itself. The fate of labor law reform would reveal the true balance of power.[73]

And indeed it did. Despite passage in the House and a 61 to 39 Democratic advantage in the Senate, the bill's sponsors were never able to muster the votes to break a determined Republican filibuster and bring the matter to a full Senate vote. Stunned by the outcome and outraged by the way capital had waged its war against the bill, longtime United Auto Workers president, Douglas Fraser, resigned from President Carter's Labor-Management Group. His resignation letter would prove remarkably prescient about what lay ahead, not just for US labor, but for the country as a whole. Wrote Fraser:

> I believe leaders of the business community...have chosen to wage a one-sided class war...against working people....The leaders of industry, commerce, and finance in the United States have broken and discarded the fragile, unwritten compact previously existing during a past period of growth and prosperity....The latest breakdown in our relationship is also perhaps the most serious. The fight waged by the business community against the Labor Law Reform bill stands as the most vicious, unfair attack upon the labor movement in more than 30 years....At virtually every level, I discern a demand by business for docile government and unrestrained corporate individualism. Where industry once yearned for subservient unions, it now wants no unions at all....Our tax laws are a scandal, yet corporate America wants even wider inequities. ...The wealthy seek not to close loopholes, but to

widen them by advocating the capital gains tax rollback that will bring them a huge bonanza.... For all these reasons ... I cannot sit there seeking unity with the leaders of American industry, while they try to destroy us and ruin the lives of the people I represent.[74]

Under extraordinarily inopportune circumstances—Democratic president, Democratic Congress—the emerging partnership between the Republican right and the newly mobilized business community had won a stunning and improbable victory. And one that could only bode serious ill for the future of organized labor. If labor could not prevail in a battle with capital at a time when Democrats controlled both houses of Congress and the White House, what possible chance could they have of exercising decisive influence under any form of divided government? Following Reagan's election two years later, it didn't take long for labor to get their answer. Barely six months after Reagan took office, air traffic controllers launched a nationwide strike, in pursuit of better wages and working conditions. In his superb book on the strike, labor historian, Joseph McCartin offers a detailed history of the ensuing struggle and a convincing assessment of what he calls "the strike that changed America."[75] In truth, it wasn't much of a struggle at all. In a decision that surprised even some conservatives, Reagan immediately invoked a provision in the Taft-Hartley Act that banned strikes by government unions and gave the striking workers 48 hours to return to their jobs, threatening them with loss of their positions if they failed to do so. Two days later, Reagan made good on his threat by firing the 11,345 air controllers who refused to abide by his order. In the end, the striking union—the Professional Air Traffic Controller Organization—lost both the battle and the war. Not only had Reagan decisively broken the strike through his action, but in October of the same year, the Federal Labor Relations Authority, decertified the union itself. Reflecting on Reagan's action in 2003, no less an authority than Alan Greenspan underscored the significance of the case. Said Greenspan:

the most important ... domestic initiative was the firing of the air traffic controllers in August 1981. The President invoked the law that striking government employees forfeit their jobs, an action that unsettled those who ... believed that no President would ever uphold that law. President Reagan prevailed...but more importantly his action gave weight to the legal right of private employers, previously not fully exercised, to use their own discretion to both hire and discharge workers. (April 9, 2003)[76]

In the wake of the abortive strike and subsequent Reagan initiatives, any semblance of a broadly equitable balance of power between capital and labor was gone. Writing in the *Wall Street Journal* in 1984, a "union avoidance" consultant cut to the heart of the matter when he wrote that the "current government and business climate presents a unique opportunity for companies...to develop and implement long-term plans for conducting business in a union-free environment."[77] With open season on unions and the Republican right and their business allies exercising ever greater control in Washington, there was little the advocates of economic—and other forms of—equality could do to stem the tide of widening class division. A substantial body of research now exists confirming a clear and consistent relationship between union strength and economic equality.[78] Strong unions promote income equality or slow the growth of inequality, while sharp declines in unionization predict rising inequality. And that, of course, is exactly what we have seen in the United States from roughly the mid-1970s to the present.

Summing Up

The 1970s tend to receive short shrift in popular and scholarly accounts of the roots of today's US political economy. When compared to the high drama of the 1960s and the clear significance of the Reagan revolution of the 1980s, the 1970s can seem oddly muddled and inconsequential. Far from being an unimportant, limbo period, however, the 1970s, as we see that decade, is a crucial, if unappreciated, bridge between the 1960s and 1980s. The bridge metaphor is especially apt when it comes to two consequential events during the decade. The first is the institutional revolution in the way we nominate presidential candidates. The new system was first implemented by the Democrats in 1972 and fully in place in both parties by 1976. But the effort to transform the system, you will remember, was actually launched by McCarthy supporters in the summer of 1968. And the significance and impact of the reforms—as the 2012 Republican reminded us anew—persist today.

The 1970s can also be seen as a crucial bridge in the political career of Ronald Reagan, who features in the next chapter. Reagan first came to political prominence in the 1960s, as the combative, right-wing governor of California, but of course, it was his two-term presidency in the 1980s that so powerfully shaped the political and economic trends that are the central focus of this book. A case can be made, however, that absent his 1976 primary challenge to the sitting president of his own party, Reagan would almost certainly not have gained the White House four years later. After all, at the time of the challenge, Reagan was already sixty-five years old and regarded with suspicion and disdain by the moderate Republican establishment that still dominated the party. It was Reagan's nearly successful primary campaign that changed the way he was seen in the party. For starters, the broad national support he received during the campaign allayed fears that he was—like Goldwater before him—unelectable. Reagan also demonstrated far more tact and ideological flexibility during the campaign than his reputation as a right-wing ideologue had led people to believe. When he capped his campaign, on the final night of the Republican convention, with one of the greatest speeches of his life, Reagan's "natural eloquence left many Republicans wondering if they had nominated the wrong man."[79] By encouraging that much more second guessing, Ford's defeat at the hands of Carter no doubt burnished Reagan's reputation all the more. We close by reiterating two key points. First, had Reagan not run in 1976, it seems unlikely that four years later the party would have turned to a sixty-nine-year-old about whom many in the party would still have had serious doubts. Finally, absent the new primary system, Reagan's 1976 challenge could never have occurred.

Beyond these two "bridging" functions of the decade, the 1970s loom as important for at least four more reasons. First, the decade marked the onset of a sustained movement by capital that shows no signs of abating and which, over the past four decades, has had as much to do with the emerging politics of inequality as any other single factor. Second, the 1970s also marked the clear beginnings of a precipitous decline in the power and political influence of organized labor. Needless to say, these two trends were very much related, with capital making the institutional assault on labor an important component of its sustained mobilizing effort. Third, the decade also marked the political "coming out party" for evangelical Christians, whose initial infatuation with Jimmy Carter in 1976 gave way by decade's end to a fervent identification with Ronald Reagan and an ever more socially conservative Republican Party. The fourth and final '70s "moment" that commands our attention is the New Left's successful capture of the Democratic Party in 1972. When we add it to all the other consequential events of the decade, the 1970s emerge as a fascinating and crucially important part of our story of how the interaction of parties and movements— among which we include the mobilization of capital—has transformed the American political economy since 1960.

5

The Reagan Revolution?

OUR CENTRAL GOAL IN THE BOOK is to trace the political dynamics and history that have shaped the two defining features—deep partisan divisions and extreme economic inequality—of the contemporary American political economy. In most discussions of the origin of these features, no single political figure looms quite as large as Ronald Reagan. We too see Reagan's legacy in today's politics of division as a highly consequential one, but one that is much more complicated, at times confounding, and certainly more interesting than the standard "before Reagan," "after Reagan" account typically allows. Three stark, summary judgments will help highlight the contradictions that we see embodied in that legacy. First, the two defining trends mentioned at the beginning of the chapter were already in evidence when Reagan took office. Reagan set in motion neither partisan polarization nor rising inequality. Second, whether measured by legislative volume or objective socioeconomic indicators, the substantive impact of Reagan's two-term presidency is surprisingly modest. He certainly did not transform the American landscape while in office. Does that mean we should regard the so-called Reagan revolution as just so much hyperbole? No, which brings us to our third and most important conclusion: Reagan's influence on the political and economic divisions that characterize life in the contemporary United States has only grown—indeed, grown significantly—in the quarter century since he left office. If it makes sense to speak of a Reagan revolution—and we think it does—it is a revolution that has owed, in our view, much more to long-term trends set in motion by his administration than to the immediate policy impacts that flowed from his eight years in office. Much of the next two chapters is devoted to highlighting what we see as the contrast between the relatively modest short-term and significant longer-term impact of the Reagan presidency. Before we get to his years in office, however, we take up the story of how he got there in the first place. It is a story that once again reflects the growing importance of movements in American electoral politics.

Movement Politics in Reagan's Rise to Power

A case can be made that no president since the end of World War II benefited more from the growing influence of movements in American politics than Ronald Reagan. Movements were critically implicated in both Reagan's primary challenge to Ford in 1976 and his decisive victory over Jimmy Carter four years later. We devoted a good deal of attention to the former story in Chapter 4; here we mean to take up Reagan's successful presidential run in 1980. Before we turn to that story, however, we want to, once again, underscore the crucial connection between Reagan's challenge to Ford in '76 and his victory four years later, and examine how both campaigns reflected the significance of the 1972 primary reforms and, more generally, the growing influence of social movements in American electoral politics.

Despite the absence of any real grass-roots pressure for reform in the Republican Party, the GOP quickly—and seemingly without significant dissent—adopted the Democratic-initiated reforms in time for the 1976 election, much to Reagan's benefit. Without the new system of binding primaries in place it is highly unlikely that Reagan would have been able to mount an effective challenge to the sitting president of his own party. And had he not been able to do so, it is very unlikely, we contend, that he would have secured the GOP nomination in 1980. Depending on one's ideological leanings, it is either frightening or tantalizing to consider the long-term consequences of this particular counterfactual.

In the end, Reagan would come up just short in '76, but in the process he succeeded in transforming his national image and standing within the party. Just as important, Ford's humiliating defeat at the hands of Jimmy Carter—a virtual unknown at the start of the 1976 primary season—weakened the centrist Republican "brand" that had defined the party in the postwar period. The effect was not unlike that visited on the Democratic Party by Humphrey's poor showing against Nixon and Wallace in 1968. Just as Humphrey's humiliating defeat had shifted the balance of power within the Democratic Party heading into 1972, Ford's loss in 1976 perfectly positioned Reagan and the mobilized movement elements of the GOP in time for 1980.

1980 and the Hybrid Movement-Party Form

With no sitting president from his own party to dislodge and with a record 35 primaries to contest, Reagan rolled to the nomination in 1980 and then to victory over Jimmy Carter behind a perfected version of the movement-party hybrid form of politics introduced in 1976. Indeed, if anything, Reagan mobilized more discrete movement groups in 1980 than he had four years earlier. Three movements contributed signifi- cantly to Reagan's triumph in 1980. These were the pro-life movement, the Christian right, and the nationwide tax revolt that had mush- roomed after the passage of California's Proposition 13 in 1978. This list takes on added significance when we note that the first two movements had granted Jimmy Carter substantial backing in 1976. Both went over- whelmingly for Reagan in 1980, representing a net gain for the GOP over the 1976 contest. To this list of movements, we add the heirs of the Wallace third-party campaigns of 1968 and 1972. While white racial conservatives perhaps were no longer a cohesive movement, Carter's success in reclaiming the South for the Democrats in 1976 made their votes a prime electoral objective for both candidates heading into the 1980 contest. We discuss all four of these movement elements below, starting with pro-life forces.

Our characterization of the shifting preferences of pro-life activists comes with something of a caveat. It is actually hard to know with any precision just how pro-life activists came down on the two candidates in 1976. At the very least, it seems clear that Carter would have been competitive with Ford on the issue, if not the consensus choice of pro-life advocates. In truth, neither candidate was the logical darling of the movement. We begin with the GOP candidate. While Ford shifted to the right on the issue under the pressure of the Reagan primary challenge—and the growing strength of the movement itself—he had previously been consistently pro-choice on the matter. And then there was First Lady, Betty Ford, who infuriated conservatives with her strident advocacy of both the Equal Rights Amendment and pro-choice views on abortion. On paper, Carter had a more liberal position on the issue than Ford, but his very public embrace of a born again Christianity left many confused as to his true views on the abortion issue. The truth is at the start of the 1976 election cycle, virtually no one outside of Georgia knew who Jimmy Carter was. In a country struggling not only with the impact of Watergate but also with a generalized post-1960s malaise, plus mounting evidence that the postwar economic boom was over, Carter was a blank slate on which a host of different constituencies could write their fondest dreams for themselves and the country as a whole. With such a modest substantive record to parse, Carter was able to remain something of a cipher throughout the campaign. Pre-election polls suggest just how successful he was at this rhetorical sleight of hand. Twenty-one percent of those responding to a September 1976 *New York Times* poll reported that Carter favored abortion rights; 36 percent claimed he opposed them.[1] Flippen captured the dynamic well when he wrote that "the media had, at various times, called Carter's position 'inconclusive' or 'muddled,' but Carter, it appeared, had successfully straddled the murky middle."[2] For such an admirably upright character, Carter proved incredibly adept at what might be called "strategic obfuscation."

Given this confusion and the conflicted nature of their positions on the issue, it is hard to imagine either candidate running away with the pro-life vote in 1976. It was a very different story four years later. If pro-life advocates had been seduced by Carter's born-again faith in 1976, his four-year presidency had stripped them of any illusions they may have had about his stance on the issue. By contrast, Reagan's strident opposition to *Roe v. Wade* endeared him to pro-life forces, motivating them not only to cast their votes for him in November but to mobilize in other ways in support of his candidacy.

Our second movement, the Christian Right, endured a very similar fall from grace in regard to Carter as the one experienced by pro-life forces. Popular narrative accounts typically identify the Iran hostage crisis as the Waterloo of the Carter presidency and the principal reason he was not returned to office in 1980. Without discounting the importance of the crisis and the enervating effect it had on his presidency, Carter's fate in 1980 had probably been sealed much earlier in his term. Even allowing for a bit of hyperbole, Balmer captures the basic storyline when he writes: "If Carter's political ascendancy represents one of the most dramatic stories in the history of American politics, the rapid turning against Carter by many of the same evangelicals who had supported him in 1976 is one of the most striking paradoxes of American politics."[3] It is now commonplace to talk about the crucial importance of "social issues" in American electoral politics. By "social issues" commentators have in mind that cluster of "moral" matters near and dear to the heart of the religious right and all manner of social conservatives. While lots of specific issues could be grouped under this broad umbrella, abortion and homosexuality are arguably the keystone issues for most social conservatives. For them, *Roe v. Wade* and the ascendant lesbian, gay, bisexual, and transgendered (LGBT) movement represent both the moral rot at the core of American society and the greatest threat to the family in US history. The important point, for our purpose, is that both issues came to occupy center stage during Carter's time in office. And by trying to carve out a middle ground between evangelicals and other social conservatives on the one hand and abortion and gay rights advocates on the other, Carter pleased no one, effectively undermining the odd coalition that had elected him in the first place.

Nor was Carter simply a victim of circumstances in this regard. Rather, in two crucial respects he helped to politicize the very issues that undermined his presidency. He did so first simply by inspiring the rise of the Christian right. His campaign and capture of the White House went a long way toward overcoming the long-standing proscription against the involvement of evangelicals in secular politics. And second, by assigning the highest priority to family issues at the beginning of his term, he set two key components of his electoral coalition—evangelicals and feminists—on a collision course. The specific initiative that made the collision inevitable was Carter's announcement, barely a year into his administration, of plans to hold a White House Conference on the Family in December of 1979. Owing to delays, the conference itself would not take place until 1980, but the planning for the event occasioned nonstop controversy, as social conservatives and pro-life advocates battled feminists and gay rights activists over all manner of issues related to the gathering. Predictably, the conference itself created all sorts of additional opportunities for controversy and for political fallout for Carter himself. Consider only the reaction of evangelist Beverly LaHaye to the proceedings: "Jimmy Carter has falsely used his born-again image to hoodwink people into thinking he is one of us. The White House Conference...does not represent the more traditionalist viewpoint of the family, but instead favors the feminist and the pro-homosexual viewpoints espoused by the liberal establishment."[4]

Nor was it only the conference and the planning preceding it that served as the coming-out party for the various issues that comprise today's "social agenda." Carter's years in office also coincided with

- singer Anita Bryant's battles with gay rights activists in Florida and her subsequent Save Our Children Campaign;
- a referendum in California—the so-called Briggs Initiative—designed to ban homosexual teachers in the state;
- the meteoric rise and subsequent assassination of gay rights activist, Harvey Milk;
- and the ongoing debates on the Hyde Amendment, which served to greatly restrict the use of federal funds to pay for abortions.

At least until the Iran hostage crisis, these were the issues that defined—and crippled—Carter's presidency. Recognizing the evangelical backlash occasioned by these controversies, "leaders of the secular New Right immediately began to devise strategies to further mobilize these evangelicals and woo them to Republican activism."[5] And this time, instead of another moderate, the party was destined to nominate a true conservative—Ronald Reagan—who would aid and abet the wooing process. The end of the decade was marked by two mutually reinforcing trends: determined efforts by party activists—men like Paul Weyrich, Richard Viguerie, and Howard Phillips—to shift the GOP decisively to the right, and a flurry of independent and over-lapping organizing efforts by Jerry Falwell, Ed McAteer, and other leaders of the religious right. Out of this latter effort "grew organizations such as the Religious Roundtable, Christian Voice, and Falwell's celebrated Moral Majority, among others."[6] Poised on the eve of the 1980 election, the "religious right" had coalesced into a formidable political force, and one now clearly aligned with the right wing of the Republican Party. "Electing Reagan, Christian Right leaders realized, was the key to accomplishing their goals. They expected his administration to roll back abortion rights, curb the gay rights movement, restore prayer in schools, and lead the nation back to morality. Abandoning their pretense of nonpartisanship, they became enthusiastic champions of the Republican ticket."[7]

For his part, Reagan sought to exploit the growing estrangement between the evangelicals and Carter by aggressively courting the religious right during the 1980 campaign. There was irony in this. Prior to 1976, most evangelicals had eschewed politics, viewing religion as a private matter that could only be sullied by association with secular political concerns. By demonstrating that faith could be combined with an active political engagement, Carter helped inspire many evangelicals to embrace politics for the first time. In doing so, he helped to introduce a potent new force into American politics. But if Carter benefited from that force the first time around, the Reagan forces were determined to appropriate the support of the religious right in 1980. This goal had more to do with reclaiming the South than appealing to evangelicals per se. Key to Carter's narrow win over Ford in 1976 was his ability to put the South back in the Democratic column following Nixon's wins there in '68 and '72. In turn, Carter's triumph in the South had been keyed by his strong support among evangelicals. "Reagan's campaign team realized the importance of winning evangelical votes, because they knew that the support of white, born-again Protestants would be the key to defeating Carter in the South."[8]

Carter and Reagan was an odd pairing. While Carter openly embraced his faith, religion appeared to play little role in Reagan's life. As Dunn and Woodward note, Reagan "attended church only on the rarest of occasions and certainly never Sunday School and absolutely never with a Bible in his hand."[9] He had also divorced his first wife and spent most of his life in that contemporary Sodom and Gomorrah known as Hollywood. Yet on the issues that concerned the religious right—abortion, gay rights, the Equal Rights Amendment—Reagan's views were far more palatable than those of Carter and the liberals in the Democratic Party.

Reagan never missed an opportunity during the campaign to high-light this difference, speaking to the National Religious Broadcasters Association at Liberty Baptist College, meeting publicly with Jerry Falwell on several occasions, and praying with a fundamentalist min-ister at a campaign rally in Mississippi. The effort paid off handsomely. The religious right mobilized en masse for Reagan. As the *New York Times* reported at the close of the campaign, "thousands of fundamen-talist Protestant churches became political centers for Mr. Reagan... as politicized evangelical groups moved into the political arena."[10] In the wake of his triumph, a flurry of polls underscored the role of the religious right in the victory. One gave Reagan a 2 to 1 edge in the votes of white evangelicals, while Miller and Wattenberg estimated that 85 percent of the "most fundamentalist" voters cast their ballots for Reagan.[11] A third poll showed that 60 percent of the white evangelicals who voted for Carter in 1976 defected to Reagan four years later.[12] In the end, Reagan not only captured the evangelical vote in 1980 but over the course of his eight years in office effectively transformed southern evangelicals from Democrats into the most loyal of Republicans, at least when it came to presidential politics. As Williams put it: "Evangelicals had been moving into the Republican Party for the previous three decades, but the GOP could not invariably count on their votes.... After 1980, fundamentalists and evangelicals would be united in supporting Republican presidential candidates."[13]

The third movement that helped Reagan capture the White House in 1980 was the nationwide "tax revolt" whose high watermark just happened to coincide with that year's presidential race. Catalyzed by the stunning triumph of California's Proposition 13 in 1978, the revolt spread like wildfire over the next two years, inspiring similar reform efforts in most states in the union. Perfectly aligned with Reagan's sig-nature attack on big government and "tax and spend liberals," the revolt motivated legions of anti-tax activists not only to vote but to campaign fervently for the GOP nominee. And once in office, we argue, the electoral threat posed by the movement helps us understand how Reagan was able to mobilize surprising bipartisan support for the centerpiece of his first year legislative blitz: the Economic Recovery Tax Act (ERTA). To understand just how important the specter of a mobilized populist anti-tax uprising was to the passage of the act, however, it will help to know a bit more about the origin and spread of the "revolt" in the late 1970s and early 1980s.

On June 6, 1978, by a margin of 62 to 34 percent, California voters overwhelmingly approved Proposition 13, fundamentally restructuring the state's system of taxation and government finance overnight. The proposition limited the annual tax on a piece of property to just 1 percent of its assessed value and further restricted increases in assessment to no more than 2 percent annually until such time as the property was sold or changed owners. Although the fiscal effects of the proposition were masked for several years by the state's large budget surplus at the time of the ballot initiative, over time the drastic reduction in property tax revenues resulting from the measure transformed California from one of the most generous states in terms of government services to one of the most miserly. To take but one noteworthy example, in the mid-1970s, when the proposition was passed, California ranked in the top third of states in terms of per capita expenditures on public education. Today, only two states—Nevada and Utah—rank *below* California.[14]

When set against the sorry record of earlier tax reform efforts in the state, the success of Proposition 13 was as improbable as it was decisive. To convey the futility of these earlier efforts, we provide a brief litany of the major initiatives in the decade leading up to the proposition. Seeking to provide property tax relief for many in southern California, Los Angeles County Tax Assessor Philip Watson sponsored an initiative in 1968 that in key ways was very similar to Proposition 13. Most important, the initiative proposed that property taxes could not exceed 1 percent of the property's assessed valuation. The initiative was resoundingly rejected by a margin of 68 to 32 percent. Watson tried again in 1972, using a different formulation, but with the same general goal of reducing the property tax burden of country residents. Once again, voters decisively rejected the initiative. In 1973, then governor Ronald

Reagan tried his hand at tax reform, proposing an amendment to the state constitution that would, through various means, have placed strict limits on the growth of government expenditures. But even Reagan's popularity with state voters wasn't enough to secure approval of the initiative. Voters rejected the measure by 54 to 46 percent. As if to punctuate this litany of failure, in 1976 "neither Philip Watson nor Paul Gann [one of the chief backers of Proposition 13] could collect enough signatures to place property tax initiatives on the ballot."[15]

Given this series of setbacks, who could have foreseen the dramatic reversal of fortune in 1978? Why did the long-suffering proponents of tax reform triumph so spectacularly in 1978 after crashing and burning on so many prior occasions? No doubt a good many factors contributed to the shift. First, quite apart from the economic aspects of the issue, it is clear that the California tax revolt also expressed a generalized distrust and anger at government that had been on the rise since the late 1960s but which had escalated sharply in the wake of the Watergate scandal. Consider the following contrast. In 1968—the year Philip Watson proposed his property tax initiative—61 percent of respondents to the American National Election Studies reported that they "trusted" the government to do the right thing "just about always" or "most of the time." Ten years later, when Proposition 13 was approved, the comparable figure stood at just 30 percent. By contrast, 68 percent reported that they trusted the government to do the right thing "none" or only "some of the time."[16] This dramatic increase in anti-government sentiment has to be seen as an important spur to the tax revolt in California and elsewhere.

Besides the general rise in popular anger at, and distrust of, government, the movement was clearly fueled by two very specific economic catalysts. The first was the red-hot California real estate market of the mid- to late 1970s, which threatened homeowners with rapidly escalating property tax bills. Between 1973 and 1978, prices for single-family homes in the Bay Area, for example, rose an average of roughly 18 percent per year. In Los Angeles the rate was even higher, averaging between 25 and 30 percent in many areas. Logically, the average increase in property tax assessments paralleled the rise in home prices. To take just two examples, assessments in San Bernardino and Orange counties rose by 28.9 and 30.1 percent per year between 1973 and 1977.[17]

Finally, serendipity—either fortuitous or disastrous depending on your view of Proposition 13—essentially assured the passage of the ballot measure. The timing had to do with the public release of the new property tax assessments for 1978. Sears and Citrin explain:

> On May 16 [1978] "city officials" in Los Angeles announced that the new assessments...would show that the total assessed value of the property in the city had increased by 17.5 percent in just one year. Since only one-third of all property was reassessed each year, this meant that the average increase per reassessment would be more than 50 percent. Many homes had not been reassessed for three years in a period of rapid inflation; their owners faced the prospect of a tax bill double the previous year. Also on May 16, Alexander Pope, the Los Angeles County Tax Assessor, announced that rather than waiting until July 17—well after election day—to learn how their property had been reassessed, voters could find out immediately by contacting his office. On May 17 the County Board of Supervisors went further, ordering Pope to mail the official reassessment notices to the county's 700,000 property owners by election day.[18]

The Board of Supervisor's action ensured that the new inflated reassessments would have maximum political effect, with shocked and angry homeowners receiving their notices literally on the eve of the election. As late as May 1–8, a statewide poll of all registered voters showed a tight contest, with proposition proponents leading opponents by 48 to 40 percent, with 12 percent undecided. But that was before the new assessments had been made public. By May 29–31, a similar poll showed the proposition now leading by a whopping 24 points, 58 to 34 percent, with 8 percent still undecided. In the end, as we have seen, the final margin was even greater than that.[19]

Of more concern to us here, however, are the consequences that followed from the stunning triumph achieved by backers of the proposition. Movements that arise unexpectedly and are seen as wildly successful tend to spread rapidly. Think only of Arab Spring and the Tea Party in the most recent period. And so it was with the tax revolt. Inspired by the success of the California insurgents, activists in a dozen states had managed to put tax reform measures on the ballot by the end of 1978 alone. Indeed, as one of the chief chroniclers of the movement notes, "in 1978, more tax-cutting initiatives appeared on state ballots than during the entire period between 1945 and 1976."[20] But that was just the beginning; the pace of tax activism actually accelerated over the next two years. As in California, many of these efforts were the work of grass-roots tax protestors; but increasingly, elected officials sought to appease and preempt the activists by proposing and passing tax reforms of their own. In the end, no less than 43 states enacted some form of property tax relief between 1978 and 1980.[21]

Given the rapid spread and accelerating pace of tax activism in these years, Ronald Reagan was perfectly positioned in 1980 to benefit from the electoral fallout occasioned by the tax revolt. Reagan's long-standing bona fides as a critic of high taxes and big government made him the darling of tax activists nationwide. But as Sears and Citrin note, "the Republicans went further, and made [Proposition 13 architect] Howard Jarvis's message the centerpiece of their 1980 presidential campaign: eliminating bureaucratic waste would make it possible to cut both taxes and public spending without the loss of valued services, and less government would enhance both the personal freedom and the personal finances of citizens."[22] Reagan's decisive win in November owed to the support of a good many constituencies, but it would be hard to overstate the importance of his appeal to those who were attuned to or active in various forms of tax activism in the run-up to the 1980 election.

The final quasi-movement group that figured prominently in Reagan's victory is the most amorphous of the four. It is arguably the most important of them as well. We refer to that loose group of southern white, racial conservatives who either took part in or were the ideological heirs of the 1968 and 1972 Wallace third-party movements. It was this group that Nixon aggressively courted during his first term in office and whose votes he largely succeeded in securing as one of the keys to his landslide win in 1972. Many of these same voters, however, returned to the Democratic fold in 1976, as native son, Jimmy Carter, reclaimed the South for the party. Reagan was determined to recapture the white South for the GOP in 1980. He was certainly aided in this by the stark contrast in the platforms of the two parties. Bartley summarizes that contrast:

The Democratic Party platform favored affirmative action, federally funded abortions, and busing, and it endorsed the Equal Rights Amendment to the point of denying party support to candidates who opposed the amendment and encouraging boycotts of states that refused to ratify it.... Reagan's Republican platform disavowed busing and abortion, ignored the Equal Rights Amendment, demanded prayer be allowed in schools, and advocated family values.[23]

But it was Reagan, through his words and his record, far more than the two platforms, who spoke most directly and effectively to the white South in 1980. He proved to be a master of speaking in code about racial matters of long-standing concern to the white South. At campaign stops in the region he reassured voters that he had long opposed government "interference" in "states' rights," reminding them that he had refused to back either the Civil Rights Act in 1964 or the Voting Rights Act in 1965.

Underscoring the central importance he attached to reclaiming the South for the GOP, Reagan chose—against his pollster's advice—to make his first post-convention campaign appearance at the Neshoba County Fair in the small town of Philadelphia, Mississippi. If the name of the town rings a bell, it's because it was the site of the infamous act of racist violence recounted in Chapter 3. To recap, in June of 1964, three civil rights workers were arrested in Philadelphia on trumped-up traffic charges, held till after dark, and then, as planned, released in the dead of night into the arms of a waiting mob. Their bodies were found in August, buried under a nearby earthen dam built for that purpose.

In his address to the overwhelmingly white crowd of 10,000 Reagan spoke in thinly veiled, reassuring code about the long-standing conflict between the federal government and the South over racial matters. As recounted by Cannon, Reagan said, "I believe in states' rights. I believe in people doing as much as they can at the private level."[24] If elected, he promised to "restore to states and local governments the power that properly belongs to them." Given the symbolic resonance of terms like "states' rights," the racial content and implications of Reagan's remarks were unmistakable in that context. Certainly they were not lost on veteran civil rights leader Andrew Young, who, in an editorial published soon after in the *Washington Post*, challenged Reagan with a number of pointed questions. After recounting the murders of Chaney, Goodman, and Schwerner in 1964, Young wondered whether "[because] these code words have been the electoral language of Wallace, Goldwater, and the Nixon southern strategy, one must ask: Is Reagan saying that he intends to do everything he can to turn the clock back to the Mississippi justice of 1964? Do the powers of the state and local governments include the right to end the voting rights of black citizens?"[25] Not surprisingly, the Reagan camp denied the charges; nonetheless the controversy helped to sharply delineate the racial politics of the two candidates. It was hardly surprising then when, in November, Reagan carried Mississippi with 61 percent of the white, and virtually none of the black, vote.

For the region as a whole, Reagan's percentage of the white vote was 61 percent. Four years later, nearly three quarters (72 percent) of all white Southerners cast their votes for Reagan. By the end of Reagan's term in office, the once "solid [Democratic] South" had become the most loyal regional component of the Republican coalition, at least in general elections. More important, having successfully reclaimed the white South and integrated both pro-life forces and the newly mobilized religious right into the party, Reagan had effectively remade the GOP into the overwhelmingly white, racially and socially conservative party it remains today. It was, as we have tried to make clear, a party remade by eviscerating the tradition of moderate Republicanism that had been the hallmark of the GOP since the late 1930s and aligning instead with the political preferences of mobilized movement conservatives at the ideological margins of the party.

The Reagan Presidency: A Revolution in Name Only

The president to whom Ronald Reagan is most often compared is Franklin D. Roosevelt. There is, as we will note, one very big difference between the two, but in most respects the comparison is apt. Both endured periods of sharp public rebuke; Roosevelt when he overreached in trying to "pack" the Supreme Court, Reagan when details of the Iran-Contra affair surfaced in November 1986. Despite these noteworthy setbacks, both presidents were generally popular over their long tenure in the White House. Indeed, their approval ratings at the close of their terms were virtually identical and remain among the highest in presidential history.

Accounting, at least in part, for their popularity was the fact that both men were superb communicators. Much has been made of Roosevelt's command of the dominant media of his day, radio, and the enormous influence he wielded through his weekly "fireside chats." Though less remarked upon, Reagan's use of television to appeal directly to the American public was only slightly less effective. More generally, Reagan's training as an actor served him well as the nation's "communicator in chief." Both Reagan and Roosevelt launched their initial terms in office with a stunning legislative blitz that decisively altered the scope and purpose of the federal government. And finally, and most important, the influence of both presidents extended well beyond their years in office. Roosevelt's conception of an active federal government committed to mitigating the effects of social disadvantage remained dominant right up until Reagan was elected, and lives on today as the guiding ethos of the Democratic Party. Similarly, Reagan's anti-tax philosophy and critique of "big government" powerfully constrained every succeeding administration and continues—in more extreme form—to motivate the Tea Party wing of the Republican Party. Indeed, it is the clash of these opposing ideologies that accounts for so much of the paralysis and dysfunction that characterizes contemporary American politics.

So what is the "one very big difference" between Reagan and FDR alluded to here? Roosevelt's decisive establishment of the activist role of government informed his entire three-plus terms in office whereas Reagan's *substantive* assault on FDRs vision was more or less confined to the first year of his presidency. We have emphasized the term "substantive" in the previous sentence to underscore an important distinction. While Reagan held *rhetorically* to his anti-tax, anti-big government message throughout his presidency, his *substantive policy-making* only sporadically accorded with this philosophy. For all intents and purpose, Reagan's assault on the American welfare state was confined to his first year in office. If this was a revolution, it started with a bang and ended with a protracted seven-year whimper.

The bang came in the form of deep cuts, enacted in 1981, to a number of once inviolate social programs, including AFDC (Aid to Families with Dependent Children) and food stamps, combined with "the largest single tax reduction bill in the history of the American republic."[26] The bill, the Economic Recovery Tax Act (ERTA), was passed by Congress and signed into law by Reagan less than six months after he had taken office. Reagan had hoped to cut taxes by 30 percent across the board, through 10 percent reductions in each of the first three years following passage of the bill, but in the end settled for 23 percent. The largest reductions were reserved for the top wage earners, with the highest marginal rate dropping from 70 to 50 percent. The bill also slashed estate taxes and cut corporate rates by $150 billion over five years. In the size of the spending reductions, the magnitude and regressive nature of the tax cuts, and the dizzying speed with which everything was enacted, Reagan essentially reversed Roosevelt's policy revolution of 48 years earlier. Unlike FDR, however, Reagan was unable to sustain his early legislative success. "Ironically," as Hacker and Pierson note, "even as Reagan's tax cuts signaled a dramatic shift in policy and message, they also represented the legislative high-water mark of the Reagan presidency."[27] Or as Gareth Davies succinctly puts it: "it is surprising to record that nearly every welfare reform initiative that President Reagan attempted between…September 1981…and the end of his presidency failed to achieve his objectives."[28]

There were multiple reasons for this failure and they varied over the life of Reagan's presidency. In his last two years in office, Reagan confronted a Democratic Congress, making it all but impossible to push through additional tax or spending cuts. By then, he was also in his mid-70s; and while never exactly a hands-on president, he was now clearly less engaged than he had been during his first term. Then too, not long after his resounding victory over Walter Mondale in 1984, the Iran-Contra scandal broke, undercutting whatever policy momentum might have come from his reelection. Without discounting these important contextual factors and distractions, however, much of the blame for Reagan's rather modest in-office revolution has to be laid to the objective failures and contradictions inherent in his initial legislative program. Beginning sometime in the mid- to late 1970s, Reagan came to believe in an extreme "supply side" view of the economic consequences that would follow from deep cuts in individual and business tax rates. Brownlee and Steuerle explain the logic of his position: "The argument was that the cuts would actually reduce budget deficits and thus relieve the upward pressure on prices, including interest rates. This deficit reduction would occur, Reagan argued, because of the huge expansion of the tax base produced by American investors and workers invigorated by big cuts in the tax rate."[29] But while Reagan insisted the supply side perspective was grounded in solid economic research, reputable economists were conspicuously absent in the ranks of those endorsing the plan. Consider the following description by a then young economist of the discipline's response to Reagan's supply side ideas at the time he took office.

> [In the early 1980s] I always got called with, "Do you have something good to say about supply-side economics?" And the fact of the matter was these guys had gone through lists and lists of people who basically told them that there was no solid economic research to support the supply-side stuff; it was a conjecture which was consistent with economic theory but had no empirical foundation.[30]

Put differently, the author of *The Consequences of Economic Rhetoric* writes: "Council of Economic Advisers Chairman Murray Weidenbaum, when asked directly what weight of influence, on a scale of one to ten, economists had enjoyed in drafting the original tax program of the [Reagan] administration, replied, 'zero.'"[31]

Likewise skeptical, Reagan's principal rival for the 1980 GOP nomination, George Bush Sr., famously derided his opponent's belief in this particular supply side perspective as so much "voodoo economics." Bush's characterization proved to be apt. To quote James Patterson on the matter:

> Contrary to Reagan's beliefs, tax cuts did not lead to escalating government revenues. Whopping increases in spending on defense, on entitlements such as Social Security and Medicare, and on interest payments to cover federal borrowing accounted for perhaps two-thirds (tax cuts the other third) of deficits that became huge in every year of Reagan's presidency.[32]

Between 1980 and 1984, as Reagan was supposedly shrinking govern-ment, the federal deficit nearly doubled, rising sharply from 2.8 percent of GDP in 1980 to fully 5 percent four years later. When coupled with the serious recession of 1981–82, the ERTA tax cuts dramatically reduced government revenues, forcing Reagan to backtrack almost immediately. The result was the 1982 Tax Equity and Fiscal Responsibility Act (TEFRA), the first major tax increase during a peacetime election year in five decades. But still the red ink kept flowing, prompting the admin-istration to redouble its efforts to find additional sources of tax revenue. This led, in July of 1984, to passage of the Deficit Reduction Act, or DEFRA which joined TEFRA as the second major tax increase in Reagan's first term in office. "Thus, Reagan took another step backward from . . . [his] dramatic measure of 1981. Taken together, TEFRA and DEFRA raised revenues on the average of $100 billion a year. . . . Increases this big had never been enacted except during major wars."[33]

During his time in office, Reagan came to be known as the "Teflon president" for his ability to remain popular despite repeated policy reversals, mistakes, and scandals. Then Democratic congresswoman from Colorado, Pat Schroeder bestowed the nickname on Reagan. Years later she explained the origin and meaning of the label. Wrote Schroeder in USA Today:

> I got the idea of calling President Reagan the "Teflon president" while fixing eggs for my kids. He had a Teflon coat like the pan. Why was Reagan so blame-free? The answer can be found in the label that did stick to him—"The Great Communicator." Reagan's ability to connect with Americans was coveted by every politician. . . . Remember how we were promised a big tax refund, a huge increase in military spending and a balanced budget? . . . When the national debt grew during his administration, you couldn't blame Reagan. He came across with that Irish twinkle. . . . Reagan's incredible ability to com-municate and his staff's genius in exploiting that ability are the reasons his presidency will be sealed forever in a Teflon coat.[34]

If anything, the gap between the popular perception of Reagan and his objective performance in office is even greater today than it was during his time in the White House. He continues to be lionized, by the extreme right especially, as the crusading opponent of big government and the inspiration for the anti-tax zealots who make up the Tea Party wing of the GOP. It is hard to square these images, however, with the actual policy outcomes of Reagan's two-term presidency. Consider the matter of "small government." In his first inaugural address Reagan famously intoned that "in the present [financial] crisis, government is not the solution to our problem. Government *is* the problem." In doing so, Reagan was simply offering up yet another version of the central argument he had been making for some 25 years, going back to his days as a spokesperson for General Electric. From the mid-1950s onward, Reagan had repeatedly assailed big government as an enervating source of personal dependence for the poor and diminished initiative for the rich. Small government and modest tax rates were necessary, he argued, to motivate and unlock the drive and entrepreneurial spirit of the American people. His central goal, as president, would be to free the people from the shackles of big government. And yet, far from cutting government expenditures, the size of both the federal budget and especially the deficit expanded dramatically during Reagan's time in office (see Table 5.1).

In absolute terms, the federal budget increased by a whopping $307.3 billion (2005 USD) between 1981 and 1989, a 2.7 percent increase per annum, exactly the same yearly increase on average as characteristic of all other postwar presidents. It was the growth in the federal deficit under Reagan, however, that poses the starkest contradiction to his image as the foe of "big government." The comparisons with his postwar predecessors are instructive. Four of Reagan's predecessors: Truman, Kennedy, Johnson, and Ford—three out of four Democrats—actually *reduced* the deficit while in office. In fact, only two postwar presidents saw larger deficit increases on their watch: Eisenhower and Nixon, notably both Republicans. The comparison with Carter, Reagan's immediate predecessor, is also instructive. The average annual rate of increase under Reagan was five and half times what it was during Carter's term in office. Overall the deficit grew by nearly 40 percent over the course of the Reagan presidency. And in absolute dollar amounts, the deficit grew by more than $65 billion (2005 USD) during his presidency; the largest increase of any president save Nixon. It is also interesting to note, in view of the ritual bloodletting that now attaches to the periodic crises over the "debt ceiling," that Reagan called on

Table 5.1 Federal Budget and Deficit, 1946–1989

Presidential Era	Fiscal Year	In Constant (FY 2005) Dollars (in Billions)			
		Total Federal Outlays	Average Per Annum Increase in Federal Outlays per Presidential Era	Budget Surplus or Deficit (−)	Average Per Annum Increase/Decrease (−) in Deficit per Presidential Era
(*Roosevelt*)	*1946*	*609.6*		−175.9	
Truman	1947	345.0		40.2	
	1948	281.3		111.5	
	1949	379.2		5.7	
	1950	399.6		−29.3	
	1951	434.7		58.3	
	1952	649.6		−14.6	
	1953	677.1		−57.8	
	1954	609.2	0.0	−9.9	−209.6
Eisenhower	1955	568.9		−24.9	
	1956	559.3		31.2	
	1957	577.1		25.7	
	1958	586.5		−19.7	
	1959	630.4		−87.9	

(*continued*)

Table 5.1 (Continued)

Presidential Era	Fiscal Year	In Constant (FY 2005) Dollars (in Billions)			
		Total Federal Outlays	Average Per Annum Increase in Federal Outlays per Presidential Era	Budget Surplus or Deficit (–)	Average Per Annum Increase/Decrease (–) in Deficit per Presidential Era
	1960	628.4		2.0	
	1961	648.5		–22.1	
Kennedy	1962	707.0	2.0	–47.3	47.2
	1963	705.0		–30.1	
Johnson	1964	740.8	2.4	–37.0	–10.9
	1965	729.4		–8.7	
	1966	810.9		–22.3	
	1967	926.3		–50.8	
	1968	1,009.3		–142.6	
	1969	976.3		17.2	
	1970	982.2	5.4	–14.3	–10.2
Nixon	1971	985.3		–108.0	
	1972	1,010.4		–102.4	
	1973	1,018.3		–61.8	

President	Year				
Ford	1974	1,027.3		−23.4	
	1975	1,149.9	3.4	−184.2	237.6
	1976	1,192.4		−236.5	
	TQ	299.1		−45.9	
Carter	1977	1,213.6	1.8	−159.1	−6.8
	1978	1,278.2		−164.9	
	1979	1,291.1		−104.3	
	1980	1,368.2		−170.9	
Reagan	1981	1,416.0	4.2	−164.9	.9
	1982	1,451.7		−249.1	
	1983	1,498.6		−385.2	
	1984	1,500.4		−326.5	
	1985	1,612.2		−361.7	
	1986	1,644.6		−367.4	
	1987	1,616.0		−241.0	
	1988	1,663.2		−242.5	
	1989	1,723.3	2.7	−230.0	4.9

Source: *Office of Management and Budget: http://www.whitehouse.gov/omb/budget/historicals*

Congress to raise the debt limit no less than 18 times during his eight years in office, the most of any modern president.

Then there is the little matter of tax increases. While Reagan did slash taxes on taking office and significantly reduced the rate for the highest earners again in 1986, he was also forced to approve two tax hikes in 1982 and 1984 to help recover the revenues lost through the 1981 Economic Recovery Tax Act. In memory as in life, Reagan is credited with the tax decreases but rarely criticized for the tax hikes. Critchlow's overall assessment of Reagan's *objective* achievements seems justified: "Reagan was genuine in his belief that the size and scope of the federal government should be reduced.... Reagan failed, however, to reshape government institutions." And yet, in the next "breath," Critchlow asserts that "there is no denying that Reagan changed the political landscape of modern America."[35] Aren't these judgments in conflict? Can both statements possibly be true? The answer is clearly "yes." However modest his objective performance in office, Reagan, through his legacy, continues to powerfully shape the landscape of contemporary American politics. In our view, Reagan's revolution has been of the "slow-release" variety, modest while in office, but accelerating ever since. To understand this odd phenomenon, we need to consider Reagan's legacy in more detail.

Reagan's Legacy and Posthumous Revolution

Reagan's influence on the US political economy is far greater today than during his presidency. In truth, during his last few years in office, Reagan was worn out and largely missing in action from the day-to-day operation of his administration. When he exited the White House in 1989, he was just shy of his 78th birthday and the oldest president in US history. He remained personally popular but was seen by most observers as a spent political force. Besides failing to affect the institutional downsizing of the federal government he had envisioned as his legacy, he had also not been able to effect a substantive philosophic makeover of his party. While George H. W. Bush had served Reagan honorably as his vice-president, he was ideologically far removed from Reagan and heir to the venerable tradition of postwar moderate Republicanism. The party's nomination of Bush as their candidate in 1988 was, in this sense, something of a rebuke to Reagan.

The contemporary view of Reagan's presidency could not be more different. The rather dispiriting end to his two-term presidency is largely forgotten, replaced by the prevailing image of Reagan as a crusading, anti-government conservative vanquishing postwar liberalism and waging a sustained, successful assault on the American welfare state. The candidates who squared off in the 2012 Republican primary fight spent almost as much time explaining how they—and not their rivals—came closest to embodying the Reagan legacy as debating substantive issues. In September of 2011 when the campaign was just heating up and Texas Governor Rick Perry appeared to be among the front runners for the nomination, Ron Paul ran an ad entitled "The One Who Stood with Reagan." Over stirring music, the ad opens with the following heroic narration: "The establishment called him extreme and unelectable. They said he [Reagan] was the wrong man for the job." The ad then goes on to attack Rick Perry for mounting an Al Gore for President effort in Texas when he was still a registered Democrat and concludes with the following stark warning: "Now America must decide who to trust: Al Gore's Texas cheerleader or the one who stood with Reagan." Perry responded by reminding people that Paul had, in fact, resigned from the GOP in 1987 in protest over Reagan's tax policies and asserting that he, not Paul, was the real heir to the Reagan legacy.

Newt Gingrich and Rick Santorum were also eager to don the Reagan mantle in 2012. At a rally in Florida in January of that year, "Mr. Gingrich hit back at former Massachusetts Governor Mitt Romney over ads that claim that the Speaker did not have a politically favorable relationship with President Reagan. He pointed to Michael Reagan, President Reagan's son, who is a Gingrich supporter as proof that his critics are wrong about this issue. 'I am delighted that tomorrow Michael Reagan will be campaigning with me. Which should tell you how false the ads were this week by Romney that suggested that I wasn't a Reagan Republican,' said Speaker Gingrich." Gingrich closed his remarks by simply asserting that "I am, in fact, the legitimate heir of the Reagan movement."[36]

Two months later, as Santorum was coming under increasing pressure to abandon his campaign and throw his support behind Romney, he offered his own version of the "I am Reagan and he's not" speech. Addressing a crowd at a Jelly Belly factory in Fairfield, California,

Santorum inveighed against Romney's moderate views, urging voters to stick with his true brand of Reagan conservatism. Said Santorum, "We as conservatives need to stand up and fight for a candidate who can win this general election, who stands solidly on the 'three-legged stool' [free enterprise, a strong defense, and conservative social policies] that brought the Reagan coalition together.... They're asking you ... to compromise your principles and to be for someone who is less corely [*sic*] convicted than Ronald Reagan because we need to win. My question is, 'win what?' Every time we run someone that the moderate establishment of the Republican Party said we need to win, we lose."[37] The implication was clear: Romney was no Reagan, but Santorum clearly was.

Even Obama went out of his way to say positive things about Reagan and his presidency. In an interview at the height of his 2008 primary battle against Hillary Clinton, Obama was asked with which presidential races and candidates he most identified. Other than the predictable comparison to John F. Kennedy, the only other specific president Obama cited positively was Ronald Reagan, saying: "I think Ronald Reagan changed the trajectory of America in a way that Richard Nixon did not and in a way that Bill Clinton did not. He put us on a fundamentally different path because the country was ready for it. They felt like with all the excesses of the 60s and the 70s and government had grown and grown but there wasn't much sense of accountability in terms of how it was operating. I think he tapped into what people were already feeling. Which is we want clarity, we want optimism, we want a return to that sense of dynamism and entrepreneurship that had been missing."[38]

Needless to say, time has been good to the Reagan legacy. But unlike his time in office, Reagan's present stature is not simply a function of image and personal likability. Quite simply, Reagan's *substantive* influence—rather modest during his two-term presidency—has increased markedly in the quarter century since he left office. The interesting question is, with Reagan himself quickly fading from public life, *how* did his substantive influence increase so dramatically after he left office? Chapter 6 can be thought of as an extended answer to this question as well as a detailed empirical examination of Reagan's unmistakable imprint on partisan polarization and trends in inequality over the past quarter century. Our work is not quite done in Chapter 5, however. We focus, for the remainder of the chapter on the *immediate* economic effects of Reagan's time in office. At first blush, mention of "immediate effects" might seem to contradict our earlier assertion that Reagan's accomplishments in office were exceedingly modest. Modest, yes, but only when measured against his revolutionary intentions and the expectations set by his first year in office. In point of fact, there *were* clear and consequential economic effects that followed from Reagan's presidency. We turn to those effects now, leaving until Chapter 6 the discussion and analysis of the longer-term unfolding of the slow-release Reagan Revolution between 1988 and 2008.

The Immediate Economic Impact of the Reagan Presidency

While the deep recession of 1981–82 may have forced Reagan to backtrack on the issue of taxes and to sign off on modest tax hikes in 1982 and 1984, the tax cuts enacted in 1981 were so massive that it would have taken a string of more substantial tax increases to offset them. If you couple ERTA with Reagan's 1986 overhaul of the tax codes, his "administration had, in fact, made the most significant changes in the tax system since World War II. And some of the important changes have proved remarkably durable.... [Most important,] income tax rates have remained significantly lower."[39] Figure 5.1 supports this summary judgment.

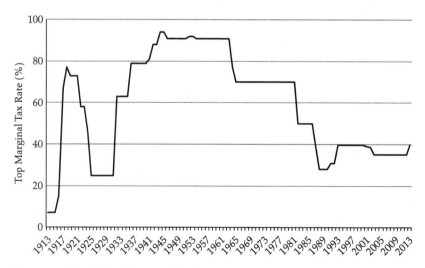

Figure 5.1 Top Federal Income Tax Rates, 1913–2013
Source: Tax Foundation

Reflecting the long policy shadow cast by FDR, the richest Americans had lived with, and generally accepted, top tax rates of at least 70 percent for nearly 50 years. When Reagan took office in 1981, the rate stood at exactly 70 percent. When he left office eight years later, the rate was but 28 percent, essentially matching the low levels that had helped fuel the roaring (and economically reckless) 1920s.

It wasn't simply the magnitude of the Reagan tax cuts, however, that so powerfully impacted the American economy. In recent years much has been made of the ever widening gap between the haves and have nots in the United States, and more pointedly, the extraordinary upward skewing of the country's income distribution. If the Occupy Movement's resonant mantra, "We are the 99%," helped broaden awareness of the trend, scholars have been tracking and generally lamenting, the hyper-concentration of wealth and income in the United States for years. As Hacker and Pierson report in their exceptional book, *Winner-Take-All Politics*, "the gains of the winner-take-all economy... have been extraordinarily concentrated. Though economic gaps have grown across the board, the big action is at the top, especially the very top."[40] And while this skewing has, if anything, accelerated in recent years, the origin of the trend bears the unmistakable imprint of the Reagan tax policies. Figure 5.2 tells the essential story.

The cumulative effect of the various changes to the tax code enacted on Reagan's watch was to produce the by now familiar skewing of the income distribution shown so clearly in Figure 5.2. If the effect of the New Deal and postwar liberalism was to narrow the income (and wealth) gap, Reagan's policies occasioned a dramatic reversal. The key catalyst in this was the 1981 Economic Recovery Tax Act. The Edsalls detail the specifics underlying the sharp reversal of economic fortune occasioned by ERTA:

> The 1981 measure...was skewed in favor of the affluent and corporations, and allowed taxes on the working poor to rise by failing to adjust for inflation two key elements of tax law designed to help those on the bottom rungs: the earned income tax credit and the standard deduction. This regressivity was then compounded by increases in the Social Security payroll tax, which not only has no progressive rate structure, but which provides no standard deduction.[41]

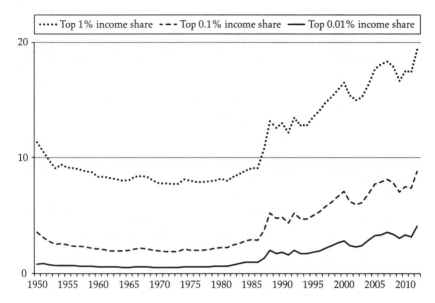

Figure 5.2 Top Income Shares, 1950–2012
Source: The World Top Incomes Database, Piketty and Saez (2007)

Tax policy wasn't the whole of the story, however. You will remember that Reagan's critique of big government had two components: the depressive effect that high taxes had on the entrepreneurial spirit of the rich and the unhealthy dependence of the poor allegedly fostered by social programs. By drastically reducing the marginal tax rate for the highest income earners, Reagan sought to address the first of these problems. He hoped to solve the second lacuna by eliminating or sharply reducing the scope of a host of government social programs. As with taxes, Reagan's ambitions in this second area far exceeded what he was able to accomplish during his time in office—a time marked not only by Democratic control of at least one branch of Congress but also significant dissent within Reagan's own party regarding his draconian plans for the American welfare state.

As with tax policy, Reagan's one notable "success" in this second area came during his first year in office, as part of the generalized legislative blitz that produced ERTA, his signature tax bill. The most significant cuts to social programs enacted during the Reagan presidency came courtesy of the 1981 Omnibus Budget Reconciliation Act (OBRA). A massive piece of legislation, OBRA essentially set Reagan's budget priorities for his first year in office. Besides huge increases in defense spending, the bill also included deep cuts to both the Aid to Families with Dependent Children and food stamp programs. Some 679,000 AFDC recipients were impacted by the reductions, with 400,000 being cut from the program and another 279,000 suffering reductions in their benefits. The cuts to the food stamp program were even deeper, with 1 million recipients losing benefits totaling $6 billion over the first three years of the reduced program.[42] In Davies words, this dramatic opening salvo, if not a full-blown "Reagan Revolution... was at least a revolutionary moment during the first six months or so, when defenders of the welfare state were on the run, overwhelmed by the president's popularity and by the widespread sense that excessive government spending lay at the heart of the nation's inflationary crisis."[43]

What a difference a year made. As the country sank into the recession of 1981–82, the perception grew that the deep tax and funding cuts of the first year had contributed to the slowdown. Reagan's popularity plummeted, undercutting his legislative momentum and emboldening proponents of social programs in both parties. Reagan would achieve no additional significant reductions in social spending during his remaining seven years in office. But as with ERTA, the size and unprecedented nature of the first year cuts had both an immediate substantive impact on the poor and, more important, a longer-term corrosive effect on the policy norms and expectations that had been set and continuously reinforced by nearly a half century of Democratic liberalism. It was this more sustained, indeed accelerating, influence on the acceptable bounds of federal policymaking between 1988 and 2008 that must be seen as the true measure and triumph of the Reagan Revolution.

Summing Up

Today Ronald Reagan's reputation as one of the most transformative presidents in American history is secure. Political observers of all ideological persuasions routinely invoke the "Reagan Revolution" to explain various features of the contemporary political economy. All too often, however, the popular narrative account of that revolution suggests a simple "before" and "after" effect of the Reagan presidency. The story, as we note in this chapter, is far more complicated, contradictory, and interesting than that. As we see it, there were actually two Reagan Revolutions, one that effectively redefined the prevailing parameters of federal policymaking and the other that dramatically transformed the ideological and demographic character of the Republican Party. Contrary to the simple "before" and "after" story, however, the fate of both revolutions was not at all clear at the time Reagan left office in 1988.

Consider the revolution in the normative contours of federal policy-making. Today's Republican Party ritualistically invokes Reagan as the inspiration for its extreme fiscal policy of "no new taxes," deep spending cuts, and an unrelenting assault on the federal deficit. And yet during his own two-term presidency, Reagan

- raised taxes 11 times;[44]
- failed to effect significant spending cuts in all but his first year in office;[45]
- saw the federal deficit nearly double during his presidency, far exceeding the increase under any previous postwar president;[46]
- and, to accommodate the run-away deficit, raised the debt ceiling a record 18 times while in office.[47]

Quite simply, in his performance in office, Reagan was dramatically less Reagan-like than any of his successors, including, we would argue, President Obama. Or to paraphrase Jeb Bush, anyone advocating Reagan's policies today could never hope to secure the Republican presidential nomination.[48]

Similarly, at the close of his presidency, Reagan's dramatic makeover of the GOP was still very much a work in progress. While nowhere near as strong as it was in its postwar heyday, the party's moderate-liberal wing remained a force to be reckoned with. Indeed, when it managed to secure the GOP nomination in 1988 for one of its own, George H.W. Bush, it appeared as if the party might be repudiating Reaganism in favor of a return to the brand of centrist Republicanism that had defined the party for the balance of the postwar period. Equally telling, the southern wing of the party—today so dominant and the source of much of the party's ideological conservatism—remained small and relatively unimportant within the GOP. In 1988, the year Reagan left office, Republicans held only 46 of 132 House seats from the region. The GOP of such Reagan-identified southern stalwarts as Newt Gingrich (GA), Tom Delay (TX), Jim DeMint (SC) and Dick Armey (TX) was still years away. As we recounted in the Chapter, by the time Reagan left Washington, he appeared to be a spent political force, his vaunted revolution pretty much reduced to the legislative output of his initial year in office. And then something quite remarkable happened; even as Reagan quickly disappeared from public view—reduced by Alzheimer's to the occasional staged family photo—his revolution gained steam. Within a decade, it had dramatically altered the ideological character of both Congress and the GOP. How did this happen with no real assistance from Reagan himself? How are we to understand the dynamics of this "slow-release" revolution? We take up this story in Chapter 6.

6

The Slow-Release Revolution

1988–2008

WE CLOSED THE LAST CHAPTER by arguing that, more than anything else, it was Reagan's success in redefining the proper role of government and resetting the boundaries of acceptable federal policy that explains how a revolution that appeared to be moribund at the time he left office was progressively realized over the next two decades. To this point, however, we have not really documented the realization of this slow-release revolution or described the processes that shaped it. These are our primary aims in this chapter. In broad relief, our argument runs as follows. While Reagan proved to be a consummate consensus politician, quite comfortable governing during an era in which bipartisan cooperation remained not just possible but necessary, he nonetheless catalyzed several processes that greatly accelerated the pace of partisan polarization in the years during and immediately following his tenure in office. These processes had the effect of pushing the Republican Party very sharply to the right, bringing a growing number of young, Reagan-identified, disproportionately southern conservatives into Congress. This meant that, notwithstanding vigorous Democratic dissent, later Congresses were much more ideologically aligned with Reagan's philosophy and policy positions than the ones he had confronted as president. By the mid-1990s, we argue, something that might be characterized as the "Reagan policy regime" was firmly in place in

Washington. That is, Reagan's stress on—if not consistent realization of—low taxes and deep cuts in social spending had become a broadly normative constraint on federal policymaking. The irony is that the institutionalization of this policy regime forces all of Reagan's successors—including Obama—to act far more Reagan-like in office than Reagan himself ever did. The effect of these policy constraints is to accelerate the pace of growing inequality across a number of institutional arenas of American life. This is the story we intend to flesh out and document in this chapter.

The Reagan Rebranding of the Republican Party and the Widening Partisan Divide

While Reagan is often depicted as a polarizing figure, the fact remains that he governed during a period when there was still considerable, if decreasing, ideological overlap between the two parties, as demonstrated in the by now familiar Poole and Rosenthal polarization time series (see Figure 6.1).

As Figure 6.1 demonstrates, throughout the 1980s, the level of partisan polarization remained relatively modest in both the House and Senate. Or to put it more positively, the extent of bipartisan cooperation in Congress during these years was far greater than today.

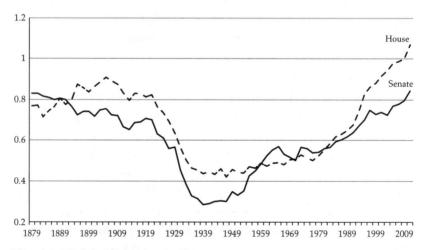

Figure 6.1 Political Polarization, 1879–2012
Source: Polarized America/voteview.com

To succeed in this era, Reagan had to operate as a pragmatic, consensus politician. It should be remembered that the stunning legislative blitz during his first year in office came at a time when Democrats controlled the House. Reagan's singular legislative victories required considerable Democratic support—support that, in the context of the relatively muted partisan divisions of the day, was forthcoming. To take but one example, 48 House Democrats crossed party lines to ensure passage of the Economic Recovery Tax Act (ERTA) in July 1981.

Nor was bipartisanship a one-way street during Reagan's years in office. On the contrary, Reagan encountered considerable opposition from the still sizable moderate contingent of the GOP congressional delegation throughout his two terms in office. In one especially note-worthy instance, David Durenberger (R-Minnesota) assailed Reagan's 1982 New Federalism initiative by posing the following pointed questions: "Does this administration—does my party—care about the poor? Is the 'new federalism' a smoke screen for a repeal of the New Deal? Is [the] private sector initiative a fig leaf to cover a lack of compassion?"[1] In the same year, Reagan's efforts to reform AFDC and enact further cuts to the food stamp program were turned aside in the Senate, in part because of the determined opposition of moderate Republican stalwart, Bob Dole. In explaining his opposition to the new cuts, Dole commented that the GOP had "already got an image across the country of harpooning the poor" and he didn't intend to make matters worse.[2] We could multiply these examples many times over; the point is that the extent of ideological overlap between the two parties remained quite high during the Reagan years. More important, and more relevant to the focus of this section, the tradition of moderate Republicanism, though clearly in decline, remained a force both within the party and Congress in the 1980s. Without ignoring the obvious impediment posed by Democratic control of the House, Republican opposition to Reagan's "extreme" agenda helps us understand why his "revolution" came to comparatively little during his years in office.

The decisive Republican shift to the right and attendant rise in party polarization came, as we can see in Figure 6.1, *after* Reagan had left the White House, with the two steepest increases coming in the 1990s and after 2008. The latter reflects the influence of the Tea

Party. Here we are concerned with the escalation of partisanship in the 1990s and especially Reagan's influence on the process. Unlike the widening *economic* gap that followed Reagan's term in office, which, we argue, followed directly from the growing influence of his substantive policies, we see Reagan's impact on the growing *partisan* divide in the 1990s as more indirect. Reagan's influence, more specifically, can be seen in three processes that together served to sharpen partisan divisions following his tenure in office.[3] Although all three of these processes are closely related, we take them up separately before discussing their combined constraining effect on the policy options available to those who have occupied the Oval Office since Reagan.

The first is the deepening connection between the GOP and the Christian right. As natural as this link seems to us now, it is worth remembering that Reagan's Democratic predecessor, Jimmy Carter, commanded the lion's share of the evangelical vote in 1976. And while it is true that Reagan took this constituency away from Carter in 1980, the Republican share of the evangelical vote—and indeed, all religious conservatives—rose sharply over Reagan's two terms in office and is even more sharply skewed toward the GOP today. Writing in 2002, Black and Black highlight the political significance of the shift: "By capturing the allegiance of the religious right, Reagan dramatically expanded the conservative base of the Republican party."[4] That is, even as he contended, during his two-term presidency, with the still sizable moderate wing of his party, Reagan was moving the GOP inexorably to the right by incorporating the ascendant Christian right into its ranks. Many of those so incorporated were movement conservatives active in the pro-life, anti-ERA battles of the period. And drawing on their activist experiences and organizing abilities, over time they came to exercise ever-greater influence over state and local party structures. In 1994 the magazine, *Campaigns and Elections*—which closely tracks various aspects of party and electoral politics—reported that 31 Republican state party organizations were under the "moderate" or "strong" control of Christian conservatives. By 2002 that number had grown to 44.[5] It was Reagan, through his consistent embrace of extreme conservative positions on all manner of social issues, who deserves much of the credit for cementing this relationship. Whatever one's normative view of the matter, it is clear that the increasing identification of the religious right with, and influence over, the GOP has been an important force pushing the party ever rightward during and after Reagan's tenure in office.

A second process responsible for the GOP's increasing conservatism was the final stage of the South's electoral shift from a solidly Democratic to a reliably Republican region—a process termed "Reagan realignment" by many. Even as the South returned solid majorities for Nixon in both 1968 and 1972, the Democrats continued to dominate House and Senate races in the region. Case in point: in 1976, Democratic candidates claimed victory in 94 of the 125 House races waged in the states and territories of the former Confederacy. And when native son Jimmy Carter reclaimed the South for the Democrats en route to the White House that same year, even the GOP breakthrough at the presidential level seemed ephemeral.

Ronald Reagan changed all that. Not only did he carry the South (save for Georgia) in routing Carter in 1980, but his coattails proved long enough that year to pick up a net of 14 House seats for the GOP. And that was only the beginning. As impressive as Reagan's 61 percent share of the southern white vote was in 1980, he upped that percentage to nearly three quarters (72 percent) four years later. Reagan's immense and growing popularity in the South drove regional realignment forward throughout the 1980s and into the 1990s. The inexorable quality of the process is captured in Table 6.1, which reports the shifting balance of Republican and Democratic House seats in the South between 1976 and 1994.

Quite simply, "Reagan's presidency was the turning point in the evolution of a competitive two-party electorate in the South."[6] Once again, though, the ultimate electoral payoff from the realignment came *after* Reagan left office—yet another slow-release process that helps us understand how his stature and influence grew that much greater with time. Within the region, the breakthrough came in 1994, when, for the first time in history, the number of Republican House members from the South outnumbered Democrats. It is simply impossible to overstate the importance of this realignment, not only for the shifting fortunes of

Table 6.1 Congressional Shifts in the South, 1976–1994

	1976		1978		1980		1982		1984		1986		1988		1990		1992		1994	
	R	D	R	D	R	D	R	D	R	D	R	D	R	D	R	D	R	D	R	D
Alabama	3	4	3	4	3	4	2	5	2	5	2	5	2	5	2	5	3	4	3	4
Arkansas	1	3	2	2	2	2	2	2	1	3	1	3	1	3	1	3	2	2	2	2
Florida	5	10	3	12	4	11	6	13	7	12	7	12	9	10	10	9	12	11	15	8
Georgia	0	10	1	9	1	9	1	9	2	8	2	8	1	9	1	9	7	4	7	4
Kentucky	2	5	3	4	3	4	3	4	3	4	3	4	3	4	3	4	2	4	4	2
Louisiana	2	6	3	5	2	6	2	6	2	6	3	5	4	4	4	4	2	5	3	4
Mississippi	2	3	2	3	2	3	2	3	2	3	1	4	1	4	0	5	0	5	1	4
Missouri	2	8	2	8	3	6	3	6	3	6	4	5	4	5	3	6	3	6	3	6
N. Carolina	2	9	2	9	4	7	2	9	5	6	3	8	3	8	4	7	4	8	8	4
S. Carolina	1	5	1	5	4	2	3	3	3	3	2	4	2	4	2	4	3	3	4	2
Tennessee	3	5	3	5	3	5	3	6	3	6	3	6	3	6	3	6	3	6	5	4
Texas	2	22	4	20	5	19	5	22	10	17	10	17	8	19	8	19	8	22	11	19
Virginia	6	4	6	4	9	1	6	4	6	4	5	5	5	5	4	6	3	8	5	6
Total	**31**	**94**	**35**	**90**	**45**	**79**	**40**	**92**	**49**	**83**	**46**	**86**	**46**	**86**	**45**	**87**	**52**	**88**	**71**	**69**
Percent Republican	**25**		**28**		**36**		**30**		**37**		**35**		**35**		**34**		**50**		**51**	

Source: Office of the Clerk (http://history.house.gov/Institution/Election-Statistics/Election-Statistics/)

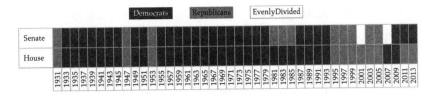

Figure 6.2 Control of Congress, 1931–2013
Source: Office of the Clerk of the House of Representatives

the two parties but for understanding the increasing imprint of Reagan's ideas on federal policymaking. Figure 6.2 tells the story.

Between 1933 and 1995, the GOP controlled the Senate, the House, or both in just five of the 31 Congresses convened in that span, underscoring the Democrat's dominance in federal policymaking for most of the period. This all changed with the Republican breakthrough in the South in the 1994 House races. In the 10 congressional sessions held since then, Republicans have controlled one or both houses of Congress eight times, or three more than they did in the preceding 64-year period. Quite simply, nothing explains the rightward shift in federal policymaking over the past two decades more than the partisan realignment of the South. We can put it even more starkly than that. Since 1930, the shifting policy fortunes of the two parties owe to a single source: whichever party has been favored by the South—make that the white South—has exercised effective policy control over the federal government.

Finally, besides solidifying the identification of the Christian Right and white Southerners with the GOP, Reagan also inspired a generation of young conservatives to align with the Republican Party as self-identified Reagan acolytes. This was no mean feat. Young voters have historically tended to vote Democratic. In the 14 presidential elections held since 1960, young voters—21–29 in the early years and 18–29 after 1972—supported the Democratic candidate all but four times. Reagan accounts for one of these exceptions. What's more, Reagan's combined share of the youth vote in his two races is greater than that of any other Republican candidate in this period. Indeed, at nearly 60 percent, Reagan's support among the young in 1984 actually exceeds the percentage he received from all voters.[7] This is really quite remarkable. Again, we tend to think of young voters as drawn to the charisma and dynamism of young progressive Democrats, such as John F. Kennedy or Barack Obama. Reagan, in sharp contrast, was neither progressive nor young. Indeed, at 69, Reagan was the oldest first-term president in US history, making his appeal among young voters all the more surprising.

This appeal, however, was much more than just a statistical anomaly. As much as anything it helps explain the unusual "slow-release" quality of the Reagan revolution. The real impact of the political generation inspired by Reagan in the 1980s comes a decade later as scores of his protégés enter politics and move the GOP and the country sharply rightward. James Patterson explains the phenomenon and its significance: "Many conservative activists, energized by Reagan's victories in the 1980s, entered electoral politics, some of them leading the GOP electoral bonanza of 1994. They also strengthened a network of organizations—the Christian Coalition, the National Taxpayers Union, the National Rifle Association, various think tanks—that bolstered conservative ideas and pressure groups at all levels of government."[8]

Nowhere was Reagan's appeal greater with young people than in the South where his "legacy was immense. [Within the region] Reagan substantially expanded grassroots Republicanism and inspired many potential Republican politicians to seek office."[9] Inspired by Reagan's charismatic conservatism of a decade earlier, the first wave of Reagan acolytes began to claim elective office in the region in the 1990s. The breakthrough year was 1994. Riding the wave of this new generation of Reagan-identified southern conservatives, the GOP made enormous inroads throughout the region. To quote Critchlow: "By the time Reagan left the presidency, the majority of southern voters already identified as Republicans. The 1994 election completed this transformation. Republicans took 119 southern legislative seats and seized the Florida Senate and the North and South Carolina lower assemblies. In addition, Republicans gained control of the majority of southern governorships."[10]

The significance of that year's election, however, is not only—or primarily—about what happened regionally. Keyed by a net gain of 19 southern seats, the GOP seized control of the US House of Representatives for the first time since 1954. McAllister nicely captures just how central Reagan as symbol was to the decisive Republican victory. He writes: "The stunning victory [in 1994]...by Republicans represented, to them at least, the Reagan agenda, part 2. Their famous 'Contract with America' borrowed heavily and unashamedly from Reagan's speeches as it outlined an economic plan that aimed to get government off the backs of the people. Populism was back, but it came with a more combative tone and methods that a new generation of baby boomer [Reagan] conservatives embraced—a take no prisoners assault on their enemies."[11] The 1990s then were witness to two significant transformations. The first is the extinction of the last vestiges of the "kinder, gentler" Republican Party—ironically embodied by Reagan—in favor of the no-holds-barred partisanship that we know all too well today. The second is the transformation of Reagan from the complex, contradictory president he was in reality to today's stylized, iconic figure.

Figure 6.3 shows the dramatic rise in Reagan's retrospective approval ratings over the course of the 1990s. As late as 1993 the American public remained evenly split on Reagan's legacy, with nearly as many Americans disapproving of his performance in office as approving. But with the resurgent GOP of the mid-1990s aggressively appropriating and stylizing Reagan's legacy, the complex figure of history morphed into the icon we know today. In short, if Reagan had seemed something of a spent political force when he left the White House in 1988, he—or rather his rehabilitated, mythic image—was alive and well in the 1990s. With the despised Bill Clinton in office and many young Reagan-inspired conservatives coming of age, a younger, insurgent GOP deployed the now-iconic Reagan as the potent symbol of their vision

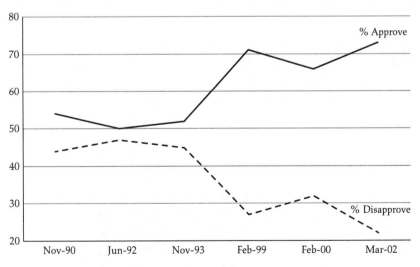

Figure 6.3 Reagan's Retrospective Approval Ratings

of an America restored to the "greatness" achieved under the former president. The high watermark of this insurgency came when the Republican breakthrough in the South in the 1994 midterm elections allowed the GOP to seize control of both houses of Congress for the first time in 40 years.

The South's ascendant brand of Reagan Republicanism didn't simply aid this effort but came, in the process, to increasingly dominate the national party. In short order, "the South would become the nation's most reliably Republican region, and its distinctive form of conservatism increasingly would dominate the GOP."[12] The new Southern face of the party was reflected in the GOP leadership in both the House and Senate following the breakthrough 1994 election. With Gingrich assuming the role of Speaker in 1995—the first Republican to hold the post in nearly four decades—a pair of Texans, Dick Armey and Tom Delay, took over the positions of House majority leader and majority whip, respectively. When Mississippi native Trent Lott won election as Senate majority leader two years later, it meant that all of the party's official congressional leadership slots were in the hands of Southerners. What a difference a decade made, to say nothing of Reagan's continuing influence over the geographic profile of the party.

While we have treated these three processes—the growing religious character of the GOP, southern realignment, and the increasing flood of self-identified young Reagan conservatives into the party—as distinct, it should be clear from what we have said that these trends were, in fact, overlapping and mutually reinforcing. The cohorts of young Reagan acolytes who began streaming into the party in the late 1980s and early 1990s were disproportionately social conservatives from the South. It would be hard to overstate the impact these overlapping trends had on the ideological character of both the GOP and Congress.

The GOP after Reagan: Taking a Hard Right

During this period, the growing alignment of the religious right, white Southerners, and young conservatives with the GOP came at the cost of the disaffection and accelerating attrition of moderate Republicans. This was especially evident in Congress. Some senators and representatives left of their own accord, unwilling to remain in an institution they no longer recognized. As one observer put it: "In the eyes of many moderates, the new crop of young, ideologically driven Republicans lacked civility and respect for Congress as an institution. One retiring Republican described them as 'rogue elephants...who don't listen to their fellow members or understand them.'"[13] Others, in a pattern that anticipated today's Tea Party tactics, were essentially forced out by challenges from young conservatives hostile to their moderate views. Not long after being ousted as the party's deputy leader in the Senate, longtime Wyoming senator Alan Simpson announced his retirement, taking a shot at the new "bug-eyed zealots" in his party as he took his leave.[14] Though he survived a similar attempt to oust him from his chairmanship of the Appropriations Committee—orchestrated by none other than Rick Santorum—another moderate stalwart, Mark Hatfield (Oregon), announced his decision to leave Congress soon after, in response to the dispiriting changes in his own party.

The irony, of course, was that in leaving Congress, the moderates only accelerated the partisan polarization they so decried while hastening the effective extinction of the GOP's distinguished and long dominant moderate wing. This was the wing that had brought the party roaring back to life after its humiliating period in the political wilderness during the 1930s. Starting in 1940, but accelerating after World War II, newly minted liberal and moderate Republicans not only replaced the few aging party conservatives who had survived the Depression era purge but began picking up seats previously held by Democrats as well. In the 75th Congress (1937–1939) the partisan balance favored Democrats by record margins of 75–17 in the Senate and 333 to 89 in the House. By the time the 80th Congress convened 10 years later, the GOP had reclaimed both houses, with margins of 51–45 and 246–188 in the Senate and House, respectively. This remarkable turnaround was the work of the party's ascendant centrist wing. This was the Republican Party of Dwight Eisenhower, Richard Nixon, Gerald Ford, Everett Dirkson, Hugh Scott, Jacob Javits, and Clifford Case. They would be joined, in the 1950s and 1960s, by the likes of Nelson Rockefeller, Charles Percy, George Romney, William Scranton, Bob Dole, John Chafee, Mark Hatfield, Howard Baker, and George H. W. Bush, to define an especially vibrant era of moderate Republicanism.

This wing of the party remained dominant through the 1970s, but with the religious right and pro-life forces increasingly active and influential in the GOP following Reagan's election in 1980, the moderates' days were numbered. By 1984, data reported in the *Congressional Quarterly* showed that their numbers had already thinned significantly. And yet, even in that year, a third of all House Republicans were accounted "moderates" in the journal's annual "Conservative Coalition" tally.[15] Though no longer dominant, the number of moderates stabilized somewhat during Reagan's second term. And when George H. W. Bush succeeded him in office in 1988, one would have been forgiven for believing the tradition of moderate Republicanism was making a comeback. The comeback would prove short-lived.

Reagan's Successors: More Reagan than Reagan

George Herbert Walker Bush was very much a product of the moderate centrist brand of Republicanism dominant in the postwar period. He was first elected to office in 1966 as a member of the House of Representatives from Texas's 7th district. Reflecting the shifting electoral geography of the South, he was the first Republican to represent the district in the House. From the beginning, Bush's voting record was characteristically moderate and occasionally more liberal than the views of his district. He voted for the Civil Rights Act of 1968, even though it was unpopular in his district and the GOP was shifting to the right on racial matters generally. He also broke with the party to support greater access to birth control. And as a first-term member of the powerful House Ways and Means Committee, he voted to end the military draft. Still, he proved a popular representative and was elected to a second term in 1968. His congressional career came to an end in 1970 when, at Nixon's urging, Bush ran for the Senate and lost to Lloyd Bentsen in a close race. For the rest of the decade Bush eschewed elective office but increased his stature and visibility by serving in a series of high profile appointed positions including US Ambassador to the United Nations, chief of the US Liaison Office in China, and director of the CIA.

In all of these positions, he burnished his reputation as a pragmatic moderate, making him a savvy choice to serve as Reagan's running mate in 1980. By tapping Bush to be his vice-president, Reagan helped to mollify and secure the support of the moderate GOP establishment that, in general, remained wary and disdainful of the former California governor. But while Bush served Reagan loyally, Kabaservice states that he was never

> comfortable with the right wing of his party or the Reaganite ideology. He called for a "kinder, gentler America," which was widely interpreted to mean a...more moderate and bipartisan politics. Bush talked about AIDS (as Reagan never had) [and] expressed sympathy for the homeless.... He secured passage of an updated and expanded version of the Clean Air Act, defied the National Rifle Association by supporting a ban on AK-47 assault rifles, and supported the 1980 Americans with Disabilities Act. Conservatives accused him of conducting a purge of the Reagan staff and refusing to appoint anyone from the [right] wing of the party.[16]

It seems clear that Bush *did* indeed want to move the GOP and the country back in a more centrist direction after the polarizing policies of the Reagan years. In the end, though, he failed to understand just how far the party had shifted to the right—and continued to do so—under Reagan's slow-release influence. After aggressively courting the right during the 1988 election, once in office, Bush quickly tacked back to the ideological center, outraging movement conservatives. The Christian right offers an instructive case in point. To help secure the support of religious conservatives, Bush tapped little known—and otherwise lightly regarded—staunch pro-life Senator Dan Quayle (R-Indiana) to be his running mate. When combined with extensive outreach to the religious right, that choice helped Bush garner 81 percent of the evangelical vote on election day, the same proportion that had cast their votes for Reagan four years earlier. But with Bush moving aggressively back to the center as president, he quickly ran afoul of the Christian right. To quote Daniel Williams:

> Bush opposed conservative evangelicals' call for funding restrictions for the National Endowment for the Arts, and he ignored their complaints when he invited gay rights activists to the White House. He selected...social liberals for his cabinet, including a pro-choice

doctor to head the Department of Health and Human Services. His first Supreme Court nominee, David Souter, proved to be a reliable vote for abortion rights.[17]

It wasn't simply the party that had moved to the right. Reagan, as we have noted, had succeeded in redefining the bounds of acceptable federal policy as well. Nothing enraged conservatives more during Bush's term in office than his retreat from his "read my lips" campaign promise never to raise taxes. Confronting an escalating deficit, in 1990 Bush acceded to a minimal increase in the top marginal tax rate, from 28 to 31 percent. Never mind that the tax increase was in exchange for Democratic support for a significant package of spending cuts, or that Reagan himself had raised taxes 11 times while in office. The difference is that Reagan had never been forced to conform to the "Reagan policy regime." Bush was the first president to confront the new policy constraints that Reagan had—over time—succeeded in establishing. By ignoring those constraints, Bush outraged the large and now dominant right wing of his party.

Given his many sins in the eyes of the large and growing right wing of his party, it came as no surprise when former Nixon speechwriter and conservative journalist, Pat Buchanan challenged Bush for the GOP nomination in 1992. Bush eventually prevailed, but not before the disastrous nominating convention in Houston exposed the deep divisions within his own party. Kabaservice nicely captures the debacle. He writes: "Buchanan spoke on the first night of the convention and declared a religious and cultural war against Democrats, feminists, and homosexuals. The convention was a public relations disaster"[18]—as was the campaign Bush waged against his Democratic opponent, Bill Clinton. While much has been made of the electoral price Bush paid for his "read my lips" apostasy in raising taxes, a good case can be made that it was Bush's inability to connect with, let alone inspire, his party's increasingly large and restive movement base that doomed him in the general election. Not only was Bush soundly beaten by Clinton, but many in the right wing of his own party cast their votes for the iconoclastic third-party candidate, Ross Perot. In the end, Bush garnered just 37.5 percent of the popular vote, matching the lowest percentage for a major party candidate since 1936.

The immediate beneficiary of Bush's humiliating defeat was his strategically positioned centrist Democratic opponent, William Jefferson Clinton. Though Clinton had been a product of the New Left when he first entered politics in the early 1970s, by the late 1980s he had aligned himself with the moderate "New Democrat" faction of his party. With no real mobilized movement wing in the Democratic Party to contend with, Clinton sought to reposition the party and reclaim the political center that the Republicans were busy abandoning. The formula had made him a popular three-term governor in a conservative southern state—Arkansas—and, aided by Bush's problems with the Republican base, and Ross Perot's third-party candidacy, it enabled Clinton to gain the White House in 1992 with just 43 percent of the popular vote. As with his predecessor, however, Clinton's honeymoon did not last very long. Distrusted by the Republican right to begin with, once in office Clinton was widely perceived as having reneged on his campaign promise to "govern from the middle." The two signature policy initiatives during his first two years in office—his "Don't Ask Don't Tell" directive to the Defense Department, and the health care reform plan announced in September 1993—outraged the right. And it helped to set in motion an orchestrated effort to turn the 1994 midterm elections into a state by state, race by race, referendum on the Clinton presidency.

The effort was the brainchild of House Minority Leader, Newt Gingrich. Gingrich and Clinton made for interesting adversaries. For all their partisan animus toward one another, their respective political journeys were shaped by much the same tug of war between movement and party politics. While Clinton had entered politics as a New Leftist and then moved to the center as the movement wing of his party atrophied, Gingrich's political evolution was the reverse of the president's. After being a fervent supporter of liberal GOP stalwart, Nelson Rockefeller, early in his career and arriving in the House as a moderate in 1978, Gingrich morphed into a self-styled Reagan conservative as the party shifted sharply to the right to accommodate its expanding movement base. It was in this latter guise that Gingrich helped to orchestrate the stunning GOP triumph of 1994. As House Minority Leader he had formulated and widely publicized the "Contract with America" in the run-up to the 1994 election. Signed by 337 Republican House candidates, the Contract was a 10-point legislative program—based heavily and explicitly on Reagan policy precepts—billed as a "covenant" with the voters. Quite cleverly, the Contract effectively "nationaliz[ed] the election, making each local contest a referendum on Bill Clinton and the perceived leftish Democratic excesses of his first two years in office."[19] How much the Contract actually swayed voters is hard to say. It did, however, garner enormous attention during the campaign, elevating Gingrich's visibility and influence in the process. Few Speakers have come to office with as much notoriety and apparent leverage as Gingrich did when the 104th Congress convened in January of 1995.

For all of his very public appropriation of the legacy and ideas of Ronald Reagan, however, Gingrich had none of the former president's personal charm or penchant for consensus politics. His was a far more confrontational, take-no-prisoners style of politics than that practiced by Reagan. If today's House Republicans have elevated legislative hostage taking and gridlock to new heights, we would do well to remember that Newt Gingrich pioneered the approach in his budget showdown with Bill Clinton in 1995. Emboldened by the electoral triumph of the previous fall, Gingrich and the new Republican House majority threatened a government shutdown unless Clinton agreed to a budget that included a trillion dollars in spending cuts and the elimination of three government departments: energy, education, and commerce. When Clinton refused, Gingrich made good on his threat to shut the government down. There were, in fact, two shutdowns, the second lasting nearly three weeks. In the end, however, the tactic backfired, with the public largely blaming Gingrich and the Republicans for the crisis. By contrast, Clinton's ratings slowly improved over the life of the showdown, allowing him to regain the political momentum he had lost as a result of the midterm elections. Less important to us than the winners and losers of the showdown, however, was the dramatic escalation in partisan bloodletting and government dysfunction that accompanied the crisis. It doesn't seem much of an exaggeration to say that in its divisive essence, the 104th Congress ushered in the brave new world of partisan politics we continue to inhabit today.

Ironically, Clinton's budget showdown with Gingrich in 1995 allowed him to regain his political footing. But even Clinton's savvy repositioning of his presidency in the aftermath of the crisis bespoke the growing influence of the extreme Republican right and the imprint of the Reagan policy regime. Kabaservice explains: "Clinton responded to the conservative upsurge with a strategy of 'triangulation,' which amounted to trying to steal the GOP's thunder by adapting some Republican ideas, including welfare reform, tax cuts for the middle class, and balanced budgets."[20] In his 1996 State of the Union Address— the first since his showdown with Gingrich—Clinton sounded positively Reagan-like when he announced that "the era of big government is over." Nor was this simply some kind of clever rhetorical sop to confuse or appease the Republican right. With his signature piece of legislation from that same year, Clinton actually outdid Reagan. In both its substance and symbolically resonant title, Clinton's 1996 Personal Responsibility and Work Opportunity Reconciliation Act, embraced two of Reagan's central policy goals: the elimination of social programs and with it the "degrading" dependence of the poor on government largesse.

Did Clinton's centrist rebranding of his presidency damp down the partisan fires that had marked his first term in office and make for a more bipartisan second term? Hardly. The Monica Lewinsky scandal and resulting impeachment imbroglio saw to that. Nothing reflects the extreme partisanship that marked the scandal and impeachment process more clearly than the nearly straight party line voting in the House on the four articles of impeachment. Two of the four articles—perjury to a grand jury and obstruction of justice—passed by margins of 228–206 and 221–212, respectively. Only four of 226 Republicans voted against all four articles, while a lone Democrat (out of 207) voted in favor of all four. Contrast that with the decidedly bipartisan vote coming out of the House Judiciary Committee during the impeachment proceedings against Richard Nixon back in 1974. In the earlier case the committee voted in favor of three articles of impeachment against Nixon. The articles and the vote tally in each case were as follows: obstruction of justice, 27–11; abuse of power, 27–11; and contempt of Congress, 23–15. More important than the aggregate tally, however, better than 40 percent of the Republicans on the committee (7 of 17) voted in support of at least one of the three articles, in essence acceding to the impeachment of the sitting president of their own party. But then again, Congress in 1998 bore little relationship to the substantially bipartisan institution in place a quarter century earlier.

In fact, the level of partisan polarization increased steadily over Clinton's tenure in office—so much so that by the time George W. Bush succeeded Clinton, the ideological distance between the two parties was at an all-time high in the House and approaching it in the Senate. The steady rightward march of the Republican congressional delegation *since* Reagan helps us understand the partisan context in which Bush came to power. With Reagan's retrospective approval ratings running around 70 percent at the time, the Reagan policy regime was stronger than ever and inviolate in the eyes of the GOP. Given this context, perhaps it should not have come as a surprise that Bush, in policy terms, wound up being the most zealous Reaganite to ever occupy the Oval Office. That was not, however, what many observers were hoping or expecting when Bush took office.

To say that Bush gained the White House amid controversy would be the mother of all understatements. As bad as the partisan divisions were at the conclusion of the Clinton presidency, the disputed Gore/Bush contest—with its ugly specter of "hanging chads" and the transparently political resolution of the crisis by the Supreme Court—left the country far more divided than before. Given the depths of those divisions and the fact that he was awarded the election while losing the popular vote prompted many to predict that Bush would have to reach out to Democrats and independents and govern from the center. In his memoir, former Republican Senator, Lincoln Chafee (R-Rhode Island) recounts how he and the remaining handful of GOP moderates left in the Senate at the time were encouraged by the election results, believing that, after having been marginalized within the GOP delegation for so long, they were destined to "play a pivotal role in passing the unifying program Bush had spoken of on the campaign trail." That was before they met with vice-president elect Dick Cheney to be briefed on the administration's plans. In his memoir, Chafee described the plan sketched by Cheney as "a shockingly divisive political agenda," adding later that the moderates' acquiescence in the plan "was the most demoralizing moment of my seven-year tenure in the Senate."[21]

Needless to say, the Bush presidency lived up to Cheney's advance billing. "As Cheney had predicted, Bush presided over a highly divisive administration and aggravated the partisan intensity of Congress and the nation.... Bush displayed little interest in compromise or bipartisanship, and moderates in the administration were humiliated at every turn."[22] But perhaps the most damning assessment of the Bush presidency came from one of the administration's very own. John Dilulio, head of Bush's Office for Faith-Based and Community Initiatives, complained that the administration "consistently talked and acted as if the height of political sophistication consisted in reducing every issue to its simplest, black-and-white terms for public consumption, then steering legislative initiatives of policy proposals as far right as possible."[23]

For all the criticism, however, a case can be made that Bush's performance in office is simply the clearest and most consistent expression of the policy aspirations articulated by Reagan but only made possible by ever more conservative GOP congressional delegations. In this sense, Bush was able to act far more Reagan-like than Reagan himself. The comparison is, in fact, instructive. Both presidents dramatically increased defense expenditures—Reagan in a renewal of Cold War tensions with the Soviet Union, Bush in support of two costly wars in Afghanistan and Iraq. Both presidents also enacted major tax cuts. The difference is that, as Reagan's tax cuts and record defense budgets began to swell the federal deficit, he felt compelled to raise taxes several times in an effort to staunch the flow of red ink. Operating in the secure context of the Reagan policy era, Bush felt no compunction to do so. Even as exorbitant cost overruns from the two wars combined with reduced tax revenues to turn the $236 billion surplus (and projected $5.6 trillion surplus over the next 10 years) he inherited from Clinton into the staggering $1.2 trillion budget deficit he bequeathed Obama, Bush apparently never considered raising taxes in an effort to slow the bleeding.[24] As Dick Cheney reportedly told Treasury Secretary Paul O'Neill, when the secretary worried about the spiraling deficit, "Reagan proved deficits don't matter."[25]

Rising Inequality and the Reagan Policy Regime

In documenting the sharp shift to the right in both the GOP and Congress after 1990, we have not simply been interested in interrogating Reagan's sustained influence on politics after he left office. Our real goal here has been to lay the necessary political and policy foundations for a more systematic exploration of Reagan's imprint on long-term trends in economic—and other forms of—inequality. The argument is straightforward: by setting in motion an ongoing shift to the right in his party, Reagan powerfully shaped the longer-term policy preferences of the Republican congressional delegation. And as those delegations became numerically larger and more conservative, so too did federal tax and spending policies come to more closely reflect Reagan's philosophy, if not his actual performance in office. The result has been the progressive solidification of a Reagan policy regime that in its impact and duration is coming to rival the policy parameters established by FDR over the course of his 13 years in office. If Roosevelt's advocacy of high taxes and social programs to mitigate disadvantage helps account for the comparative equality achieved in the postwar period, Reagan's ideological emphasis on low taxes and deep cuts to social programs must be counted as the major factor promoting the sharp increases in inequality we have seen over the past three to four decades. We have not, however, yet documented those increases or sought to link them to the increasingly conservative fiscal policies coming out of Washington after Reagan left office in 1988. That is our goal for the balance of the chapter.

Redefining Policy Expectations

As with his influence on partisan polarization, the real economic impact of the Reagan presidency came after he left office. While Reagan's legislative innovations served to reverse five decades of reductions in income and other forms of inequality, had the result of this reversal been confined to his time in office, the aggregate effect would have been relatively minor. But that, of course, is not what happened. If anything, as the by now familiar Piketty and Saez time series clearly demonstrates, income inequality grows more rapidly after Reagan leaves office than when he occupied the White House (Figure 6.4).

No doubt, many factors are implicated in this, but Reagan's role in decisively reshaping the federal policy environment has to be counted as among the most important influences propelling the trend. Even as he was falling well short of realizing his revolutionary vision for a transformed federal government, Reagan was busy undermining, through his words and actions, the policy parameters that, since FDR, had

Figure 6.4 Income Inequality, 1913–2012
Source: The World Top Incomes Database, Piketty and Saez (2007)

defined what was possible in the realms of federal tax and spending policy. With substantial assists from both the late 1970s "tax revolt" and the inflationary crisis of the same period, Reagan effectively transformed "the meaning of 'taxes.' ... No longer the resource with which to create a beneficent federal government, taxes had come ... to signify the forcible transfer of hard-earned money away from those who worked, to those who did not."[26] In this same view, social programs were simply the vehicles used to effect this illegitimate "transfer" rather than humane efforts by government to mitigate disadvantage, as they had been seen over the course of the previous half-century. It was in this sense that Martin Anderson, writing in 1988, could argue that it was now "largely irrelevant" who succeeded Reagan because "prospects are nil for ... big, new social welfare programs."[27] Critchlow puts it even more succinctly when he writes that "whatever qualifications are placed on the Reagan revolution [during his time in office], there is no denying that Reagan changed the political landscape of modern America."[28]

The irony is, so successful was Reagan in resetting policy norms and expectations that, as we showed in the previous section, a case can be made that all of his successors—including Obama—have been forced to conform more closely to Reagan's general economic vision than Reagan ever had to himself. As Mann and Ornstein assert, "the steps [Reagan] took in office ... were so far outside the policy and procedural bounds of the contemporary GOP that [he could not]...win a Republican nomination today."[29] Consider only the matter of taxes. Just as Roosevelt's popularity and perceived effectiveness as a leader had helped Americans accept high tax rates, Reagan effectively demonized elevated rates, making it politically risky for all succeeding presidents to use taxes to address the increasingly out of control federal deficit. This despite the fact that "Reagan was a serial violator of what we could call 'Axiom One' for today's GOP, the no-tax-increase pledge: he followed his tax cuts of 1981 with tax increases in nearly every subsequent year of his presidency."[30] But then there is the "do as I say, not as I do" Reagan policy regime that constrains all succeeding presidents in the matter of taxes.

Most analysts still believe that George H. W. Bush lost his reelection bid in 1992 by going back on his "read my lips" pledge not to raise taxes, even though the resulting increase was minuscule, raising the top rate from just 28 to 31 percent. Bill Clinton did manage to increase the top rate to 39.6 percent during his first term in office—which helped produce budget surpluses for the first time in some 30 years—but this still meant that the highest wage earners were paying roughly half the rate their counterparts had from 1936 to 1964. More ominously, the budget bill that included Clinton's modest tax hike received exactly zero votes from Republicans in the House and Senate, a harbinger of the gridlock to come in the years ahead. Finally, despite record-setting deficits—fueled by two cripplingly expensive wars—George W. Bush never saw fit to increase taxes during his term in office. But nothing illustrates the tenacious—if dysfunctional—hold that a stylized, extreme version of Reagan's anti-tax legacy continues to impose on federal policymaking than the fierce and generally effective opposition that President Obama faced in trying to enact a modest tax increase on the wealthiest Americans during the early days of his second term in office. Despite strong public support for the measure and the seeming mandate afforded by his reelection, the best Obama could muster was a return to the Clinton era tax rates, but only on individuals making more than $425,000 per year as head of household, and $400,000 as single filers.[31]

The ultimate poster child for Reagan's ongoing policy influence, however, comes in the area of social programs rather than taxes. We refer to the 1996 Personal Responsibility and Work Opportunity

Reconciliation Act (PRWORA), Clinton's effort to "end welfare as we know it." The name itself bespeaks the bill's debt to Reagan's critique of the personal dependence and irresponsibility allegedly encouraged by government social programs. It is no coincidence that Gareth Davies begins his assessment of Reagan's long-term influence on the "Welfare State" with the following observation. At the close of his presidency, writes Davies, Reagan's legacy "looked unimpressive: after a stirring beginning, he achieved hardly any of his policy objectives. Yet by 1996 something that looked a lot like a Reagan welfare revolution had materialized, following enactment of the Personal Responsibility and Work Opportunity Reconciliation Act."[32] In general, Clinton's election in 1992 "exposed how much Reagan had altered the political landscape.... Clinton won only because he sounded as though he had abandoned the liberalism of the older Democrats and embraced a new way, a third way between the old liberals and the old conservatives."[33] The "slow-release" Reagan Revolution was now constraining Democrats in the same way New Deal liberalism had dictated the acceptable policy parameters for Eisenhower and, to a large extent, Nixon. The uphill battle on all tax and spending matters that Obama has been forced to wage since taking office makes it clear that we continue to live very much in the Reagan policy shadow. But we are getting ahead of ourselves. Having accounted for the immediate impact of Reagan's policies during his term in office and the clear imprint of his innovations on the policies embraced by his successors, we ask what effect has the sustained Reagan "policy regime" had on various forms of inequality in the United States since he took office?

Inequality in Contemporary America: "It's [Not Just] the Economy Stupid"

As the Occupy Movement spread rapidly around the United States in the fall of 2011, it became commonplace to credit the movement with "changing the conversation" and broadening awareness of increasing inequality in the country. It should be clear by now that we see Reagan's sustained impact on tax and spending policies as deeply implicated in that trend, which has now been with us for the better part of four decades. We use the balance of the chapter to document these trends.

There is an overwhelming tendency to view the issue of inequality in contemporary America in narrowly economic terms. This is reflected, not only in the general ignorance of the political processes that have encouraged inequality but also in the proclivity to define the growing chasm between the "haves" and "have nots" exclusively in financial terms. We too regard the evidence of escalating disparities in wealth and income in the United States as clear, compelling, and the most important single dimension of the inequality story. It is not, however, the only one. On the contrary, in virtually every significant area of American life, the trends mirror the by now familiar economic story. The gap between the most and least advantaged—or, more accurately, the most advantaged and the rest of the country—has been steadily widening in a host of institutional arenas. In a very real sense, the master narrative of the past 40 years is the ever widening material gap between rich and poor and the abandonment of any meaningful commitment to the ideal of an egalitarian society. As a result, the "have nots" are not simply poorer than their fellow citizens but are saddled with a host of deficits that compound and magnify the overall burden and impact of their generally disadvantaged position. We hope to illustrate the additive nature of inequality in the contemporary United States using evidence from the institutional realms of health and education. We begin, though, by highlighting the major economic trends of the past three or four decades.

Economic Inequality

Scholarly treatments of the economic trends of the past few decades tend to quickly devolve into a mind-numbing set of technical analyses, backed by countless tables and figures. By contrast, Andrew Hacker's visual metaphor is starkly refreshing. "Imagine," he says, "a giant vacuum cleaner looming over America's economy, drawing dollars from its bottom to its upper tiers. Using U.S. Census reports, I estimate that since 1985, the lower 60 percent of households have lost $4 trillion, most of which has ascended to the top 5 percent, including a growing tier now taking in $1 million or more each year."[34] But as dramatic as these numbers are, Hacker's starting point of 1985 misses the onset of the larger economic trend by roughly a decade. The Piketty and Saez time series data (see Figure 6.3) provide the longer-term perspective missing from Hacker's otherwise bracing metaphor.

Figure 6.4 documents the dramatic over-time changes in income disparity within the United States. Two trends stand out in the figure. The first is the general decline in income inequality from roughly the mid-1930s to the early 1970s. The trend line turns ever so slightly upward in the mid- to late 1970s, but consistent with the account offered earlier, the decisive, sustained rise in inequality owes to the initial implementation and gradual strengthening of the Reagan policy regime since 1981. That is the second trend reflected in Figure 6.4. How did things change so dramatically in a relatively short span of time?

To begin to explore these issues, we take our cue from the Occupy Movement. Its slogan, "We are the 99%," points us in the right direction. As Hacker and Pierson report in *Winner-Take-All Politics*, "the gains of the winner-take-all economy... have been extraordinarily concentrated. Though economic gaps have grown across the board, the big action is at the top, especially the very top."[35] The evidence for what Hacker and Pierson term the "sustained hyper-concentration" of income is clear and compelling. Consider Figure 6.5, which plots the growth in real income earnings, between 1950 and 2012 of ever more rarified slices at the very top of the income distribution.

The findings shown in Figure 6.5 are based on *The World Top Incomes* research by Piketty and Saez, who used data from IRS returns to map the rapidly improving fortunes of the most highly compensated Americans. The really striking feature of the figure is just how consistently—

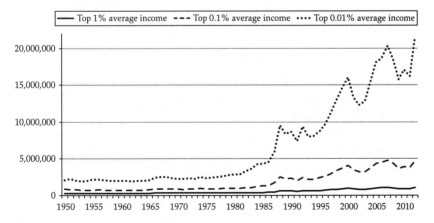

Figure 6.5 Average Incomes of Top Earners, 1950–2012
Source: The World Top Incomes Database, Piketty and Saez (2007)

and dramatically—the gains escalate as one ascends the income distribution. Over the past 30 years, the "1%-ers" have nearly tripled their average income earnings. But that's modest, even, when compared to the "hyper" wealthy. Those in the top .1 percent and .01 percent now earn four and a half, and nearly seven times, respectively, that of their counterparts of three decades earlier! As the figure clearly illustrates, the gains are highly concentrated at the top of the income distribution. Hacker and Pierson underscore this point when they ask us to

> consider the astonishing statistics. From 1979 until the eve of the Great Recession, the top one percent received 36 percent of all gains in house-hold income.... Economic growth was even more skewed between 2001 and 2006, during which the share of income gains going to the top one percent was over 53 percent. That's right: more than 50 cents of every dollar in additional income pocketed by Americans over this half decade accrued to the richest 1 in 100 households.[36]

What happens as we descend the income ladder over this same period of time? We suspect the answer will not come as a surprise. Figure 6.6 shows that the change in the average household after-tax income was quite different for those at the top than for the rest of the country.

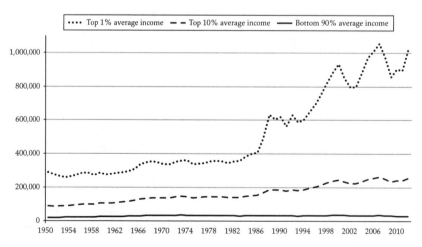

Figure 6.6 Comparative Income Earnings, 1950–2012
Source: The World Top Incomes Database, Piketty and Saez (2007)

The dramatic gains experienced by those at the top of the distribution are once again clearly visible in the figure. While incomes of the top 1 percent tripled, and top 10 percent nearly doubled, earnings throughout the rest of the country—the "bottom" 90 percent—remained stagnant. In fact, for most workers, real wages are slightly *lower* today on average than they were 30 years ago. Consider one final piece of evidence. Figure 6.7 puts the more recent period of rising inequality in stark historical relief by comparing the central income dynamic of the postwar period with the very different one described here.

Reflecting the combined effect of a booming economy and the highly progressive tax policies characteristic of the postwar period, all regions of the income distribution did exceedingly well between 1947 and 1975. Two findings are worth noting, however: no one did better in this period than the middle class and, everyone did slightly better than the very rich. The highly unequal stepwise pattern of income gains after 1975 affords a stark contrast to the earlier period and accords closely with our earlier discussion. Consistent with the evidence presented

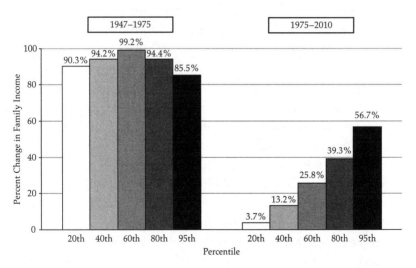

Figure 6.7 Change in Incomes by Percentile: 1947–1975 compared to 1975–2010
Source: US Census Bureau (2011). Table F-1. Income Limits for Each Fifth and Top 5 Percent of Families, from Historical Incomes Table. Retrieved from http://www.census. gov/hhes/www/income/data/historical/index.htm. Reproduced from Russell Sage

here, the gains in this second period are concentrated in the upper reaches of the income distribution.

Locating the source of the shift is not, however, the same as explaining it. The received wisdom in this regard is that these changes reflect natural economic processes independent of government action and the politics that shape them. No less an authority on the economy than former Labor Secretary Henry Paulsen affirmed this view when, on the eve of the Great Recession, he told an audience at Columbia University that "as our economy grows, market forces work to provide the greatest rewards to those with the needed skills in the growth areas.... This trend... is simply an economic reality, and it is neither fair nor useful to blame any political party."[37] Given the economy over which Paulsen was then presiding and the attention that was starting to be paid to the issue of inequality, it is tempting to interpret his remarks in political terms—as little more than a transparent effort to undercut criticism of the Bush administration. In point of fact, however, the general perspective invoked in his remarks has long been the prevailing view among most policymakers and economists, Democrats no less than Republicans, liberals as well as conservatives.

The economy, or so we have been told, is akin to a force of nature, a natural system largely impervious to the efforts of governments to control it. Indeed, the best thing governments can do is get out of the way and let the natural "efficiencies" of the market take hold. And so how exactly are we to understand that giant sucking sound and the resulting hyper-concentration of wealth at the upper reaches of the American class structure? As Democratic candidate John Kerry sought to make this an issue during the 2004 presidential race, the chief economist for Wells Fargo effectively chastened the candidate when he flatly asserted that "this really has nothing to do with Bush or Kerry, but more to do with the longer-term shift in the structure of the economy."[38] Okay, we'll play along. What specific changes in the "structure of the economy" could account for the rapid transformation of the American income structure that has occurred over the past three to four decades? Two linked processes, one global, the other more individual in nature, are routinely cited as the causes of this transformation. The larger process is economic globalization; the more micro is something economists call "skill-based technological change" (SBTC). The argument runs something like this: as the economy has globalized, the manufacturing sector has shrunk dramatically in the United States (and Europe) and expanded rapidly across the developing world. One consequence of this has been the loss of the well-paid, high-skill manufacturing jobs that fueled much of the postwar economic boom in the United States. The loss of these jobs has effectively hollowed out the middle of the American occupational structure, leaving an increasingly bimodal economy in its place. At the bottom is the large and varied low-skill, low-pay service economy that employs most Americans (and countless undocumented immigrants who claim jobs that most Americans disdain). At the top is a rapidly evolving "knowledge economy" that demands both ever increasing levels of formal education and sophisticated technical knowledge, especially facility with the new information technologies.

We don't for a minute dispute this basic portrait of the transformation of the US occupational structure. These changes are real and have made it harder and harder for the poor and the working class to find stable, remunerative employment in an economy that features an ever shrinking supply of high-skilled, blue-collar jobs. At the same time, this cannot fully explain the increasing inequality and hyperconcentration of wealth and income at the very top of the class structure, especially when we compare trends in the United States to those in other comparator countries. As of 1970, the United States was broadly comparable to other advanced economies when it comes to income inequality. Today it is an outlier on that dimension, with only Mexico, Turkey, and Chile among all 34 OECD countries ranking higher on income inequality.[39] The explanation for this dramatic shift in our relative position among comparable countries is, of course, the striking increase in income inequality in the United States over the past three to four decades. We see this same trend at the very top of the income distribution. By putting the matter, again, in stark cross-national relief, Figure 6.8 calls into question the conventional account summarized earlier.

Figure 6.8 compares the income shares received by the top 1 percent wage earners in a dozen advanced economies, including all OECD countries for which there are comparable data. In 1970, the United States is bunched in the middle of the distribution, with the top wage earners in seven other countries commanding a larger share of income

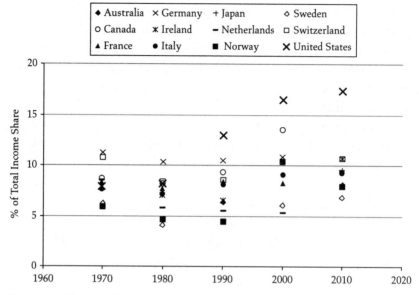

Figure 6.8 Country Comparisons of Top 1% Income Share, 1970–2010
Source: The World Top Incomes Database

than those in the United States. This is entirely consistent with our earlier characterization of the United States as fairly typical of other advanced economies during this period on the dimension of aggregate inequality. Reflecting the dramatic increase in income inequality, by 1990 the United States is already an outlier; and by 2010 it stands distinctly alone in terms of the share of income going to the top wage earners.[40] And lest you think that the onset of the recession in 2008 changed this basic picture, think again. If anything, as numerous studies confirm, the economic cost of the downturn has been born overwhelmingly not by the wealthy, but by the already struggling middle and lower classes. Consistent with this claim, as of 2012, nearly one-fifth of the country's wealth was concentrated among the top 1 percent, a steady 5 percent per annum increase since the peak of the recession in 2010.[41]

So what? What is the significance of the rather dramatic shift in the relative position of the United States across this time period? It is simply impossible to reconcile the conventional account sketched earlier with the data reported in Figure 6.8. As advanced economies, all of the countries included in the figure have been undergoing the same general economic transformation as the United States. They too have been subject to the pressures of a globalizing economy. More important, there is no reason to believe that the demands of the knowledge economy—that is, the returns to education or technological skills—should be appreciably greater in the United States than in the other countries shown in the figure. The point is that the influence of these twin processes

> should be seen over long spans of time and, more important for the present discussion, across national borders. After all, other rich nations have computers and the Internet too...and most rich nations are more exposed to the global economy than we are. If [skill-based technological change] SBTC did it here, it should have done it elsewhere, where the same technological and global shifts were taking place....Yet gaps in skills, as measured by years of schooling, are not larger in the United States than they are in other affluent nations. They are actually smaller. Inequality is dramatically higher in the United States not because of greater skill gaps or greater returns to education, but because within-group inequality is greater than it is in other rich nations. Indeed, there is more inequality among workers with the same level of skills...in the United States than there is among all workers in some of the more equal rich nations.[42]

The last point made by Hacker and Pierson is worth highlighting. There is no simple relationship between education and technological knowledge and wealth or income. Yes, the richest individuals in the United States are well educated, but no more so than many who find themselves many rungs lower on the income distribution. The same is true for level of technological knowledge. Based on their detailed analyses of income growth over the past four decades, economists Ian Dew-Becker and Robert Gordon found little support for the skill-based technological change account. As they put it in summarizing their findings, "most of the shift in the income distribution has been from the bottom 90 percent to the top 5 percent. This is much too narrow a group to be consistent with a widespread benefit from SBTC."[43] They also note serious problems with the SBTC account when it comes to explaining variation in income gains and losses across occupations. How, for example, are we to make sense of the fact that compensation for chief executive officers (CEOs) increased 100 percent between 1989 and 1997, while the income of engineers declined slightly over the same period of time?[44] Without discounting the importance of broad economic processes, there is simply no way to make sense of these stark within-group variations in compensation or the equally puzzling cross-national differences in income concentration by reference to the SBTC account. We concur with the likes of Hacker and Pierson and Bartels: absent serious attention to the not so invisible hand of the American state over the past 40 years—especially since the onset of the Reagan presidency—it is simply impossible to understand the extreme inequality that presently characterizes the United States.[45] Indeed, much of our focus in the book—highlighted in the first half of this chapter—has been on the evolution of a distinctive Republican politics of inequality, advanced somewhat haphazardly by Nixon, far more systematically under Reagan, and essentially institutionalized in the years since Reagan left office. But throughout our discussion of the GOP's politics of inequality, our focus has been primarily economic in nature. Before we bring the chapter to a close, we want to make good on our earlier promise to briefly document two other forms of inequality that have worsened over the same period of time—and for the same general reasons—as the growing financial divide.

Health Disparities

As the authors of a recent article in the *Annual Review of Public Health* note, interest in the topic of "health disparities" has itself mushroomed in recent years. Adler and Rehkopf report that "in the 1980s [health disparities] was a key word in only one article, and in the 1990s there were fewer than 30 such articles. In contrast, during the five years from 2000 through 2004, more than 400 such articles appeared."[46] Without suggesting any causal connection, it is nonetheless interesting to note that attention to the topic has kept pace with the growing public awareness of the general issue of inequality.

A major report issued by the US Department of Health and Human Services in 2000 defined health disparities as "differences that occur by gender, race or ethnicity, education or income, disability, geographic location or sexual orientation."[47] Of these characteristics, we focus on those that link to social class; that is, education and income, with occasional reference to race as well. The simple relationship of low socioeconomic status (SES) to a host of health disparities has, of course, been known for years.[48] By now a massive literature documenting class-related disparities exists, not just for the United States but for a host of other countries as well.[49] Given the ubiquitous influence of social class on virtually all aspects of social life, we should hardly be surprised by the basic relationship between SES and health. The animating question here, however, is slightly different. Does the severity of health disparities correlate with increases or decreases in economic inequality? Or framed in more contemporary terms, is there evidence that health disparities have grown apace of the widening income and wealth gap documented earlier? The answer is yes. To take but a few examples, we highlight trends in mortality and life expectancy, particularly among infants.

Pappas et al. were among the first researchers to take note of an apparent link between socioeconomic status and increasing health disparities. The focus of their groundbreaking article was over-time changes in the mortality rates of the most and least advantaged segments of the US population. Using both income and education as measures of social class, the authors show that the inverse relationship between SES and mortality was significantly greater in 1986 than in 1960.[50] In a particularly interesting article, Krieger et al. compare rates of "premature mortality" (that is, deaths among persons under 65) and "infant mortality" (deaths under age 1) in all US counties for 1960–2002. When it comes to differences in mortality by the class and racial makeup of those counties, their conclusions mirror the aggregate trends in income inequality discussed earlier. To quote the authors: "between 1960 and 2002, as U.S. premature mortality and infant death rates declined in all county income quintiles, socioeconomic and racial/ethnic inequities in premature mortality and infant death . . . shrank between 1966–1980, especially for U.S. populations of color; thereafter, the relative health inequities widened."[51] This sharp reversal in health outcomes closely mirrors the income trends reviewed earlier. As we showed, aggregate differences between those at the top and the bottom of the income distribution declined in the postwar period until sometime in the mid-1970s, increasing sharply after that. While the magnitude of these opposing trends is somewhat different in the two cases—that is, income versus mortality—their timing and direction run very much in parallel.

Perhaps no public health researcher has devoted as much empirical attention to the issue of health disparities—and especially recent increases in disparities—than Gopal Singh. In 2006, Singh and his co-author, Mohammed Siahpush, published an article entitled "Widening Socioeconomic Inequalities in U.S. Life Expectancy, 1980–2000." The title summarizes the central finding, but the details underscore just how striking the results are. In 1980–82, life expectancy at birth was, on average, 2.8 years shorter for the poorest segment of the US population compared to the most advantaged; by 1998–2000, the gap had grown to 4.5 years, a 60 percent increase in less than two decades.

Singh has also spent a good deal of time analyzing changes over time in the magnitude of a number of socioeconomic disparities related to childhood mortality. In 2007 he and Michael Kogan published an article in the *American Journal of Public Health* documenting significant increases in the relative mortality risk of socioeconomically disadvantaged infants in a host of categories. They summarize their findings as follows: "despite marked declines in child mortality, socioeconomic gradients...in overall child mortality increased substantially during the study period. During 1969–1971, children in the most deprived socioeconomic quintile had 52, 13, 69, and 76 percent higher risks of all-cause, birth defect, unintentional injury, and homicide mortality, respectively, than did children in the least deprived socioeconomic quintile. The corresponding relative risks increased to 86, 44, 177, and 159 percent, respectively from 1998 to 2000."[52] The same authors report very similar results for a study of over-time changes in the relative risk of different socioeconomic groups to infant, neonatal, and post-neonatal mortality. Once again, they show that "although absolute disparities have narrowed over time, relative socioeconomic disparities in infant mortality have increased since 1985."[53] Nor do these articles constitute the sum total of evidence in support of the general thesis. On the contrary, these articles are but the tip of a much larger iceberg. It is significant that Lisa Berkman titled her recent review article on the topic, "Social Determinants of Health in the United States: Are We Losing Ground?"[54] In her subsequent review of the literature, Berkman leaves little doubt that she thinks the answer to the question posed by her subtitle is "yes." As with income and wealth shares, the last few decades have seen a sharp increase in a host of class-related health disparities.

Based on what we know about the general causes of health disparities, should we really be surprised that the health trends closely mirror the economic patterns of the past three to four decades? We think not. After all, what are the major determinants of socioeconomic disparities in health? In their widely cited review of the literature, Adler and Newman identify three broad categories of causal factors: environmental exposure, health behavior, and health care. While it is hard to see how the major economic trends of the past three to four decades could have significantly impacted the first of these factors, the other two are much more subject to the influence of the growing class disparities in wealth and income. While socioeconomic differences in some health behaviors—such as smoking—appear to owe more to engrained subcultural norms than to fiscal resources, others—such as healthy diets and gym memberships—are powerfully shaped by both sets of factors.[55] As the economic gap has widened in this country, so too has the relative ability of the most and least advantaged segments of the US population to bear the costs associated with a host of important health behaviors. But it is the third and last of the aforementioned factors—health care— that bears the strongest imprint of the major economic trends of the past three to four decades. There is simply a myriad of ways in which economic disadvantage translates into substandard, limited, or no access to health care whatsoever. For starters, poverty constrains health-related expenditures the same way it does all other forms of consumer behavior. With so little discretionary income, the poor may be forced to forgo medicines, doctor's appointments, or other health-related expenses. But even if they are willing to bear the costs of, say, a visit to a doctor, the poor may struggle to find a doctor to visit. At the aggregate level, states with greater income inequality also have fewer primary care doctors per capita.[56] But nothing underscores the powerful impact of economic disadvantage on health more than its powerful effect on health care coverage. Among those who are uninsured, 63 percent are from low-income families (less than $50,000 household income), even though this demographic makes up only 42 percent of the country.[57] More worrisome still is the 35 percent of children (under 18) in poverty who are uninsured.[58] It is the strength of this relationship that makes the dramatic increase in the number of uninsured in recent decades so relevant to the issue of class disparities in health. Figure 6.9 documents the rise in the number of uninsured Americans between 1987 and 2011. Based on the important work on the topic by sociologist and physician Donald Barr, the figure depicts the harsh reality of the significant and steady increases in the numbers of those uninsured over the past quarter century.

Taken together—the increasing number of the uninsured and the disproportionate number of low-income families in that category— the class implications of the two trends are stark and sobering. With the absolute number of uninsured on the rise and an ever-larger percentage of that group drawn from the ranks of the poor, should we really be surprised that so many socioeconomic health disparities have increased in recent years? We close on an obvious, but critically important, topical note. As stark and worrisome as these health disparities are, we can

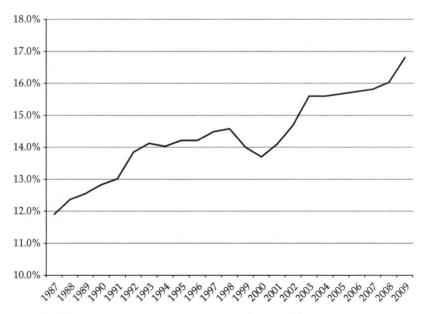

Figure 6.9 Percentage of the Population Uninsured, 1987–2009
Source: Data from U.S. Census Bureau; data previous to 2000 adjusted for change in methodology. Don Barr, Introduction to US Health Policy: The Organization, Financing and Delivery of Health-Care in America (Baltimore: Johns Hopkins University Press, 2011)

expect them to grow that much worse should the Affordable Health Care Act be effectively rescinded or somehow defunded.

Educational Inequality

We have always relied on our schools to level the socioeconomic playing field—to serve as the key institutional vehicle of upward mobility in the United States. While still criticizing widening gaps in other areas, we might yet reconcile ourselves to those trends if we could be reassured that class inequities in educational access and achievement were still narrowing. Then at least we could take some comfort in knowing that the traditional leveling function of education would, in time, begin to erode some of the disparities reviewed so far. This is not happening, however. On the contrary, the trends in education essentially mirror what we have seen in the other two areas. As Goldin and Katz document in their exhaustive history of education in the 20th century, US educational institutions functioned as a generally effective vehicle of class mobility for the first three quarters of the century.[59] The last three or four decades, however, have seen sharp increases in class-based disparities in any number of areas of educational preparation, access, and achievement. Space constraints preclude anything close to a full review of these trends, but we can convey something of the breadth and consistency of these trends.

From early childhood educational achievement through access to, and completion of, higher education and finally broad summary measures of number of years of schooling completed, we find growing disparities across the full span of academic life. We begin with what we know about trends in the "income achievement gap"—that is, the socioeconomic disparity in performance on standardized achievement tests—since World War II. In a recent summary chapter, Sean Reardon painstakingly reviews virtually all of the reading and math tests administered to nationally representative samples of US students since the advent of standardized testing. The socioeconomic trends in both math and reading achievement are virtually identical and, perhaps most tellingly, map neatly onto the more general pattern of rising economic inequality reviewed here. Between roughly 1950 and the mid-1970s, the income achievement gap held basically steady in reading and actually declined slightly in math.[60] After 1975, however, the size of the gap has grown significantly in both subjects. "Among children born around 1950, test scores of low-income children lagged behind those of their better-off peers by a little over half a standard deviation, about 60 points on an SAT-type test. Fifty years later, this gap was twice as large."[61] The fact that the black/white gap in test scores has dropped sharply over this same period of time only underscores the importance of Reardon's analyses on class inequities.

At the other end of the educational time line, we also find increasing disparities related to college education. For instance, Reardon et al. "find that low- and middle-income students are . . . extremely under-represented in the most selective colleges. Students from top income quintile families are seven to eight times more likely to enroll in a highly selective college than students from bottom quintile families."[62] More relevant to our focus on over-time change, however, is the fact that "this disparity appears to have grown over time, as more and more seats in highly selective schools have been occupied by students from high income families."[63] In another review chapter in the Duncan and Murnane volume, Bailey and Dynarski document a widening gap in college graduation rates between children from high- and low-income families. While rates for the children from high-income families jumped 21 percent for children born between the early 1960s and the early 1980s, the comparable increase for children at the low end of the income distribution was just four percentage points.[64] So in rates of access to, and graduation from, college, the disparity between the richest and poorest students also appears to have risen in recent decades.

Given these disparities, it is hardly surprising that the socioeconomic gap in the overall length of an individual's educational career has also widened over time. And here the increasing disparity in number of years of school completed appears to bear the clear statistical imprint of the general trend of rising income inequality. In a 2001 *American Journal of Sociology* article, Susan Mayer documented a very close association between a rise in income inequality and a significant increase in the disparity in mean number of years of school completed by low- and high-income students. In a chapter published 10 years after Mayer's article, Duncan and Murnane effectively extend her analyses, showing that the income gap in years of completed schooling has grown apace of the general rise in economic inequality in the United States.[65]

For those interested in exploring the general topic of educational disparities in greater depth, you could not do better than the definitive Duncan and Murnane volume on the subject, published in 2011, under the provocative title, *Whither Opportunity? Rising Inequality, Schools and Children's Life Chances*. Besides expanding greatly on the relatively modest number of specific studies referenced here, the volume also devotes a great deal of attention to the all-important issue of mechanisms. And while they are not always able to statistically connect this or that mechanism to growing class-based disparities on some educational dimension, the evidence they adduce for such links is invaluable, if still suggestive. Among the mechanisms explored in the volume are these:

- increasing class segregation in the composition of schools between 1972 and 1988;[66]
- much higher rates of student turnover in schools located in poor areas, creating lots of distractions and disruptions that undermine the educational process;[67]
- higher rates of teacher turnover and lower numbers of highly qualified credentialed teachers further compromise the educational effectiveness of schools serving large numbers of traditionally disadvantaged students.[68]

In truth, however, no mechanism may be more implicated in the growing socioeconomic inequities in education than simply the stark and ever increasing class disparities in wealth and income documented earlier. As a result of these economic trends "the resources available to low-income families to pay for their children's preschool, for access to good public schools or to private education, and for college investments have fallen farther behind those of affluent families."[69] But it is not simply the severe monetary constraints imposed on the poorest families that are relevant here. Just as important are the myriad ways the richest families can deploy their expanding resources to enhance and enrich their children's educational opportunities even more than before.

It seems only appropriate to give Duncan and Murnane the last word in this section. They close the way we started, by underscoring the distinctive significance of education to the consideration of trends in inequality in the contemporary United States. As they remind us

> American society relies on its schools to level the playing field for children born into different circumstances. More than any other institution, schools are charged with making equality of opportunity a reality. During a period of rising inequality, can schools play this critical role effectively? Or has growing income inequality affected families, neighborhoods, and labor markets in a manner that undercuts the effectiveness of schools serving disadvantaged populations?[70]

Based on the evidence reviewed here—and covered in much more depth in their book—it seems clear how the authors would answer their own questions. Far from fulfilling their traditional role as vehicles of upward mobility, schools also appear to have succumbed to the master trend in inequality that should, by now, be all too familiar. Rather than reducing inequality, our schools are now themselves magnifying and widening class disparities.

Summing Up

As Ronald Reagan prepared to take office in January 1981, the American political landscape still bore the unmistakable imprint of the liberal policy regime initiated by FDR during his first term in office. At 70 percent, the tax rate on the highest income earners remained at or near the elevated levels first put in place by Roosevelt. While nowhere near as large or generous in its entitlements as comparable European systems, the American welfare state had nonetheless grown more or less continuously—under Republican presidents no less than Democrats—since its modest beginnings in the New Deal. In general, the norms and expectations that had shaped policymaking for nearly half a century remained largely in place. Government action to mitigate disadvantage and "level the playing field" was still viewed positively by a majority of the American public. And reflecting 50 years of policymaking shaped by these liberal, ameliorative norms, levels of inequality in the United States remained low by American standards, and more or less average when viewed in comparative perspective. Finally, reflecting the stability of these policy parameters, the overall level of party polarization remained comparatively low as well, higher perhaps than in the golden era of bipartisanship during and immediately after World War II, but well below levels seen throughout most of the country's history.

Things could not be more different today. Even after the bruising, down-to-the-wire battle over the expiring Bush tax cuts at the close of 2012, Obama was only able to nudge the marginal tax rate on the highest income earners back to the 39.6 percent mark set by Clinton. In truth, any semblance of a general consensus on policy norms and expectations is long gone, replaced by two ultimately antithetical conceptions of government. Almost all Democrats continue to believe in some version of the liberal vision of an ameliorative state acting to advance and protect the interest of all Americans while the great majority of Republicans continue to push for no new taxes and deep cuts to programs they see as promulgating dependence by ever larger swaths of the American public. Reflecting the oil and water nature of these two views, party polarization now sits at levels not seen since the run up to the Civil War. These divisions have, in turn, led increasingly to government paralysis, with the 112th Congress (2011–13) passing fewer bills than any since 1940 and the 113th responsible for the first government shutdown in two decades. Finally, three decades of low taxes and deep cuts to social programs, have transformed the United States from a very typical country to the status of statistical outlier in its level of income inequality relative to all other comparable developed economies.

Very little of this change occurred on Reagan's watch. In fact, as we were at pains to point out in Chapter 5, the objective impact of Reagan's two-term presidency was relatively modest. Beset by a crippling early recession, spiraling deficits, the Iran-Contra scandal, and no shortage of determined, bipartisan opposition during his time in office, Reagan's significant achievements were largely confined to the first six months of his presidency. But that doesn't make his revolution any less significant for largely unfolding after he left office. On the contrary, it is testament to Reagan's enduring influence that most of the dramatic changes that we can plausibly attribute to him did not depend on his direct leadership. Instead, we see the longer-term effects of his revolution mediated by the three processes touched on in the chapter. First, by aggressively courting the religious right Reagan set in motion a longer-term effort by movement conservatives to wrest control of state party organizations from their secular—generally more moderate— counterparts. The result has been a steady rightward shift in the party, fueled by the embrace of ever more extreme positions on social issues. Second, and overlapping with the first process, Reagan effectively completed the electoral realignment of the South initiated by Nixon in 1968. Even as a majority of southern whites were voting Republican in presidential contests in the late 1960s and 1970s, the region remained fundamentally Democratic in all other respects. Reagan changed all of this; his popularity with southern whites was so great as to gradually transform the states of the former Confederacy from the most loyal Democratic to most reliable Republican region of the country. When the GOP finally claimed the majority of southern House seats in 1994, their advantage in the region was a scant two seats, 71–69. Today that margin has grown to 65 seats (108 to 43). By contrast, elsewhere in the country, Democrats outnumber Republicans 158 to 126. Quite simply, the GOP controls the House because of its dominance in the South. The great majority of Tea Party–aligned House members also hail from the South. As of January, 2013, 33 of the 48 members of the House Tea Party Caucus were from the former Confederate states or territories. And of the 80 House members who signed a letter to John Boehner urging him to shut the government down if Obamacare was not defunded—a group that conservative commentator Charles Kraut-hammer dubbed the "suicide caucus"—just over half came from southern districts.[71] Third, Reagan's charismatic leadership set in motion longer-term processes of socialization and recruitment that have brought countless self-identified, young Reagan conservatives into the ranks of the GOP over the past three decades. As those legions of young conservatives streamed into the party from the South or the religious right, the once proud tradition of moderate Republicanism has withered and died. By effectively rebranding the GOP as the party of small government, no taxes, and extreme views on social issues, Reagan helped create a culture that simply proved untenable for the party's once vibrant moderate/liberal wing. When Olympia Snowe (R-Maine) retired from the Senate in 2013—prompted by her increasing alienation from her party and frustration at the general gridlock in

Washington—it left the Republican congressional delegation without a single moderate member.

The combined force of all of these processes has made the Reagan Revolution an ongoing, living force in American politics, stronger today than ever before. It is almost certainly, however, a revolution that Reagan would not recognize as his own. For all his stark ideological rhetoric, Reagan, as president, proved to be a consummate, consensus politician. In his memoir of his time in the White House, David Stockman, Reagan's budget director, laments the administration's failure to achieve its revolutionary economic aims, essentially laying the blame at the president's door. Reagan, Stockman writes, "had no business trying to make a revolution because it wasn't in his bones. . . . [He] was a consensus politician, not an ideologue."[72] While most would view Reagan's willingness to compromise and work with others to find common, bipartisan, ground a virtue, Stockman sees it as a failing. It is this rigid adherence to extreme ideological positions—that is, no new taxes ever, no increase in the debt ceiling—that continues to divide the country, cripple governance, and distort and do violence to Reagan's presidential legacy. But nothing served to lock the GOP into this extreme position, or illustrate the continuing force of social movements in American politics, more than the events of Barack Obama's presidency. We take up that story in Chapter 7.

7

The Obama Years

Uncivil War

POLITICS AND GOVERNANCE has and always will be a blood sport of sorts. Given what is at stake, how could it be otherwise? Politics invariably involves decisions that impact the distribution of valued resources and opportunities, which in turn, shape the life chances of all groups in society. It also centers on complex issues inextricably linked to the principal sources of meaning and identity in people's lives. Quite simply, the material and symbolic stakes at the heart of policymaking are often enormous, accounting for the intense passions and deep divisions that frequently characterize the political arena. Although the United States has been generally spared the recurring violence that marks many political systems, it is certainly no stranger to convulsive political crisis and intense partisan animus. Even if we confine ourselves to just the last half century, we find no shortage of compelling examples.

We begin with the extraordinary passions aroused by the war in Vietnam. Those passions drove a president—Johnson—to withdraw from a presidential race that only a year or so before he seemed assured of winning. They also fueled four "days of rage" in the streets surrounding the Democratic National Convention in Chicago in 1968 and the effective suspension of much of American higher education following the shooting of student anti-war demonstrators at Kent State in April of 1970. Then there was the wrenching and sustained drama of Watergate, which brought the machinery of federal government to a standstill and ultimately occasioned the only resignation of a sitting president in the country's history. Or consider the revelation in November of 1986 that officials in the Reagan White House had arranged the sale of weapons to Iran, in part to funnel money to guerrilla groups fighting the Sandinista regime in Nicaragua (the "contras"). Both actions—the weapons sale and active support of the contras—were illegal at the time. The resulting two-year "Iran-contra scandal" emboldened Reagan's critics, hamstrung his administration, and led to the indictment of 14 White House officials. We close our abbreviated "greatest hits" list with the inflamed partisan passions that marked the sordid business of the Clinton impeachment proceedings. Much like the Iran-contra affair, the impeachment process held the administration and, by extension, the country hostage for better than a year. On December 19, 1998—on the basis of overwhelming party line voting—Clinton became the first elected president in US history to be impeached by the House.

These are all worthy examples of political crisis and intense partisan contention. Indeed, several of them would probably survive to reappear on any ultimate top 10 list of political crises in the history of the United States. And yet, when it comes to party polarization and government dysfunction, we contend that all of them pale in comparison to the acrimony, bitterness, and willful sabotage of policymaking that has characterized Barack Obama's time in office. Only the bitter run-up to the Civil War clearly surpasses the past six years for partisan bloodletting and the constant threat of governmental paralysis. The number of bills signed into law during a congressional term represents one very general way of measuring the effectiveness and efficiency of federal policymaking. If we assume that the need or demand for legislative action is roughly equal across every Congress, then the more bills passed in a session, the higher the level of government functioning. By that measure, the last two Congresses, the 112th (2011–13) and 113th (2013–15), have been among the least productive in recent history. Figure 7.1 tells the sorry story.

The 113th is still in session, but the 112th earned the dubious distinction of enacting fewer pieces of legislation than any of its postwar predecessors, with only 284 bills approved over the two-year span. By contrast, the 10 sessions of Congress that convened between 1948 and 1968 *averaged* close to 1,400 enactments per session.

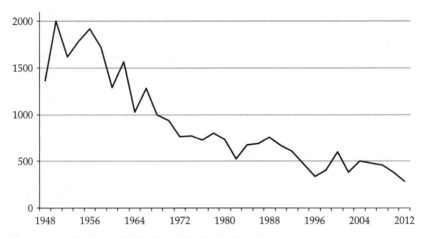

Figure 7.1 Number of Bills Passed by Each Congress, 1947–2012
Source: Office of the Clerk (library.clerk.house.gov/resume.aspx)

The Obama years should not, however, be seen as an undifferentiated whole. On the contrary, the partisan rancor and governmental dysfunction have escalated steadily over the course of his time in office and currently sit at what would seem to be the highest levels of his presidency. This chapter offers a detailed sketch and critical analysis of the Obama years, highlighting the escalating conflict and governmental paralysis alluded to. We see the Obama years comprised of three quite different periods, each corresponding to a discrete session of Congress. The first period includes both Obama's initial election in 2008 and the 111th Congress, which afforded him Democratic majorities in both the House and Senate. Shaped by the rise of the Tea Party in 2009 and the midterm elections of the following year, period two is marked by the deepening partisan divisions and intransigence of the 112th Congress. And finally, there is the present period—corresponding to the 113th Congress— defined not only by the yawning chasm between Republicans and Democrats but increasingly by the open warfare *within* the GOP. What accounts for the dramatic escalation in partisanship and dysfunction over these three periods? After first recounting the major events of the past six years, we close the chapter with an extended answer to this question; an answer that will effectively recast the events of the Obama years in terms of the book's two central themes. We contend that nothing has shaped the convulsive developments of the past six years so much as America's ongoing struggle with race and the by now familiar tug of war between movements, parties, and governmental institutions. Or to put it more concretely, it is the rise and growing radicalization of a racially inflected Tea Party movement that is largely responsible for the deepening divisions and government dysfunction that characterize the contemporary United States.

The Calm before the Storm: The 2008 Election and the 111th Congress

If the Obama years have been marked by deepening partisan division and escalating institutional dysfunction, they certainly didn't begin that way. In fact, the entire 2008 election cycle proved remarkably civil and orderly. Very quickly the Democratic primaries devolved into a historic battle between the first credible black and female presidential candidates in US history, Barack Obama and Hillary Rodham Clinton. Not surprisingly, given the stakes, there was no shortage of sharp exchanges and the usual charge that the other side was engaging in negative campaigning, or even thinly veiled racist or misogynistic attacks. On the whole, however, the primary battle was marked by substantive debate of very high quality and overriding respect between the two candidates; respect that would later lead Obama to appoint Hillary Clinton as his immensely popular secretary of state.

As for the Republicans, the election cycle was marked by only the slightest hints of the fear and loathing that would later fuel the Tea Party. While the "birther" controversy over whether Obama was truly an American citizen did, indeed, surface during the election, it appears to have been sparked by anonymous e-mails sent out by Hillary Clinton supporters late in the Democratic primary battle rather than any of the GOP candidates.[1] And to his credit, the eventual Republican nominee, John McCain, was much—and deservedly—praised for forcefully rejecting ugly attacks on Obama during a town hall meeting in Minnesota on October 10, 2008. In the most publicized exchange, McCain actually takes the microphone from a woman who seeks to defame Obama by calling him "an Arab." McCain forcefully rebuffs her saying, "No ma'am, he's a decent family man and citizen." But the more significant exchange, in our view, came earlier in the same town hall meeting when a man prefaces his question by saying that he and his wife "are scared of an Obama presidency." Although McCain could just as easily have ignored the man's preface and simply answered his question, he did not. Instead, despite being roundly booed for his remark, he chose to reassure the man with the following words: "I have to tell you, [Obama] is a decent person and a person you don't have to be scared of as president of the United States."

The ideological tone of the 2008 GOP primary battle was also markedly different from the one that played out four years later. Besides McCain, the race featured the 2012 nominee, Mitt Romney, and minister and former governor of Arkansas, Mike Huckabee. As he would in 2012, Romney sought to reassure primary voters that he was a "true conservative" and not the Massachusetts "moderate" his critics claimed. Under the pressures of the primary campaign, McCain too veered to the right, distancing himself from some of the moderate positions he had earlier embraced on such issues as immigration and the environment. For all the conservative tenor of the primary battle, however, the tone and substance of all three candidates' campaigns were far less strident and ideological than the positions the candidates would adopt in 2012.

In the end, McCain won handily, capturing two thirds of the delegates and nearly half of all votes cast in the primaries, and wrapping up the nomination well in advance of the Republican convention. And then there was the historic general election itself. While there was much talk of the vaunted "Bradley effect"[2] as the election neared, and credible speculation that America's deeply ingrained racism would, in the end, sabotage Obama's chances, the anticipated last-minute erosion of support never materialized. Instead, Obama scored a decisive and historic victory that left many older Americans—regardless of how they voted—amazed by what had transpired. Obama received 53 percent of the popular vote and more than two thirds of the electoral votes en route to a comfortable win. Comparisons to past Democratic candidates underscore just how historic the victory was. Obama's percentage of the popular vote was the largest for a Democratic candidate since Johnson's landslide win 44 years earlier. More impressive still, the total number of votes received by Obama—some 69.5 million—was the largest in US history and 10 million greater than the largest total ever recorded by a Democratic candidate. When George and Laura Bush warmly welcomed the Obamas to the White House on January 20, 2009, most Americans could be forgiven for believing that the country had not only turned a historic corner with respect to race, but that maybe—just maybe—a broader unity and consensus could be forged in the wake of the strident partisanship of the Bush and Clinton years. Sadly, "most Americans" would be proven wrong.

Robert Draper opens *Do Not Ask What Good We Do*, his 2012 portrait of the 112th House of Representatives, with a telling account of a dinner gathering of a number of Republican heavyweights held the very night the Obamas were making the rounds of the inaugural balls on January 20, 2009. The assembled GOP brain trust—including the likes of Eric Cantor, Paul Ryan, Jim DeMint, and Kevin McCarthy—used the occasion to fashion a general plan to reclaim the White House in 2012. The basic outline of the plan was clear: seek to obstruct the president's policy agenda at every turn, attack vulnerable Democrats relentlessly, reclaim the House in 2010 and use it to paralyze policymaking en route to winning the White House and the Senate in 2012. As Newt Gingrich, another of that night's attendees intoned as the dinner was breaking up, "You'll remember this as the day the seeds of 2012 were sown."

It did not quite work out that way, with the Democrats holding on to both the White House and the Senate in 2012, but the general vision of a united, unyielding, and obstructionist GOP congressional delegation and a triumphant return to power in the House in 2010, proved prescient. Still, with the Democrats in control of both houses of Congress during Obama's first two years in office, the president was able, despite the willful intransigence of Republican lawmakers, to compile an impressive record of legislative achievement. Besides his signature policy enactment, the 2010 Patient Protection and Affordable Care Act, Obama's first two years in office also saw passage of two bills designed to counteract the effects of the 2008 financial meltdown, the American Recovery and Reinvestment Act of 2009 and the 2010 Tax Relief, Unemployment Insurance Reauthorization and Job Creation Act. Obama was also able to secure passage of legislation to strengthen the oversight and regulation of Wall Street (e.g., Dodd-Frank Wall Street Reform and Consumer Protection Act) and to repeal the military's "Don't Ask, Don't Tell" policy. Add to that the New START arms control treaty with Russia and the effective end of the American military presence in Iraq and you have, in the estimation of many observers, the most successful first two years in office by any president since Reagan. But one of Obama's chief achievements, the legislative and financial measures that stabilized the economy following the meltdown of 2008, also helped to catalyze a populist backlash that was destined not only to make the remainder of his first term in office that much more difficult, but, more importantly, usher in the era of extreme partisan division and dysfunction in which we are still mired.

Let the (Tea) Party Begin

Like many social movements, the rising tide of collective action that would come to be known as the Tea Party developed out of disparate strands of protest in the early months of 2009. And while subsequent events and the characteristics of movement participants would in time make it clear that antipathy toward Obama is central to the movement, the nominal trigger for the protests was diffuse anger at the federal "bailout" of Wall Street and generalized opposition to "big government." Among the events generally credited with galvanizing the new movement are the following:

- January 24, 2009—Trevor Leach, chairman of the Americans for Liberty in New York State, organizes a "tea party" to protest the "obesity tax" proposed by Governor David Patterson.
- February 16, 2009—Conservative blogger and activist Keli Carender organizes a "Porkulus Protest" in Seattle to protest the stimulus bill signed into law by President Obama the following day.
- February 19, 2009—CNBC business reporter Rick Santelli delivers an on-air rant against the federal government's plan to refinance mortgages, suggesting that traders should hold a "tea party" on July 1 and dump the derivatives into the Chicago River.

From there the use of the term and the pace of grass-roots action in the name of the Tea Party Movement spread rapidly, punctuated by nationwide protests on April 15, 2009, that drew an estimated 300,000 people.

As with all movements that suddenly burst on the scene, the Tea Party inspired wildly varying accounts of its origins. To those on the right, the movement was a spontaneous expression of grass-roots patriotic populism. To many on the left, the "movement" was derided as an "astroturf" imposter rather than a genuine bottom-up populist uprising. These critics saw the hand—and deep pockets—of right-wing elites like the Koch brothers and longtime Republican operative Dick Armey behind the "movement." A documentary on the movement released by the Media Education Foundation in 2011 best expressed this cynical view. The title tells you all you need to know about the filmmaker's take on the movement: *The Billionaires' Tea Party: How Corporate America Is Faking a Grassroots Revolution.*

As more systematic scholarship on the Tea Party has come out, however, it seems clear that the true nature of the movement lies somewhere between the two views. In their important 2012 book, Skocpol and Williamson offer what we see as the most accurate portrait of the movement. They characterize it as

> neither a top-down creation nor a bottom-up explosion. This remarkable political outpouring is best understood as a combination of three intertwined forces. Each force is important in its own right, and their interaction is what gives the Tea Party its dynamism, drama and wallop. Grassroots activism is certainly a key force, energized by angry, conservative-minded citizens who have formed vital local and regional groups. Another force is the panoply of national funders and ultra-free-market advocacy groups that seek to highlight and leverage grassroots efforts to further their long-term goal of remaking the Republican Party, pushing it towards the hard right on matters of taxation, public spending, and government regulation. Finally, the Tea Party cannot be understood without recognizing the mobilization provided by conservative media hosts who openly espouse and encourage the cause.[3]

It is true, though, that if the movement was initially known primarily by its large, loud, and colorful mass protests and demonstrations, by 2010 the Tea Party had largely morphed into an electoral movement committed to advancing its goals—ousting Obama, repealing the Affordable Care Act, reducing taxes, and downsizing if not dismantling government—through electoral means. Initially these means centered on recruiting candidates committed to Tea Party aims to run against offending Democrats. Fairly quickly, however—and accelerating over time—this conventional party dynamic was augmented by efforts to identify suspect Republicans for ouster in favor of movement-approved candidates. What is remarkable is just how quickly and effectively the movement implemented this electoral strategy. Indeed, if we date the movement's "coming out" party to the April 15, 2009, nationwide "tax protests," it took the Tea Party little more than 18 months to forcefully assert its presence on the national electoral stage.

The 2010 Midterm Elections

If nothing is certain but death and taxes, losses in midterm elections by the party occupying the White House is as close to a sure bet as we have in American politics. Only twice since Roosevelt's victory in 1932 has the party in control of the White House not suffered losses in either or both houses of Congress in the midterm election. Moreover, both exceptions occurred under very unusual circumstances. The first came in 1934 at the height of the Depression when popular anger at those deemed responsible for the crisis—that is, Republicans—remained very high. The second came in 2002, as partisan rancor gave way for a time to a national unity forged in the crucible of the 9/11 terrorist attacks. In all other off-year elections—21 in all—the party in power suffered losses in the House, Senate, or typically both. But even by these normal standards, the Democratic losses in the 2010 midterm elections were very large. Only once since 1930 were the losses in the House greater than the 63 seats lost by the Democrats in 2010. More important, the gains were more than enough for the GOP to regain control of the House, denying to Obama the advantages of the unified government he had enjoyed during his first two years in office. The Republicans also gained six Senate seats, six statehouses, and an estimated 700 additional seats in state legislatures.[4] The losses left the Democrats reeling and the heady triumph of 2008 a distant memory for many.

On their face, the Democratic losses would seem to offer ample evidence of the electoral impact of the Tea Party. On the other hand, given the expected nature of midterm losses, how can we be sure the Republicans wouldn't have achieved the gains under any circumstances, especially given the dire economic straits the country was in at the time of the election? It is worth remembering that when Obama took office in January 2009, the US unemployment rate stood at 7.6 percent, bad in comparison to the 4.9 figure of exactly a year earlier, but nothing compared to the 10.2 percent it would hit in October of 2009. Worse yet, sitting at 9.8 percent, the figure had barely budged when the country went to the polls in the midterms a year later. Never mind that the economic meltdown had commenced on George W. Bush's watch. Given how bad things were in November of 2010, it is not unreasonable to imagine that the Democrats would have been punished for the recession with or without the help of the Tea Party. We are quite sure they would have been, but the magnitude of the setbacks and the fact that the losses occurred at all levels of government—local, state, and national—strongly support the view that the Tea Party significantly escalated the midterm losses we might have expected under normal circumstances. We strongly agree with the bottom line assessment of the movement's effect offered by Skocpol and Williamson:

> While the conventional wisdom about the Tea Party as driver of the GOP victories sometimes gets carried away, we think the doubters underestimate the impact of combined Tea Party forces on GOP momentum going into November 2010. Most basically, grassroots Tea Party protests and local network-building helped the Republican Party escape the defeatism that pervaded party ranks after the massive defeats the Republicans suffered in 2008.... Moreover, the huge media coverage for Tea Party complaints about "big government" spending and bailouts... helped Republicans and conservatives to reset national agendas of debate. People stopped talking about "change we can believe in" and started talking about government tyranny.[5]

To these two components of the movement must be added the third emphasized by Skocpol and Williamson: the moneyed elites who bankrolled the various insurgent Tea Party candidates to the tune of countless millions. It is doubtful that these elites would have been anywhere near as active and generous in 2010 absent the grass-roots energy supplied by the movement. To us, however, the more compelling evidence of the movement's influence in American politics comes after the election in the form of the unprecedented gridlock and dysfunction characteristic of the 112th Congress.

The 112th Congress: The First Debt Ceiling Crisis and Other Adventures

If Republicans in the 112th Congress were to distinguish themselves by raising brinksmanship and legislative hostage taking to new heights, we would do well to remember that the will to obstruct was already in place before the Tea Party contingent arrived on the scene in January of 2011. Recall that it had been central to the general plan embraced by the Republican brain trust who dined together on the night of Obama's initial inaugural back in 2009. The intent to obstruct and block policymaking had also been acknowledged—in surprisingly forthright fashion—by Senate Minority Leader Mitch McConnell (R-Kentucky) who on the eve of the midterm elections stated in an interview that "the single most important thing we want to achieve is for President Obama to be a one-term president." It is true, however, that the recapture of the House and the arrival of the Tea Party reinforcements allowed GOP lawmakers to achieve previously unknown levels of obstruction and dysfunction. No less distinguished and bipartisan observers of Congress than Thomas Mann and Norman Ornstein describe the resulting 112th Congress in the following unequivocal terms: "what followed was an appalling spectacle of hostage taking—most importantly, the debt ceiling crisis—that threatened a government shutdown and public default, led to a downgrading of the country's credit, and blocked constructive action to nurture an economic recovery or deal with looming problems of deficits and debt."[6] And just to make sure that readers didn't follow convention and blame both sides equally for the mess, the authors go on to make it clear where they think the central problem lies:

> However awkward it may be for the traditional press and non-partisan analysts to acknowledge, one of the two major parties, the Republican Party, has become an insurgent outlier—ideologically extreme; contemptuous of the inherited social and economic policy regime; scornful of compromise; unpersuaded by conventional

understanding of facts, evidence, and science; and dismissive of the legitimacy of its political opposition. When one party moves this far from the center of American politics, it is extremely difficult to enact policies responsive to the country's most pressing challenges.[7]

The extreme partisanship and intent to obstruct were evident in the first significant vote taken by the new Senate. The vote, on January 26, 2010, was on a resolution to appoint an 18-member bipartisan task force charged with crafting a comprehensive plan to address the nation's record deficit. Procedurally the task force was to be "fast tracked"; that is, its plan would bypass all committees and be brought straight to the House floor for an up-or-down vote. The resolution was co-authored by Judd Gregg (R-New Hampshire) and Kent Conrad (D-North Dakota) with significant bipartisan support, in the form of numerous co-sponsors from both parties. And while McConnell was not one of those co-sponsors, he had for at least a year been touting the Gregg-Conrad proposal as the "best way to address the crisis.... It deserves support from both sides of the aisle."[8] And yet, on the day in question, the resolution went down to defeat when the Senate fell 7 votes shy of the 60 needed to end a determined Republican filibuster on the matter. If Republicans helped craft and co-sponsor the resolution, who was behind the filibuster? Mann and Ornstein capture what they call the "Alice-in-Wonderland" quality of the episode and the 112th Congress more generally:

> Among those who voted to sustain the filibuster and kill the resolution were Mitch McConnell and John McCain. [They were] . . . joined in opposition by six other original co-sponsors, all Republicans. Never before have co-sponsors of a major bill conspired to kill their own idea. . . . Why did they do so? Because President Barack Obama was for it, and its passage might gain him political credit.[9]

Although it wasn't apparent at the time, the willful sabotage of the resolution marked the beginning of the first debt ceiling crisis of the Obama presidency. Why would the Republicans block the very approach to the problem they had been advocating for some time? Denying Obama a political victory is no doubt part of the answer, as Mann and Ornstein suggest. But we see another, arguably more,

important calculus at work here. Now that they controlled the House—
and a much more rigidly ideological House at that—Republican leaders
were prepared to gamble that they could extract greater concessions
from the White House on spending by playing chicken on the debt
ceiling than they could through the kind of comprehensive, bipartisan
"grand bargain" promised by the Conrad-Gregg proposal. This is not to
say that all the frustrating twists and turns and dispiriting drama that
accompanied the actual summer 2011 debt ceiling negotiations were
knowingly and precisely orchestrated by the Republicans; only that
their twin desires to inflict partisan injury on Obama while enacting
deep cuts in federal funding emboldened them to threaten a government default, regardless of its impact on the fragile economy.

If the January defeat of the Conrad-Gregg resolution set the debt
ceiling debacle in motion, the actual crisis played out in the summer,
escalating with the approach of the date—August 2—that Treasury
Secretary Timothy Geithner had set as the official default. Since others
have already recounted, in gory detail, the tortured negotiations that
defined the crisis, we are spared that depressing assignment.[10] More
important, in any case, than the blow-by-blow specifics of the crisis is
an understanding of the recurring strategic dynamic that shaped the
impasse, not just over the debt ceiling but on all significant financial
matters during the 112th Congress.

For all our stress on the centrifugal force that movements often exert on
parties and, by extension, policymaking, one would be hard-pressed to
find a better example of this dynamic in recent years than the impact that
the Tea Party has had on the Republican Party and Congress since 2010.
Consider only the Republicans' unprecedented approach to the debt
ceiling. From 1960 through 2010 Congress raised the debt ceiling 78 times,
49 of them with a Republican in the White House, and although on a few
of those occasions negotiations had been heated, "no [previous] debt limit
increase had any preconditions attached."[11] In both 2011 and again in 2013,
Republicans insisted there would be. Here we focus on the first of those
crises. In 2011, the Republicans were prepared to hold the debt ceiling
hostage to extract maximum concessions from the White House on
budget cuts. But while the emphasis throughout the crisis was on the
impasse between the two parties, the key recurring dynamic in the crisis
owed more to the party-movement cleavage within the GOP than simple

partisanship. For all their seeming intransigence, veteran GOP lawmakers—Boehner and McConnell, for sure, but apparently even such young guns as Eric Cantor (R-Virginia), Paul Ryan (R-Wisconsin), and Kevin McCarthy (R-California)—were not disposed to let the country default on its obligations. The same could not be said, however, for the majority of freshmen GOP House members who rode the Tea Party wave into Washington the previous fall. It was their presence in the House that made the Republican threat of default so credible. Those movement conservatives and first-term House members were perfectly prepared to let the government default if that is what it would take to bring the bloated federal establishment to heel.

Three times during the crisis, efforts to fashion some kind of bipartisan agreement collapsed when it became clear that the Republican leadership in the House would not be able to deliver the votes required to secure the bargain. In each case, the irresistible force of routine—if extreme—party politics collided with the immovable object of a social movement. Only at the 11th hour and with serious arm-twisting was a deal finally forged, but only because the really tough decisions on entitlement reform, budget cutting, and new revenues were referred to a 12-member "super committee" created as part of the agreement. Predictably, that committee would come to naught, disbanding later in the year after failing to reach bipartisan accord on even the basic framework for any kind of "grand bargain." In short, the resolution of the debt ceiling crisis amounted to no resolution at all. The deal did little more than kick the fiscal can just a bit farther down the road, presaging the ongoing series of fiscal and governance crises that culminated in the government shutdown and second debt ceiling debacle of fall 2013.

The day after the agreement was announced, Wall Street offered its own no confidence vote on the state of the federal government when the Dow Jones Industrial Average dropped 266 points, wiping out in a single day all the gains that had accrued to that point in the year. Standard and Poor's followed suit two days later, downgrading the country's credit rating for the first time in US history. It explained its action by noting that the "political brinksmanship of recent months highlights what we see as America's governance and policy making becoming less stable, less effective, and less predictable than what we previously believed."[12] And while the economic blowback from the debacle was perhaps less than some had feared, the economy did stall in the last quarter, only adding to the misery of the millions of Americans whose lives had been disrupted by the worst economic crisis since the Great Depression.

Far from being anomalous, the debt ceiling crisis was only the most widely publicized instance of legislative brinksmanship during the 112th Congress. Space constraints preclude a full accounting of all the congressional misadventures that occurred in 2011 and 2012, but mention of a few others affords a fuller picture of just how ubiquitous dysfunction and extreme partisanship were during these years. The serial machinations over the "continuing resolution" early in the session proved to be something of a dry run for the later debt ceiling crisis. Historically, such resolutions—which allow Congress to continue stop-gap funding of routine government functions when they have not been able to enact all necessary spending bills on time—have been a Congressional staple, a pragmatic response to the complex exigencies of federal spending, just as raising the debt ceiling has been routine and generally noncontroversial. But not on Obama's watch; reflecting their resolve to oppose him at every turn, the Republicans intentionally passed resolutions of much shorter duration than in the past. In all, six resolutions were enacted for fiscal 2011 alone. The practical effect of this was to keep the threat of some form of shutdown continuously alive as House Republicans orchestrated a series of mini-crises that kept the country and its fragile economy on tenterhooks much of the year.

Negotiations over the last of these six resolutions were the most contentious and protracted, stretching over two months and, in a preview of both subsequent debt ceiling crises, resolved only an hour before the midnight April 8 deadline set by Congress. And once again, voting on the bill bore the clear imprint of the movement-party split within the GOP. Even with $38 billion in budget cuts as the price the Democrats and the administration had to pay to secure the continuing resolution, 59 movement conservatives in the House defied GOP leadership and voted against the measure. The fact that that many House Republicans were willing to vote "no" was not only an embarrassment to John Boehner and Paul Ryan—who had fashioned the agreement—but a harbinger of the open warfare to come in the party.

It may be, however, that the real measure of the willful GOP obstruction of governance in the 112th Congress is reflected best not in the series of 11th hour legislative crises it orchestrated but in the way it used two traditionally routine procedural mechanisms—the filibuster and confirmation of executive appointments—to impede policymaking and frustrate the administration at every turn. Consider the filibuster. For older Americans—or fans of classic movies—the term is likely to conjure up images of an exhausted and hoarse Jimmy Stewart in *Mr. Smith Goes to Washington*, heroically deploying the filibuster as the tool of the little guy to break the power of a corrupt politician from his home state. Many others will associate it—less nobly perhaps—with the battle over racial matters in Congress, as southern senators spoke in concert for days to block consideration of civil rights legislation. Either way, the tendency is to think of the filibuster as something of an anachronism; a procedural throwback to an earlier period in Congress. Nothing could be further from the truth. As Figure 7.2 shows, use of the filibuster—and the need for cloture motions to close off debate—has risen dramatically in recent years, closely tracking increasing party polarization in Congress.

In all of 1965–66, as the Senate wrestled with highly charged civil rights issues, the total number of cloture motions filed was just eight. In Obama's first year in office, that number soared to nearly 140. It is worth quoting Mann and Ornstein at length on the matter:

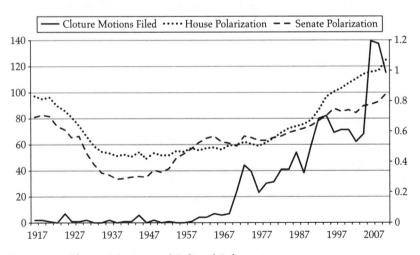

Figure 7.2 Cloture Motions and Political Polarization, 1917–2012
Sources: United States Senate (Senate.gov); Polarized America/voteview.com

Since Obama's inauguration in 2009, the filibuster is more often a stealth weapon, which minority Republicans use not to highlight an important national issue but to delay and obstruct quietly on nearly all matters, including routine and widely supported ones. It is fair to say that this pervasive use of the filibuster has never before happened in the history of the Senate.... This is more evidence that senators have distorted a practice designed for rare use—to let a minority of any sort have its say in matters of great national significance—to serve other purposes. One purpose is rank obstruction, to use as much precious time as possible on the floor of the Senate to retard progress on business the majority wants to conduct.[13]

We offer up the Worker, Homeownership, and Business Assistance Act of 2009 as a poster child for the legislative dysfunction ushered in by Obama's election. The bill, whose main goal was simply to extend unemployment benefits at the height of the recession, faced no opposition in the Senate whatsoever. In fact, the bill would ultimately pass unanimously (98–0) in November of 2009, but not before being subjected to two filibusters. Each filibuster lasted two days before cloture motions could be introduced to close off debate. Under Senate rules, however, even successful cloture motions require an additional 30 hours of post-cloture debate. When all was said and done, a bill that was opposed by no one took four torturous weeks to work its way through the Senate. Why would the Republicans mount a filibuster against a bill they unanimously supported? The answer is as straightforward as it is depressing. Harkening back to Senate Minority Leader Mitch McConnell's goal of making Barack Obama a one-term president, the misuse of the filibuster in this, and many other cases, was simply designed to gum up the works in hope that, at a time of real economic crisis, the American public would get so frustrated with the lack of results in Washington that they would take it out on the ruling Democrats. No doubt the stunning success enjoyed by the GOP in the 2010 midterm elections convinced Republicans that the strategy was working. This may help, in part, to explain why the level of dysfunction and willful obstruction reached new heights in the 112th and 113th Congresses.

The misuse of the filibuster has had an especially deleterious effect on the often mundane but important procedural matter of presidential appointments, which historically, have tended to be routine and noncontroversial. Consider the matter of judicial appointments and in particular, the stark contrast in the Senate's response to the nominees proposed by Reagan and Obama. Reagan as we noted in Chapter 6 (see note 3), broke with convention and took an unprecedented ideological approach to judicial appointments. To achieve his aim of remaking the federal judiciary, Reagan put in place a systematic process for identifying and vetting potential nominees. At the heart of the system were formal interviews with judicial candidates that were unprecedented and controversial in their explicit political aim. The interviews amounted to an ideological litmus test that candidates had to pass in order to be put forward for judicial vacancies. Needless to say, Reagan's unprecedented ideological approach to judicial appointments was controversial. Still, with a few notable exceptions—such as the Bork Supreme Court nomination—Reagan's appointments were acted on with dispatch and considerable bipartisan cooperation. Two figures are worth noting here. First, during Reagan's initial term in office, roughly 90 percent of his circuit court nominees were confirmed. Second, on average, it took the Judiciary Committee just 20 days to bring Reagan's judicial nominees to the full Senate floor for consideration. This speed allowed Reagan to appoint more judges than any other president in history. How times and Senate norms have changed. Mann and Ornstein ask us to

> consider President Obama's nomination of Judge Barbara Milano Keenan to the U.S. Court of Appeals for the Fourth Circuit. Judge Keenan's qualifications were impeccable; as a judge on Virginia's Supreme Court, she was widely praised. But her confirmation in March 2011 was subject to filibuster and a cloture motion that passed 99–0, followed by a similar 99–0 confirmation vote. In the case of Judge Keenan, her confirmation occurred a full 169 days after her nomination, and 124 days after the Judiciary Committee unanimously reported her nomination to the floor.[14]

Despite unanimous GOP support for Judge Keenan, Republican senators did everything they could to delay action on her nomination for as long as possible. As with the Worker, Homeownership, and Business Assistance Act of 2009, the intent was the same: to frustrate the administration and minimize Obama's influence over policymaking.

As much as we might deplore this intentional delay of unopposed judicial candidates, the practice pales in comparison to what we see as a far more troubling and arguably anti-democratic misuse of the filibuster to block certain executive appointments brought forth by Obama. Two examples will serve to make the point. The first was Donald Berwick, whom the administration nominated to head the Centers for Medicare and Medicaid Services, the institution charged with implementing much of the Affordable Care Act. Despite Berwick's stellar credentials as both scholar and practitioner, GOP senators vowed to block his appointment. Obama countered by making Berwick a "recess appointment," which allowed him to bypass Senate confirmation but also greatly reduced the term of his appointment and his institutional authority. Frustrated by these restrictions, Berwick resigned his post, leaving the position vacant and slowing the implementation of the new health care reforms. That, of course, was exactly what the Republican senators were hoping for. But let's be clear; this is significantly different from delaying the inevitable confirmation of a clearly qualified judicial appointee. By virtue of their oath of office, senators vow to "support and defend the Constitution of the United States." It seems to us that seeking to compromise or impede the implementation of a federal law violates the spirit if not the strict letter of the aforementioned oath.

Nor was this an isolated incident. Emboldened by their success in effectively frustrating Berwick's appointment, Senate Republican leaders made it clear that they were committed to blocking any candidate the administration brought forward to head the Consumer Financial Protection Bureau (CFPB) mandated by the Dodd-Frank Wall Street Reform and Consumer Protection Act. The reason: their general opposition to the law, never mind that it had already been enacted by Congress in the previous term. Elizabeth Warren served ably as interim head of the CFPB from September 2010 through July of 2011. Based on her knowledge and experience in the interim post, Warren would seem to have been the logical choice for the permanent position, but knowing how determined Republican senators were to block her appointment, Obama chose not to bring her name forward. (Warren had the last laugh, however, gaining entrance to the very body that had frustrated her appointment, by virtue of her highly publicized win over Scott Brown in their 2012 Massachusetts Senate race. We suspect that more than a few GOP senators wish they had encouraged her nomination after all.) But that wasn't quite the end of the CFPB story. President Obama nominated Richard Cordray for the post. At his confirmation hearing, Republican senators treated Cordray, a former Ohio attorney general, much more kindly than they had Warren. Indeed, they were nearly unanimous in their praise for the qualifications and general character of the nominee, all the while making it perfectly clear that Cordray had no more chance to be confirmed than Warren. In the end, Obama was, once again, forced to make Cordray a recess appointment, reducing his tenure and authority in the bureau he had been appointed to head. We close this section by quoting Mann and Ornstein's bottom-line normative judgment on the Republican tactics on display in these and other instances:

> Whether lawmakers like or dislike laws, they are under oath to carry them out. They can move, under their Article 1 powers, to repeal the laws, amend the laws, or even cut off funding for them....And, of course, they are free to run in the next election against those laws. But to use the hold and filibuster to undermine laws on the books from being implemented is an underhanded tactic, one reflecting, in our view, the increasing dysfunction of a parliamentary-style minority party distorting rules and norms of the Senate to accomplish its ideological and partisan ends.[15]

Mann and Ornstein's take on the matter stands for us as a compelling summary judgment of the state of willful Republican obstruction during the whole of the 112th Congress.

The 113th Congress: Open Warfare in the GOP

Given that one of the main aims motivating Republican obstruction had been to limit Obama to one term, one might have thought that his reelection would have tempered the extreme partisanship characteristic of his first four years in office. It did not. Hope for a bit more legislative cooperation on pressing, popular issues such as gun control and immigration reform quickly faded as partisan lines hardened and gridlock set in once more. Even as public support for gun control jumped sharply in the wake of the December 2012 killing of 20 children and 6 staff members at Sandy Hook Elementary School, the president and

Democratic proponents of reform were unable to muster the necessary support in the Senate to even expand background checks on those buying guns, let alone restrict the sale of assault weapons or high-capacity magazines. And, after a promising bipartisan start in the Senate, the immigration reform effort was effectively tabled in the far more conservative, Republican-controlled House. But nothing signaled the continuation of the extreme partisanship and legislative dysfunction of Obama's first term more than the government shutdown and second debt ceiling crisis that unfolded in the fall of 2013.

At first blush, the fall fiasco seemed like déjà vu, very much apiece with the serial crises that marked Obama's first term. The similarities were striking. As before, the Republicans sought to hold hostage familiar fiscal deadlines—the need to pass a new continuing resolution by October 1 and the looming debt ceiling deadline of October 17—to force concessions from the administration. The crisis was once again centered in and initiated by the Republican-controlled House, with House Speaker John Boehner again unable or unwilling to bring his hard-core Tea Party contingent to heel to resolve the crisis. Finally, the fall events were only resolved through an 11th hour high-wire act that rattled the American public and world markets while inflicting damage on the still struggling US economy.[16]

For all the similarities, however, the 2013 shutdown and debt ceiling fiasco was different in two crucial respects from the serial crises recounted earlier. First, while all previous crises had involved Republican efforts to reduce the deficit by imposing new spending cuts on the administration, the 2013 gambit had as its goal the effective dismantling of a piece of legislation enacted three years earlier—the Affordable Care Act— affirmed as constitutional by the Supreme Court in 2012, and partially implemented at the time of the shutdown. But it isn't simply the substitution of one goal for another that we mean to highlight here.[17]

Second, and perhaps owing to the unprecedented—and quixotic— nature of the new goal for which the activists were willing to risk government default, the 2013 crisis was marked by a sharp escalation in intramural conflict and open enmity within Republican ranks. In effect, the crisis marked the point in time when the tensions that had been building since the 2010 midterm elections between the Tea Party activists and more traditional party loyalists flared into open warfare.

Race and the Tug of War between Movement and Party

The striking escalation in partisan bloodletting and governmental dys-function over the course of the past six years bear the clear imprint of the two central structuring forces that we have sought to highlight in the book: the continuing—indeed *increasing*—significance of race in American politics; and the dynamic interaction of, and tension between, movement and party as forms and logics of politics. More to the point, we see the rise and radicalization of a racially inflected Tea Party movement as largely responsible for the deepening crisis in American political life.

The *Increasing* Significance of Race

In the aftermath of Obama's victory over Romney in the 2012 general election, there was much talk about how the Republicans were out of touch with the shifting demography of the United States; how they had become a party of older, white voters and unless they found ways to attract minority and younger voters, they were doomed to suffer the same fate in future elections. And while this analysis is demonstrably true, the skewed racial demography of the Republican Party is hardly new. Since Nixon and others first used a thinly veiled politics of racial reaction to court southern white voters and other racial conservatives in the mid- to late 1960s, the GOP has been moving steadily to the right and becoming ever more dependent on a racially skewed demographic base. This is not to say that today's GOP is, in racial terms, the same as it was in 1972 or during Reagan's years in office, or even under George W. Bush. On the contrary, we claim that, owing much to the Tea Party, the current Republican Party is *more* racially conservative and demo-graphically exclusive than at any point in the past 50 years. But before we take up these claims, we want to first emphasize the essential conti-nuity we see reflected in the racial politics embraced by the GOP over the past half century.

We begin with the briefest recap of the story we told in Chapter 3 of the dramatic shift in the racial geography of American politics. On the eve of the 1960s, the racial politics of the two major parties was, notwithstanding cosmetic differences, largely unchanged since the con-solidation of Jim Crow laws in the late 1800s. The GOP congressional delegation remained far more racially liberal than its Democratic counterpart. Notwithstanding a certain rhetorical embrace of the need for civil rights reform, Democratic presidential aspirants remained generally committed to accommodating the racial sensibilities of the party's Dixiecrat wing. Accordingly, the white South remained the most loyal and strategically important component of the Democratic electoral coalition. And while African Americans had also aligned with the Democrats during Roosevelt's time in office, the "black vote" remained at least somewhat competitive, with Eisenhower attracting roughly 40 percent of all black voters in 1956.

The political environment that had sustained this particular system of racial politics was irrevocably altered by the revival and dramatic expansion of the civil rights movement in the spring of 1960 and the reactive rise of the white resistance countermovement in that same year. Consistent with our stress on the centrifugal force of movements in US history, over the course of the 1960s these companion struggles pushed the two parties in opposite directions. Subject to the unrelenting pressure of the civil rights revolution, the Democrats shifted left, first tentatively and reluctantly under Kennedy and then much more quickly and dramatically with Johnson in the White House. At the same time, and despite protests from the dominant centrist, pro-civil rights wing of the party, the GOP began to shift to the right in an effort to claim the votes of a white South angered by the Democrats' increasingly aggressive advocacy of civil rights reform. And when the southern resistance movement morphed into the nationwide "white backlash" of the mid- to late 1960s, the rightward shift of the GOP only accelerated. Running on what he called his "southern strategy," Nixon claimed the White House in 1968 and then spent much of his first term in office perfecting a politics of racial reaction to cement his appeal with white Southerners and racial conservatives elsewhere in the country. In their 1991 book, *Chain Reaction*, the Edsalls succinctly describe the racial politics that animated the Republican "brand" pioneered by Nixon. In their words:

> Race was central, Nixon and key Republican strategists began to recognize, to the fundamental conservative strategy of establishing a new polarization of the electorate, a polarization isolating a liberal, activist, culturally permissive, rights oriented, and pro-black Democratic Party against those unwilling to pay the financial costs of this reconfigured social order.[18]

The strategy was to depict the GOP as the party of the law-abiding, tax-paying, "silent (mostly white) majority" and demonize the Democrats as the party of liberals and the undeserving (disproportionately minority) poor whose dependence on social programs was taking money out of the pockets of hard-working, overtaxed (white) Americans. Sound familiar? It should since this very same critique was invoked by Mitt Romney in his famous—or infamous—disputation on the "47 percent" at a fund-raising event during the 2012 presidential campaign. Romney's intent, in making the remark, was to stress just what a difficult challenge he faced in the election, given the dependence of large segments of the American public on "big government." As he saw it, "there are 47 percent of the people who will vote for the president no matter what.... [They] are dependent upon government [and] believe that they are victims, who believe that government has a responsibility to care for them, who believe they are entitled to health care, to food, to housing...you name it."[19]

Interestingly, while Romney apologized and sought to distance himself from his remarks when they first became public, he returned—even more explicitly—to the same themes in his first press appearance following the election. In fact, if anything, his post-mortem comments on his defeat were much more explicitly racial than his original remarks had been. Eschewing the normal practice of congratulating his opponent for the win and commending him for a campaign well run, Romney instead blamed his defeat on the policy "gifts" that Obama had bestowed on the very "dependent" segments of the population to whom he had alluded in his initial "47 percent" commentary. But this time he named those groups, "especially the African American community, the Hispanic community, and young people," going into considerable detail about how specific policies benefited each group, thus effectively buying their votes.

We could offer countless examples of essentially the same thinly veiled, racialized attack on liberal social programs, unfair taxes, and the undeserving, dependent poor offered up by prominent Republicans spanning the last five decades, but we will confine ourselves to the following examples.

- In 1969, Nixon adviser Kevin Phillips sought to articulate in *The Emerging Republican Majority* the strategic logic that had propelled Nixon to victory in 1968 and, as the book's title suggested, ensure

Republican political dominance for the foreseeable future. The goal was to fashion a centrist coalition defined in large part by opposition to the civil rights movement and the social programs that were seen as favoring undeserving minorities. Central to the strategy was a critique of the Democrats as the party of high taxes, social programs, and the minority voters who benefited from them. The following quote nicely captures the general thrust of the argument. Wrote Phillips: "The Democratic Party fell victim to the ideological impetus of a liberalism which had carried it beyond programs taxing the few for the benefit of the many to programs taxing the many on behalf of the few."[20] In the coded language of the emerging racial politics of the GOP, the "many" were understood to be white and the "few" were black (or other minorities) and undeserving.

• One of the highlights of Ronald Reagan's standard stump speech during his 1976 primary challenge to Gerald Ford was an outrageous story about an unnamed "welfare queen" from Chicago who had amassed a small fortune by using multiple social security cards to fraudulently collect welfare and other government benefits. Here was Reagan's actual description of the woman: "There's a woman in Chicago.... She has 80 names, 30 addresses, 12 Social Security cards.... She's got Medicaid, getting food stamps and she is collecting welfare under each of their names. Her tax-free cash income alone is over $150,000."[21] It was a great story and one perfectly calibrated to curry the support of outraged white voters; too bad it wasn't really true. There was a woman in Chicago whose circumstances vaguely resembled Reagan's foil, but only if you wildly exaggerated her behavior. In the end, though, it didn't matter what the truth was; the story of the "welfare queen" quickly attained the status of an urban legend, believed to be true by nearly everyone. Why did the story survive if it wasn't really true? Probably because it played on the racial stereotypes and prejudice of many white voters. While Reagan did not mention the race of the culprit, the colorful details with which he embellished the story—the woman lived on the South Side of Chicago, drove a Cadillac, and so on—left little doubt in the listener's mind that the woman was black.

• The leading 2012 Republican presidential candidates also afford us a wealth of examples. Earlier, we made note of Romney's contribution to the genre. For his part, Newt Gingrich accused Obama of being a "food-stamp president," adding that "poor people should want paychecks, not handouts." But most explicit of all was Rick Santorum, who offered up the following quote: "I don't want to make black people's lives better by giving them someone else's money."[22]

For all the consistency of the rhetoric of the GOP over the past four to five decades, a growing body of evidence supports the conclusion that the party's racial politics have grown that much more extreme during the Obama years. Analyzing data from the American National Election Studies, Tesler and Sears show that the racial attitudes of those who identify with the two major parties are now more polarized than ever.[23] Consistent with that finding, a host of analyses of the 2008 election results suggest that a nontrivial number of white voters cast ballots for John McCain who otherwise would have probably voted for President Obama.[24] Based on various statistical models, one analyst estimated that Obama would have received anywhere from 2 to 12 additional percentage points of the vote had the racial attitudes of the American electorate been "neutral."[25] For all the evidence showing the influence of anti-black attitudes on voting behavior and party identification in 2008, those attitudes have, if anything, strengthened and polarized even more over the course of Obama's first term in office. Most tellingly, Pasek and his colleagues show that Republican identifiers in 2012 expressed significantly greater anti-black attitudes than their counterparts in 2008.[26]

The question is: where did this upsurge in "old-fashioned racism" come from? Based on the best survey data on support for the Tea Party, it seems reasonable to credit the movement for at least some of the infusion of more extreme racial views and actions into American politics. We begin by considering the racial attitudes of Tea Party supporters and what that suggests about the animating racial politics of the movement wing of the Republican Party. In this, we rely on two sources of data: the multi-state surveys of support for the Tea Party conducted by Parker and Barreto in 2010 and 2011 and Abramowitz's analysis of the October 2010 wave of the American National Election Studies.[27]

We start with a key finding from the Parker/Barreto study. Fifty-six percent of those survey respondents who identified as Republicans in their study were also Tea Party supporters. In and of itself, this is a remarkable figure, suggesting that Tea Party views are close to being modal among rank-and-file Republicans. But given what we know about the tendency of party activists to embrace more extreme views, we can be sure that even this figure understates the influence of Tea Party attitudes in the Republican Party. That is, if Tea Party adherents and sympathizers constitute 56 percent of all Republicans, it's almost certain—given the typically more extreme views of party activists—that a much higher proportion of party activists are aligned with the movement. Indeed, Parker and Barreto report findings very much in line with this conclusion. They show that Tea Party supporters are significantly more likely than other respondents to vote or engage in "non-voting [political] behavior."[28] In reporting these results, Parker and Barreto essentially echo the conclusion advanced earlier. In their words: "if our findings on Tea Party supporters are in any way indicative of the political engagement and mobilization of the Tea Party, we know why Republicans have listened to them: they are more likely than other segments of the mass public to pursue politics as a means of voicing their grievances."[29] Given the disproportionate influence of the Tea Party within the GOP, it becomes all the more important to understand the attitudes that appear to be motivating those who identify with and support the movement. To date, no one has studied this issue as systematically as Abramowitz and Parker and Barreto. Their findings are especially important for the strong, consistent support they afford of the central role that race appears to play in shaping the views of movement adherents.

Tea Party defenders have been understandably sensitive to charges that the movement is fueled by racist attitudes. Supporters typically rebut such charges by arguing that the movement is simply animated by traditional conservative values and/or conventional partisanship. And to be sure, these factors do differentiate Tea Party supporters from all other respondents in both the Parker and Barreto and Abramowitz studies. But when the explanatory power of those factors is assessed simultaneously with a host of other independent variables, their influence tends to wane in comparison to a few key variables with clear racial implications. We begin with the Parker and Barreto study. In their analyses three variables with clear racial implications emerge as especially important in explaining variation in support for, and active engagement in, the movement. These are "fear of Obama," "racism," and what Parker and Barreto term a "social dominance orientation."[30]

The first two variables should be clear on their face. Tea Party supporters are far more likely than all other respondents to express fear and antipathy toward Obama and what Parker and Barreto refer to as "racial resentment" (i.e., "racism") toward blacks. The concept of "social dominance orientation (SDO)," however, requires some explanation. Developed by the psychologist Jim Sidanius, the concept has been defined as a "preference for inequality among social groups."[31] SDO is essentially the opposite of egalitarianism. Those who embrace a "social dominance orientation" deny that "all men are created equal" and instead see some groups as clearly superior to, and more deserving than, others. While not exclusively racial in emphasis, the concept nonetheless has clear racial implications, especially when it occurs in combination with the two previous variables. No doubt, race is one of the dimensions along which proponents of "social dominance" believe society should be structured. Given this racial dimension, it is hardly surprising, then, that SDO also bears a strong predictive relationship with support for the Tea Party. It is worth noting, though, that of all the variables included in the Parker/Barreto study, the strongest single predictor of Tea Party support is fear and antipathy toward the first African American president in US history.

Abamowitz's analyses of the 2010 ANES data yield results that are very consistent with the Parker/Barreto findings. In particular, Abamowitz finds three variables to be especially strong predictors of attitudinal support for the Tea Party. Two of the three—"dislike of Obama" and "racial resentment"—essentially mirror the first two variables in the Parker/Barreto study. Abramowitz's conclusion echoes that of Parker and Barreto: "these results clearly show that the rise of the Tea Party movement was a direct result of the growing racial and ideological polarization of the American electorate. The Tea Party drew its support very disproportionately from Republican identifiers who were white, conservative, and very upset about the presence of a black man in the White House."[32]

Support for the Tea Party is thus decidedly not the same thing as conventional conservatism or traditional partisan identification with the Republican Party. Above all else, it is race and racism that runs through and links all three variables discussed here. Whatever else is motivating supporters, racial resentment must be seen as central to the Tea Party and, by extension, to the GOP as well in view of the movement's significant influence within the party. Nor is the imprint of race and racism on today's GOP only a matter of attitudes. It was also reflected in the party's transparent efforts to disenfranchise poor and minority voters in the run-up to the 2012 election. It may well be that the country has never seen a more coordinated *national* effort to constrain the voting rights of particular groups than we saw in 2012. Throughout the country, Republican legislators and other officials sought to enact new laws or modify established voting procedures which, in virtually all instances, would have made it harder—in some cases, much harder—for poor and minority voters to exercise the franchise.

Not surprisingly, some of the most egregious examples of these voter suppression efforts took place in key battleground states, where the electoral stakes were especially high. We offer up two especially brazen examples of these efforts. In Florida, convinced that early voting had allowed Obama to carry the state in 2008, the Republican legislature reduced the number of days of early voting from 14 to 8 heading into the election. They also outlawed it altogether the Sunday before the election, thereby eliminating the long-standing "souls to the polls" tradition in the African American community, in which black churches used that Sunday to transport their congregations to early voting polling places. As a result of the Sunday cancellation, the early voting lines on that last Saturday grew unconscionably long. In some cases, voters waited in line for eight hours to cast their ballots. And yet, as the situation deteriorated on Saturday, Republican governor, Rick Scott, rebuffed even bipartisan pleas to lift the ban on Sunday balloting. But the GOP efforts were not confined to the run-up to the election. On election day itself, "the Miami Herald documented the difficulties that numerous [minority] voters encountered until they simply gave up, and said that there was no question that voter suppression had taken place."[33]

But for us, the clear poster child of the vote suppression effort was Ohio, as orchestrated by its Republican Secretary of State Jon Husted. Elizabeth Drew describes the lengths to which Husted went to try to limit African American voting in hope of delivering the state for Romney:

> The Ohio legislature reduced the number of weekends for early voting from five to one...[b]ut Husted took further steps to limit the black vote, which was what this was all about. He tried to prevent early

voting in urban (for which read black) areas—while expanding opportunities in areas dominated by whites. . . . After his plan was shot down, Husted simply banned early voting on all three days before the election. . . . A federal court then ordered Husted to restore early voting on those critical three days. . . . [In response] Husted sharply reduced the hours during which votes could be cast on the three days. . . . Finally, in a last-gasp effort to hold down votes for Obama, at 7:00 PM on the Friday before the election Husted ordered that applications for provisional ballots be filled out by the would-be voter instead of the usual polling officials. If the early voters made a mistake filling out the rather complicated request form, their ballots would be rejected. Husted had invented his own literacy test. But on Tuesday, election day, the same federal judge . . . rejected [Husted's latest maneuver].[34]

It is worth noting that the judge punctuated his order with the following pointed commentary on Husted's behavior: "For an executive of the state to [flout] state law in arbitrarily reassigning a poll worker's statutory duty to a voter, with the result being disenfranchisement of the voter is 'fundamentally unfair and constitutionally impermissible.' "[35]

We have devoted a great deal of attention in the book to the conservative racial politics that have defined the Republican Party at least since the Nixon administration. But nothing in the 40 years between Nixon's first election in 1968 and Obama's ascension to the White House in 2008 could have prepared us for the extreme racial attitudes and behaviors exhibited by the GOP during Obama's time in office. It is hard to imagine a starker rebuke to all those who wanted to believe that, with the election, the country had finally put its troubled racial past behind it. Far from the imagined post-racial society Obama's election was supposed to herald, we find ourselves living through the period of greatest racial tensions and conflict since the 1960s and early 1970s.

Power in Movement

As we have emphasized throughout the book, since the revitalized civil rights struggle (and its companion white resistance countermovement) reintroduced the form to American politics in 1960, social movements have exerted a powerful force on the two major parties and, by extension, electoral politics and policymaking in this country. Much of the influence of movements in American politics owes, as we have stressed, to their ability to push the major parties off center and toward their ideological margins. The Tea Party represents one of the very best and most consequential examples of this dynamic in US history. Much of our account earlier in the chapter of the escalation in partisan tensions and legislative paralysis during the Obama years spoke implicitly to the powerful effect that the Tea Party has had on American politics and governance since the movement burst on the scene in 2009. Here, though, we want to give a more systematic account of the evidence of that influence.

For starters, there is the striking shift to the right after 2010 in the composition of the Republican congressional delegation, or more precisely its House members. We have relied, at several points in the book, on Poole and Rosenthal's time-series data to track changes in party polarization in the United States since the 1930s. The basic trajectory captured by Figure 1.2 should, by now, be familiar. After an extended period of significant ideological convergence during World War II and the immediate postwar period, the parties began to gradually diverge in the 1960s and 1970s, but with an especially sharp upturn in the early to mid-1990s. By the time of Obama's election in 2008, Congress was more deeply divided than at any time since the run-up to the Civil War. One might have thought we would have reached some kind of ceiling when it came to partisanship, with little room for increasing division, but alas, no. As dramatic as the uptick was in the 1990s and 2000s, the steepest slope follows the 2010 midterm elections and the arrival of the Tea Party contingent. Just how conservative was the Tea Party class of 2010? Political scientist Adam Bonica estimates that nearly 80 percent of the GOP freshmen in the 112th Congress would have been in the extreme right wing of the party's House delegation in the already right-shifted 111th Congress.[36] The details of Bonica's innovative analysis are shown in Figure 7.3, which locates all the continuing, exiting, and entering House members in the 112th Congress along an ideological axis that runs from just beyond –1.5 on the extreme left to just beyond 1.5 on the extreme right.

The contrast in the shifting composition of the two parties could not be starker. For all intents and purposes, the ideological makeup of the Democratic House remained unchanged over the two Congresses.

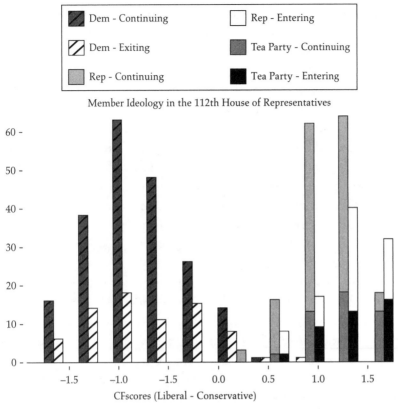

Figure 7.3 Partisan Shifts in Congress, 2010 to 2011
Source: Bonica, Adam. 2013. "Mapping the Ideological Marketplace."American Journal of Political Science. doi: 10.1111/ajps.12062.

On the other hand, Skocpol and Williamson characterize the shift in the House Republican delegation between the 111th and 112th Congress as a "rightward lunge." As they put it, "this GOP House contingent turns out to have ushered in a new phase in the extreme ideological polarization of U.S. politics."[37] But it is not the general profile of the GOP House delegation that concerns us so much as the impact of the Tea Party on the ideological makeup of the Republican House. As Figure 7.3 shows, Republican holdovers from the 111th Congress were generally far to the right of their Democratic counterparts. And yet, as generally conservative as the GOP veterans were, their incoming Republican colleagues were significantly to the right of them. And, in the aggregate, none were more extreme than those publicly aligned with the Tea Party.

Skocpol and Williamson put the election in historic perspective: "the ideological shift from the 111th to the 112th Congress was extraordinary—indeed, larger than any previous shift from one House to the next."[38] Bonica's data make it clear that the unprecedented nature of the shift was primarily the work of the Tea Party movement, which had indeed, moved the GOP House further to the right than it had ever been before.

So much for the results of the 2010 midterm elections; the real question is how did the Republican "lunge rightward" impact the legislative process? It is impossible to answer that question directly. We devoted considerable space at the outset of the chapter to a recap of the litany of willful obstruction and partisan dysfunction characteristic of the last two Congresses. Indeed, as we showed in Figure 7.1, the 112th Congress owns the dubious distinction of having enacted the fewest pieces of legislation since World War II.

We are certainly not affixing the blame for this woeful state of affairs on the freshmen Tea Party solons alone. Increased partisanship and rancor is, sadly, more the norm than the exception. We do, however, think that their presence contributed to the paralysis responsible for the meager output in both direct and indirect ways. The direct contribution is straightforward. Traditional party politics is, in the end, pragmatic and geared to compromise, albeit on terms favorable to the party in question. Movement politics, on the other hand, is typically motivated by ideological purity and a singular commitment to non-negotiable ends. In short, to a committed activist, compromise is akin to betrayal. To the extent that the loyalty of a majority of the Republican House freshmen—and some number of returning House members—was to the Tea Party movement rather than the GOP, the willingness to compromise that is so crucial to the crafting and passage of legislation has been in very short supply in the 112th and 113th GOP House delegations.

Draper's revealing portrait of the House during the first year of the 112th Congress offers numerous examples of the "true believer," activist mentality motivating the great majority of Tea Party freshmen.[39] In an early confrontation between Republican House leaders and the Tea Party contingent over the size of budget cuts the GOP should demand as a price for the February 2011 "continuing resolution," freshman after freshman refused to consider any alternative to the arbitrary $100 billion figure they had settled on. When leadership argued that its proposal to cut $33 billion would be both more realistic and still constitute a significant victory, Raul Labrador (R-Idaho), brushed aside the alternative figure saying, "To me, $100 billion isn't the ceiling. It's the floor. And $33 billion... that's under the floor." Another first term Tea Party adherent, Steve Southerland (R-Florida) concurred, adding "there is a limit to how far I will follow. I may lose in 2012—but I will not lose me."[40] But perhaps the clearest expression of this unyielding, activist stance came from second term Tea Party loyalist Jason Chaffetz (R-Utah). In a *Washington Post* article immediately following the 11th hour debt ceiling vote in late July 2011, Chaffetz, "who voted against both Boehner's first proposal and the final bill, said he was well aware of how the leadership had used his and others' willingness to let a default happen as a negotiating chip, and said he didn't mind at all. 'We weren't kidding around either,' he said. 'We would have taken it [the government] down.'"[41] Needless to say, this is more the defiant stance of a movement activist than a conventional party politician.

The *Washington Post* article also makes clear the indirect contribution that the Tea Party adherents appear to have made to the unprecedented paralysis that has gripped the last two Congresses. Emboldened by the extraordinary bargaining leverage afforded them by the Tea Party loyalists, GOP House leaders were themselves willing to engage in more willful obstruction and legislative brinksmanship than ever before. The combined effect of these two influences—indirect no less than direct— was to effectively inoculate the House GOP from the disease of compromise. In the words of conservative *Washington Post* commentator Michael Gerson, there "are always compromises in governing. But they are harder to make when one element of a political coalition views compromise itself as the problem."[42]

The "rightward lunge" of the Republican Party was not simply evident in Congress. It was also on full display in the 2012 GOP presidential primaries. Earlier we recounted the comparatively civil tone and moderate substance of the 2008 Republican primary process. It would be an understatement to say that in 2012, civil was often replaced by uncivil and that moderate had been almost entirely supplanted by extreme. It seems clear that this change in tone and substance was largely attributable to the Tea Party and its radicalizing effect on the Republican base. Let's be clear on what the implication of this "radicalization" was for the primary process. As we note at several points in the book, primary voters tend to be more ideologically extreme than all registered voters.[43] Second, and more important, Parker and Barreto's data show that 56 percent of those who identified with the GOP were Tea Party supporters. The implication should be clear. If Tea Party supporters constitute a majority of Republican identifiers and primary voters tend to be more ideologically extreme than the median voter, there is good reason to believe that a substantial majority of those who voted in the 2012 primaries were Tea Party adherents. The percentage would, of course, have varied from state to state, but overall, it seems reasonable to assume that perhaps as many as two thirds of all primary voters would have been broadly sympathetic to the movement. This alone should help us understand why the tone and substance of the primary contests were so much more extreme than in 2008. Two examples will help underscore the stark contrast between 2008 and 2012.

In our brief account of the 2008 race, we recounted John McCain's firm—and laudable—efforts to set the record straight when two questioners at a town hall meeting attacked Obama's character. Contrast McCain's strident defense of Obama with the following extended account of Rick Santorum's behavior when confronted with a very similar situation at a town hall meeting during the Florida primary:

> At a Rick Santorum town hall meeting in Lady Lake, Florida moments ago, a woman stood up to declare that she doesn't like to refer to "President Obama as president because, legally, he is not." While the audience gasped and clapped at the comment, Santorum restrained himself, refusing to utter a critical word. The lady continued, Obama "totally ignores" the Constitution, prompting a nod of approval from Santorum. Then she went even further with her conspiracy rant: "He is an avowed Muslim." [applause] "And my question is: why isn't something being done to get him out of our government? He has no legal right to be calling himself President." In an exemplary show of cowardice, Santorum did not tell the woman that she had her facts wrong or even bother to distance himself from the previous comments.
>
> Instead, he did the opposite, giving sanction to her views. "I'm doing my best to get him out" of office, Santorum said, "and you're right about—he uniformly ignores the Constitution." The tail

continued to wag the dog as the lady pressed Santorum for tougher language about Obama's unconstitutionality. Santorum meekly responded, "I agree with you in the sense that he is—he does things that are against the values and the founding principles of our country."[44]

The second incident also took place in Florida, during a presidential debate held at the State Fairgrounds on September 12, 2011. The debate moderator, Wolf Blitzer, asked Ron Paul a hypothetical question about whether an uninsured but otherwise healthy 30-year-old man in a coma should be treated. Paul responded as follows: "What he should do is whatever he wants to do and assume responsibility for himself. That's what freedom is all about, taking your own risk. This whole idea that you have to compare and take care of everybody else…" At this point, the audience erupted in cheers, effectively cutting off Paul's answer. Hoping to clarify what Paul was saying Blitzer then posed the logical follow-up question: "Congressman, are you saying that society should just let him die?" Several in the audience responded by shouting out "yeah," followed by more applause. Paul himself never directly answered the follow-up question, but his response to the moderator strongly suggested that he agreed with the sentiments expressed by the audience.[45]

These, of course, are just two incidents. No doubt, one could claim that they were hardly representative of the campaign as a whole, that we have simply cherry-picked the most extreme examples we could to distort the primary process. We demur. While the events were extreme and certainly not representative of the entire process, they nonetheless speak to an ideological extremism that was on display throughout the primary process. In general, commentators spoke consistently during the campaign of the extreme views on display in the debates and town hall meetings, generally attributing the tone and substance of the proceedings to the influence of the Tea Party. But we needn't rely on incidents alone to support the view that the 2012 primary campaign was more extreme and attuned to the movement base of the party than the 2008 contest. The best evidence of this comes from the candidates who competed in the two races and, most important, the aggregate results of the two primary contests.

Comparing the field of primary candidates in 2008 and 2012 helps underscore just how much the Tea Party had moved the GOP to the right in those four years. In 2008 the field quickly reduced to three main candidates: John McCain, Mitt Romney, and Mike Huckabee. In the end, McCain won handily. And while McCain did work to distance himself from some of his earlier moderate views on issues such as immigration and campaign finance reform, his record of independence and bipartisan sponsorship of legislation was well known to voters. Much like McCain, Romney too tacked to the right during the primaries but was never really able to dispel his image as a "Massachusetts moderate." In short, with McCain and Romney garnering three quarters of all delegates and nearly 70 percent of all primary votes cast, it seems reasonable to say that the ideological center of gravity of the 2008 race was decidedly centrist, at least by today's Republican standards. Another interesting piece of comparative evidence supports this view. Libertarian Ron Paul was a candidate in both 2008 and 2012 and arguably the most conservative contender in both fields. In 2008 he tallied just 35 delegates, or 1.6 percent of the total. Four years later his share was better than four times that amount (6.7 percent). And the amount of attention he received was many times greater than that accorded him in 2008.

Besides Paul, the 2012 field at various times also included candidates much further to the right than any of the 2008 contenders. These included such Tea Party favorites as Michelle Bachman, Rick Perry, and Rick Santorum, who in the end proved to be Mitt Romney's most formidable opponent. Taking up a series of substantive positions well to the right of those embraced by McCain, Romney, and Huckabee four years earlier, Santorum wound up capturing no fewer than 11 states before suspending his financially strapped campaign in April. At the time of his withdrawal from the race, Santorum had garnered 25 percent of all primary votes cast, compared to some 40 percent for Romney. In the end, Santorum's total fell to just 20 percent of all votes cast, with Romney claiming a bare majority of primary voters. There is, however, another way to look at the results and the general strategic dynamic on offer in the campaign. The Republican establishment backed Romney, seeing in him the only candidate who would likely have a chance against Obama in the general election. On the other hand, the party's movement base was never able to generate much enthusiasm for

Romney and kept searching for a candidate behind whom they could unite. At various times Bachman, Perry, Gingrich, Paul, and Santorum assumed that mantle. Together these five candidates claimed nearly half of all primary votes cast (46 percent), and this despite the fact that the race effectively ended in early April, allowing Romney to rack up large vote margins in the 19 contests that followed. More significantly, while the nomination was still being actively contested, these "insurgent" candidates combined to tally nearly 60 percent of all primary votes cast.

These numbers highlight a split within the GOP that simply wasn't there in 2008, at least not in any organized way. In describing the impact that movements have had on American politics, we have often employed the phrase "tug of war between movement and party." The 2012 primary results are just more evidence of the tug of war between two forms of politics and two visions of Republicanism that the Tea Party triggered and continues to wage within the GOP. While most of the emphasis during the first debt ceiling crisis was on the impasse between Republicans and Democrats, the far more salient split in 2013 was between movement-identified activists and party-identified House and Senate members within the GOP. The central strategic dynamic in the 112th Congress involved generally unsuccessful efforts by the Republican leadership to impose party discipline on movement conservatives. Add to the primary results the open warfare between movement- and party-oriented GOP members of Congress in 2013–14, and the efforts by grass-roots Tea Party groups to target and replace insufficiently zealous Republican incumbents with movement conservatives, and you begin to understand just how intense, ongoing, and consequential the battle for the GOP has become. "Tea Party activists," to quote Skocpol and Williamson, "have designs on the Republican Party. They want to remake it into a much more uncompromising and ideologically principled force. As Tea Party forces make headway in achieving this ideological purification, they spur *movement* of the Republican Party ever further to the right."[46]

True enough, but as we saw in the second debt ceiling fiasco, there are limits to how far the Republican establishment is willing to move right to accommodate the Tea Party agenda. In the end, the pyrrhic effort of Ted Cruz, coupled with the apparent willingness of the House radicals to allow the government to default, triggered a very public backlash by the party establishment and the moneyed right-wing elites who had helped fund the rise of the movement in the first place. It's as if, having sought for three to four years to appropriate and channel the energy and passion of the movement to advance their own agendas, the traditional party elite finally realized that the movement's aims might actually threaten their own interests. This realization has transformed the simmering tensions between the movement and establishment wings of the party into something much closer to open warfare. This was made evident during the 2013 government shutdown by the anger and contempt directed at freshman senator Ted Cruz (R-Texas) by a good many of his Republican colleagues. Typical of the comments was the following offered by Orrin Hatch (R-Utah), the senior Senate Republican, when asked about the strategy of shutting down the government in an effort to defund Obamacare. Said Hatch: "Let's face it, it was not a good maneuver...and that's when you've got to have the adults running things."[47] Republican Senator Charlie Dent of Pennsylvania also took a swipe at Cruz and other movement activists, punctuating his remarks with the following admonition: "It's time to govern. I don't intend to support a fool's errand at this point."[48] Perhaps most pointed of all was Representative Peter King's (R-New York) characterization of Cruz as a "fraud," and repeated pleas to his fellow Republicans to ignore the Tea Party extremists and vote to end the shutdown. As to who should be blamed for the debacle, King was equally blunt. Said King: "Ted Cruz should be blamed and anybody that follows him."

Nor did the open hostility and partisan vitriol subside at the resolution of the crisis. Just three weeks later, the deep rift in the party was on full display in a handful of elections contested in November 2013. For example, in Alabama where longtime GOP House member Jo Bonner had unexpectedly retired earlier in the year, a special election was held in November to select a Republican candidate to run in a December contest against Democrat Burton LeFlore. The special election pitted longtime party regular Bradley Byrne against extreme conservative and Tea Party identified Dean Young. After winning the election by a slim margin, Byrne reached out to Young urging them to work together to unify the party. As recounted in a *New York Times* article, Young was having none of it. "In a sign of just how difficult that unity may be, Mr. Young...said again at his election night gathering that he would not vote for Byrne in the general election, and would not even call him to concede defeat. Maintaining the defiant tone that attracted his supporters in the first place, Mr. Young [added] . . . 'this is the first warning shot that goes out across the nation.' "[49] The sudden onset of this not so civil war in the GOP has "heralded a very public escalation of a far more consequential battle for control of the Republican Party, a confrontation between Tea Party conservatives and establishment Republicans that will play out in . . . 2014 and 2016."[50]

The next skirmish in the intramural battle was waged in February 2014 when party leaders preempted another eleventh hour fiscal showdown by orchestrating passage of a "clean" debt ceiling bill in both the House and Senate. Predictably, the series of clearly coordinated moves to effect passage of the measure infuriated movement activists and Tea Party loyalists in Congress. Jenny Beth, co-founder of the Tea Party Patriots excoriated House Speaker, John Boehner, saying: "a clean debt ceiling is a complete capitulation on the speaker's part and demonstrates that he has lost the ability to lead the House of Representatives, let alone his own party. It is time for him to go."[51] But to us, the more telling reaction to the bill was the one offered by House Tea Party stalwart, Tim Huelskamp (R-Kansas). Also directing his wrath at Boehner, Huelskamp charged that the speaker "gave the president exactly what he wanted," adding that the outcome was "going to really demoralize the base."[52] Implicit in Huelskamp's remark is the suggestion that the GOP establishment may have taken much of the wind out of Tea Party sails by preempting yet another fiscal crisis.

Postscript: Looking Ahead To 2014

So what are the likely implications of all of this for the 2014 midterm elections and beyond? In view of the battle now being waged for control of the Republican Party, we really need to take up two distinct questions. First, who is likely to prevail in Republican House and Senate primaries—Tea Party or more "moderate" party-oriented candidates? Second, given the outcomes of the primary contests, what should we expect when Republicans and Democrats square off in November? Moreover we will want to answer these questions separately for the House and Senate.

House Races

In the wake of the 2013 government shutdown and debt ceiling crisis, much was made of polls showing that the public placed more of the blame for the debacle on the Republican House than on President Obama or Senate Democrats. One representative poll showed 53 percent blaming Republicans and only 31 percent faulting the president, with only 24 percent of those surveyed professing a "favorable opinion" of Republicans.[53] Numbers like these prompted some to suggest that the GOP might be vulnerable to losing the House in 2014.[54] We see almost no chance of this happening. For one thing, most Americans care little for politics and as a result, have very short memories when it comes to even fairly recent events. For them, the 2013 government shutdown and debt ceiling fiasco are ancient history. And let's not forget that close on the heels of that crisis came the disastrous rollout of the Affordable Care Act, which has to be counted as at least as damaging to the Democrats as the shutdown was to the GOP. Perhaps most important of all, congressional Republicans did themselves a huge strategic favor by signing off on the two-year budget agreement negotiated by Paul Ryan (R-Wisconsin) and Patty Murray (D-Washington) in December of 2013 and passing a "clean" debt ceiling bill in February of the following year. By finally achieving the party discipline that had eluded them since the 112th Congress convened in 2011, the GOP spared itself one final public relations disaster just months before the 2014 midterms.

The real problem for the Democrats is simply the number of seats they would have to win to retake the House. With Republicans currently enjoying a 234 to 201 advantage, the Democrats would need to claim a net of 17 seats to regain control. Up until very recently, a swing of 17 seats was certainly not out of the question. But with the most recent wave of gerrymandering drastically reducing the number of competitive House districts, the ability of either party to take a large number of seats from the other has been drastically reduced. There is, to be fair, one cause for optimism among Democrats concerning the November House race. Of the very few true swing districts that will be contested in the fall, the great majority are currently in Republican hands. Of the 35 seats that the Cook Political Report see as very much up for grabs in November, 25 are currently "barely Republican," and 10 "barely

Democratic." So at least from a strict numeric standpoint, the Republicans are more vulnerable to losses in the fall than are the Democrats. But even this glimmer of hope for Democrats comes with a sobering chaser. Even if the Democrats were to pull off the impossible and claim, say, 15 of the current GOP "swing" seats, they would still find themselves 2–3 seats shy of the number needed to take possession of the House. Bottom line: the Democrats are almost certain to remain the minority party in the House come January of 2015.

The more interesting and consequential question for us, however, is how will the two warring factions of the GOP fare in their head to head primary contests in advance of the November elections? There are two schools of thought on the question. Based on their proven ability to mount successful primary challenges against longtime GOP stalwarts, it is not unreasonable to think that the Tea Party faithful would have a significant edge heading into this year's all-important intraparty scrum. Or put another way, up to this point, the party establishment has shown neither the inclination nor the ability to challenge the Tea Party at its own game. Lacking the grass-roots ground game honed by the Tea Party, the establishment has never really tried to recruit and run more moderate party-oriented candidates against Tea Party incumbents. This year they are trying to do just that. And this, coupled with a huge edge in funding, is the basis for the view that holds that this will be the year in which the GOP establishment begins to reverse the ideological tide of the last few years.

Where do we come down on the matter? We think there is much to recommend both views. We suspect the results of the GOP primaries will, in fact, be mixed, with neither side coming away with a clear victory. That said, we tend to side with those who think we may well have seen the high-water mark of the Tea Party phenomenon and that, in finally mobilizing against the movement over the past year, the GOP establishment is slowly regaining control of the party. In politics, as in sports, momentum is everything. For three years the movement wing of the party had been able to maintain that momentum, effectively setting the legislative agenda in Congress, while cowing party leaders in the process. By finally bringing the Tea Party insurgents to heel at the close of the shutdown crisis, and quickly following that up with a two-year budget deal in December 2013 and the February debt ceiling bill, the establishment appears to have regained the upper hand.

This does not, however, mean that we should expect major changes in the ideological character or loyalties of the GOP House delegation as a result of the mid-term elections. Our conviction is based on three factors. First, notwithstanding the lengths to which the GOP establishment has gone to mount a ground game in this year's midterms, the Tea Party remains better organized at the grass-roots level than party regulars. Second, midterm and primary elections both tend to suppress voter turnout. Should the combination of the two wind up reducing voter turnout all the more, it would grant a significant advantage to the party's mobilized movement wing. Finally, one has to take into account the comparative vulnerability of establishment and Tea Party incumbents to primary challenge. And here again, the Tea Party incumbents would seem to have an edge over their establishment counterparts. Quite simply, the majority of Tea Party incumbents hail from some of the safest of safe GOP districts. And why are they so "safe?" The answer: because the ideological leanings of the electorate in these districts are also very extreme and therefore likely to prove hostile to a primary challenge by an establishment opponent. To a large extent, then, the Tea Party House members find themselves in the enviable position of being reasonably well insulated from the threat of a primary challenge. On balance then, we expect to see the result of this year's GOP primary battles as more or less a draw. If that, in fact, is how things turn out, we can expect the final slate of Republican House candidates in 2014 to be ideologically very similar to the current GOP House delegation.

What can we expect when the Democratic and Republican House candidates square off in November? It is almost certain, in our view, that the GOP will remain in control of the House, even if the Democrats, as seems likely, are able to pick up a few more seats in the process. It is entirely likely, however, that the Democrats will confront an even more extreme GOP delegation come January 2015 than they do at present. The Tea Party incumbents are drawn so heavily from safe districts that their chances of being unseated in November are exceedingly small. Assuming they survive any primary challenge the Tea Party may mount, the more moderate GOP House members—and especially those who come from more competitive districts—are vulnerable to whatever diffuse anti-Republican sentiment may inform the November contests. Thus even if the tide has turned in the battle for control of the Republican

Party, it is still possible for the proportion of House seats claimed by the insurgents to increase as a result of the mid-term elections.

Senate Races

Including the two independents who caucus with the party, the Democrats currently enjoy a 10- seat edge in the Senate (55 to 45). When combined with the diffuse anti-Republican sentiment generated by the gridlock and dysfunction of the Obama years, one might think the Democrats would be just as likely to retain control of the Senate via the 2014 midterms as the GOP is of maintaining its edge in the House. As logical as this may sound, we see control of the Senate as very much up for grabs in 2014. The numbers tell the story. Of the 35 seats to be contested in the election, 21 are currently in Democratic hands, reversing the situation in the House and making the party more vulnerable to losses in the Senate than the GOP. Then there is the all-important issue of the relative vulnerability of the incumbents up for reelection in both parties. In our view, the GOP incumbents would seem to have the clear edge in this regard. Of the 14 Republican seats up for reelection this year, only one— Susan Collins' seat in Maine—is from a state won by President Obama in 2012. The other 13 are in states carried by Mitt Romney by at least five percentage points. By contrast, at least 9 of the 21 seats currently held by Democrats appear to be in play heading into the election. Retirements have a lot to do with this. Five Senate Democrats are stepping down this year. Three of these—Baucus (Montana), Rockefeller (West Virginia), and Johnson (South Dakota)—are in Republican-leaning states. The other two—Harkin (Iowa) and Levin (Michigan)—are in more traditionally Democratic states, but polling suggests that these races could also be competitive. Adding to the Democrats' woes, four of the remaining 16 incumbents also seem to be locked into very tight races. Mark Pryor (Arkansas) looks to be the most vulnerable of these four, but the other three—Begich (Alaska), Landrieu (Louisiana), and Hagan (North Carolina)—also hail from generally red states and are likely in for close contests as well.

Still, the GOP path to control of the Senate is a narrow one. To pull it off, they will need to pick up a net gain of six seats. Whether they are able to do so may come down to how well establishment "moderates" fare in their primary battles against Tea Party challengers. The most closely watched race in this regard is the one in Kentucky between Senate Minority Leader Mitch McConnell and his Tea Party opponent Matt Bevin. But Tea Party challengers are making things more interesting—and complicated—for the GOP in no fewer than five other states. In Mississippi, incumbent Thad Cochran is hoping to fend off a primary challenge by Tea Party candidate Chris McDaniel. In Nebraska, another Tea Party loyalist, Ben Sasse, has squared off against two moderates in hopes of capturing the seat being vacated by retiring GOP senator Mike Johanns. State senator Lee Bright has taken up the Tea Party mantle in his battle to unseat GOP incumbent Lindsay Graham in South Carolina. In explaining his motivation for challenging Graham, Bright alluded to the resolution of the 2013 government shutdown in issuing what amounted to a not so veiled warning to the Republican establishment. Said Bright: "We know which senators fought for liberty, and which ones caved to Obama. We have a list."[55] Add to these three races the Tea Party challenges being mounted against Lamar Alexander in Tennessee and Pat Roberts in Kansas, and exactly half of the GOP incumbents are doing battle with the party's insurgent wing. With the exception of Mississippi and South Carolina, victories in even one or two of these states by the Tea Party candidate would almost certainly dim the hopes of the GOP of taking control of the Senate. Capturing a small, carefully redrawn House seat is one thing; for an extreme Tea Party candidate to prevail in a much larger, statewide Senate race is quite another. Here is where our sense of the shifting momentum in the battle between the movement and establishment wings of the party may be especially relevant. If, in fact, we have seen the high watermark of the Tea Party, we would expect to see the "moderates" prevail in the great majority of this fall's Republican Senate primary contests. Should they do so, then the GOP would have a real chance of taking over the Senate heading into 2015. And if it does, the gridlock and dysfunction of the 113th Congress would likely pale in comparison to what we could expect to see in Obama's last two years in office.

The prospect of even more partisan bloodletting and government dysfunction raises real questions about the viability of American democracy. In Chapter 8 we bring the book to a close with an extended discussion of the normative implications raised by the unprecedented events of the past six years.

8

Restoring American Democracy

HAVING SPENT THE BULK of the book detailing the long, strange journey that has brought us to the mess we presently find ourselves in, we want to turn now to what we see as the serious implications of the current situation for the viability of American democracy. Throughout the book, we have defined the mess in terms of two defining features of the contemporary United States: extreme inequality and unprecedented partisan polarization. While problematic in and of themselves, these two features combined also pose very serious threats, in our view, to the health and well-being of this country's democratic ideals and practices. In this chapter, we want to account these threats and, in bringing the book to a close, offer some thoughts on what could be done to restore our badly frayed democracy. Animating our purposive survey of these threats is what we see as the single most important normative principle at the heart of democratic theory: the foundational notion of political equality.

Inequities in Voice

Equality is fundamental to the theory of democratic governance. Here, however, we refer not to economic equality, but equality of voice in civic life. Political theorist Robert Dahl cuts to the heart of the matter when he asserts "that a key characteristic of democracy is the continued responsiveness of the government to the preferences of its citizens, considered as *political equals*."[1] Our normative disdain for autocratic forms of government stems from the fact that "the consent of the governed" counts for so little compared to the power wielded by the select few. When we proudly proclaim that democracy flows from "the will of the people," we don't mean *some* of the people, or that the will of some counts for more than others. And while we acknowledge that this ideal has never been fully realized in the United States, we want to believe that our history represents an inexorable, progressive march toward the realization of that goal. Among the most troubling aspects of the present political moment in America is the accumulating evidence that we have been moving *away* from this ideal for some time. Here we take up what we see as the two most important sources of political inequality in the contemporary United States.

Minority versus Majority Views

The American democratic experiment bears the imprint of the revolutionary struggle that gave it life. Confronting what they came to regard as the tyranny of King George and the British majority, the founding fathers went to great lengths to ensure that minority views would be institutionally protected in the US system. The goal was not to promote an even more perverse tyranny of the minority but simply to safeguard the fundamental equality of voice—regardless of one's views—deemed essential to a democracy. In practice, however, safeguarding minority views while acceding to the will of the majority is exceedingly hard to do and has occasioned a great deal of conflict over the course of our history.

In a recent article in *Daedulus*, former longtime House member Mickey Edwards (R-Oklahoma) provides a useful framework for thinking about the tricky relationship between majority and minority views and the broader issue of political equality. Elected officials, writes Edwards "have only three options available to them; they may (a) side with the more numerous faction (that is, majority rule); (b) take advantage of their own positions in government to impose their own views, regardless of the wishes of the citizens; or (c) find a way to forge a compromise between the competing visions."[2] Compromise is, of course, the preferred option, though with Congress in its present gridlocked state, very difficult to achieve. Of the remaining two options, majority rule—though not without problems—is clearly preferable to the second option. As Edwards argues: "the second option is contrary to the democratic impulse. Edmund Burke was correct in arguing that elected officials are not to be rubber stamps for their constituents but should instead bring their own expertise, experience, and judgment to the decisions they make. *But to ignore completely the wishes of the citizens is to render the concept of representation moot.*"[3] And yet, we contend, this disregard for popular preferences has come increasingly to characterize federal policymaking. In effect, the views of the majority have been increasingly marginalized in favor of those of a relatively small and nonrepresentative ideological minority. This is exactly the reverse of what Downs and Black told us the all-powerful "median voter" would ensure against in our winner-take-all two party system. Extreme views, they argued, would be marginalized in deference to the wishes of the moderate majority who occupied the center of the country's ideological distribution.

The expected centrist bias in federal policymaking has not, however, been much in evidence in recent years. In support of our argument we offer three concrete examples of the present day disconnect between centrist majority views and the far more extreme cast of current government policy.

1. **Gun Control**—Since 1980 the popular consensus has favored more restrictive gun control laws. Figure 8.1 reports the last 33 years of Gallup polls on the matter.

With the exception of a brief period between 2009 and 2012, a solid majority of Americans has voiced a preference for stricter "laws covering the sale of firearms." And yet, with only the occasional legislative breakthrough, the will of the majority has been frustrated on the issue time and time again. The most recent demonstration of popular powerlessness came in the wake of the horrific shooting of 26 children and teachers at Sandy Hook Elementary School in Newtown, Connecticut, in December of 2012. Fueled by widespread shock and outrage, public support for stricter gun control laws jumped sharply in the wake of the shootings. This in turn, forced Congress to confront the issue in a meaningful way for the first time since 1994 when it enacted a 10-year ban on assault weapons as part of the broader Violent Crime Control

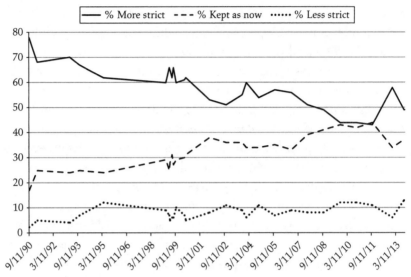

Figure 8.1 Public Opinion on Gun Control, 1990–2013
Source: Gallup

and Law Enforcement Act. In the end, though, all the outrage and all the pressure that the likes of former Representative Gabby Gifford— herself a victim of gun violence in 2011—could exert on Congress mattered little. On April 17, 2013, the Senate defeated a compromise plan to expand background checks on firearms sales as well as a proposal to ban high-capacity gun magazines and certain models of assault weapons—this despite a host of polls showing Americans strongly in favor of the bill on the eve of the vote.[4]

Even in the Senate—the less polarized of the two congressional chambers—the vote split overwhelmingly along party lines, with just four Republicans joining 50 of 55 Senate Democrats in support of the bill. With 60 votes required to bring the matter to the floor, this left supporters of the legislation still 6 votes shy of the number needed to consider the measure. In the wake of the setback, any number of commentators and political figures lamented the clear rebuke to the "will of the majority." As President Obama put it, "The American people are trying to figure out: how can something have 90% support and yet not happen?"[5]

2. **Immigration**—Our second issue has special contemporary relevance. Not only has the issue of immigration and immigration reform

received a great deal of media attention in recent years—and especially since the wave of immigrant rights protests in 2005 and 2006—but save for the debt ceiling, no issue would seem to have received more legislative attention from the current Congress. Almost the first item of business taken up by the Senate after the 113th Congress convened in January 2013 was comprehensive immigration reform. Motivated, no doubt in part, by the striking demonstration in 2012 of the growing electoral significance of the Hispanic vote, a bipartisan immigration reform bill passed the Senate by a 68–32 margin and was forwarded on to the House in late June of 2013. And there it is has languished ever since, another victim of the paralysis that has gripped the House since the midterm elections of 2010. Notwithstanding dire warnings from GOP pollsters concerning the electoral price the party will pay for failing to embrace the need for comprehensive reform, the determined opposition of the Tea Party contingent in the House has once again tied Boehner's hands and dimmed the prospect for any legislative progress on the issue.

As with our other two issues, public support for immigration reform is substantial and appears to have increased in recent years. The critical question here is whether the United States should create a legal path forward by which those in the country illegally can become citizens. In a September 2013 PEW poll, nearly three quarters of those surveyed (73 percent) agreed that "immigrants currently in the country illegally who meet certain requirements, should have a way to stay legally."[6] In the same poll, exactly 75 percent of respondents reported that they felt it would be better for the economy if these immigrants were allowed to become legal workers. These results, however, represent only a single point in time. What about public opinion trends over time?

As you can see in Table 8.1, public support for granting illegal immigrants a way to "remain in the U.S. and become citizens" has held steady at roughly two thirds of those surveyed since 2006, the first time Gallup asked that particular question. Moreover, during that same period of time, the central policy concern of those surveyed has shifted significantly. In 2006, 53 percent of all respondents wanted the federal government to focus its efforts at "halting the flow of illegal immigrants." By contrast, only 43 percent thought the government's focus should be on developing a plan for resolving the legal status of those in

Table 8.1 Public Opinion on Immigration, 2006–2011

Question: "What percent of respondents think that illegal immigrants should remain in the U.S. and become citizens if they meet certain requirements over a period of time?"

2011 June 9–12:	64%
2007 March 2–4:	59
2006 June 8–25:	66
2006 May 5–6:	61
2006 April 7–9:	63

Source: Gallup

the country illegally. By the summer of 2013, those two percentages had effectively reversed, with 55 percent now attaching priority to finding a path forward for those illegally in the country, versus 41 percent who remained primarily concerned with safeguarding the border.[7] However, as with our other two issues, the strong and growing support for immigration reform has not been enough to compel Congress to act.

3. **Abortion**—The final example of the disconnect between contemporary policymaking and the "will of the people" concerns the issue of abortion. Unlike our other two issues, however, virtually all of the action on the matter has been happening at the state and local, rather than the federal level. That makes it a bit harder to succinctly capture the growing divide between public opinion on the matter and the current state of abortion policy in the country. Still, there is absolutely no question about the direction in which that policy is moving.

While most of the attention accorded the Tea Party has focused on Congress and the impact that the flood of movement-identified freshmen has had on the House since their arrival following the 2010 midterm elections, the movement's real impact has been at the state and local level. And no issue reflects this localized impact more than the conflict over abortion rights. A new report by the Guttmacher Institute, which has long tracked policy changes in the area, documents a flood of anti-abortion legislation in the three years following the Tea Party's breakthrough in the 2010 elections. Since then, 30 states have enacted more than 200 new pieces of restrictive legislation. Nor does the pace of the legislative frenzy show any signs of abating. Indeed, in 2013 alone,

22 states adopted 70 different restrictions. The specific restrictions include late-term abortion bans, requirements that doctors performing abortions have admitting privileges at local hospitals, and prohibitions on abortion coverage by the new health exchanges. Texas was only the most visible and contentious of the states enacting the new laws. As the *New York Times* reported:

> The many strands of attack came together in Texas, which in a tumultuous special session in July required doctors performing abortions to have local hospital admitting privileges, imposed costly surgery-center standards on abortion clinics, sharply limited medication abortions and adopted a 20 week ban [on abortions]. The admitting privileges requirement immediately forced about one-third of some 30 clinics in the state to stop performing abortions and left much of South Texas without any abortion clinics.[8]

A federal judge temporarily halted enforcement of the new law, but Texas successfully appealed the ruling, effectively reinstating the new restrictions, pending trial.

The impact of the new restrictions should be all too clear. Access to abortion—a right legally conferred by *Roe v. Wade*—is probably less available now than at any time since the ruling. Perhaps more important, that access is now highly variable geographically, with women in large swaths of the country effectively unable to exercise a right still nominally guaranteed them.

Given the theme of this section, it will come as no surprise that the trend toward ever more restrictive abortion rights has happened even as public preferences have grown incrementally more liberal over time. The survey data shown in Figure 8.2 provides the relevant support for this claim.

The data also affirm the overwhelmingly moderate, centrist view of Americans on this, as with so many other issues. Over the past 40 years, the modal position of the general public on abortion has barely budged, with somewhere between 50 and 60 percent of survey respondents favoring abortion "under certain circumstances." The other two more "extreme" preferences on the issue—"legal under all circumstances" and "illegal under all circumstances"—have remained distinctly minority views. Interestingly,

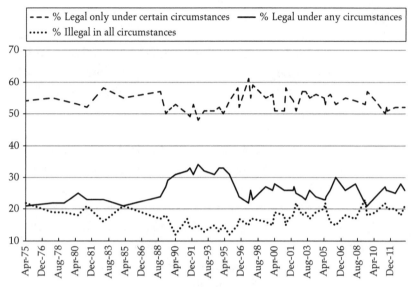

Figure 8.2 Public Opinion on Abortion, 1975–2013
Source: Gallup

however, even as a woman's access to abortion has been dramatically reduced in recent years, the actual percentage of those favoring outlawing abortions under all circumstances has been slowly declining. In 1975, the proportions of those favoring complete legalization and abolition of abortion were identical, with roughly 20 percent of the general public embracing both "extreme" views. In the most recent survey on the matter, those favoring legalization outnumbered "abolitionists" by a 28 to 18 margin. More to the point, 80 percent of survey respondents favored either the "status quo" position—that is, legal under some circumstances—or complete legalization. And yet the relentless assault on abortion rights continues, further marginalizing the policy preferences of the once vaunted "median voter."

The Tyranny of the Minority: Subverting the Will of the Majority

As fashioned by the founding fathers, the US system was designed to safeguard minority rights and views, even as it attended to the will of the majority. However, as the disparities in voice documented in this chapter make clear, we find ourselves increasingly in a situation where the extreme ideological views of a distinct minority dominate policy, effectively marginalizing the centrist preferences of the majority. But it is worse than that. Not content simply to aggressively advocate their minority views, a good many policymakers are engaging in efforts to either subvert the legislative process or mute the voice of others. Most strikingly, the contemporary GOP—and especially its movement wing—has, since Obama took office, embraced a politics of obstruction and willful sabotage designed to subvert the process by which other views might be voiced and acted upon. It is one thing to aggressively promote one's own views; it is quite another to intentionally suppress the expression of others. We briefly touched on these efforts in the previous chapter; here we describe them in more detail.

Legislative Paralysis

Even as they fought a revolution based on appeals to popular representation and the will of the people, America's founding fathers—at least most of them—were terrified of the "mob" (read "people") and loath to grant meaningful participation to the great majority of the new society. From the very beginning, the structure of the American system reflected this ambivalence. A good many features of the system—from the odd institution of the Electoral College to the very notion of checks and balances—were designed to insulate it from popular pressure and to ensure that change, when it did come, would be piecemeal and slow. But no one should mistake the present gridlock in Congress for the ideal of slow, deliberative, incremental change. Paralysis was never the intention, and yet, in recent years, that is essentially what we have at the federal level.

The contrast with the postwar period could not be greater. The broad consensus that prevailed in those years transformed Congress into a bipartisan legislative engine responsible for a steady string of consequential enactments that reshaped the country in powerful and lasting ways. From the GI Bill, funding for the United Nations, and the Marshall Plan in the immediate aftermath of World War II, to the 1956 Highway Act in the middle of the period, to the landmark civil rights bills of 1964 and 1965 and the creation of Medicare and Medicaid—also in '65—the period is among the most productive and favorably regarded in congressional history. As consensus gave way, however, to increasing partisan division in the 1980s, and especially 1990s, the pace of significant congressional action slowed dramatically. In recent years, it would be kind to characterize that pace as a crawl. As we document in Chapter 7 (see Figure 7.1), the 112th Congress (2011–13) earned the dubious distinction of being the least productive— as measured by bills passed—Congress in modern US history.

Figure 8.3 affirms the close connection between polarization and the pace of congressional enactments. The strong inverse relationship between partisan polarization and the pace of congressional action could not be clearer. As polarization has increased, especially after the mid-1990s, the rate of legislation has dropped precipitously. It turns out that this general relationship also holds for the most significant pieces of congressional legislation. As part of his seminal study of postwar law-making, political scientist David Mayhew created an annual count of "landmark" congressional enactments. In their book, McCarty, Poole, and Rosenthal plot those enactments against their polarization time series. As they report, the figure "reveals a striking pattern. Congress enacted the vast majority of its significant measures during the least polarized period. The ten least polarized congressional terms produced almost sixteen significant enactments per term, whereas the ten most polarized terms produced just slightly more than ten. The gap would be

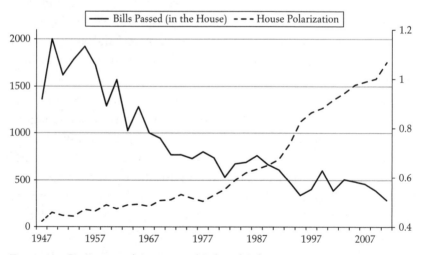

Figure 8.3 Congressional Activity and Political Polarization, 1947–2012
Sources: Office of the Clerk; Polarized America/voteview.com

even bigger except for the enormous legislative output following the September 11 terrorist attacks."[9]

Not content to look only at the simple relationship between polarization and legislation, McCarty has sought to measure the impact of polarization on legislative output, controlling for a number of other tried and true variables. In all of his models, however, polarization bears a strong, significant relationship with legislative output, with the least polarized Congresses enacting somewhere between 60 and an incredible 166 percent more legislation than in the most polarized of sessions.[10]

Without for a minute discounting the significance of his research, it is nonetheless worth noting that McCarty's findings are based on data sets that exclude the last six congressional sessions, which just happen to be among the most polarized sessions in the annals of Congress. Corresponding to the Obama years, the last three of these sessions, in particular, have set a new standard of polarization—a new low, if you will—by which all future Congresses may be judged. Moreover, consistent with McCarty's findings, the last two sessions (112th and 113th) have also ranked among the least productive in congressional history.[11] In short, given the absence of these especially polarized Congresses from his analysis, it is very likely that McCarty's results actually understate the impact of polarization on legislative output.

Willful Sabotage of Policymaking

An inability to reach agreement on legislation due to strongly held views on substantive matters is one thing; open enmity and a willful commitment to sabotage the proposals of a sitting president is quite another. And that is more or less the situation the country has been in since Obama took office in January 2009. As Drew put it: "For the first time, defeat of the incoming president in the next election became the opposition party's explicit governing principle. If that meant blocking measures to improve the economy, or preventing the filling of important federal offices to keep the government running, so be it. Wrecking became the order of the day. Confrontation became the goal in itself."[12]

Having devoted much of Chapter 7 to a narrative account of Republican efforts to block, undermine, and otherwise paralyze policymaking during Obama's time in office, we can afford to be fairly brief here.

We begin by revisiting a few of the "greatest hits" from Chapter 7—that is, the best examples of willful obstruction by the GOP between 2009 and 2014.

- On January 26, 2010, the Senate votes on a resolution to create an 18-member bipartisan task force to fashion a comprehensive plan to address the debt crisis. Though co-authored by a Republican, Judd Gregg, and backed by a rash of GOP co-sponsors, the resolution fails when it falls 7 votes shy of the 60 needed to end a determined Republican filibuster against the measure. In all, seven Republican co-sponsors of the resolution vote to sustain the filibuster, effectively killing the measure they proposed. "Never before have co-sponsors of a major bill conspired to kill their own idea. Why did they do so? Because President Barack Obama was for it, and its passage might gain him political credit."[13]
- Senate Republicans effectively block executive appointments on at least three occasions in transparent efforts to undermine the implementation of new laws—including the Affordable Care Act—with which they disagree.
- And then there were the two "debt ceiling" crises, arguably the "mother of all" obstructionist acts engineered by the GOP during Obama's presidency. Congress had raised the debt ceiling no fewer than 78 times since 1960 and in none of these cases had those opposed to the increase insisted on any preconditions for raising the limit. But in 2011 and again in 2013 the old rules didn't apply. Emboldened, or pressured, by the Tea Party insurgents in the House, the Republicans were seemingly prepared to let the country default on its obligations. In the end, in both cases, a deal of sorts was brokered at the 11th hour—a deal that did nothing to resolve the underlying fiscal issues—but the damage to our financial standing and, more important, to a fragile economy, had already been done.

The meager legislative output characteristic of the Obama years owes at least as much to willful Republican sabotage of policymaking as it does to the ideological chasm between the two parties. Nor can the obstruction be blamed entirely on the wave of movement conservatives swept into the House in the 2010 midterm elections. On the contrary, as made clear by the story recounted in the previous chapter about the dinner of GOP leaders on inauguration night 2009, the intent to obstruct was in place at the time Obama first took office. Comments by GOP leaders early in Obama's first term merely confirmed the intention. In July of 2009, South Carolina Senator Jim DeMint told party activists that his goal was to "break" Obama and make the president's health care bill "his Waterloo." And then there was Mitch McConnell's (R-Kentucky) even more explicit acknowledgment that his central aim as Senate Minority Leader was to limit Obama to a single term.

In pursuing this strategy, congressional Republicans appear to have taken a page from Newt Gingrich, who was the first to add willful sabotage to the GOP playbook. Mann and Ornstein recall a fascinating incident involving Gingrich from 1978. The two authors had recruited a group of freshman representatives to participate in a series of informal dinner conversations, the better to understand their evolving sense of the legislative process and the institution they had recently joined. One of those invited to take part in the dinners was Newt Gingrich, then a newly minted House member from Georgia. The specific incident recounted by Mann and Ornstein involved an extended discourse by Gingrich on how he would go about breaking the stranglehold the Democrats had enjoyed over the House for nearly a quarter of a century. Mann and Ornstein pick up the story: "Gingrich's...core strategy was to destroy the institution in order to save it, to so intensify public hatred of Congress that voters would buy into the notion of the need for sweeping change and throw the majority bums out. His method: to unite his fellow Republicans in refusing to cooperate with Democrats in committee and on the floor."[14] Never mind that Gingrich employed this strategy, as we saw in Chapter 6, with ultimately disastrous consequences for the GOP in his 1995 budget showdown with Bill Clinton. Nevertheless, the Republican Party—or at least its movement wing—has been willing to deploy the same strategy again and again with Obama in the White House. Nothing fits the record of GOP delay, obstruction, and legislative hostage taking during Obama's time in office better than the original strategic vision spelled out by Gingrich.

As we bring this section to a close, it is important to highlight the antidemocratic nature of the current GOP strategy. We see three specific threats to democratic ideals and/or practice embodied in the strategy. The first is simply the intentional sabotage of the legislative process. If the heart of a democratic system is policymaking by the people, as carried out by their democratically elected representatives, then the willful sabotage of that process is inherently nondemocratic. Intentionally undermining public confidence in the central representative institution of American governance constitutes a second clear threat to the health and well-being of the democratic system. The third threat is the most general and perhaps the most important; it is the privileging of ends over democratic means. Just like Gingrich in 1978, the movement wing of today's GOP justifies the willful obstruction and sabotage of democratic practice—representative policymaking—as necessary to attain its ends. At its heart democracy prizes means over ends; in reversing the emphasis, many current lawmakers threaten the fundamental logic and practice of a democratic system.

Restricting Electoral Voice

This anti-democratic inversion of means and ends is also reflected in the many GOP efforts undertaken in recent years to restrict the electoral influence of traditionally Democratic voters. We touched on these efforts in the previous chapter, but only briefly and with a focus on how they reflect the GOP's long-standing embrace of a politics of racial reaction. But Republican initiatives in this regard have been broader in their demographic focus and more varied in form than simply efforts to restrict the black vote. More specifically, the GOP has sought to restrict Democratic electoral voice through two general strategies pursued on a systematic, nationwide basis. The two strategies have involved the passage of new, restrictive state voting laws that effectively target presumptive Democratic constituents; and creative gerrymandering by Republican-controlled state legislatures to concentrate and thereby dilute the "urban" (read: Democratic) vote, while distributing the rural and suburban (read: Republican) vote to maximize electoral effect. Of the two approaches, the former has received the most attention, even if the latter has had the greater impact. The intent, however, is the same in both cases: altering the rules and geographic structure of voting to suppress or mute the electoral voice of traditional Democratic voters (e.g., racial minorities, the poor, and young people). We take up each approach in turn, beginning with the epidemic of proposed new voting laws in the run-up to the 2012 election.

In our brief discussion of the topic in Chapter 7, we focused specifically on the efforts of GOP officials in Florida and Ohio—perhaps the two most crucial battleground states—to restrict the black vote. But these two states represent only the tip of a very large iceberg of new restrictive voting laws proposed, overwhelmingly by GOP lawmakers, between 2010 and 2012. The Brennan Center at the New York University School of Law has been especially vigilant in tracking proposed changes to electoral laws around the country. According to data reported on the Center's website, from the beginning of 2011 through September of 2012 at least 180 bills were introduced in 41 states. Ultimately, 25 new laws and 2 executive actions were adopted in 19 states. In total, these states represented 231 electoral votes, or 85 percent of the total needed to win the presidency. In the view of the authors of the summary, "this amounted to the biggest threat to voting rights in decades."[15] The most common of the new laws were statutes requiring voters to obtain new identification cards in order to cast ballots in the 2012 general election. The nominal justification offered for the ID requirement was the prevention of voter fraud, though as many commentators noted, there was something inherently fraudulent in the rationale itself. Many of the states seeking to implement these laws had no reported cases of voter fraud in the past few decades. In general, voter fraud had been a non-issue in the United States until it was conveniently seized upon by Republican lawmakers as cover for the new laws.

On occasion, however, even they—in moments of carelessness or bravado—went "off message" and owned up to the transparent aim of the new ID laws or restrictions on voting. After orchestrating the passage of Pennsylvania's especially restrictive voter ID law, Mike Turzai, the GOP leader of the state's House of Representatives, couldn't help but boast a bit. Said Turzai, "Voter ID, which is going to allow Governor Romney to win the state of Pennsylvania. Done."[16] Then there was the adviser to Ohio's Republican Governor, John Kasich, who defended the governor's decree drastically limiting early voting, by saying that "we shouldn't contort the voting process to accommodate the urban—read African-American—voter- turnout machine."[17] Most recently, a Republican official in North Carolina was forced to resign after touting ID cards as a way to reduce voting by "a bunch of lazy blacks that wants the government to give them everything."[18] But these rare admissions merely confirm what was already clear to any neutral observer. "The point," as Drew noted, was simply "to make it more difficult for constituent groups of the Democratic Party—blacks, Hispanics, low-income elderly, and students—to exercise their constitutionally guaranteed right to vote."[19]

In the absence of more systematic studies of the flurry of restrictive voting measures, it is hard to offer an overall assessment of their impact on the 2012 election. While in the end, legal rulings blocked implementation of a number of the laws, scores were in effect on Election Day. And even when the new restrictions were set aside, confusion in the minds of voters may well have had much the same effect on turnout as if the laws had been in place. This was especially true in locales where GOP officials deliberately sought to sow or promote confusion. In Wisconsin, for instance, where free ID cards issued by the Department of Transportation (DOT) would satisfy the state's new voter ID requirement, DOT officials were told to withhold information about the cards. And then there were the many cities where intimidating billboards suddenly appeared in predominantly black and Hispanic neighborhoods suggesting that photo IDs would be required to vote, even when this was not the case. Finally there were the long lines in many states—products of drastic GOP cuts in early voting hours—and the suppressive effect they may have had on voters. Some commentators have insisted that the racially restrictive aims in these cases inspired minority voters to persevere to spite those behind the laws.[20] But these assertions tend to be based on anecdotes, impressions, and most important, a partisan investment in the claim. Again, to our knowledge, no systematic assessment of the impact of the new laws on turnout in 2012 has been published to date. Past studies, however, have generally confirmed that ID laws do indeed seem to impact minority voters and other traditional Democratic constituents more than their Republican counterparts.[21] Notwithstanding these findings, it is clear that the worst fears of observers concerning significant suppressive effects were not realized in 2012.

One thing is certain: the fact that Obama managed to win should not be taken as prima facie evidence of the ineffectiveness of the restrictive measures. In any case, far more significant to us than the laws' objective impact is the clear and brazen threat to democratic practices posed by the measures. In Chapter 7 we advanced the intentionally provocative claim that "it may well be that the country has never seen a more coordinated national effort to constrain the voting rights of specific groups than we saw in 2012." The key word in the sentence is, of course, "national." In sheer brutality and sustained will, nothing, we hope, will ever match the 80- to 90-year effort by the white South to deny the franchise to African Americans. Still, that was a regional effort. The fact that Republican officials throughout the country colluded in a thinly veiled effort to make it significantly harder for many millions of Americans to exercise their constitutional right to vote should be a serious concern to us all.

In fact, the threat of a similar but more effective effort being mounted in the future grew significantly in June of 2013 when the Supreme Court, in *Shelby County (Ala.) v. Holder*, invalidated the crucial "pre-clearance" provision of the Voting Rights Act of 1965. To be more precise, the Court left the "pre-clearance" section in place but declared that the formula used to determine which jurisdictions were required to secure federal approval before they could make changes in voting laws was "based on decades-old data and eradicated practices." So even as the Court left section 5 intact, it effectively terminated the "pre-clearance" requirement, by invalidating the formula used to trigger a "pre-clearance" review. The practical implications of the ruling were made all too evident the very day *Shelby County (Ala.) v. Holder* was handed down. Within hours of the ruling, Texas Attorney General Greg Abbott announced that the state's controversial voter ID law, which had been struck down as unconstitutional by a federal court panel, authorized under the "pre-clearance" section of the act, would be immediately implemented. Let that sink in for a moment. A law that had been declared unconstitutional was quickly reinstated following the Supreme Court decision. The implications of this are as worrisome as they are clear on the face of Texas's action in the wake of the ruling. If the nationwide voter suppression campaign of 2012 proved less effective than many had feared (or hoped), among the main reasons for this was the fact that several of the most restrictive new laws—including the Texas ID law—were struck down, under pre-clearance review, in advance of the election. With the threat of such review now removed, those motivated to make it that much harder for minorities, the poor, and young voters—Democratic constituencies all—to cast ballots in 2014 and 2016, will have a freer hand to do so.

Inequities in Voice as a Function of Money

Having devoted a great deal of attention to the various ways in which minority views have come to exert what we see as an inordinate influence over politics and policymaking, we turn our attention to the second great source of political inequality in the contemporary United States: money. Money plays an enormously complicated and multi-faceted role in our political system. As such, it has spawned a literature all its own, including a number of recent books devoted exclusively to the topic.[22] With all the issues before us in the present volume, we can't possibly hope to explore the matter in all its complexity. Given the goal of this last chapter we will limit our focus to the serious threat that money can pose to our democratic ideals. Two ideals are particularly relevant here. The first is the aforementioned principle of *political equality*. The second is another ideal central to the aims of the founding fathers that has not yet figured in our discussion. We refer to this as the principle of *dependence*.

We normally think of dependence as a bad thing and in the *Federalist Papers*, virtually every usage of the term reflects a negative connotation. There is, however, one exception to this convention. In *The Federalist* No. 52, we are told that in a representative democracy, the elected representatives should be "dependent upon the People alone." Lessig elaborates: "the House of Representatives (and after the Seventeenth Amendment, so, too, the Senate) was intended to have a specific dependency. . . . *Dependent*—meaning answerable to, relying upon, controlled by: *Alone*—meaning dependent upon nothing or no one else. . . . [A] representative democracy that developed a competing dependency; conflicting with the dependency upon the people would be 'corrupt.'"[23] Ever cold-eyed realists, the framers were smart enough to realize that formal political equality—"one man, one vote"—would mean little if instead of being attuned to, or dependent upon, the People, the elected representatives were beholden to a competing "dependency." Indeed, the framers took specific steps to safeguard against the development of competing dependencies. In the balance of this section, we hope to convince you that today both of the aforementioned principles are seriously compromised by the influence of money in our political system. We begin with the principle of *political equality*.

If we only focused explicitly and at length on the widening economic gap in the United States in Chapter 6, the general trend has been on our radar throughout the book. We revisit the phenomenon here, though, because it clearly bears on the issue of political equality as well. We begin with a few preliminaries. Well-meaning Americans embrace very different normative views of economic inequality. There are those who hold that, as a nation, we should do all we can through social programs and the equalization of various kinds of opportunities to reduce economic disparities. The underlying assumption here is that more egalitarian societies are inherently more stable and unified and therefore less prone to conflict than ones featuring enormous wealth gaps between rich and poor. Others will argue, however, that government efforts to promote equality depress the entrepreneurial spirit, encourage enervating personal dependence on government, and in general hamper economic growth. The best way, they contend, to unlock human potential is to reduce government interference to allow for unfettered competition. If the price of this competition is inequality, so be it; the general social good will still be furthered through the resulting economic prosperity and individual freedoms. While acknowledging the legitimacy of these very different normative views of *economic* inequality, we see no such diversity of permissible opinions when it comes to *political* equality. In a democracy, the principle of political equality should be inviolate. Any social arrangement that compromises the principle undermines democracy and should be cause for concern. Therein lies the rub; what if economic inequality can be shown to promote political inequality? If so, then the diversity of normative views on the former should, in our view, yield to the simple normative requirements of the latter. Even if a sizable economic gap between rich and poor is not in and of itself objectionable, it becomes highly problematic if it compromises the principle of political equality central to democratic governance. That, of course, is what the evidence suggests has been happening in the United States for some time: increasing economic disparities are producing growing inequities in political voice as well. The rich, as we showed in Chapter 6, are not simply getting richer, but are coming to exercise ever greater influence over the political system as well.

While anecdotal accounts of the corrupting influence of money on politics are popular in the media, we begin by recounting the results of two systematic empirical studies of the topic by political scientists. Chronologically, the first of the studies was conducted by Martin Gilens in the early 2000s. The empirical centerpiece of the study was nearly 2,000 survey questions measuring the policy preferences of Americans on a wide range of issues. Gilens coded the responses to differentiate the policy preferences of different segments of the US public, with special attention to broad socioeconomic groupings. He then sought to assess the statistical relationship between the policy preferences of these different SES groups and the actual policies adopted in various issue areas. His analyses yielded two principal findings. First, across all issue areas, he found a very strong association between actual policy and the policy preferences of the most affluent survey respondents. By contrast, the views of the less affluent bore a much weaker relationship to the actual course of policy than was true for the affluent. The second finding is arguably more important. When he restricted his analyses to only those issues on which the views of the most and least affluent respondents diverged, Gilen found that actual policy almost always reflected an upper-class bias. In his own words, "influence over actual policy outcomes appears to be reserved almost exclusively for those at the top of the income distribution."[24] His overall normative take on the findings is more pointed still: "representational biases of this magnitude call into question the very democratic character of our society."[25]

More recently, Larry Bartels has reported very similar findings, but from a study quite different in design from Gilens's. Using survey data collected for the Senate Election Study conducted by the American National Election Studies (ANES) research team in 1988, 1990, and 1992, Bartels, like Gilens, sought to assess the general relationship between citizen policy preferences and the voting behavior of policy-makers. But whereas Gilens did this in general terms for the country as a whole, Bartels was able to fine-tune his analysis and focus in on the relationship between constituent preferences and senatorial voting behavior on a state-by-state basis. Still, his central research question was the same as that of Gilens. Are senators equally responsive to the policy preferences of all of their constituents, regardless of their socioeconomic circumstances? The answer is no. Bartels reports the results of a number of analyses, but his findings are broadly similar throughout. They also closely mirror Gilens's results. Differentiating between low-, middle-, and high-income constituents, Bartels also finds that the voting behaviors of the senators are far more statistically "responsive" to the views of the affluent than to low- and middle-income constituents. Perhaps more damning are his results at the other end of the SES continuum. "In contrast [to the results for the high-income group], the views of low-income constituents had *no* discernible impact on the voting behavior of their senators."[26] While the statistical relationship between voting behavior and the views of the most affluent constituents was much stronger for GOP senators than their Democratic colleagues, the general association held for both groups.

It is important to note that Bartels also sought, in his analyses, to control for how knowledgeable and engaged in the political process constituents were. He used questions from the ANES Senate Election Study to measure variation on three dimensions of political engagement: knowledge, contact with elected officials, and voter turnout. Perhaps, one might argue, the responsiveness of senators to the views of these three broad groups of voters simply reflects significant differences in the latters' efforts to engage the political process. While we still might lament the clear class bias in voting behavior, it would be hard to fault the senators for simply attending more closely to the views of their more active and knowledgeable constituents. This is not, however, what Bartels found. Significant differences in responsiveness remained even after controlling for these factors. It seems even the knowledgeable, engaged poor get ignored by their elected representatives.

So if it isn't class-based differences in knowledge and engagement that largely account for the variable responsiveness of senators, what is it about the most affluent voters that prompt elected officials to attend so closely to their views? There is no single answer to this question, but it is hard to imagine that the extraordinary financial resources at the disposal of the richest voters aren't a significant part of the story. The wealthy are simply in a much better position to bend the will of the system to their views through financial means than are other groups of voters. In politics, as in most things, money talks; and when money talks, elected officials—as Bartels has shown—listen. What makes the Bartels findings all the more worrisome is that they are based on data from the late 1980s and early 1990s; that is, before the extraordinary increases in income inequality of the last two decades greatly magnified class disparities in this country; and before the Supreme Court saw fit in its 2010 *Citizens United v. Federal Election Commission* ruling to remove all legal constraints on political giving by the richest corporations and individuals in the United States. Reflecting on these two developments, we can only imagine how much larger the disparities in voice are in contemporary America than they were a quarter of a century ago, when the data on which Bartels based his study were first collected.

What of the second principle? Even if Bartels and Gilens had not turned up evidence of glaring class inequities in political voice in the United States, we would still be concerned about the ideal of congressional *dependence*. One could imagine a world in which citizens were formally equal in voice but generally ignored by a Congress attuned to a competing "dependency." We should be so lucky. In fact, the evidence suggests that ours is a system beset not only by significant class disparities in political influence but also by a legislative branch distant from the People and increasingly attuned to—*dependent upon*—those who fund their never-ending reelection campaigns and the lobbyists who broker these connections. It was not always this way. As Lessig and others document, the present system—which Lessig terms the "Fund Raising Congress"—has really been in place only since the 1990s.[27] Prior to that time, the temporal and financial exigencies of election and reelection campaigns were relatively modest. "Campaigns," to quote Ornstein and Mann, "generally were confined to the latter half of election years."[28] And until the last 25 years or so, the money required to mount a campaign was surprisingly modest, especially for House races. As late as 1974, the mean amount spent on a House reelection campaign was just $56,000; by 2010 that amount had risen to $1.3 million (Huffington 210 : 130). "In 1974 the total spent by all candidates for Congress (both House and Senate) was $77 million.... By 2010 it was $1.8 billion."[29] Not to put too fine a point on it, that is better than a 2300 percent increase in campaign expenditures, compared to an overall inflation rate of 370 percent for the same period.[30]

A host of factors have contributed to this out-of-control escalation in campaign costs, none more important than the increasingly competitive partisan balance in Congress after 1994 and the advent of ever more sophisticated—and significantly more expensive—campaign tactics (e.g., political polling, TV ads, media and other consultants, etc.). Far more important to us than the causes of the spiraling costs, however, are the effects that have followed from the financial pressures they impose on members of Congress. Lessig, among others, describes a system in which the demands of nonstop campaigning force senators and especially representatives to devote more and more time to courting donors and especially cultivating relationships with lobbyists who serve as the key brokers in the system. Not surprisingly, given the central role they play in this system, the growth over time in lobbyists closely parallels the aggregate rise in campaign costs. Hacker and Pierson report that in 1971 there were just 175 firms with registered lobbyists in DC.[31] By 2009 that number had grown to 13,700, with annual expenditures of $3.5 billion, or roughly $6.5 million per member of Congress.[32]

Mind you, the workings of this system are far cleaner than the sordid influence peddling of earlier periods. Gone for the most part is the naked quid pro quo exchange of money for votes or other political favors. Such instances are rare and often uncovered and punished. In a very real sense, however, the corrupting influence of money on contemporary politics is far more ubiquitous and insidious for being so much more subtle and indirect than during the "bad old days." The workings of the system are complex and far too complicated to examine in detail here; in any case, they are described in compelling detail elsewhere.[33] What these books and the broader literature on the topic also make clear is just how much the increasing financial demands—and enticements—of the system are coming to constitute exactly the kind of competing dependence about which the framers were so concerned.

In compelling and convincing detail, Lessig documents three significant effects of the growing dependence of members of Congress on this system. The first is simply the distraction to members of having to spend what Lessig estimates at anywhere from 30 to 70 percent of their time and energy on fund-raising activities.[34] In fact, it may well be that the actual percentage is closer to the upper than the lower end of Lessig's range. As former House member and future senator Mike Barnes (D-Maryland) told Philip Stern, "As I spoke to political consultants, they all said I should not even consider running for the Senate if I weren't prepared to spend 80 or 90 percent of my time raising money. It turned out they were absolutely correct."[35] Or consider the view of former Senate majority leader, Robert Byrd (D-West Virginia): "Senators start hosting fundraisers years before they next will be in an election. They all too often become fundraisers first and legislators second."[36]

The second effect of the extraordinary amounts of money now flowing into the political system is the unmistakably corrosive effect these funds have on the public's general regard for, and *trust* in, members of Congress. In a poll conducted soon after the *Citizen's United* decision was announced, 74 percent of respondents agreed that "special interests" exert too much influence on Congress. An even larger number, 79 percent, agreed that members of Congress are "controlled" by those who finance their campaigns, while only 18 percent believed elected officials listened to voters more than donors.[37] Even if somehow the appearance of impropriety and undue financial influence is not objectively true, the subjective impact of these widely shared perceptions is an important, and corrosive, force in contemporary politics.

It is, however, the third effect identified by Lessig—*distortion*—that poses the biggest threat to democratic ideals. If the financial demands of the current system merely distracted members of Congress, we could live with that, but an increasing body of evidence strongly suggests that with distraction comes distortion of legislative priorities. As members of Congress devote more and more time to fund-raising and to cultivating relationships with the lobbyists who lubricate the entire system, they inevitably attend more closely to the interests of lobbyists and donors and less and less to those of the general public. This is entirely consistent with the stark policy "disconnect" that Baumgartner and his colleagues found when they systematically compared the public's view of the "most important problems facing the country today" with data "reflecting the concerns of the Washington lobbying community." In their own words, "the bad news is that the wealthy seem to set the agenda.... [resulting in] little overall correspondence between the congressional agenda and the public's agenda."[38] In place of the framer's intended dependence on the People, Congress is increasingly dependent on those wealthy, vested interests who have mastered the exigencies of the new "Fund-Raising Congress." Don't believe us? Perhaps those who know best, the members of Congress, will convince you. Consider only the following four all too typical quotes:

- Representative Eric Fingerhut (D-Ohio): "The completely frank and honest answer is that the method of campaign funding that we currently have... has a serious and profound impact on not only the issues that are considered in Congress, but also on the outcome of those issues."[39]
- Representative Joe Scarborough (R-Florida): "Across the spectrum, money changed votes. Money certainly drove policy at the White House during the Clinton administration, and I'm sure it has in every other administration."[40]
- Representative Pete DeFazio (D-Oregon): "You pretty much have to neglect your job.... You're spending all this time on telephones, talking mostly to people you don't know, you've never met."[41]
- Senator, Fritz Hollings (D-South Carolina): "I had to collect $30,000 a week, each and every week, for six years. I could have raised $3 million in South Carolina. But to get $8.5 million I had to travel to New York, Boston, Chicago, Florida, California, Texas and elsewhere. During every break that Congress took, I had to be out hustling money. And when I was in Washington, or back home, my mind was still on money."[42]

Political Inequality and the Current Legitimacy Crisis

In the waning days of the Soviet system, it was common to speak of a "legitimacy crisis" in the USSR and other Warsaw Pact countries. The speed with which the system collapsed seemed to only confirm the judgment. For all its sheer size and menacing presence, the Soviet system seemed, in the final analysis, to be an edifice built on the softest of sand. The system simply lacked the popular legitimacy necessary for long-term survival. In the wake of the collapse, we in the United States smugly celebrated this difference, asserting with pride that it was the enormous popular support for the American way of life and governance that in the end differentiated the two systems and allowed us to prevail in the Cold War.

We would not for a minute claim that the levels of public distrust of, and estrangement from, the American political system have reached the epidemic proportions we saw in the dying days of the Soviet system. There is, however, compelling and growing evidence to suggest that we are in the midst of a serious legitimacy crisis of our own. Since the American National Election Studies polling began in the 1950s and '60s, Americans have never held such consistently low regard for government institutions across the board or expressed more distrust or lack of confidence in government as they do now. A wealth of survey data support this claim, including time-series data on (1) trust in the federal government, (2) approval of Congress, (3) perceptions of how much public officials "care what people think," and (4) opinions on the extent to which people "have a say in what the government does." Over-time data on all four of these issues are shown in Figures 8.4 through 8.8.

Rather than discuss each figure in turn, we think it makes more sense to treat the data holistically, as a not-so-surprising general expression of mounting public anger and frustration at the stark inequities in political

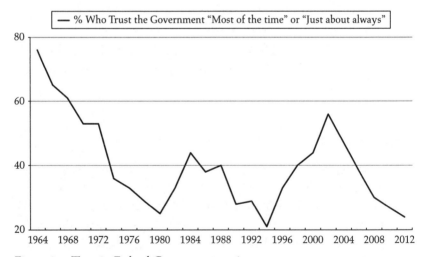

Figure 8.4 Trust in Federal Government, 1964–2012
Source: American National Election Studies
* *In 1958, 73% reported high trust in the government; survey not conducted in 1960, 1962, 2006, and 2010; data for 2006 and 2010 are interpolated*

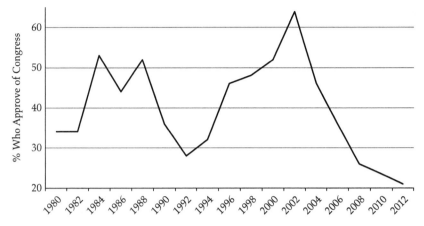

Figure 8.5 Congressional Approval (ANES), 1980–2012
Source: American National Election Studies

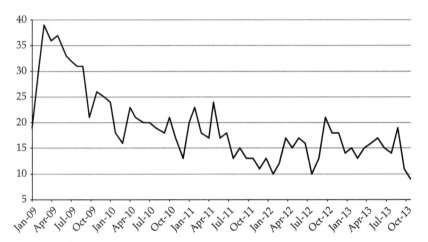

Figure 8.6 Congressional Approval, 2009–2013
Source: Gallup

voice documented previously. Given the dominant policy influence of nonrepresentative, extreme views on a host of issues, should we really be surprised by the unprecedented levels of popular anger, distrust, and cynicism among the general public? Are we really naïve enough to believe that the stark disconnect between current federal policy and public opinion on a host of issues is lost on the American people? Or that African Americans and other racial minorities have somehow missed the recent spate of transparent efforts to limit their electoral

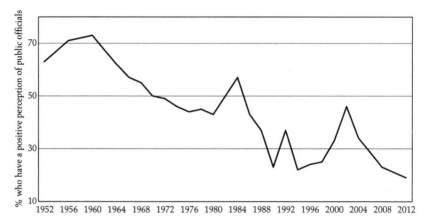

Figure 8.7 Positive Perception of Public Officials, 1952–2012
Source: American National Election Studies
* *Note that a new variable ("neither agree nor disagree") was introduced in 1988, artificially decreasing responses of positive perceptions; data for 1954,1958, 1962, 2006, and 2010 were interpolated*

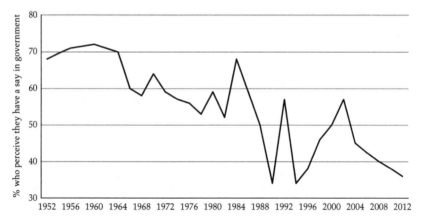

Figure 8.8 Perceptions of Say in Government, 1952–2012
Source: American National Election Studies
* *Note that a new variable ("neither agree nor disagree") was introduced in 1988, artificially decreasing responses of positive perceptions; data for 1954, 1958, 1962, 2006, and 2010 were interpolated*

voice? The trends highlighted here suggest otherwise and together paint an entirely consistent picture of the relationship of the general public to the federal government.

The picture isn't pretty, but before we turn to it let us contrast today's worrisome profile with the very different image suggested by the data from the earliest period shown in the figures. In the late 1950s and 1960s, the great majority of Americans professed trust in the federal government. Small wonder, since throughout the 1950s and well into the '60s some 70 percent of those polled *disagreed* with the following two statements: "people don't have a say in what the government does" and "public officials don't care what people think." With both parties hewing to the middle of the ideological continuum, it was easy for the "median voter" to feel that elected officials were responsive to her views, and, in turn, to trust the federal government "to do the right thing." Alas, the American National Election Studies only started tracking the public's approval rating of Congress in 1980, but based on the other three time-series we think it's almost certain that a majority of Americans would have given Congress high marks in the 1950s and 1960s.

Needless to say, things look very different today. As we first noted in Chapter 1, trust in the federal government is at a near all-time low. From a high of 76 in 1964, the percentage of Americans who profess to trust the federal government to do the right thing "just about always" or "most of the time," shrank to just 24 percent, according to the ANES survey conducted in 2012. That figure dropped to 19 percent in October 2013 in the midst of the government shutdown and debt ceiling fiasco.[43]

The other numbers reported in Figures 8.5 through 8.8 help us understand why trust in government is now such an endangered species. It's hard to trust government when you see it as fundamentally corrupt and unresponsive to your views. Fifty-five percent of Americans polled in 2010 thought that "quite a few people running the government are crooked"[44] and roughly two thirds of those surveyed agreed that "public officials don't care what people think."[45] But if Americans see government as generally unresponsive and not worthy of their trust, they reserve special contempt for Congress. Reflecting the dysfunctional gridlock that has characterized the last few congressional sessions, public approval of the institution has reached new lows. At the height of the fall 2013 government shutdown and debt ceiling fiasco, a scant 9 percent of Americans approved of the way Congress was discharging its duties.[46] We will bring this rather depressing discussion to a close with one final, especially worrisome, piece of data. Since the late 1990s the PEW Research Center has been asking Americans how they "feel" about the federal government. To express their "feelings," respondents are provided with the following three response categories: "basically content," "frustrated," or "angry." In Table 8.2 we report the over-time changes in the distribution of these responses.

Table 8.2 Feelings about the Federal Government, 2000–2013

	Feb 2000	Nov 2001	Mar 2004	Oct 2006	Jan 2007	Sept 2010	Mar 2011	Aug 2011	Sept 2013
Angry	10	8	13	20	16	23	14	26	26
Frustrated	54	34	52	54	58	52	59	60	51
Basically Content	33	53	32	21	21	21	22	11	

Source: Pew Research Center

Consider the change in the emotional "temperature" of the country since 2000. While only a third of all respondents reported feeling "basically content" in that year's poll, that proportion is still three times higher than the comparable figure for the latter two dates: August of 2011 and September 2013. More than a quarter of those surveyed in the recent period said they were "angry" at the current state of the country, up from just 10 percent in 2000. When the percentage of citizens who say they are "angry" outnumber those who report feeling "basically content" by a factor of two and a half, we think our claim that the United States is in the throes of a legitimacy crisis is not farfetched at all.

Angry, frustrated, alienated, and deeply distrustful of government: anyone who cares about the health and well-being of American democracy should be extremely concerned by the portrait that emerges from these data. With substantial majorities of Americans agreeing that they "don't have a say in what the government does" and that elected officials "don't care what they think," we are convinced that much of this worrisome attitudinal fallout owes to the clear inequities of voice—the fundamental lack of political equality—documented in this chapter. Quite simply, the great majority of Americans do not believe their voice matters; that the essential principle of political equality does not apply in the contemporary United States. While the last 40 years have seen a steady erosion in public trust and confidence in government, the last decade or so would seem to demarcate a qualitatively different period in the relationship between the federal government and the American public. Without being alarmist, we can't help but wonder how long these widespread feelings can persist without giving rise to even more visible threats to the political system. The pressing question now is what can be done to restore the fundamental principle of political equality? How can we begin to convince people that their views do matter and that the government is at least minimally responsive to their preferences? With no illusions about the extraordinary challenges that stand in the way of even modest progress toward this general goal, we nonetheless want to bring the book to a close by offering a number of proposals for concrete change that could help to restore, at least minimally, the political equality so essential to a democracy.

What's to Be Done? Restoring Political Equality in the United States

We are not so naïve as to imagine that the ideal of political equality can be easily or completely achieved. In truth, it has always been an ideal in progress, a principle toward which we, as a nation, have only intermittently and imperfectly strived. Our commitment to the ideal has been strong in some eras and weak in others. Sadly, our own time belongs in the latter category. The shame of the current situation is not just that inequities of voice exist—after all, they always have—but that we seem to accept them so readily. Indeed, those working to further restrict the voice of others operate openly and without apology. Quite simply, we have strayed so far from the ideal of political equality in this country that much work needs to be done just to begin the process of restoring it.

A complete discussion of democratic restoration would need, in our view, to address a host of topics, which would minimally include media reform, the reinvigoration of the civic function of our schools, review of congressional procedures, and the re-democratization of our electoral system. All of these are important topics, but we confine ourselves to only the last of these topics. As you will see, this "single" topic is complicated enough in its own right. Indeed, there are multiple features of our electoral system contributing to inequities in political voice. We take up each in turn, beginning, in reverse order of the problems listed, with the influence of money in politics.

The Corrupting Influence of Money

The evidence that disparities in wealth promote inequities in political voice is now voluminous and seemingly incontrovertible. We barely scratched the surface of that evidence earlier in the chapter. It is one thing, however, to document a problem and quite another to fashion effective remedies, especially when the problem is as big and multi-faceted as this one. And what makes reform in this area especially problematic at present is the ideological makeup of the three institutions that have historically exercised principal oversight in the areas of campaign spending and campaign finance reform: the Federal Election Commission, the Supreme Court, and Congress. At present, all three are hostile to reform. In what follows then, we briefly note the ideological hurdle that each of these institutions presently pose to meaningful reform before going on to suggest the longer-term remedies that eventually might be effected through each body.

We begin with the Supreme Court. With conservatives enjoying a fairly stable 5–4 majority on most controversial cases, the ideological makeup of the Court is not, at present, conducive to reforms that would in any way constrain the ability of wealthy individuals or organizations (corporations, unions, political action committees, etc.) to contribute money to candidates or political campaigns. Just how much the present Court is opposed to any restrictions on financial giving for political purposes was made abundantly clear in its decision in *Citizens United v. Federal Election Commission*. The decision turned on two highly controversial analogies: that corporations are akin to people, and campaign contributions—however large and potentially corrupting—are a form of free speech. By extension any restriction on campaign giving should be prohibited as a threat to the First Amendment right of free speech granted to all people (which now apparently includes corporations).

It seems fair to say that no Supreme Court decision in recent memory has been as roundly criticized as the ruling in *Citizens United*, with 65 percent of the public "strongly" opposed and 72 percent in favor of reinstating limits. That is perhaps reflected in the public's all-time low opinion of the Supreme Court.[47] Nor was the criticism confined only to those on the left. One especially striking and perceptive critique of the decision was authored by longtime Republican House member Jim Leach of Iowa. Wrote Leach:

> Brazenly, in *Citizens United*, the Court employed parallel logic to the syllogism embedded in the most repugnant ruling it ever made,

the 1857 *Dred Scott* decision. To justify slavery, the Court in *Dred Scott* defined a class of human beings as private property. To magnify corporate power a century-and-a-half later, it defined a class of private property (corporations) as people. Ironies abound.

Despite overwhelming evidence to the contrary, the mid-nineteenth-century Court could see no oppression in an institution that allowed individuals to be bought and sold. In the *Citizens United* ruling, despite overwhelming evidence to the contrary, the Court implied that corporations were somehow oppressed—in this case considered to be censored—and therefore should be freed to buy political influence.... How are corporations oppressed? Do corporate leaders not have free speech and the right to give campaign contributions like all other citizens?

Have they and the political action committees... that they control not already been over-empowered to infuse millions into the political process? Is it an accident that as the influence of moneyed interests has increased in American politics, the gap between the rich and the poor has widened?[48]

Concern over the corrupting influence of money has been around as long as democracy itself. The severity of the threat, however, has varied from era to era. Today the unholy combination of extreme inequality and unlimited political giving by the wealthy makes the issue all the more critical. But while the Supreme Court may, in the short run, be an obstacle to meaningful reform in this area, other avenues of legal challenge are open to reformers. For instance, even as it was removing restrictions on political giving by the wealthiest individuals and organizations, the Supreme Court, was simultaneously affirming, in its *Citizens United* decision, two other important provisions of the law regulating campaign donations. These are provisions requiring "disclosure" of donors and the "separation" of the PACS and other partisan expenditure groups from the candidates and campaigns they support. In truth, both the spirit and letter of these provisions are routinely contravened in the contemporary United States; but that's the point. Drawing on the Supreme Court's affirmation of these requirements, reformers should aggressively press to see that these provisions are more closely adhered to. Long term, however, the ultimate judicial goal should be clear: mounting a challenge to the legal basis of the *Citizens United* decision.

As the source of all federal laws, Congress is clearly the most important policymaking body in the area of political giving and campaign finance. Unfortunately, owing to the present poisoned partisan state of the institution, meaningful legislation in this area is about as likely as a sudden reversal of Supreme Court opinion in the matter of *Citizens United*. The fate of the proposed DISCLOSE Act, introduced into the Senate in 2010, tells you all you need to know about the prospects for significant congressional reform in this area. Concerned that the *Citizens United* decision would only exacerbate the corrupting influence of money in American politics, reformers in the Senate sought through the DISCLOSE Act to greatly strengthen the disclosure regime governing campaign contributions. Perhaps the distorting influence of the flood of new money into politics could be mitigated somewhat by more stringent disclosure requirements; or so the reformers hoped. In the end, however, the bill fell victim to the partisan gridlock we have come to expect from Congress. Mann and Ornstein describe the denouement of the reform effort:

> The Democrats' united effort to create a robust disclosure regime after *Citizens United* was thwarted on a filibuster in the Senate in 2010 when all fifty-nine Democrats voted for the DISCLOSE Act, but could not get a single Senate Republican, including reformers like John McCain and Olympia Snowe, to provide the necessary sixtieth vote to overcome the filibuster.[49]

Given that the laws regulating campaign finance and political giving are set at the federal level, reformers have little choice but to continue to pressure Congress to address the clear threat that unprecedented flows of essentially unregulated money into our system poses to the principle of political equality. Congress has acted decisively in this area on numerous occasions in the past and will no doubt, do so again, but only if reformers continue to put pressure on both houses to enact and enforce legislation designed to strengthen the "disclosure" and "separation" provisions affirmed in the *Citizens United* decisions. There is, to be sure, no substitute for serious restrictions on how much money individuals and organizations can contribute to political candidates and campaigns, but until such restrictions are enacted, it is absolutely essential that stringent laws regarding donor disclosure and the separation of PACs, candidates, and campaigns are in place.

Mann and Ornstein mince no words in assigning blame for the failure of the Senate to pass the DISCLOSE Act. "The leaders," they say, "in the effort to evade disclosure laws have been Republicans."[50] Small wonder since it is the GOP that profits most from the flood of unregulated money into the political system. The source of most of that money—corporations and the individual wealthy—tend to be ideological conservatives. So it should come as no surprise that the Republicans are also implicated in the dysfunction of our third and final institution involved in regulating campaign finance and political giving. Indeed, if Congress and the Supreme Court have a role to play in this area, no institution is more directly charged with ensuring the integrity of the electoral system than the Federal Election Commission (FEC).

Created in 1975 as an amendment to that year's Federal Election Campaign Act, the FEC describes its duties as "to disclose campaign finance information, to enforce the provisions of the law such as the limits and prohibitions on contributions, and to oversee the public funding of Presidential elections." In theory yes, but, at present, partisan politics has rendered the FEC inert. The structure and composition of the agency are partly to blame for this. The FEC is composed of six commissioners, no more than three of whom can be from the same political party. In practical terms this means three Republican and three Democratic commissioners. Were we living in an era of bipartisan cooperation, this particular compositional formula might not be problematic. But we are not and it is. While commissioners are appointed by the president, they need to be confirmed by the Senate. Therein lies the rub. Senate Minority Leader Mitch McConnell (R-Kentucky) "has made it clear that protecting the FEC as it now exists—that is, as a lawless agency—is a top priority for him."[51] More specifically, McConnell has worked hard to secure the appointment of three Republican commissioners committed to the nullification of federal election law. You see the problem; with four votes required to take any action, the FEC has itself been nullified as an effective regulatory agency. So not only does the current composition of Congress rule out the possibility of any new campaign finance legislation, the partisan capture of the FEC obviates effective enforcement of existing laws. This must change and the president has the power to effect that change, though he would probably have to use his power of recess appointment to do so. More important, he would have to be willing to essentially go to war with the Senate Minority Leader to restore the integrity of the FEC. Given all the challenging issues on his plate, we can certainly understand that the president does not want to pick this particular fight at the present time, but at some point—sooner rather than later—the effective independence of the FEC must be reestablished if we are to restore the integrity of our election system.

There is a depressing, broken-record quality to our brief survey of the current state of efforts to oversee and regulate the corrupting influence of money in our electoral system. The ideological composition of all three institutions—the Supreme Court, Congress, and the FEC—has made each a de facto proponent of a laissez-faire electoral system, one in which there are no real restrictions on political giving and no real requirements for donor disclosure or the effective separation of expenditure organizations from the candidates and campaigns they bankroll. The threat to the principle of political equality in all of this should be only too obvious. In the long run, effective reform will probably require changes in the partisan composition of these bodies. Until then, reformers will need to work through other more tangential agencies, such as the Federal Communications Commission, the Securities and Exchange Commission, the Internal Revenue Service, and the Justice Department, to do what they can to mitigate the distorting effects of the present system. Eventually, we would love to imagine that some comprehensive "clean money" or "voter-owned" election system could be fashioned for the country as a whole. While any number of variants of such a system have been proposed over the years, virtually all of them agree on three central features: (1) substantial public funding of elections, (2) stringent limits on how much money individual contributors can donate to campaigns, and finally (3) no, or extremely limited, organizational donations to candidates. While fully endorsing such an approach, we are not, at the moment, optimistic about its realization. As Mann and Ornstein so aptly put it: at the moment "the path to significant restrictions on an out-of-control money system...is steeply uphill."[52]

Ongoing Efforts to Limit the Franchise

Nothing in recent years has posed a starker contradiction to the principle of political equality than the epidemic of voter suppression efforts mounted in the run-up to the 2012 election. We have devoted a great deal of attention to the nondemocratic consequences that follow from primaries and other low turnout elections. Even in presidential contests, we barely engage half of the American citizenry. As former House member, Mickey Edwards (R-Oklahoma), put it, "the percentage of Americans who contribute to, work in, and even vote in public elections is disappointingly low, especially for a nation that likes to think of itself as the world's foremost beacon of democracy."[53] Given the "disappointingly low" numbers that take part in the electoral process, it is unthinkable that groups would conspire to reduce those numbers still further, but that, of course, is exactly what transpired between 2010 and 2012. Moreover, now that the Supreme Court has seen fit to effectively eliminate the requirement for "preclearance" review of any proposed changes to voting procedures, we are betting these efforts will intensify in the run-up to the 2014 and 2016 elections. The overwhelming majority of these efforts have, of course, been orchestrated by Republican groups and elected officials, intent on making it more difficult for traditional Democratic voters—especially racial and ethnic minorities—to exercise the franchise. As we point toward future elections, the Republicans have little choice but to redouble their efforts to suppress minority votes. As shown in Figure 8.9, the rapidly changing demographic face of the United States underscores the strategic urgency of these efforts.

When Nixon first succeeded in transforming the GOP into a party composed disproportionately of white racial conservatives, the white share of the country's population stood at just under 85 percent. Hispanics, by contrast, were but 4.5 percent of the population. When Reagan solidified the racial cast of his party by completing the electoral realignment of the white South, whites still constituted better than three quarters of the nation's population. As Obama geared up for his reelection campaign, however, the white percentage of the population had shrunk to just 63 percent, with the black and Hispanic share approaching half the white total. By the time Americans cast their

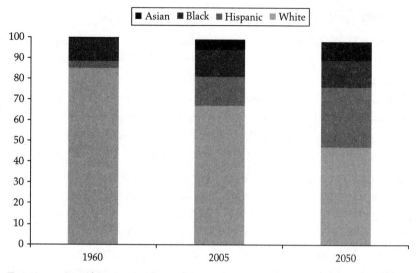

Figure 8.9 Racial Demographics of the United States, 1960–2050
Source: Pew Research Center

ballots in 2016, whites will constitute little more than 60 percent of the population. Quite simply, the demographic noose is tightening on the GOP. In the wake of Mitt Romney's loss in 2012, there was, of course, lots of bold talk about the Republicans embracing diversity and becoming a more inclusive party. While entirely sensible from a detached, strategic perspective, it strains credibility to think it could actually happen. The demographic and ideological makeup of today's GOP will make it very hard to turn the Republican ship around anytime soon. Having painted themselves into this particular demographic corner, Republicans have little choice but to do all they can to limit the votes of racial minorities. For that reason, we should expect to see an even more intensive vote suppression effort than we saw in 2012. Unfortunately, with the elimination of the preclearance provision of the Voting Rights Act, voter rights activists have been deprived of perhaps the single most valuable tool they have used in the past to outlaw or otherwise block these efforts. Those who care about the integrity of our electoral system and the severe threat these efforts pose to the principle of political equality will need to again be vigilant and prepared to use whatever legal means they have at their disposal to challenge vote suppression efforts when and wherever they arise, and to counter with voter registration and get-out-the-vote efforts of their own.

The Electoral Implications of Felon Disenfranchisement

Before we leave the topic of race and voter suppression, we would do well to consider the decidedly nonrandom electoral implications of the unprecedented expansion in the US prison population that has taken place over the past four to five decades. Figure 8.10 captures the extraordinary dimensions of the "incarceration epidemic" that has unfolded in this country since the late 1970s.

Figure 8.10 shows that the number of those imprisoned in the United States has increased more than fourfold over the past three decades, or 10 times faster than the rate of growth for the country as a whole. And these figures—taken from the Bureau of Justice Statistics—may actually underestimate the rate of growth in the prison population. Leading experts, including the International Centre for Prison Studies and the Sentencing Project, put that number closer to 2.2 million incarcerated today, or a 500 percent increase over the past three decades.[54] The latter figure would equate to an incarceration rate of roughly 716 per 100,000 in population, making the United States the leading jailer in the world.[55]

In the final analysis, however, our primary concern has more to do with *who* than *how many*. If the demographic composition of our prison population essentially mirrored the country as a whole, we wouldn't be having this particular "conversation." Needless to say it

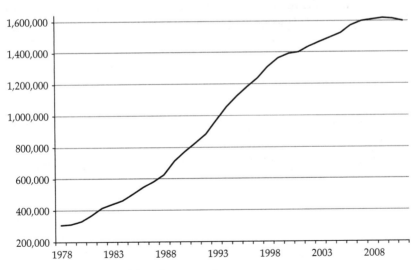

Figure 8.10 Incarcerated Population, 1978–2011

does not. The following sorry litany of facts taken from a publication of the *American Sociological Association* entitled "Race, Ethnicity, and the Criminal Justice System," tells the skewed demographic story:

- Incarceration rates of blacks in 1999 were 2.8 times the rates in 1980, and 8.2 times the incarceration rate for non-Hispanic whites.
- An estimated 16.6 percent of adult black males in 2001 were current or former state or federal prisoners—twice the rate for Hispanic males (7.7 percent), and 6 times that for white males (2.6 percent).
- 60 percent of all inmates in US prisons in 2004 were minorities (black inmates were an estimated 41 percent of all inmates, Hispanics, 19 percent, with whites only 34 percent) even though blacks and Hispanics made up only about a quarter of the population).
- And at current incarceration rates, about 1 in 3 black males, 1 in 6 Hispanic males, and 1 in 17 white males are expected to go to prison at some point during their lifetime.[56]

The standard story generally offered to account for both the massive expansion in the prison population and the striking racial/ethnic imbalances in that population has to do with the "war on drugs." Launched in the 1970s and expanded under Reagan in the 1980s, the war, or so the story goes, explains the extraordinary growth in total inmates and the higher rate of incarceration for, say, blacks than whites. Never mind that self-reported data on drug usage among high school seniors has consistently shown whites to have significantly *higher* rates of all manner of drug usage—that is marijuana, cocaine, and crack—than blacks.[57] However interesting it may be, the detailed story of race, the war on drugs, and the incarceration epidemic is beyond the scope of this book. In any case it has been explored in full by a host of other scholars.[58]

That leaves just one remaining piece of the puzzle to complete our story. Quite simply, the laws governing the voting rights of felons or ex-convicts are far harsher or more restrictive in the United States than in virtually all other Western democracies. While it is true that most nations in the world do not allow prisoners to vote, the United States is among the rare few who restrict voting *after* a person's prison term has been completed. Closer to home, most Western democracies expressly safeguard the rights of prisoners to vote, with many more allowing voting under certain circumstances.[59]

So not only do we imprison a much higher percentage of our population, but in general we also restrict their voting rights much more than other countries do. These two facts alone would seem to constitute yet another threat to the principle of political equality. Why should those in prison—and especially those who have paid their debt to society and been released—be denied political voice? But when we add the final piece of the puzzle, that is, the stark racial disparities in the prison population, we are no longer talking about a simple inequity in voice between felons and nonfelons, but a much more complicated pattern that reinforces our earlier concern about ongoing attempts to restrict the voting rights of racial and ethnic minorities. Nor is this more complicated pattern only a matter of abstract normative concern. In recent years, scholars have systematically accounted for the significant, nonrandom political impact of felon disenfranchisement. Uggen and Manza's findings are representative in this regard:

> Because felons are drawn disproportionately from the ranks of racial minorities and the poor, disenfranchisement laws tend to take more voters from Democratic than from Republican candidates. Analysis shows that felon disenfranchisement played a decisive role in U.S. Senate elections in recent years. Moreover, at least one Republican presidential victory would have been reversed if former felons had been allowed to vote, and at least one Democratic presidential victory would have been jeopardized had contemporary rates of disenfranchisement prevailed during that time.[60]

The remedy should be clear; even if we are not prepared to make major reforms to our criminal justice system to reduce the size of the prison population or address the stark racial disparities in rates of arrest, conviction, and sentencing, we should, at the very least, bring our laws regarding felon voting in line with those of other Western democracies. Until we do, we will not only be denying political voice to most convicts and many ex-convicts, but perpetuating a form of racial discrimination in electoral participation that has already been shown to carry with it significant partisan bias.

Gerrymandering

While the myriad Republican efforts to restrict the voting rights of traditional Democratic voters drew lots of critical scrutiny in the run-up to the 2012 general election, less attention was focused on the most recent epidemic of gerrymandering and the nondemocratic implications of it. Redrawing electoral boundaries to advantage the party in power is, of course, a time-honored American political tradition. That may help explain why these recent efforts received scant attention relative to the GOP's transparent vote suppression tactics, but the truth of the matter is that we should be much more concerned about gerrymandering than about voter suppression. While the literature on the impact of voter identification (ID) laws generally confirms the partisan bias noted by critics, it also suggests that the suppressive effects are fairly modest.[61] The same cannot be said for the recent epidemic of gerrymandering. On the contrary, it seems clear that the recent restructuring of House districts has had the effect of making the entire system much less competitive, essentially rendering the issue of political voice meaningless in the great majority of locales. The trend is shown all too clearly in Figure 8.11.

If we define "landslide" and "strong" districts as noncompetitive, nearly 45 percent of all House races remained competitive in 1992 (188 of 435). As of 2012, that number was just 20 percent (88 of 435). The decline in true "swing" districts was even steeper, dropping from nearly a quarter of the total in 1992 (103 of 435) to a scant 8 percent (35 of 435) 20 years later. For all intents and purposes, the great majority of Americans now exercise little electoral voice when it comes to those who represent them in the House. But this dramatic increase in the number of "safe districts" has done more than simply mute electoral voice; it has also served to greatly enhance the influence of the movement wing of the Republican Party. The point is, in noncompetitive districts, the only election that really matters is the primary. In safe Republican districts, whoever wins the GOP primary is virtually assured of going to Washington. And given the exceedingly low turnout numbers characteristic of primaries, this greatly favors the Tea Party–backed candidates who appeal to the nonrepresentative, ideologically extreme voters who tend to turn out for such contests. In turn, this

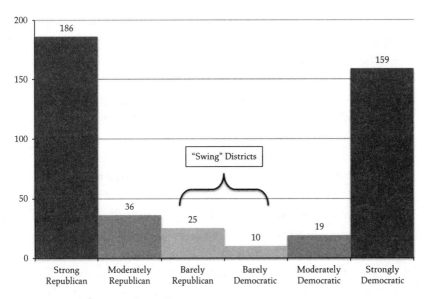

Figure 8.11 Safe versus Swing Districts
Source: Cook's Report: http://cookpolitical.com/story/5604

dynamic is key to understanding how the House has become the central impediment to federal policymaking in recent years. With so many movement conservatives now coming to the House from safe Republican districts, there is simply no electoral incentive for them to moderate their views once in office. Facing no electoral threat, they are subject neither to party discipline nor to general public opprobrium. As a result, they remain free to hold firm to their narrow ideological agenda, rendering Congress increasingly irrelevant and inert in the process.

Nor is the absence of any real choice in most House districts the only cost of gerrymandering. In a recent article in *Daedalus,* former Republican House member Mickey Edwards of Oklahoma highlights two other nondemocratic consequences of the practice. The first reflects his own experience of gerrymandering as a first-term Republican House member in a state still very much under the control of the Democrats. Ironically, the opposition's transparent efforts to redraw House districts to preserve their advantage also benefited Edwards. Nonetheless he came away from the experience with a very jaundiced view of the practice. Writes Edwards:

After I won a congressional seat that had been held for nearly a half-century by the other party... my district was redrawn from a single square-shaped county in the middle of the state to a large upside-down "L" stretching from central Oklahoma to the Kansas border and halfway over to Arkansas, the only purpose being to put as many fellow Republicans into my district and thus make the other districts safer for Democrats. The result was to place tens of thousands of wheat farmers, cattle ranchers, and small-town merchants in a new district where they would be represented by an urban congressman, familiar with big-city issues and unfamiliar with the economic interests of his new constituents. So much for the founders' intended representativeness.[62]

Unfortunately, the kind of willful disregard of geographic integrity described by Edwards has become more or less the norm among the partisan legislators charged with redrawing district boundaries. The game is simple enough: using ever more sophisticated sources of geographic data, seek out and concentrate your voters in several "safe" districts while conceding one large noncompetitive district to their side. The results are districts that, like Edwards' example, lack any kind of fundamental social or cultural coherence. On a lighter note, the lengths to which partisan lawmakers go to fashion safe districts often results in wonderfully comic spatial contortions. A few of our favorites appear in Figure 8.12.

Besides reducing the competitiveness of districts and often their social and geographic integrity, redrawing boundaries also tends to powerfully reinforce partisan polarization, further reducing the prospects for the kind of minimal bipartisanship so crucial to and sadly so rare in today's legislative process. Again, Edwards explains:

Running in a district with no serious likelihood of losing to a member of an opposing party, a [representative] becomes even more dependent on remaining in the good graces of members of his or her own party.... Compelled by the pressures of partisan redistricting to stick to the party line, elected officials are further discouraged from reaching across the aisle to find common ground or forging compromises with members of another party.[63]

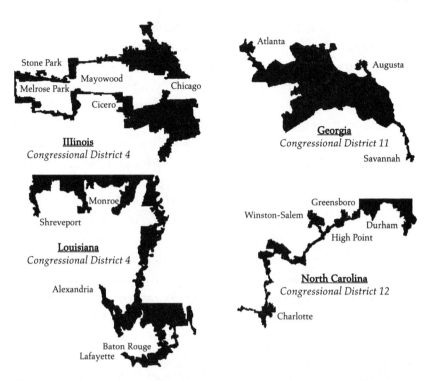

Figure 8.12 Gerrymandered Districts
Source: Graphics from "1990s Supreme Court Redistricting Decisions," Peter S. Wattson

Increased polarization, diminished electoral voice, and freakish district boundaries that undermine the concept of representative government: can anything be done to redress these distortions of democratic ideals and practice? Yes, indeed the answer is simple, straightforward, and already in place in 13 states. It is only fitting that we give the last word to Edwards. These thirteen states, he writes, "have taken this power away from their state legislatures, either entirely or to some degree, and placed much of the redistricting authority in the hands of independent, nonpartisan redistricting commissions. Every state should do the same: drawing district lines should be about able representation, not partisan advantage."[64] Amen.

The Electoral College

And while we are at it, why not consider abolishing the Electoral College, arguably the ultimate voice-suppressing institution in

American politics? Our opposition to the Electoral College is very
similar to our central objection to gerrymandered House districts. If
you reside in a noncompetitive district, you essentially have no electoral
voice in the composition of the House. The same, of course, is true
when it comes to presidential elections, except that the stakes could be
seen as considerably higher. The contrast here is between "safe" and
"battleground" states. Provided one can stand the invading media army
and the nonstop barrage of candidate ads, we imagine the residents of
battleground states derive a heady sense of political importance from
being courted so intensively in the months leading up to a general
election. Nor is this some kind of illusion. In an especially close
election, the voters in one or more of these states may really determine
the outcome of the contest. But what about all those citizens who reside
in safe states? Consider the loyal Republican who lives in California or
the stalwart Mississippi Democrat? Every four years, voting for them is
an exercise in political powerlessness, at least when it comes to the presidential race. This stark dichotomy between "voice" and "no voice"
might not be so bad if most states were competitive enough to qualify
as battleground states. Needless to say, they are not, which means the
preferences of the vast majority of Americans are marginalized every
four years.

Consider the case of the 2012 election, which by US standards, was
closer than most. If we define "battleground" states as those where the
final margin of victory was 5 percent or less, only 6 of the 50 states
qualify. They were Colorado (4 percent), Florida (1 percent), North
Carolina (3 percent), Ohio (2 percent), Pennsylvania (5 percent), and
Virginia (3 percent). Moreover, the mean margin of difference in the
remaining 44 states was a whopping 19 percent. Even with such pop-
ulous states as Florida, Pennsylvania, and Ohio in the mix, the total
population of the 2012 battleground states was barely 20 percent of the
country's total. That means four out of every five Americans exercised
no real electoral voice in a hotly contested, highly consequential, and
comparatively close presidential contest. Why do we persist in an
arrangement that promotes a singularly unnecessary form of political-
electoral inequality? Why not empower every registered voter by doing
away with the Electoral College? If the normative goal of restoring fundamental electoral equality doesn't excite you, what about the likely

jump in voter registration and participation rates and the prospect of meaningful attention to the key issues in the race in *all 50 states*? If we are serious about addressing today's legitimacy crisis and restoring a fundamental sense of individual political equality and efficacy to this country, no single reform would deliver on this promise more than this last one.

The Tyranny of the Primary (and Other Low Turnout Elections)

Our current system of presidential primaries was born of the very principle of political equality that serves as our normative touchstone here. The institutional reform movement of 1968–72 that birthed the present system was motivated by the desire to democratize the selection of convention delegates, wrest control of the presidential nomination process from party elites, and "let the people decide" by means of binding primaries and caucuses. And as binding primaries became the norm in presidential contests, their use in House and Senate races expanded as well. Without a doubt the widespread use of primaries is far more democratic—far more in keeping with the principle of political equality—than the old system, at least as measured by the number of citizens who take part in the process. And yet, it seems increasingly clear that this nominally more democratic system is implicated in a host of perverse, unanticipated effects that are contributing to the extreme, polarized quality of our legislative bodies, including Congress. The problem owes to two features of primary elections touched on earlier: low turnout and the nonrepresentative character of primary voters.

These features are ideally suited—as we've noted at several points in the book—to magnifying the influence of the ideologically extreme, movement wing of a party. The New Left took advantage of the primaries to secure the Democratic Party nomination for the movement-identified George McGovern in 1972. In recent decades, however, it is the movement wing of the GOP that has been the most consistently active, pushing the party to the right through the strategic exploitation of the primary system. And no group of activists has been more strategically savvy in taking advantage of the movement bias of the primaries and other low-turnout elections than Tea Party forces. By recruiting and backing Tea Party candidates for elective office at all levels of the system and mounting primary challenges targeting suspect GOP incumbents, the movement has succeeded in moving the party and a host of legislative bodies—most notably the House of Representatives—sharply to the right since it burst on the scene in 2009. The net effect of this rightward lunge has been to sharply increase partisan polarization and magnify the inequities in ideological voice documented earlier. The result, across an increasing number of policy domains, is the influence of nonrepresentative minority views over the will of the (moderate) majority.

The current nondemocratic implications of our primary system pose a tricky normative challenge for reformers. At first blush, it might seem tempting to blame today's movement conservatives for exploiting the biases inherent in the primary system to promote nonrepresentative ideological views. Nonsense. Movements, of whatever ideological stripe, are not the problem. Quite the opposite; throughout American history, social movements have been a critical vehicle for safeguarding or advancing the rights and views of all manner of minorities—ethnic, racial, religious, or ideological. As such, they have generally served to promote, rather than undermine, the principle of political equality. More pragmatically, Tea Party and other conservative activists can hardly be faulted for taking advantage of the unique opportunities afforded movements by the primary system. No, the problem lies with the anemic turnout typical of primaries, and indeed, all too many elections in the United States. What can be done to address this endemic problem? For starters, it is incumbent on those liberal groups or movements that are especially exercised by the alleged right-wing bias of the primary system to recognize that the system is in fact, ideologically neutral and affords them the same opportunities for amplified voice as it does movement conservatives. One could make a case, for example, that when it burst on the scene in the fall of 2011, the Occupy Movement enjoyed more momentum and broad public support than did the Tea Party.[65] Had Occupy chosen to appropriate and channel this support into a sustained, focused attack on the tax and spending policies that have so advantaged the "1 percent," we might well be talking as much about them today as we do the Tea Party. But they didn't and we are not. Instead, by committing itself to a dead end, pyrrhic strategy of actualizing and defending democratic encampments against the social control appetites of authorities, Occupy soon lost favor with the general public and any chance of developing into a significant force in American politics. The problem then is not movements per se but the lack of strategic vision that informs them. Indeed, in a country afflicted by chronically low levels of mass political engagement, we see movements—of whatever ideological persuasion—as very much part of the solution rather than the problem. That is, they remain an especially promising vehicle for encouraging popular participation in politics. Nothing would please us more than to see a variety of movement groups focusing their efforts on the need to increase voting in the primaries and other low turnout elections.

That said, however, turning primaries into contests to see which nonrepresentative ideological minority can exercise more influence does nothing to address the real issue: the marginalization of the "median voter." How much better things would be if we could achieve much higher voting rates across the board. And we certainly could if we were willing to follow Australia's lead and make voting in most elections compulsory. Concerned that declining rates of voter turnout were beginning to undermine the principle of representative democracy, in 1924 Australia enacted a law requiring all citizens 18 years and older to participate in federal and state elections. Just to be clear, the law does not actually require citizens to vote, only to register to vote, appear at a polling station, and deposit a ballot in a secret ballot box. Still, the change in the law increased voter turnout in Australia from around 55 to over 90 percent. More important, as Mann and Ornstein point out, the new law "changed campaign discourse. Politicians of all stripes have told us that when they know that their own base will turn out en masse, and will be balanced by the other party's base, they shift their efforts to persuading voters in the middle."[66] This would have the positive effect of reducing the felt powerlessness and frustration of the median voter, without in any way suppressing minority views. But quite apart from its immediate salutary effect of muting the current ideological tenor of American electoral politics, it is simply hard to imagine a normative objection to a reform that would so clearly advance the goal of political equality.

Even if we did not want to go quite that far, there are other electoral reforms we could enact that would also have the effect of moderating extreme views in favor of a more equitable contest reflecting the distribution of preferences across the full ideological spectrum. Indeed, as Mann and Ornstein note, these "other electoral reforms" are already selectively in place in the United States:

> Another option is to expand the use of open primaries and combine them with preference voting. Several states...now use open primaries, in which all candidates from all sides run together; the top two finishers go on the ballot for the general election. Add in preference voting, whereby voters rank their choices in order of preference...and it reduces the chances of an extreme candidate winning a top-two finish because multiple non-extreme candidates divide the votes of the more populous, moderate electorate. Another advantage of an open primary is that lawmakers who cast contentious votes would be less intimidated by threats of a primary challenge funded by ideological organizations if they knew the primary electorate would be expanded beyond a small fringe base.[67]

We are agnostic about the comparative virtues of these various options. Some version of the Australian law would obviously represent the fullest electoral embodiment of the principle of political equality. On the other hand, it would obviously be easier to expand reforms (e.g., open primary, preference voting) that have already achieved some degree of legal and institutional standing in the United States, and more important, have been shown to temper the extreme character of the closed primary.[68] The more important point is, when it comes to the ideological bias of the primary, we do have options.

Summing Up

At the outset of the book, we defined the current mess the country is in as a function of two central features: extreme material inequality and deep and rapidly increasing partisan polarization. All along, though, we have been centrally concerned with a third dysfunctional feature of the present day United States. We refer to the sorry state of American democracy. It is this third problematic aspect of the contemporary United States that has occupied our attention in this final chapter. Although we see the drastic erosion of our democratic ideals and practices as largely deriving from the other two trends, the causal arrow is now, in our view, very much reversed. The key, we believe, to gaining any kind of meaningful traction on the substantive economic and political issues that divide us must come from efforts to restore and revitalize our democratic ideals and practices. Nothing will be more vital to this effort than restoring a sense of shared citizenship in this country. Divisions are one thing. The country has been deeply divided many times before, but with the exception of the earliest days of the republic and the Civil War period, 1855–1876, we would be surprised if there has ever been another extended period in the history of the nation marked by the levels of deep distrust and fundamental denial of political and social equality that characterize the present moment.

In an interview conducted shortly after Walter Cronkite's death in 2009, his former CBS colleague Dan Rather expressed great admiration for Cronkite's journalistic values and integrity, noting that one would be hard-pressed to guess from the objective quality of his reporting that his own views were decidedly liberal. He also went on to note that despite Cronkite's liberal views, the president he—that is Cronkite—most admired was the moderate Republican Eisenhower. But then again, Rather quickly added, Cronkite grew up in a period when you supported your president, regardless of which party he came from. And in doing so, you partook of a sense of shared national identity and citizenship that is all but absent from contemporary American life. Could there be a starker contrast to Cronkite's bipartisan embrace of a Republican president than the vitriol and disrespect visited upon our current sitting president by a dismayingly large segment of the American public? The "birther" controversy is simply the best known—and most resilient—of the various paranoid fantasies that deny to Obama the basic legitimacy accorded a fellow citizen. Six years into his term as our president, and in the face of incontrovertible evidence to the contrary, 25 percent of the American public—and 45 percent of Republicans—continue to insist that Obama is not an American citizen and therefore a usurper of his position.[69] Another 17 percent persist in believing that the president is a Muslim.[70] Finally, and quite unbelievably, Public Policy Polling reports that as many as one in ten—and one in five among Republicans, claim that he's the "anti-Christ."[71] And then there is the steady stream of breathtaking personal attacks on the president by

Republican officials and opinion leaders. There was Representative Mike Coffman's (R-Colorado) considered judgment that "in his heart...[Obama]'s not an American."[72] But that pales beside the charges leveled at the president by Glenn Beck and Rush Limbaugh. For his part, Beck asserted that Obama had "over and over again" revealed himself "as a guy who has a deep-seated hatred for white people or the white culture.... This guy is, I believe, a racist."[73] And Limbaugh? He would have us believe that the president of the United States hates the very country he is helping to govern. In Limbaugh's own words: "I think it can now be said without equivocation... that this man hates this country. He is trying—Barack Obama is trying—to dismantle, brick-by-brick, the American dream."[74]

We are now defined much more by our divisions than by any sense of national unity. As Parker and Barreto's 2013 survey of Tea Party adherents makes clear, animus toward a wide range of "others" informs the movement and by extension a significant swath of the Republican Party.[75] Similarly, a good many Democrats deny legitimacy to those on the right. To the extent that a basic civility and respect for one's fellow citizens has now given way to a series of "us/them" divisions—infused with real hatred and distrust—we worry that we may be in danger of destroying the minimal mutual trust and respect required for democratic self-governance.

As we bring the book to a close, we reflect on the temporal arc of our narrative. We began our story in the postwar period, an era generally revered on the right as something of a golden age in American life; a time of shared patriotism, prosperity, and faith. Allowing for a bit of oversimplification, it was all of that, but it was also a time of unprecedented cooperation between the two parties and of bipartisan support for expanding social programs and the tax policies needed to fund them. More important, it was a period in which Democrats and Republicans alike were committed to the proposition that among the central functions of the federal government was the mitigation of disadvantage and the expansion of opportunities for all Americans. And with a huge assist from our privileged position in the postwar global economy, it worked.

In Figure 6.7 we compared the percentage gains experienced by different segments of the income distribution for two periods: 1947 to 1975 and 1975 to 2010. The central income dynamics characteristic of the two eras could not have been more different. Reflecting the combined effect of a booming economy and the fiscal policies of the postwar period, all regions of the income distribution did exceedingly well between 1947 and 1975. As we noted in Chapter 6, however, no one did better in this period than the middle class, and everyone did slightly better than the very rich. Contrast that with the starkly different and highly unequal stepwise pattern for the more recent period.

How much stronger we were as a nation when the rising tide of the postwar economy was lifting all boats and when the great majority of citizens took pride in the expanding reach of the American dream. How much weaker we are today as a result of the deep and growing economic and political divisions documented in this book. To reclaim our greatness as a country, we must begin to bridge these divides. This process must start with our politics and in particular with our elected officials searching for common ground, in spite of their differences. If they won't, we will have no choice but to compel them to do so through grass-roots action of our own. Throughout the book we have highlighted the normal centrifugal force of movements in pushing the two major parties toward their ideological margins. So successful have movements been in recent decades that those parties—especially the GOP—now largely reside at the margins. What is needed now is a *centripetal* movement to reclaim and reinvigorate the political middle and repair our badly frayed democracy.

NOTES

Chapter 1

1. http://www.npr.org/templates/story/story.php?storyId=18489466.
2. http://www.politico.com/news/stories/1108/15301.html.
3. Parker and Barreto 2013; Pasek et al. forthcoming; Tesler forthcoming; Tesler and Sears 2010.
4. Gallup Poll on "Most Important Problem" (http://www.gallup.com/poll/165302/dysfunctional-gov-surpasses-economy-top-problem.aspx).
5. Emerging from the Piketty and Saez World Top Incomes Database, see "Striking It Richer: The Evolution of Top Incomes in the United States" by Saez, first published in *Pathways Magazine* at Stanford's Center on Poverty and Inequality, and the September 3, 2013, update (http://elsa.berkeley.edu/~saez/saez-UStopincomes-2012.pdf).
6. McCarty, Poole, and Rosenthal 2006.
7. Lepore 2013.
8. Cox 1990.
9. Burden 2001; Cohen et al. 2008; Fiorina 1999; Fiorina et al. 2005.
10. Doherty 1998.
11. Roberts and Roberts 1998.
12. Fiorina 1999, p. 3.
13. The clear exception to this rule is Sid Tarrow who, besides being a distinguished comparativist, has also been among the most influential social movement scholars since the emergence of the field in the 1980s. Tarrow has long argued for a perspective on politics that sees movements, parties, interest groups, and governmental institutions as mutually

constitutive. His recent chapter with the first author is only the latest in a long string of publications to advance this perspective. McAdam and Tarrow 2013; see also Tarrow 2011.

14. One important exception to the disciplinary divide described here is conceptual and empirical work by John Zaller and a number of colleagues that at least implicitly acknowledges the important role that movements often play in shaping party politics (Bawn et al. 2012; Cohen et al. 2008). In an interesting 2012 conceptual article, Bawn et al. (p. 571) "propose a theory of political parties in which interest groups and activists are the key actors, and coalitions of groups develop common agendas and screen candidates for party nominations based on loyalty to their agendas. This theoretical stance contrasts with currently dominant theories, which view parties as controlled by election-minded politicians." This conception is very similar to our argument that party politics in the United States is typically shaped by an ongoing tug of war between more party- and movement-oriented coalitions of actors. "Election-minded politicians" tend to be more oriented to party and inclined to appeal to the moderate center of the ideological continuum. But parties, as the authors note, are also home to more ideologically extreme elements. Bawn et al. call these elements "extreme policy demanders." Among the most important of these extreme policy demanders are movement groups and activists, who exert significant centrifugal force on the parties, even as "election-minded politicians" and their allies seek to respond to the centripetal incentives represented by the "medium voter."

15. Crotty and Jackson 1985; Polsby 1983; Walker 1988.
16. DiMaggio et al. 1996, p. 738.
17. Abramowitz 2013; Abramowitz and Saunders 2005; Hetherington 2011; Hetherington and Weiler 2009; Niemi, Weisberg, and Kimball 2011.
18. Fiorina, Abrams, and Pope 2005; Fiorina and Levendusky 2006; Fiorina and Abrams 2008.
19. Fiorina and Abrams 2008, p. 563.
20. Abramowitz 2006.
21. McCarty, Poole, and Rosenthal 2006.
22. McVeigh 2009; Rhomberg 2004.
23. Phillips-Fein 2009; McGirr 2001; Scher 1996.
24. Bloom and Martin 2013.
25. Farris 2012, p. 186.
26. Kabaservice 2012.
27. Goldman 1970, p. 102.
28. Quoted in Carson 1981, p. 126.
29. McAdam 1988, p. 120.
30. Shafer 1983, p. 4; emphasis in original.
31. Aldrich 1995; Brady et al. 2007; Burden; Fiorina et al. 2005.

Chapter 2

1. Kabaservice 2010.
2. Feinstein and Schickler 2008; Schickler et al. 2010.

3. Lizza 2012, p. 38.
4. Poole and Rosenthal 2007, p. 136.
5. Poole and Rosenthal 2007, pp. 103–4.
6. Poole and Rosenthal 2007, p.104.
7. This is not to ignore the many exclusionary practices of the New Deal legislation, as noted by Katznelson (2005).
8. Quoted in McAdam 1999a, p. 83.
9. Mettler 2005.
10. Fredik Logevall 2012, p. 184.
11. Myrdal 1970, p. 35.
12. Schickler et al. 2010.
13. Poole and Rosenthal 2007, p. 104.
14. Tynes 1996, pp. 118–19.
15. McAdam 1999a, pp. 77–81.
16. A consortium of scholars at Stanford, Pennsylvania State University, and the University of Arizona compiled a detailed time-series data set on "public protest" in the United States spanning the years 1960 to 1995. Commonly referred to as "yankdat," the actual data from the project are available at yankdat.com.
17. The data were collected as part of an ambitious research project designed to empirically map the growth of social movement activity in the United States from roughly 1950 to 1970 (the data were later extended to 1980 by Craig Jenkins). Carried out at State University of New York, Stonybrook, in the 1970s, the project employed graduate students—including the first author—to code all relevant "social movement" events reported in the *New York Times* for "their" movement for a specified range of years. Alas, the project never yielded the broad empirical overview of public protest in the United States in the postwar period that had been intended. Of the various movements studied, only civil rights/black power and the farm worker's struggle were the subjects of published empirical work (Jenkins and Perrow 1977; Jenkins 1985; McAdam 1982, 1999a).
18. These data were also generated for the aforementioned "insurgency project," and served as part of the evidentiary basis for the first author's dissertation and subsequent 1982 book.
19. Kleidman 1993, ch. 5.
20. Phillips-Fein 2009; McGirr 2001; Scher 1996.
21. Richard Flacks 1971, p. 2.
22. Quoted in Anderson 1995, p. 38.
23. Cohen 1993; Kelley 1990; Korstad 2003.

Chapter 3

1. American National Election Studies: http://electionstudies.org/nesguide/text/tab5a_1.txt.
2. McAdam 1999b.

3. McAdam 1988, p. 142.
4. Feinstein and Schickler 2008; Schickler et al. 2010.
5. McAdam 1999a, p. xx.
6. Leuchtenburg 2005, p. 46.
7. Quoted in McAdam 1999a, p. 84.
8. McCullough 1992.
9. See Dudziak 2000; Layton 2000; Skrentny 1998.
10. In stressing the considerable extent to which Cold War foreign policy considerations informed Truman's civil rights policies, we are not for a minute blind to the influence of naked electoral calculus as well. By the mid- to late-1940s, political strategists were fully aware of the rapid expansion and growing electoral significance of the "black vote." Indeed, in the wake of the 1944 election, Roosevelt's narrow victory was in part credited to his support among African American voters (Brooks 1974: 121).
11. Quoted in Woodward 1966, p. 132.
12. Cook 1981, pp.173–77; Dudziak 2000, ch. 4.
13. McAdam 1999a, p. 86.
14. Lawson 1976, p. 256.
15. Hall 2009.
16. McAdam 2009, pp. 67–68.
17. Hubbard 1968, p. 5.
18. King 1963, pp. 34–35.
19. Hubbard 1968, p. 5.
20. Watters 1971, p. 266; emphasis added.
21. McAdam 1999a, p. 178. Famously, Kennedy paid ironic tribute to Connor—and indirectly to the strategic dynamic under discussion—when he hosted King and other civil rights leaders at the White House during the August 1963 March on Washington. In an offhanded remark to King, during a discussion of the civil rights bill then before Congress, Kennedy indicated that "our judgment of Bull Connor should not be too harsh. After all, in his own way, he has done a good deal for civil rights legislation this year" (quoted in King, p. 144).
22. The high regard for Kennedy among African Americans is out of proportion to the late president's objective civil rights record. On taking office, Kennedy had little or no commitment to the issue. His main policy aims had much more to do with foreign policy than domestic matters. Like his Democratic predecessors Truman and Roosevelt, Kennedy's main goal when it came to race was finessing the issue so as not to antagonize the strategically critical southern wing of his party. In time, the relentless force of the movement made this impossible, compelling Kennedy to more fully embrace the need for civil rights reform. At best, then, his record in this area was mixed and much less consistently pro–civil rights than that of his successor, Lyndon Johnson, who nonetheless does not seem to be held in near the same regard by blacks as JFK.

23. One might object to this characterization, pointing to the prolonged and agonized response to Lincoln's assassination in 1865. The difference in the two cases, however, owes to the barely suppressed righteous satisfaction—if not outright joy—that greeted Lincoln's death in the South. There was no such regional "dissent" from the genuine outpouring of grief evoked by Kennedy's murder.

24. McAdam 1999a, p.168.

25. Dittmer 1995; Payne 1996.

26. Guyot quoted in Raines 1083, p. 287.

27. Atwater 1964, p. 16.

28. Forman quoted in McAdam 1988, p. 40.

29. Holt 1965, p. 167.

30. Quoted in White 1965, p. 279.

31. Harris 1982, p. 74.

32. Quoted in Romaine 1970, pp. 335–36.

33. Quoted in Carson 1981, p. 126.

34. Edsall and Edsall 1992; Carmines and Stimson 1989.

35. Cohen et al. 2008, p. 140.

36. Quoted in Middendorf 2006, p. 15.

37. Cohen et al. 2008.

38. Lambert 1993, p. A34.

39. Carmine and Stimson 1989, p. 69.

40. Carmines and Stimson 1989, p. 70.

41. Indeed 94 percent of the actions represented in the figure took place in the states of the former Confederacy (McAdam 1999a).

42. The lie in all the drama of that long ago day in Tuscaloosa was that the "confrontation" had been scripted in advance by Wallace in private conversation with John and Bobby Kennedy. The latter agreed to allow Wallace to "stand in the school house door"—as he had promised he would do during his January inaugural address—if he agreed to step quietly aside the following day. He did, but not before the subterfuge allowed him to emerge as the hero of the embryonic white resistance movement.

43. Brink and Harris 1967, p. 182.

44. Killian 1975, p. 132.

45. Brink and Harris 1967, p. 111.

46. Brink and Harris 1967, pp.111–14.

47. Samuel Lubell 1964, pp. 127–28.

48. Brink and Harris 1967, p. 108.

49. Converse et al. 1969, p. 1105.

50. Phillips 1969, p. 37.

51. Phillips 1969, p. 287.

52. Edsall and Edsall 1992, p. 82.

53. Quoted in Edsall and Edsall 1992, pp. 82–83.

54. Edsall and Edsall 1992, p. 82.

55. Quoted in Ambrose 1989, pp. 316–17.

56. Edsall and Edsall 1992, pp. 82.

57. Although nearly 50 years have elapsed since Nixon was first elected, one can hardly miss the eerie parallels between the preclearance issue then and now. In the late 1960s, white elected officials in the South at all levels were scrambling to retain political control in the face of rapidly rising numbers of black voters. Had Nixon been able to do away with the preclearance requirement, the challenge confronting the region's long-standing white political elite would have been eased considerably. All sorts of possibilities for creative redistricting or alterations in voting rules would have opened up, had the need to secure Justice Department approval for any such changes been eliminated. Fast forward to today: nationwide the GOP faces the challenge, not of newly registered black voters, but of a shrinking white electorate and a rising tide of Democrat-aligned non-white voters. What hasn't changed is the GOP response to this new demographic challenge. As before, their efforts to retain political and electoral control continue to turn on a steady stream of demographically gerrymandered districts and a flood of racially restrictive new voting laws. There is, however, another difference between these otherwise familiar efforts, then and now. Forty-three years after Nixon failed in his bid to overturn the preclearance requirement of the Voting Rights Act, the Supreme Court did just that by decreeing in *Shelby County, Alabama v. Holder, Attorney General et al.* that the formula used to determine which districts were subject to review was out of date and therefore invalid. The practical significance of the decision should be clear on its face. Heading into the 2014 midterms and 2016 general election, white racial conservatives are going to face much less federal "interference" in their efforts to fashion electoral districts and procedures motivated by a desire to mute the voice of Democratic leaning minority voters. The more things change, the more they remain the same.

58. Edsall and Edsall 1992, p. 84.

59. census.gov.

60. Goldman 1970, p. 102.

Chapter 4

1. Shafer 1983.

2. Robert Michels 1962 [1911]; Ron Aminzade 1993.

3. Bruhn 2008; Heaney and Rojas 2012.

4. Skocpol and Williamson 2012.

5. DeBenedetti 1990, p. 227.

6. DeBenedetti 1990, p. 228.

7. August 1968 Gallup Poll: http://www.gallup.com/poll/19924/war-through-partisan-lenses.aspx.

8. DeBenedetti 1990, p.209.

9. It seems almost as surreal today as it did in 1968 to recall that a scant five days after Johnson withdrew from the race, Martin Luther King Jr. was shot and killed in Memphis, Tennessee.

10. Shafer 1983, p. 15.

11. Shafer 1983, p. 19.

12. Shafer 1983, p.25; emphasis added.

13. Shafer 1983, pp. 25–40.

14. Quoted in Shafer 1983, p. 34; emphasis in original.

15. Shafer 1983, p. 38.

16. In 1956, Adlai Stevenson received just 42 percent of the popular vote in his rematch with Dwight Eisenhower.

17. Kingdon 1984.

18. Shafer 1983, p. 42.

19. There were, of course, new staff hires as well, but in making these hires McGovern was clearly intent on reinforcing the radical reform bent of the original Hughes staffers. The most important of these additional hires was the appointment of Kenneth Bode as full-time director of research for the Commission. Bode too had an activist background, had come out of the McCarthy campaign, and shared with the veteran staff a distrust and antipathy toward the Democratic Party establishment. Together with veteran Hughes staffer, Eli Segal, who served as counsel to the commission, Bode was probably the most influential member of the McGovern staff.

20. Shafer 1983, p. 73.

21. Shafer 1983, p. 210.

22. Quoted in Shafer 1983, pp.146–47; emphasis added.

23. Quoted in Crotty and Jackson 1985, p. 33.

24. Quoted in Shafer 1983, pp. 219–20; emphasis in original.

25. Quoted in Shafer 1983, p. 250.

26. Crotty and Jackson 1985, p. 16.

27. Shafer 1988, p. 163.

28. Shafer 1988, p. 47.

29. Crotty and Jackson 1985, p. 49.

30. Aldrich 1995; Brady et al. 2007; Burden 2001; Fiorina et al. 2005.

31. Shafer 1983, p. 427.

32. Democratic Party Platform, 1972 from The American Presidency Project: http://www.presidency.ucsb.edu/ws/index.php?pid=29605.

33. In the 1984 election, Ronald Reagan soundly defeated Democratic candidate Walter Mondale winning 58.8 percent compared to 40.6 percent of the popular vote—slightly more than McGovern—but with Mondale claiming just 13 electoral votes—four shy of McGovern—from the District of Columbia and Minnesota.

34. http://elections.nytimes.com/2008/results/president/national-exit-polls.html.

35. Watergate is generally represented as an aberration, a byproduct of the singular, paranoid world view that marked Richard Nixon as perhaps the most psychologically distinctive, if not troubled, president in US history. Without for a minute discounting the role that Nixon's distinctive psychology no doubt played in the campaign of dirty tricks and political espionage that triggered the scandal, in our view a case can be made that Watergate also bears the clear imprint of the increasingly radical movement activity that marked Nixon's first term. Consider the two most celebrated targets of the illegal activities engaged in by Nixon's team of Watergate "plumbers." In one instance, the plumbers broke into the office of Daniel Ellsberg's psychiatrist and stole files related to his case. Nixon's obsession with Ellsberg stemmed from his leaking of the top-secret "Pentagon Papers" to the *New York Times,* among other papers. By calling into question the administration's prosecution of the Vietnam War, the secret report aided the anti-war cause, which, of course, was exactly Ellsberg's intent in releasing the "Papers." And what of the break-in at the offices of the Democratic National Committee in the Watergate complex that triggered the scandal and gave it its name? We have already documented the increasing influence of New Left activists within the Democratic Party in the years corresponding to the covert activities countenanced by Nixon. The point is, Nixon's actions occurred in the context of escalating anti-war and related campus protests, and clear evidence of growing New Left influence within the "enemy camp" (read: Democratic Party). His actions have to be seen against, and partially as a reaction to, the growing influence of movements in American politics.

36. American National Election Studies: http://www.electionstudies.org/nesguide/toptable/tab5a_1.htm.

37. Critchlow 2011, p. 103.

38. Critchlow 2011; Kabaservice 2012.

39. Quoted in Jenkins 2006, pp. 96–97.

40. Critchlow 2011, p. 123.

41. Ford's wife, Betty, further infuriated both groups by her outspoken advocacy of the ERA and abortion rights for women.

42. Critchlow 2011, p. 123.

43. The true last hurrah of 20th century moderate Republicanism would come with George Herbert Walker Bush's election in 1988.

44. And the first candidate from the South was Lyndon Johnson, who gained the White House only when JFK was shot and killed in office in 1963.

45. Gallup Poll (AIPO), October 17–20, 1975, retrieved from the Roper Center for Public Opinion Research, University of Connecticut: http://www.ropercenter.uconn.edu/data_access/ipoll/ipoll.html.

46. Gallup Poll (AIPO), September 1956–October, 1975, retrieved from the Roper Center for Public Opinion Research, University of Connecticut: http://www.ropercenter.uconn.edu/data_access/ipoll/ipoll.html.

47. Quoted in Flippen 2011, p. 4.
48. Quoted in Harding 2000, p. 22.
49. Quoted in Flippen 2011, pp.77, 79.
50. Williams 2010, p. 125.
51. Flippen 2011, p. 80.
52. Quoted in Marley 2007, p. 43.
53. Flippen 2011, p. 96.
54. No other American president has ever consented to an interview with *Playboy* magazine. Why Carter agreed to do so remains something of a mystery. Perhaps he thought it might reassure those voters who were worried by his fervent embrace of his "born again" faith. Whatever the intent, the result was a disaster. Carter was comfortably ahead of his Republican rival, Gerald Ford, at the time he agreed to the interview, but Ford began to slowly close the gap as the election drew near. Timed for maximum impact, *Playboy* ran the interview in its November 1976 issue, which hit newsstands just two weeks before the election. The public response was strong and immediate, with most commentators sharply critical of Carter's remarks. The most famous—or infamous—of those remarks was his admission that he had "lusted in his heart" for many women. The full quote follows: "Because I am just human and I am tempted and Christ set some almost impossible standards for us. The Bible says, 'Thou shalt not commit adultery.' Christ said, I tell you that anyone who looks on a woman with lust has in his heart already committed adultery. I've looked on a lot of women with lust. I've committed adultery in my heart many times. . . . This is something that God recognizes, that I will do and have done, and God forgives me for it. But that doesn't mean that I condemn someone who not only looks on a woman with lust but who leaves his wife and shacks up with somebody out of wedlock. Christ says, don't consider yourself better than someone else because one guy screws a whole bunch of women while the other guy is loyal to his wife. The guy who's loyal to his wife ought not to be condescending or proud because of the relative degree of sinfulness." The controversy very nearly derailed his campaign. Polls showed his lead over Ford narrowing sharply in the two weeks leading up to the vote. In the end, though Carter survived the ill-timed, ill-considered interview, edging Ford by a slim 50 to 48 percent margin in the popular vote.
55. Edsall and Edsall 1992, p. 134.
56. Hacker and Pierson 2010, p. 117.
57. Quoted in Phelps-Fein 2009, pp.158, 160.
58. Hacker and Pierson 2010, p. 118.
59. Burris 2010, p. 248.
60. Burris 2010.
61. Burris 2010; Neustadtl and Clawson 1998; Su et al. 1995.
62. Burris 2010, p. 251.

63. Neustadtl and Clawson 1998.
64. Francia et al. 2003.
65. Brown et al. 1995,
66. Francia et al. 2003 reported in Burris 2010, p. 255.
67. Burris 2010.
68. Hacker and Pierson 2010, p. 134.
69. Hacker and Pierson 2010, pp. 60–61.
70. In addition to the severity of anti-labor activism by capital and conservative policymakers, the specific institutional features of the labor regimes in different industrial countries also help us understand cross-national variation in the decline of labor. With respect to Canada and the United States, no one has studied these institutional contributions to union decline more closely than the sociologist Barry Eidlin. It is worth quoting him at length on the consequential institutional differences in the labor regimes in these two countries. As he notes (2013, p. 1), the specific institutional incorporation of labor "created different labor regimes in the U.S. and Canada, governed by different organizing logics. In the U.S., labor was incorporated as an interest group into a labor regime governed by a pluralist idea. In Canada, labor was incorporated as a class representative into a labor regime governed by a class idea. This led to a Canadian labor regime that legitimized class issues and facilitated addressing them and a U.S. labor regime that delegitimized class issues and prevented addressing them. As employer aggression flared in both countries in the 1970s, the Canadian regime proved better able to hold employers in check and protected workers' collective bargaining rights. As a result, union density stabilized in Canada, while plummeting in the U.S."
71. Hacker and Pierson 2010, p. 59.
72. Edsall 1984.
73. Hacker and Pierson 2010, p. 129.
74. Quoted in Zinn and Arnove 2009, pp. 530–33.
75. McCartin 2011.
76. http://www.federalreserve.gov/boarddocs/speeches/2003/200304092/default.htm.
77. Quoted in Hacker and Pierson 2010, p. 59.
78. Atkinson 2003; Hicks and Misra 1993; Western 1997.
79. Critchlow 2011, p. 150.

Chapter 5

1. *New York Times*, February 13, 1976, p. 29 as reported in Flippen, p. 106.
2. Flippen 2011, p. 106.
3. Balmer 2008, pp. 104–105.
4. Quoted in Clendinen and Nagourney 1999, p. 423.
5. Wilcox 1992, p. 11.
6. Flippen 2011, p. 23.

7. Williams 2010, p. 187.
8. Williams 2010, p. 189.
9. Dunn and Woodward 1990, p. 123.
10. *New York Times*, November 6, 1980.
11. Busch 2005, p. 128; Miller and Wattenberg 1984.
12. Flippen 2011, p. 106.
13. Williams 2010, p. 193.
14. Statistics for 1976–77 come from the US Census Bureau. Rankings for the most recent data, 2010, are reported by the Editorial Projects in Education Research Center, which makes adjustments based on cost of living by state.
15. Sears and Citrin 1982, p. 21.
16. ANES: http://electionstudies.org/nesguide/text/tab5a_1.txt.
17. Sears and Citrin 1982, p. 22.
18. Sears and Citrin 1982, p. 28.
19. Sears and Citrin 1982, p. 29 (Table 2.1).
20. Lo 1990, p. 2.
21. Peterson 1982, p. 184.
22. Sears and Citrin 1982, p. 2.
23. Bartley 1995, pp. 455–56.
24. Cannon 1991, p. 270.
25. Quoted in Black and Black 2002, p. 217.
26. Darman 1996, p. 70.
27. Hacker and Pierson 2010, p. 187.
28. Davies 2003, p. 211.
29. Brownlee and Steuerl 2003, p. 157.
30. Quoted in Reay 2012, p. 71.
31. Galbraith 1988, p. 224.
32. Patterson 2003, p. 363.
33. Brownlee and Steuerle 2003, p. 168.
34. Schroeder in *USA Today*, June 6, 2004.
35. Critchlow 2011, p. 186.
36. *Washington Times*: http://www.washingtontimes.com/blog/watercooler/2012/jan/29/picket-newt-i-am-legitimate-heir-reagan-movement-n/#ixzz2SA7G5pTZ.
37. Seema in *Los Angeles Times*, March 29, 2012.
38. http://www.nytimes.com/ref/us/politics/21seelye-text.html.
39. Brownlee and Steuerle 2003, p. 173.
40. Hacker and Pierson 2010, p. 15; emphasis in original.
41. Edsall and Edsall 1992, p. 159.
42. Davies 2003, p. 211.
43. Davies 2003, p. 211.
44. http://www.politifact.com/virginia/statements/2012/jun/25/gerry-connolly/rep-gerry-connolly-says-reagan-raised-taxes-during/.

45. Davies 2003, p. 211.
46. The deficit increased from $79B in 1981 to $152.6B in 1989 (see Table 5.1); Sources: Department of Commerce (Bureau of Economic Analysis), Department of the Treasury, and Office of Management and Budget.
47. http://www.politifact.com/truth-o-meter/statements/2011/jul/26/barack-obama/obama-says-reagan-raised-debt-ceiling-18-times-geo/.
48. http://www.theguardian.com/world/2012/jun/11/bush-reagan-republicans-moderate-live.

Chapter 6

1. "Reagan Pushes New Federalism," *Evening News*, July 13, 1982, 2A.
2. *Washington Post*, June 12, 1982, A-4.
3. There was, in fact, a fourth process that contributed to the "slow-release," ongoing nature of the Reagan Revolution. This had to do with Reagan's success in systematically remaking the ideological character of the federal judiciary. Prior to Reagan, most presidents had treated judicial appointments as either a form of party patronage, or adopted what O'Brien (2003: 329) calls "a 'bi-partisan approach' to judicial recruitment." The presidents—including Eisenhower, Ford, Carter, and Clinton—who adhered to this latter approach tended, according to O'Brien (2003: 329), to emphasize "first and foremost, their nominees' professional competence. Some... attention was given to rewarding party faithful, along with some consideration of symbolic representation of race and gender on the federal bench. But none of these presidents imposed rigorous ideological screening for their nominees." Reagan, however, did so, making ideological conformity to "a jurisprudence of original intent" a virtual requirement for judicial appointment. Knowing that his legislative program would be controversial and anathema to many liberal jurists, Reagan, from the beginning, consciously set about to remake the ideological character of the federal bench. His aim in this was clear: "to," as his Attorney General Edwin Meese III once put it, "institutionalize the Reagan revolution so it can't be set aside no matter what happens in future presidential elections" (quoted in O'Brien 2003: 327). In orchestrating this effort, Reagan successfully reversed the general liberal direction that had characterized federal jurisprudence since the mid-1930s and, in so doing, catalyzed a conservative judicial countermovement that grew after he left office and remains a powerful political/legal force today.
4. Black and Black 2002, p. 219.
5. Conger and Green 2002.
6. Black and Black, p. 26.
7. http://www.nytimes.com/1988/10/31/us/political-memo-gop-makes-reagan-lure-of-young-a-long-term-asset.html?pagewanted=all&src=pm.
8. Patterson 2003, p. 369.
9. Black and Black 2002, p. 370.
10. Critchlow 2011, p. 247.

11. McAllister 2003, p. 56.
12. Kabaservice 2012, p. 376.
13. Kabaservice 2012, p. 378.
14. Shanahan and Benson 1995, p. 22.
15. Kabaservice 2012, p. 367.
16. Kabaservice 2012, pp. 372–73.
17. Williams 2010, p. 221.
18. Kabaservice 2012, p. 374.
19. Kabaservice 2012, p. 376.
20. Kabaservice 2012, p. 378.
21. Chafee 2008, pp. 6–10.
22. Kabaservice 2012, p. 383.
23. Quoted in Hacker and Pierson 2005, p. 4.
24. For a good comparison across presidential terms, see http://useconomy. about.com/od/usdebtanddeficit/p/US-Debt-by-President.htm.
25. Quoted in Susskind 2004, p. 291.
26. Edsall and Edsall 1992, p. 214.
27. Anderson 1988, p. 438.
28. Critchlow 2011, p. 186.
29. Mann and Ornstein 2012, p. 53.
30. Mann and Ornstein 2012, p. 53.
31. taxfoundation.org.
32. Davies 2003, p. 209.
33. McAllister 2003, p. 56.
34. Hacker 2012, p. 34.
35. Hacker and Pierson 2010, p. 15; emphasis in original.
36. Hacker and Pierson 2010, p. 3.
37. Quoted in Bartels 2008, p. 29.
38. Quoted in Bartels 2008, p. 29.
39. OECD *Society at a Glance 2011—OECD Social Indicators*: http://www .oecd.org/els/societyataglance.htm.
40. Note that we do not have comparable data for Canada or Germany in 2010, though we are quite confident their rates are significantly lower.
41. Top World Incomes Database.
42. Hacker and Pierson 2010, p. 37; emphases in original.
43. Dew-Becker and Gordon 2005, p. 73.
44. Dew-Becker and Gordon 2005, p. 74.
45. Hacker and Pierson 2010; Bartels 2008.
46. Adler and Rehkopf 2008, p. 236.
47. U.S. Department of Health and Human Services in 2000, p. 14.
48. Williams et al. 2010.
49. http://www.who.int/social_determinants/thecommission/finalreport/en/ index.html.
50. Pappas et al. 1993.

51. Krieger et al. 2008, p. 227.
52. Singh and Kogan 2007a, p. 1658.
53. Singh and Kogan 2007b, e928.
54. Berkman 2009.
55. Adler and Newman 2002, p. 60.
56. Shi et al. 1999.
57. Data reported are for 2011 and come from the U.S. Department of Health Statistics: http://aspe.hhs.gov/health/reports/2012/uninsuredintheus/ib.shtml and the U.S Census Bureau's Current Population Survey: http://www.census.gov/hhes/www/cpstables/032012/health/h01_000.htm.
58. As of 2010 reported by the US Census Bureau, Current Population Survey.
59. Goldin and Katz 2008.
60. Reardon 2011, pp. 95–96.
61. Duncan and Murnane 2011, p. 5.
62. Reardon et al. 2012.
63. Reardon et al. 2012, p. 1.
64. Bailey and Dynarski in Duncan and Murnane 2011.
65. Duncane and Murnane 2011.
66. Altonji and Mansfield 2011.
67. Raudenbush et al. 2011.
68. Boyd 2011.
69. Duncan and Murnane 2011, p. 5.
70. Duncan and Murnane 2011, p. 7.
71. "Where the tea party conservatives live," *Washington Post*, October 15, 2013: http://www.washingtonpost.com/blogs/the-fix/wp/2013/10/15/where-the-tea-party-conservatives-live/.
72. Stockman 1986, p. 7.

Chapter 7

1. *Politico* provides an overview of the origins and ongoing debate on the "birther" issue: http://www.politico.com/news/stories/0411/53563.html.
2. The concept of the "Bradley effect" refers to the discrepancy between actual voting behavior and the percentage of white survey respondents who report that they plan to vote for a particular black candidate. The term was coined in the aftermath of the 1982 California gubernatorial race between the Democratic candidate, African American Tom Bradley and his GOP opponent, George Deukmejian. Bradley had a comfortable lead in the polls leading up to the election but wound up losing by a narrow margin to Deukmejian, largely because whites voted for him in far fewer numbers than the poll data suggested they would.
3. Skocpol and Williamson 2012, pp. 12–13.
4. Skocpol and Williamson 2012, p. 4.
5. Skocpol and Williamson 2012, p. 160.
6. Mann and Ornstein 2012, p. xii.

7. Mann and Ornstein 2012, p. xiv.

8. Quoted in Mann and Ornstein 2012, p. ix.

9. Mann and Ornstein 2012, p. x.

10. Draper 2012; Mann and Ornstein 2012.

11. Mann and Ornstein 2012, p. 7.

12. Quoted in Mann and Ornstein 2012, p. 4.

13. Mann and Ornstein 2012, pp. 88–90.

14. Mann and Ornstein 2012, p. 92.

15. Mann and Ornstein 2012, p. 100.

16. The US Office of Management and Budget estimated that the shutdown cost an estimated $2–6 billion. Tax refunds were delayed (est. $4B); fewer private sector jobs were created during the shutdown (est. 120,000 jobs); import and export licenses were put on hold; private sector lending to individuals and businesses was disrupted (est. $1.2 million in requests could not be processed); federal loans to small businesses, homeowners, and housing and healthcare facility developers were disrupted (another $140 million in small business loans); an estimated $500 million in revenues was lost when National Park Service tourism was shut down; and $2.5 billion in compensation was paid out for a combined total of 6.6 million furloughed days for federal government employees: http://www.whitehouse.gov/sites/default/files/omb/reports/impacts-and-costs-of-october-2013-federal-government-shutdown-report.pdf.

17. Furthermore, a case could be made that the goal of defunding or effectively crippling the Affordable Care Act is, in fact, inconsistent or opposed to the earlier GOP stress on deficit reduction and fiscal responsibility. There is a school of thought, endorsed by the Office of Management and Budget (http://cbo.gov/publication/44008) and a good many health economists, that the law will actually reduce health care expenditures and the federal deficit over the long run. From this perspective, the shift in goal could be read not only as a significant escalation in partisan warfare but also a striking abandonment of the central policy aim that had seemingly motivated GOP strategy during the previous congressional session.

18. Edsall and Edsall 1991, p. 98.

19. *Mother Jones* was the first to break the story: www.motherjones.com/politics/2012/09/secret-video-romney-private-fundraiser.

20. Phillips 1969, p. 37.

21. For a more complete story, as well as a contemporary analysis, see CNN reports: www.cnn.com/2012/01/23/politics/welfare-queen/.

22. CBS was one of the many news sources to capture this story: www.cbsnews.com/news/santorum-targets-blacks-in-entitlement-reform/.

23. Tesler and Sears 2010.

24. Highton 2011; Hutchings 2010; Pasek et al. 2009; Piston 2010; Schaffner 2011.

25. Pasek et al. 2012, p. 4.
26. Pasek et al. 2012, p. 2.
27. Parker and Barreto 2013; Abramowitz 2013.
28. Parker and Barreto 2013, ch. 6.
29. Parker and Barreto 2013, p. 221.
30. Parker and Barreto 2013, p. 90.
31. Pratto et al. 1994, p. 741.
32. Abramowitz 2013, p.118.
33. Drew 2012, p. 26.
34. Drew 2012, p. 26.
35. Quoted in Drew 2012, p. 26.
36. Bonica 2010.
37. Skocpol and Williamson 2012, pp. 169–70.
38. Skocpol and Williamson 2012, p. 170.
39. Draper 2012.
40. Quoted in Draper 2012, p. 76; emphases in original.
41. *Washington Post*, August 8, 2011.
42. Quoted in Skocpol and Williamson 2012, p. 185.
43. Abramowitz 2010; Aldrich 1995; Brady et al. 2007; Burden 2001; Fiorina et al. 2005.
44. http://thinkprogress.org/politics/2012/01/23/409656/at-florida-town-hall-rick-santorum-cowardly-panders-to-woman-who-alleges-obama-is-an-avowed-muslim/.
45. http://abcnews.go.com/blogs/politics/2011/09/tea-party-debate-audience-cheered-idea-of-letting-uninsured-patients-die/.
46. Skocpol and Williamson 2012, p. 155; emphasis added.
47. Martin et al. 2013, p. 1.
48. Peters and Weisman 2013.
49. Campbell Robertson, "Byrne Wins Republican Runoff in Alabama House Race," *New York Times*, November 5, 2013.
50. Martin et al. 2013, p. 1.
51. Weisman and Parker 2014, p.1.
52. Weisman and Parker 2014, p. 1. Emphasis added.
53. NBC/Wall Street Journal poll as reported by Mark Murray, "NBC/WSJ Poll: Shutdown Debate Damages GOP," *NBC News*, October 10, 2013: http://firstread.nbcnews.com/_news/2013/10/10/20903624-nbcwsj-poll-shutdown-debate-damages-gop; original poll data: http://msnbcmedia.msn.com/i/MSNBC/Sections/A_Politics/_Today_Stories_Teases/Oct_poll.pdf.
54. http://election.princeton.edu/2013/10/10/a-prediction-for-2014-house-elections-take-1/.
55. Coll 2013, p. 37.

Chapter 8

1. Dahl 1971, p. 1; emphasis added.
2. Edwards 2013, p. 86.

3. Edwards 2013, p. 87; emphasis added.
4. As reported by CNN, a CNN/ORC International poll showed 86 percent of the public supporting some form of background checks that are not currently required; an ABC News/Washington Post survey also reported 86 percent of Americans favoring background checks for gun sales on the internet and at gun shows. The survey also reported that 86 percent of gun-owning households support increases to gun control (politicalticker. blogs.cnn.com/2013/04/17/public-opinion-gets-trumped-in-gun-control-defeat/). The week following the rejection of the legislation, 65 percent of those polled said that the Senate should have passed the measure, and 83 percent said that if they were allowed to vote on the issue in future elections, they would require background checks for all gun purchases (www.gallup.com/poll/162083/americans-wanted-gun-background-checks-pass-senate.aspx).
5. "Public Opinion Gets Trumped in Gun Control Defeat," CNN, April 17, 2013: http://politicalticker.blogs.cnn.com/2013/04/17/public-opinion-gets-trumped-in-gun-control-defeat/.
6. http://www.pewresearch.org/key-data-points/immigration-tip-sheet-on-u-s-public-opinion/.
7. http://www.gallup.com/poll/1660/immigration.aspx#1.
8. Eckholm, Erik. "Access to Abortion Falling as States Pass Restrictions," *New York Times,* January 14, 2014, A1.
9. McCarty, Poole, and Rosenthal, p. 181.
10. To test for the possibility that polarization only impacts "landmark" bills, McCarty applied the same multivariate models to data collected by William Howell and colleagues on all postwar congressional enactments. Howell and his colleagues assigned each bill to one of four categories, based on the importance of the legislation. McCarty tested his models against all four categories of enactments. Significantly, only the least important, most trivial of bills bore no effect of polarization. For the other three categories, McCarty's results were very similar to his findings regarding Mayhew's "landmark enactments" (McCarty 2007).
11. Office of the Clerk: http://library.clerk.house.gov/resume.aspx.
12. Drew 2013, p. 63.
13. Mann and Ornstein 2012, p. ii.
14. Mann and Ornstein 2012, p. 33; emphasis added.
15. Brennan Center: http://www.brennancenter.org/publication/voting-law-changes-election-update
16. Quoted in Toobin 2013, p. 17.
17. Quote in Gourevitch 2012, p. 18.
18. Quoted in Harwood 2013, p. A17.
19. Drew 2012, p. 26.
20. Drew 2012.
21. Cobb et al. 2010; Pitts 2012; Pitts and Neumann 2009.

22. Birnbaum 2000; Clawson et al. 1998; Kaiser 2009; Lessig 2011.
23. Lessig 2011, p. 128; emphases in original.
24. Gilens 2005, p. 794.
25. Gilens 2005, p. 778.
26. Bartels 2008, p. 260; emphasis in original.
27. Lessig 2011.
28. Ornstein and Mann 2000, p. 222.
29. Lessig 2011, p. 91.
30. The extraordinary escalation in the cost of running for office is almost certainly related to another trend that also undermines the principle of political equality. While there has long been a class bias associated with running for public office, Carnes (2012) in his recent book, *White Collar Government,* offers stark evidence of just how much stronger that bias has become in recent years.
31. Hacker and Pierson 2010, p. 118.
32. Huffington 2010, p. 129.
33. Birnbaum 2000; Kaiser 2009; Lessig 2011.
34. Lessig 2011.
35. Stern 1992, p. 130.
36. Quoted in Lessig 2011, pp. 347–48.
37. Huffington 2010, p. 129.
38. Baumgartner et al. 2009, pp. 257–58.
39. Makinson 2003.
40. Schram 1995, p. 89.
41. Makinson 2003, p. 6.
42. Hollings 2006.
43. http://www.people-press.org/2013/10/18/trust-in-government-interactive/.
44. Gallup: http://www.gallup.com/poll/5392/trust-government.aspx.
45. ANES: http://www.electionstudies.org/nesguide/toptable/tab5b_3.htm.
46. Gallup: http://www.gallup.com/poll/165809/congressional-approval-sinks-record-low.aspx.
47. http://articles.washingtonpost.com/2010-02-16/politics/36773318_1_corporations-unions-new-limits.
48. Leach 2013, pp. 96–97.
49. Mann and Ornstein 2012, pp. 75–76.
50. Mann and Ornstein 2012, pp. 75–76.
51. Mann and Ornstein 2012, p. 154.
52. Mann and Ornstein 2012, p. 152.
53. Edwards 2013, p. 90.
54. http://www.prisonstudies.org/country/united-states-america; http://www.sentencingproject.org/template/page.cfm?id=107.
55. http://www.prisonstudies.org/highest-lowest?area=all&category=wb_poprate.
56. *American Sociological Association* 2007, p. 17.

57. ASA 2007, p. 7.
58. Tonry 1995 and Bobo and Thompson 2006, for example.
59. Rottinghaus 2003, p. 22.
60. Uggen and Manza 2002, p. 777.
61. Cobb et al. 2010; Hood and Bullock 2012; Pitt 2013; Pitt and Neumann 2009.
62. Edwards 2013, p. 91.
63. Edwards 2013, p. 88.
64. Edwards 2013, p. 91.
65. Pew Research Center: http://www.people-press.org/2011/10/24/public-divided-over-occupy-wall-street-movement/.
66. Mann and Ornstein 2013, p. 22.
67. Mann and Ornstein 2013, p. 22.
68. Gerber and Morton 1998; McGhee 2010; Kanthak and Morton 2001; Wright and Schaffner 2002.
69. http://www.cbsnews.com/8301-503544_162-20056061-503544.html.
70. http://www.huffingtonpost.com/2012/07/26/obama-muslim_n_1706522.html.
71. http://www.huffingtonpost.com/2013/04/03/americans-believe-obama-anti-christ-global-warming-hoax_n_3008558.html.
72. http://www.huffingtonpost.com/2012/05/18/rep-mike-coffmans-obama-i_n_1527662.html.
73. http://www.huffingtonpost.com/2009/07/28/fox-host-glenn-beck-obama_n_246310.html.
74. Quoted in Klein 2012, p. 53.
75. Parker and Barreto 2013.

REFERENCES

Abramowitz, Alan I. 2006. "Disconnected or Joined at the Hip?" Pp. 72–85 in
  Pietro S. Nivola and David W. Brady (eds.), *Red and Blue Nation? Volume I:
  Characteristics and Causes of America's Polarized Politics.* Washington, DC/
  Stanford, CA: Brookings Institute Press and Stanford University Press.
Abramowitz, Alan I. 2010. *The Disappearing Center: Engaged Citizens,
  Polarization, and American Democracy.* New Haven, CT: Yale University Press.
Abramowitz, Alan I. 2013. *The Polarized Public? Why American Government Is so
  Dysfunctional.* Boston: Pearson.
Abramowitz, Alan I., and Kyle L. Saunders. 2005. "Why Can't We All Just Get
  Along? The Reality of a Polarized America." *The Forum: A Journal of Applied
  Research in Contemporary Politics* 3.
Abramowitz, Alan I., and Kyle L. Saunders. 2008. "Is Polarization a Myth?"
  Journal of Politics 70: 542–55.
Adler, Nancy E., and Katherine Newman. 2002. "Socioeconomic Disparities in
  Health: Pathways and Policies." *Health Affairs* 21: 60–76.
Adler, Nancy E., and David H. Rehkopf. 2008. "U.S. Disparities in Health:
  Descriptions, Causes, and Mechanisms." *Annual Review of Public Health*
  29: 235–52.
Akard, Patrick. 1992. "Corporate Mobilization and Political Power." *American
  Sociological Review* 57: 597–615.
Aldrich, John. 1995. *Why Parties? The Origin and Transformation of Political
  Parties in America.* Chicago: University of Chicago Press.
Aldrich, John. 2009. "The Invisible Primary and Its Effects on Democratic
  Choice." *PS: Political Science and Politics* 42(1): 33–38.

Altonji, Joseph G., and Richard K. Mansfield. 2011. "The Role of Family, School, and Community Characteristics in Inequality in Education and Labor-Market Outcomes." Pp. 339–58 in Greg J. Duncan and Richard J. Murnane, eds., *Whither Opportunity? Rising Inequality, Schools, and Children's Life Chances*. New York: Russell Sage Foundation and Chicago: Spencer Foundation.

Ambrose, Stephen E. 1989. *Nixon: The Triumph of a Politician 1962–1972*. Vol 2. New York: Simon and Schuster.

American Sociological Association. 2007. *Race, Ethnicity, and the Criminal Justice System*. Department of Research and Development, American Sociological Association.

Aminzade, Ronald. 1993. *Ballots and Barricades: Class Formation and Republican Politics in France, 1830–1871*. Princeton, NJ: Princeton University Press.

Anderson, Martin. 1988. *Revolution*. San Diego: Harcourt Brace Jovanovich.

Anderson, Terry H. 1995. *The Movement and the Sixties*. New York: Oxford University Press.

Anzia, Sarah. 2013. *Timing and Turnout*. Chicago: University of Chicago Press.

Atkinson, A. B. 2003. "Income Inequality in OECD Countries: Data and Explanations." *CESifo Economic Studies* 49: 479–513.

Atwater, James. 1964. "If We Can Crack Mississippi..." *Saturday Evening Post*, July 25.

Bailey, Martha J., and Susan M. Dynarski. 2011. "Inequality in Postsecondary Education." Pp. 117–32 in Greg J. Duncan and Richard J. Murnane (eds.), *Whither Opportunity? Rising Inequality, Schools, and Children's Life Chances*. New York: Russell Sage Foundation and Chicago: Spencer Foundation.

Balmer, Randall. 2008. *God in the White House: How Faith Shaped the Presidency from John F. Kennedy to George W. Bush*. New York: HarperCollins.

Bartels, Larry M. 2008. *Unequal Democracy: The Political Economy of the New Gilded Age*. New York: Russell Sage Foundation.

Bartley, Numan V. 1995. *The New South: 1945–1980*. Baton Rouge: Louisiana State University Press.

Baumgartner, Frank R., Jeffrey M. Berry, Marie Hojnacki, David C. Kimball, and Beth L. Leech. 2009. *Lobbying and Policy Change: Who Wins, Who Loses, and Why*. Chicago: University of Chicago Press.

Bawn, Kathleen, Martin Cohen, David Karol, Seth Masket, Hans Noel, and John Zaller. 2012. "A Theory of Political Parties: Groups, Policy Demands and Nominations in American Politics." *Perspectives on Politics* 10: 571–97.

Berkman, Lisa F. 2009. "Social Epidemiology: Social Determinants of Health in the United States: Are We Losing Ground?" *Annual Review of Public Health* 30: 27–41.

Birnbaum, Jeffrey H. 2000. *The Money Men: The Real Story of Fund-raising's Influence on Political Power in America*. New York: Crown.

Black, Duncan. 1958. *A Theory of Committees and Elections*. New York: Cambridge University Press.

Black, Earl, and Merle Black. 2002. *The Rise of Southern Republicans*. Cambridge, MA: Belknap Press of Harvard University Press.

Bloom, Joshua, and Waldo Martin. 2013. *Black against Empire: The History and Politics of the Black Panther Party*. Berkeley: University of California Press.

Bobo, Lawrence B., and Victor Thompson. 2006. "Unfair by Design: The War on Drugs, Race, and the Legitimacy of the Criminal Justice System." Social Design 73(2): 445.

Bonica, Adam. 2010. "Introducing the 112th Congress." *Ideological Cartography*, November 5, 2010. Available at: http://www.ideologicalcartography. com/2010/11/05/introducing-the-112th-congress/

Bonica, Adam. 2013. "Mapping the Ideological Marketplace." *American Journal of Political Science*.

Boyd, Don, Hamp Lankford, Susannah Loeb, Matthew Ronfeldt, and Jim Wycoff. 2011. "The Effect of School Neighborhoods on Teachers' Career Decisions." Pp. 377–96 in Greg J. Duncan and Richard J. Murnane (eds.), *Whither Opportunity? Rising Inequality, Schools, and Children's Life Chances*. New York: Russell Sage Foundation and Chicago: Spencer Foundation.

Brady, David W., Hahrie Hahn, and Jeremy C. Pope. 2007. "Primary Elections and Candidate Ideology: Out of Step with the Primary Electorate?" *Legislative Studies Quarterly* 32: 79–106.

Breines, Wini. 1982. *Community and Organization in the New Left, 1962–1968*. New Brunswick and London: Rutgers University Press.

Brink, William, and Louis Harris. 1967. *Black and White*. New York: Simon and Schuster.

Brooks, Thomas R.1974. *Walls Came Tumbling Down: A History of the Civil Rights Movement, 1940–1970*. Englewood Cliffs, NJ: Prentice-Hall.

Brown, C. W. Jr., L. W. Powell, and C. Wilcox. 1995. *Serious Money: Fundraising and Contributing in Presidential Nomination Campaigns*. New York: Cambridge University Press.

Browning, Joan C. 2000. *Shiloh Witness*. Pp. 37–81 in Constance Curry et al. (eds.), *Deep in Our Hearts: Nine White Women in the Freedom Movement*. Athens: University of Georgia Press.

Brownlee, W. Elliot, and C. Eugene Steuerle. 2003. "Taxation." Pp. 155–81 in W. Elliot Brownlee and Hugh Davis Graham (eds.), *The Reagan Presidency: Pragmatic Conservatism and Its Legacies*. Lawrence: University Press of Kansas.

Bruce, Steve. 1988. *The Rise and Fall of the New Christian Right: Conservative Protestant Politics in America 1978–1988*. Oxford: Clarendon Press.

Bruhn, Kathleen. 2008. *Urban Protest in Mexico and Brazil*. New York: Cambridge University Press.

Burden, Barry C. 2001. "The Polarizing Effects of Congressional Primaries." Pp. 95–115 in Peter F. Galderisi, Marni Ezra, and Michael Lyons (eds.), *Congressional Primaries and the Politics of Representation*. Lanham, MD: Rowman and Littlefield.

Burlage, Dorothy Dawson. 2000. "Truths of the Heart." Pp. 85–130 in Constance Curry et al. (eds.), *Deep in Our Hearts: Nine White Women in the Freedom Movement*. Athens: University of Georgia Press.

Burris, Val. 2001. "The Two Faces of Capital: Corporations and Individual Capitalists as Political Actors." *American Sociological Review* 66: 361–81.

Burris, Val. 2010. "Corporations, Capitalists, and Campaign Finance." Pp. 247–62 in Kevin T. Leicht and J. Craig Jenkins (eds.), *Handbook of Politics: State and Society in Global Perspective.* New York: Springer.

Busch, Andrew E. 2005. *Reagan's Victory: The Presidential Election of 1980 and the Rise of the Right.* Lawrence: University Press of Kansas.

Cannon, Lou. 1991. *President Reagan.* New York: Simon and Schuster.

Cannon, Lou. 2000. *President Reagan: The Role of a Lifetime.* New York: Simon and Schuster.

Carmines, Edward G. and James Stimson. 1989. *Issue Evolution: Race and the Transformation of American Politics.* Princeton, NJ: Princeton University Press.

Carnes, Nicolaus. 2013. *White Collar Government.* Chicago: University of Chicago Press.

Carson, Claybourne. 1981. *In Struggle: SNCC and Black Awakening of the 1960s.* Cambridge, MA: Harvard University Press.

Carson, Claybourne, et al. (eds.). 2003. *Reporting Civil Rights,* Vols. 1–2. New York: Library of America.

Chafee, Lincoln. 2008. *Against the Tide: How a Compliant Congress Empowered a Reckless President.* New York: Thomas Dunn.

Clawson, Dan, and Alan Neustadtl. 1989. "Interlocks, PACs, and Corporate Conservatism." *American Journal of Sociology* 94: 749–73.

Clawson, Dan, Alan Neustadtl, and Mark Weller. 1998. *Dollars and Votes: How Business Campaign Contributions Subvert Democracy.* Philadelphia: Temple University Press.

Clendinen, Didley, and Adam Nagourney. 1999. *Out for Good: The Struggle for a Gay Rights Movement in America.* New York: Simon and Schuster.

Cobb, Rachael V., D. James Greiner, and Kevin M. Quinn. 2010. "Can Voter ID Laws Be Administered in a Race-Neutral Manner? Evidence from the City of Boston in 2008." *Journal of Political Science* 7: 1–33.

Cohen, Marty, David Karol, Hans Noel, and John Zaller. 2008. *The Party Decides: Presidential Nominations Before and After Reform.* Chicago: University of Chicago Press.

Cohen, Robert. 1993. *When the Old Left Was Young.* New York: Oxford University Press.

Coll, Steve. 2013. "Party Crashers." *The New Yorker,* November 4, pp. 37–38.

Conger, Kimberly H., and John C. Green. 2002. "Spreading Out and Digging In: Christian Conservatives and State Republican Parties." *Campaigns and Elections,* February.

Converse, Philip E., Warren E. Miller, Jerrold G. Rusk, and Arthur C. Wolfe. 1969. "Continuity and Change in American Politics: Parties and Issues in the 1968 Election." *American Political Science Review* 63: 1083–105.

Cook, Blanche Wiesen. 1981. *The Declassified Eisenhower: A Divided Legacy.* Garden City, NY: Doubleday.

Cottle, Thomas J. 1971. *Time's Children*. Boston: Little, Brown.

Cox, Gary W. 1990. "Centripetal and Centrifugal Incentives in Electoral Systems." *American Journal of Political Science* 34: 903–35.

Craig, Robert H. 1992. *Religion and Radical Politics*. Philadelphia: Temple University Press.

Critchlow, Donald T. 2011. *The Conservative Ascendancy: How the Republican Right Rose to Power in Modern America* (2nd ed.). Lawrence: University Press of Kansas.

Crotty, William, and John S. Jackson III. 1985. *Presidential Primaries and Nominations*. Washington, DC: CQ Press.

Crowley, Michael. 2012. "A House Divided." *New York Times Book Review*. July 22.

Curry, Constance, et al. 2000. *Deep in Our Hearts: Nine White Women in the Freedom Movement*. Athens: University of Georgia Press.

D'Emilio, John. 2003. *Lost Prophet: The Life and Times of Bayard Rustin*. New York: Free Press.

Dahl, Robert A. 1971. *Polyarchy: Participation and Opposition*. New Haven, CT: Yale University Press.

Darman, Richard. 1996. *Who's in Control? Polar Politics and the Sensible Center*. New York: Simon and Schuster.

Davies, Gareth. 2003. "The Welfare State." Pp. 209–32 in W. Elliot Brownlee and Hugh Davis Graham (eds.), *The Reagan Presidency: Pragmatic Conservatism and Its Legacies*. Lawrence: University Press of Kansas.

DeBenedetti, Charles. 1990. *An American Ordeal: The Antiwar Movement of the Vietnam Era*. Syracuse, NY: Syracuse University Press.

Dew-Becker, Ian, and Robert J. Gordon. 2005. "Where Did the Productivity Growth Go? Inflation Dynamics and the Distribution of Income." Paper presented at the 81st meeting of the Brookings Panel on Economic Activity, Washington DC, September 8–9.

DiMaggio, Paul, John Evans, and Bethany Bryson. 1996. "Have Americans' Social Attitudes Become More Polarized?" *American Journal of Sociology* 102: 690–755.

Dittmer, John. 1995. *Local People: The Struggle for Civil Rights in Mississippi*. Urbana: University of Illinois Press.

Doherty, Carroll. 1998. "Lots of Inertia, Little Lawmaking as Election '98 Approaches." *CQ Weekly*, July 18, 1927.

Downs, Anthony. 1957. *An Economic Theory of Democracy*. New York: Harper and Row.

Draper, Robert. 2012. *Do Not Ask What Good We Do*. New York: Free Press.

Drew, Elizabeth. 2012. "Determined to Vote." *New York Review of Books*, December 20, pp. 26–28.

Drew, Elizabeth. 2013. "The Stranglehold on Our Politics." *New York Review of Books*, September 26, pp. 61–64.

Dudziak, Mary L. 2000. *Cold War Civil Rights: Race and the Image of American Democracy*. Princeton, NJ: Princeton University Press.

Duncan, Greg J., and Richard J. Murnane. 2011. "Introduction: The American Dream, Then and Now." Pp. 3–23 in Greg J. Duncan and Richard Murnane (eds.), *Whither Opportunity? Rising Inequality, Schools, and Children's Life Chances.* New York: Russell Sage Foundation and Chicago: Spencer Foundation.

Duncan, Greg J., and Richard J. Murnane (eds.). 2011. *Whither Opportunity? Rising Inequality, Schools, and Children's Life Chances.* New York: Russell Sage Foundation and Chicago: Spencer Foundation.

Dunn, Charles W., and J. David Woodward. 1990. "Ideological Images for a Television Age: Ronald Reagan as Party Leader." Pp. 115–31 in Dilys M. Hill, Raymond A. Moore, and Phil Williams (eds.), *The Reagan Presidency.* London: Macmillan.

Easterlin, Richard. 1980. *Birth and Fortune.* New York: Basic Books.

Ebbinghaus, Bernhard, and Jelle Visser. 2000. *The Societies of Europe: Trade Unions in Western Europe since 1945.* London: Palgrave Macmillan.

Eckholm, Erik. 2014. "Access to Abortion Falling as States Pass Restrictions." *New York Times,* January 14, A1.

Edsall, Thomas Byrne. 1984. *The New Politics of Inequality.* New York: W. W. Norton.

Edsall, Thomas Byrne, and Mary D. Edsall. 1991. *Chain Reaction: The Impact of Race, Rights, and Taxes on American Politics.* New York: W. W. Norton.

Edwards, Mickey. 2013. "What Is the Common Good? The Case for Transcending Partisanship." *Daedalus* 142: 84–94.

Eidlin, Barry. 2013. "Class vs. Special Interest: Labor Regimes and Union Strength in the U.S. and Canada, 1911–2011." Unpublished paper.

Ellwood, Robert S. 1994. *The Sixties Spiritual Awakening: American Religion Moving from Modern to Postmodern.* New Brunswick, NJ: Rutgers University Press.

Evans, John H. 2003. "Have Americans' Attitudes Become More Polarized? An Update." *Social Science Quarterly* 84: 71–90.

Farris, Scott. 2012. *Almost President: The Men Who Lost the Race but Changed the Nation.* Guilford, CT: Globe Pequot Press.

Feinstein, Brian D., and Eric Schickler. 2008. "Platforms and Partners: The Civil Rights Realignment Reconsidered." *Studies in American Political Development* 22: 1–31.

Findlay, James F. Jr. 1993. *Church People in the Struggle: The National Council of Churches and the Black Freedom Struggle, 1950–1970.* New York: Oxford University Press.

Fiorina, Morris P. 1999. "Whatever Happened to the Median Voter?" Paper presented at the MIT Conference on Parties and Congress, October 1999.

Fiorina, Morris P., and Samuel J. Abrams. 2008. "Political Polarization in the American Public." *Annual Review of Political Science* 11: 563–88.

Fiorina, Morris P., Samuel J. Abrams, and Jeremy C. Pope. 2005. *Culture War? The Myth of a Polarized America.* New York: Pearson Longman.

Fiorina, Morris P., and M. Levendusky. 2006. "Disconnected: The Political Class versusthe People." Pp. 49–71 in Pietro S. Nivola and David W. (eds.), *Red and Blue Nation? Volume I: Characteristics and Causes of America's Polarized Politics.* Washington, DC/Stanford, CA: Brookings Institute Press and Stanford University Press.

Flacks, Richard. 1971. *Youth and Social Change.* Chicago: Markham.

Flippen, J. Brooks. 2011. *Jimmy Carter, the Politics of Family, and the Rise of the Religious Right.* Athens: University of Georgia Press.

Francia, P. L., J. C. Green, P. S. Herrnson, L. W. Powell, and C. Wilcox. 2003. *The Financiers of Presidential Elections.* New York: Columbia University Press.

Galbraith, James K. 1988. "The Grammar of Political Economy." Pp. 221–39 in Arjo Klamer, Dierdre N. McCloskey, and Robert M. Solow (eds.), *The Consequences of Economic Rhetoric.* New York: Oxford University Press.

Galea, Sandro, Melissa Tracy, Katherine J. Hoggatt, Charles DiMaggio, and Adam Karpati. 2011. "Estimated Deaths Attributable to Social Factors in the United States." *American Journal of Public Health* 101: 1456–65.

Ganz, Marshall. 2000. "Resources and Resourcefulness: Strategic Capacity in the Unionization of California Agriculture, 1959–66." *American Journal of Sociology* 105: 1003–62.

Ganz, Marshall. 2009. *Why David Sometimes Wins.* New York: Oxford University Press.

Garrow, David J. 1986. *Bearing the Cross: Martin Luther King, Jr., and the Southern Christian Leadership Conference.* New York: William Morrow.

Garrow, David J. 1998. *Liberty and Sexuality: The Right to Privacy and the Making of Roe v. Wade.* Berkeley: University of California Press.

Gerber, Elisabeth R., and Rebecca B. Morton. 1998. "Primary Election Systems and Representation." *Journal of Law, Economics and Organization* 14: 304–24.

Gilens, Martin. 2005. "Inequality and Democratic Responsiveness." *Public Opinion Quarterly* 69: 778–96.

Ginsberg, Benjamin, and Martin Shefter. 1999. *Politics by Other Means: Politicians, Prosecutors, and the Press from Watergate to Whitewater* (rev. ed.). New York: W. W. Norton.

Glad, Betty. 1980. *Jimmy Carter: In Search of the Great White House.* New York: W. W. Norton.

Golden, M., Lange, P., & Wallerstein, M. 2002. Union Centralization among Advanced Industrial Societies: An Empirical Study. Dataset available at http://www.shelley. polisci. ucla. edu/data.

Goldin, Claudia D., and Lawrence F. Katz. 2008. *The Race between Education and Technology.* Cambridge, MA: Harvard University Press/Belknap Press.

Goldman, Peter. 1970. *Report from Black America.* New York: Simon and Schuster.

Goldstone, Jack A. 1991. *Revolution and Rebellion in the Early Modern World.* Berkeley: University of California Press.

Gourevitch, Philip. 2012. "Republican vs. Republican." *The New Yorker,* September 3, pp. 17–18.

Hacker, Andrew. 2012. "We're More Unequal Than You Think." *New York Review* 59(3): 34–36.

Hacker, Jacob S., and Paul Pierson. 2010. *Winner-Take-All Politics*. New York: Simon and Schuster.

Hacker, Jacob S., and Paul Pierson. 2005. *Off Center: The Republican Revolution and the Erosion of American Democracy*. New Haven, CT: Yale University Press.

Hall, Jacquelyn Dowd. 2005. "The Long Civil Rights Movement and the Political Uses of the Past." *Journal of American History* (91.4): 1233–63.

Hall, Richard, and Alan V. Deardorff. 2006. "Lobbying as Legislative Subsidy." *American Political Science Review* 100: 69.

Harding, Susan Friend. 2000. *The Book of Jerry Falwell: Fundamentalist Language and Politics*. Princeton, NJ: Princeton University Press.

Harris, David. 1982. *Dreams Die Hard*. New York: St. Martins.

Harwood, John. 2013. "Behind the Roar of Political Debates, Whispers of Race Persist." *New York Times*, October 31, p. A17.

Hayden, Casey. 2000. "Fields of Blue." Pp. 333–75 in Constance Curry et al. (eds.), *Deep in Our Hearts: Nine White Women in the Freedom Movement*. Athens: University of Georgia Press.

Heaney, Michael T., and Fabio Rojas. 2007. "Partisans, Nonpartisans, and the Antiwar Movement in the United States." *American Politics Research* 35: 431–64.

Heaney, Michael T., and Fabio Rojas. 2012. *Party in the Street: The Antiwar Movement and the Democratic Party after 9/11*.

Hetherington, Marc J. 2001. "Resurgent Mass Partisanship: The Role of Elite Polarization." *American Political Science Review* 95: 619–31.

Hetherington, Marc J. 2009. "Putting Polarization in Perspective." *British Journal of Political Science* 39: 413–48.

Hetherington, Marc J., and Jonathan D. Weiler. 2009. *Authoritarianism and Polarization in American Politics*. New York: Cambridge University Press.

Hicks, Alexander, and Joya Misra. 1993. "Political Resources and the Growth of Welfare in Affluent Capitalist Democracies, 1960–1982." *American Journal of Sociology* 99: 668–710.

Highton, B. 2011. "Prejudice Rivals Partisanship and Ideology When Explaining the 2008 Presidential Vote across the States." *PS: Political Science and Politics* 44: 530–35.

Hollings, Fritz. 2006. "Stop the Money Chase." *Washington Post*, February 19.

Holt, Len. 1965. *The Summer that Didn't End*. New York: William Morrow.

Hood, M. V., and Charles S. Bullock III. 2012. "Much Ado about Nothing? An Empirical Assessment of Georgia Voter Identification Statute." *State Politics and Policy Quarterly* 12: 394–414.

Hout, Michael, and Alexander Janus. 2011. "Educational Mobility in the United States since the 1930s." Pp. 165–86 in Greg J. Duncan and Richard J. Murnane (eds.), *Whither Opportunity? Rising Inequality, Schools, and Children's Life Chances*. New York: Russell Sage Foundation and Chicago: Spencer Foundation.

Howell, William, Scott Adler, Charles Cameron, and Charles Riemann. 2000. "Divided Government and the Legislative Productivity of Congress, 1945–1994." *Legislative Studies Quarterly* 25: 285–312.

Hubbard, Howard. 1968. "Five Long Hot Summers and How They Grew." *Public Interest* 12: 3–24.

Huffington, Arianna. 2010. *Third World America*. New York: Crown.

Hulsether, Mark. 1999. *Building a Protestant Left: "Christianity and Crisis" Magazine, 1941–1993*. Knoxville: University of Tennessee Press.

Hutchings, V. L. 2010. "Change or More of the Same? Evaluating Racial Attitudes in the Obama Era." *Public Opinion Quarterly* 73: 917–42.

Jackson, Thomas F. 2007. *From Civil Rights to Human Rights: Martin Luther King, Jr., and the Struggle for Economic Justice*. Philadelphia: University of Pennsylvania Press.

Jenkins, J. Craig. 1985. *The Politics of Insurgency: The Farm Worker Movement in the 1960s*. New York: Columbia University Press.

Jenkins, J. Craig, and Charles Perrow. 1977. "Insurgency of the Powerless: Farm Worker Movements (1946–1972)." *American Sociological Review* 42: 249–68.

Jenkins, Philip. 2006. *Decade of Nightmares: The End of the Sixties and the Making of Eighties America*. New York: Oxford University Press.

Johnson, Charles S. 1941. *Growing Up in the Black Belt*. Washington, DC: American Council on Education.

Jones, Landon. 1980. *Great Expectations*. New York: Ballantine Books.

Jones, Rachel K., and Kathryn Kooistra. 2011. "Abortion Incidence and Access to Services in the United States, 2008." *Perspectives on Sexual and Reproductive Health* 43: 41–50.

Kabaservice, Geoffrey. 2012. *Rule and Ruin*. New York: Oxford University Press.

Kaiser, Robert. 2009. *So Damn Much Money*. New York: Alfred A. Knopf.

Kanthak, Kristin, and Rebecca Morton. 2001. "The Effects of Primary Systems on Congressional Elections." In Peter Galderisi and M. Lyons (eds.), *Congressional Primaries and the Politics of Representation*. Lanham, MD: Rowman and Littlefield.

Katznelson, Ira. 2005. *When Affirmative Action Was White*. New York: W. W. Norton. Company.

Kelley, Robin D. G. 1990. *Hammer and Hoe: Alabama Communists during the Great Depression*. Chapel Hill: University of North Carolina Press.

Killian, Lewis M. 1975. *The Impossible Revolution, Phase II: Black Power and the American Dream*. New York: Random House.

King, David C. 1997. "The Polarization of American Parties and Mistrust of Government." In Joseph S. Nye Jr., Philip D. Zelikow, and David C. King (eds.), *Why People Don't Trust Government*. Cambridge, MA: Harvard University Press.

King, Martin Luther, Jr. 1963. *Why We Can't Wait*. New York: Harper and Row.

Kingdon, John W. 1984. *Agendas, Alternatives and Public Policies*. Boston: Little, Brown.

Kleidman, Robert. 1993. *Organizing for Peace: Neutrality, the Test Ban, and the Freeze*. Syracuse, NY: Syracuse University Press.

Klein, Ezra. 2012. "Block Obama." *New York Review of Books,* September 27, pp. 52–54.

Korstad, Robert Rodgers. 2003. *Civil Rights Unionism*. Chapel Hill: University of North Carolina Press.

Krieger, Nancy, David H. Rehkopf, Jarvis T. Chen, Pamela D. Waterman, Enrico Marcelli, and Malinda Kennedy. 2008. "The Fall and Rise of US Inequities in Premature Mortality: 1960–2002." *PLoS Medicine* 5: 227–41.

Krieger, Nancy, D. R. Williams, and N. E. Moss. 1997. "Measuring Social Class in U.S. Public Health Research: Concepts, Methodologies, and Guidelines." *Annual Review of Public Health* 18: 341–78.

Lawson, Steven F. 1976. *Black Ballots: Voting Rights in the South, 1944–1969*. New York: Columbia University Press.

Layton, Azza Salama. 2000. *International Politics and Civil Rights Policies in the United States, 1941–1960*. New York: Cambridge University Press.

Leach, Jim. 2013. "*Citizens United*: Robbing America of Its Democratic Idealism." *Daedalus* 142: 95–101.

Lepore, Jill. 2013. "Long Division: Measuring the Polarization of American Politics." *The New Yorker,* December 2, pp. 75–79.

Lesch, H. 2004. "Trade Union Density in International Comparison." In *CESifo Forum* 4: 12–18. Munich: Ifo Institute for Economic Research, University of Munich.

Lessig, Lawrence. 2011. *Republic Lost: How Money Corrupts Congress—and a Plan to Stop It*. New York: Twelve.

Leuchtenburg, William E. 2005. *The White House Looks South*. Baton Rouge: Louisiana State University.

Lewis, David L. 1978. *King: A Biography* (2nd ed.). Urbana: University of Illinois Press.

Lizza, Ryan. 2012. "The Obama Memos." *The New Yorker,* January 30.

Lo, Clarence Y. H. 1990. *Small Property versus Big Government: Social Origins of the Property Tax Revolt*. Berkeley: University of California Press.

Logevall, Fredik. 2012. *Embers of War: The Fall of an Empire and the Making of America's Vietnam*. New York: Random House.

Lomax, Louis E. 1962. *The Negro Revolt*. New York: Harper and Row.

Lubell, Samuel. 1964. *White and Black, Test of a Nation*. New York: Harper and Row.

Makinson, Larry. 2003. "Speaking Freely." Center for Responsive Politics.

Mann, Thomas E., and Norman J. Ornstein. 2012. *It's Even Worse Than It Looks: How the American Constitutional System Collided with the New Politics of Extremism*. New York: Basic Books.

Mann, Thomas E., and Norman J. Ornstein. 2013. "Finding the Common Good in an Era of Dysfunctional Governance." *Daedalus* 142: 15–24.

Marley, David John. 2007. *Pat Robertson: An American Life*. New York: Rowman and Littlefield.

Martin, Issac William. 2013. *Rich People's Movements: Grassroots Campaigns to Untax the One Percent.* New York: Oxford University Press.

Martin, Jonathan, Jim Rutenberg, and Jeremy W. Peters. 2013. "Fiscal Crisis Sounds the Charge in G.O.P.'s 'Civil War'". *New York Times,* October 20, 2013.

Marx, Gary T. 1971. "Religion: Opiate or Inspiration of Civil Rights Militancy among Negroes?" Pp. 161–71 in Gary T. Marx (ed.), *Racial Conflict.* Boston: Little, Brown.

Mayer, Susan E. 2001. "How Did the Increase in Economic Inequality between 1970 and 1990 Affect Children's Educational Attainment?" *American Journal of Sociology* 107: 1–32.

Mayhew, David R. 1991. *Divided We Govern: Party Control, Lawmaking, and Investigations, 1946–1990.* New Haven, CT: Yale University Press.

Mays, Benjamin and Joseph W. Nicholson. 1969. *The Negro's Church.* New York: Arno Press and the New York Times.

McAdam, Doug. 1982. *Political Process and the Development of Black Insurgency, 1930–1970.* Chicago: University of Chicago Press.

McAdam, Doug. 1983. "Tactical Innovation and the Pace of Insurgency." *American Sociological Review* 48: 735–54.

McAdam, Doug. 1988. *Freedom Summer.* New York: Oxford University Press.

McAdam, Doug. 1989. "The Biographical Consequences of Activism." *American Sociological Review* 54: 744–60.

McAdam, Doug. 1999a. *Political Process and the Development of Black Insurgency* (2nd ed.). Chicago: University of Chicago Press.

McAdam, Doug. 1999b. "The Biographical Impact of Activism." Pp. 117–46 in Marco Giugni, Doug McAdam, and Charles Tilly (eds.), *How Social Movements Matter.* Minneapolis: University of Minnesota Press.

McAdam, Doug. 2009. "The U.S. Civil Rights Movement: Power from Below and Above, 1945–1970." Pp. 58–74 in Adam Roberts and Timothy Garton Ash (eds.), *Civil Resistance and Power Politics.* Oxford: Oxford University Press.

McAdam, Doug, and Ronnelle Paulsen. 1993. "Social Ties and Recruitment: Toward a Specification of the Relationship." *American Journal of Sociology* 99: 640–67.

McAdam, Doug, and Sidney Tarrow. 2013. "Social Movements and Elections: Toward a Broader Understanding of the Political Context of Contention." and Contentious Politics: Building Conceptual Bridges." Pp. 325–246 in Jacquelien Van Stekelenburg, Conny M. Roggeband, and Bert Klandermans (eds.), *The Future of Social Movement Research.* Minneapolis: University of Minnesota Press.

McAllister, Ted V. 2003. "Reagan and the Transformation of American Conservatism." Pp. 40–60 in W. Elliot Brownlee and Hugh Davis Graham (eds.), *The Reagan Presidency: Pragmatic Conservatism and Its Legacies.* Lawrence: University Press of Kansas.

McCartin, Joseph. 2011. *Collision Course: Ronald Reagan, the Air Traffic Controllers, and the Strike that Changed America.* New York: Oxford University Press.

McCarty, Nolan. 2007. "The Policy Consequences of Political Polarization." Pp. 223–55 in Paul Pierson and Theda Skocpol (eds.), *The Transformation of American Politics.* Princeton, NJ: Princeton University Press.

McCarty, Nolan, Keith T. Poole, and Howard Rosenthal. 2006. *Polarized America.* Cambridge, MA: MIT Press.

McCullough, David. 1992. *Truman.* New York: Simon and Schuster.

McGhee, Erin. 2010. "Open Primaries." *At Issue.* Public Policy Institute of California, February.

McGirr, Lisa. 2001. *Suburban Warriors: The Origins of the New American Right.* Princeton, NJ:. Princeton University Press.

McVeigh, Rory. 2009. *The Rise of the Ku Klux Klan: Right-Wing Movements and National Politics.* Minneapolis: University of Minnesota Press.

Medoff, Marsall H. 2009. "The Relationship between State Abortion Policies and Abortion Providers." *Gender Issues* 26: 224–37.

Mehta, Seema. 2012. "Rick Santorum Invokes Ronald Reagan at Jelly Belly Factory in California." *Los Angeles Times,* March 29.

Mettler, Suzanne. 2005. *Soldiers to Citizens: The GI Bill and the Making of the Greatest Generation.* New York: Oxford University Press.

Michels, Robert. 1962. *Political Parties.* New York: Collier Books.

Middendorf, J. William, II. 2006. *A Glorious Disaster: Barry Goldwater's Presidential Campaign and the Origins of the Conservative Movement.* New York: Basic Books.

Miller, A. H., and M. P. Wattenberg. 1984. "Politics from the Pulpit: Religiosity and the 1980 Elections." *Public Opinion Quarterly* 48: 302–17.

Mokdad, Ali H., James S. Marks, Donna F. Stroup, and Julie L. Gerberding. 2004. "Actual Causes of Death in the United States, 2000." *Journal of the American Medical Association* 291: 1238–45.

Monheit, A. C., and J. P. Vistnes. 2000. "Race/Ethnicity and Health Insurance Status: 1987 and 1996." *Medical Care Research and Review* 57: 11–35.

Myrdal, Gunnar. 1944. *An American Dilemma.* New York: Harper and Row.

Myrdal, Gunnar. 1970. "America Again at the Crossroads." Pp. 13–46 in Richard P. Young (ed.), *Roots of Rebellion: The Evolution of Black Politics and Protest since World War II.* New York: Harper and Row.

Neustadtl, Alan, and Dan Clawson. 1988. "Corporate Political Giving: Does Ideology Unify Business Political Behavior?" *American Sociological Review* 53: 172–90.

Niemi, Richard G., Herbert F. Weisberg, and David C. Kimball (eds.). 2011. *Controversies in Voting Behavior.* Washington, DC: CQ Press.

Nixon, Richard. 1978. *The Memoirs of Richard Nixon.* New York: Grosset and Dunlap.

O' Brien, David M. 2003. "Federal Judgeships in Retrospect." Pp. 327–54 in W. Elliot Brownlee and Hugh Davis Graham (eds.), *The Reagan Presidency: Pragmatic Conservatism and Its Legacies.* Lawrence: University Press of Kansas.

Oldfield, Duane Murray. 1996. *The Right and the Righteous: The Christian Right Confronts the Republican Party.* New York: Rowman and Littlefield.

Ornstein, Norman J., and Thomas E. Mann (eds.). 2000. *The Permanent Campaign and Its Future.* Washington, DC: AEI Press.

Pappas, Gregory, Susan Queen, Wilbur Hadden, and Gail Fischer. 1993. "The Increasing Disparity in Mortality between Socioeconomic Groups in the United States, 1960 and 1986." *New England Journal of Medicine* 329: 103–109.

Parker, Christopher S., and Matt A. Barreto. 2013. *Change They Can't Believe In: The Tea Party and Reactionary Politics in Contemporary America.* Princeton, NJ: Princeton University Press.

Pasek, Josh, Jon A. Krosnick, and Trevor Thompson. 2012. "The Impact of Anti-Black Racism on Approval of Barack Obama's Job Performance and on Voting in the 2012 Presidential Election." Unpublished paper.

Pasek, Josh, A. Tahk, Y. Lelkes, J. A. Krosnick, B. K. Payne, O. Akhtar, and T. Thompson. 2009. "Determinants of Turnout and Candidate Choice in the 2008 U.S. Presidential Election: Illuminating the Impact of Racial Prejudice and Other Considerations." *Public Opinion Quarterly* 73: 943–94.

Patterson, James T. 2003. "Afterword: The Legacies of the Reagan Years." Pp. 355–75 in W. Elliot Brownlee and Hugh Davis Graham (eds.), *The Reagan Presidency: Pragmatic Conservatism and Its Legacies.* Lawrence: University Press of Kansas.

Payne, Charles. 1996. *I've Got the Light of Freedom.* Berkeley: University of California Press.

Peters, Gerhard. 1999–2012. "Federal Budget Receipts and Outlays." John T. Woolley and Gerhard Peters (eds.), *The American Presidency Project.* Santa Barbara: University of California.

Peters, Jeremy W., and Jonathan Weisman. 2013. "Senate Action on Health Law Moves to Brink of Shutdown." *New York Times*, September 29, 2013.

Peterson, George E. 1982. "The State and Local Sector." In J. L. Palmer and I. V. Sawhill (eds.), *The Reagan Experiment.* Washington, DC: Urban Institute Press.

Phillips-Fein, Kim. 2009. *Invisible Hands: The Making of the Conservative Movement from the New Deal to Reagan.* New York: W. W. Norton.

Phillips, Kevin. 1969. *The Emerging Republican Majority.* New Rochelle, NY: Arlington House.

Piketty, Thomas, and Emmanuel Saez. 2003. "Income Inequality in the United States, 1913–1998. *Quarterly Journal of Economics* 118: 1–39.

Piston S. 2010. "How Explicit Racial Prejudice Hurt Obama in the 2008 Election." *Political Behavior* 32: 431–51.

Pitts, Michael J. 2013. "Photo ID, Provisional Balloting and Indiana's 2012 Primary Election." *University of Richmond Law Review* 47: 939–57.

Pitts, Michael J., and Matthew D. Neumann. 2009. "Documenting Disfranchisement: Voter Identification during Indiana's 2008 General Election." *Journal of Law and Politics* 25.

Piven, Frances Fox, and Richard A. Cloward. 1979. *Poor People's Movements.* New York: Vintage Books.

Polsby, Nelson W. 1983. *Consequences of Party Reform.* New York: Oxford University Press.

Poole, Keith T., and Howard Rosenthal. 2007. *Ideology and Congress*. New Brunswick, NJ: Transaction.

Prasad, Monica. 2006. *The Politics of Free Markets: The Rise of Neoliberal Economic Policies Britain, France, Germany, and the United States*. Chicago: University of Chicago Press.

Prasad, Monica. 2012. "The Popular Origins of Neoliberalism in the Reagan Tax Cut of 1981." *Journal of Policy History* 24: 351–83.

Pratto, Felicia, Jim Sidanius, Lisa M. Stallworth, and Bertram F. Malle. 1994. "Social Dominance Orientation: A Personality Variable Predicting Social and Political Attitudes." *Journal of Personality and Social Psychology* 45: 741–63.

Raines, Howell. 1983. *My Soul Is Rested*. New York: Penguin Books.

Raudenbush, Stephen W., Marshall Jean, and Emily Art. 2011. "Year-by-Year and Cumulative Impacts of Attending a High-Mobility Elementary School on Children's Mathematics Achievement in Chicago, 1995 to 2005." Pp. 359–76 in Greg J. Duncan and Richard J. Murnane (eds.), *Whither Opportunity? Rising Inequality, Schools, and Children's Life Chances*. New York: Russell Sage Foundation and Chicago: Spencer Foundation.

Reardon, Sean F. 2011. "The Widening Academic Achievement Gap between the Richand the Poor: New Evidence and Possible Explanations." Pp. 91–115 in Greg J. Duncan and Richard J. Murnane (eds.), *Whither Opportunity? Rising Inequality, Schools, and Children's Life Chances*. New York: Russell Sage Foundation and Chicago: Spencer Foundation.

Reardon, Sean F., Rachel Baker, and Daniel Klasik. 2012. "Race, Income, and Enrollment Patterns in Highly Selective Colleges, 1982–2004. Stanford, CA: Center for Education Policy Analysis, Stanford University.

Reay, Michael J. 2012. "The Flexible Unity of Economics." *American Journal of Sociology* 118: 45–87.

Reddick, L. D. 1959. *Crusader without Violence: A Biography of Martin Luther King, Jr.* New York: Harper and Brothers.

Rhomberg, Chris. 2004. *No There There: Race, Class, and Community in Oakland*. Berkeley: University of California Press.

Roberts, Cokie, and Steven Roberts. 1998. "GOP Strategy: Make Clinton a Bad PosterBoy." *San Jose Mercury News*, September 28, p. 6B.

Romaine, Anne Cook. 1970. "The Mississippi Freedom Democratic Party through August, 1964." Masters thesis, University of Virginia.

Rossinow, Doug. 1994. "The Break-Through to New Life: Christianity and the Emergence of the New Left in Austin, Texas, 1956–1964." *American Quarterly* 46: 309–40.

Rottinghaus, Brandon. 2003. "Incarceration and Enfranchisement: International Practices, Impact and Recommendations for Reform." *International Foundation for Election Systems*, Washington, DC.

Saez, Emmanuel. 2008. "Striking It Richer: The Evolution of Top Incomes in the United States." *Pathways Magazine* (Stanford Center for the Study of Poverty and Inequality), Winter, pp. 6–7.

Sale, Kirkpatrick. 1973. *SDS*. New York: Random House.

Saletan, William. 2004. *Bearing Right: How Conservatives Won the Abortion War*. Berkeley: University of California Press.

Schaffner, B.F. 2011. "Racial Salience and the Obama Vote." *Political Psychology* 32: 963–88.

Scher, Abby.1996. "Cold War on the Home Front: Middle Class Women's Politics in the Age of McCarthy." Ph.D. Dissertation, Department of Sociology, The New School.

Schickler, Eric, Kathryn Pearson, and Brian D. Feinstein. 2010. "Congressional Parties and Civil Rights Politics from 1933 to 1972." *Journal of Politics* 72: 672–89.

Schram, Martin. 1995. "Speaking Freely." Center for Responsive Government.

Schroeder, Patricia. 2004. "Nothing Stuck to 'Teflon' President." *USA Today*, June 6.

Sears, David O. and Jack Citrin. 1982. *Tax Revolt: Something for Nothing in California*. Cambridge, MA: Harvard University Press.

Shafer, Byron E. 1983. *Quiet Revolution: The Struggle for the Democratic Party and the Shaping of Post-reform Politics*. New York: Russell Sage Foundation.

Shafer, Byron E. 1988. *Bifurcated Politics: Evolution and Reform in the National Party Convention*. Cambridge, MA: Harvard University Press.

Shanahan, Michael, and Miles Benson. 1995. "Moderates Can't Stand Heat, Leave Kitchen." *Cleveland Plain Dealer*, December 14, 1995, p. 22A.

Shepsle, Kenneth A., and Mark S. Bonchek. 1997. *Analyzing Politics: Rationality, Behavior, and Institutions*. New York: W. W. Norton.

Shi, L., et al. 1999. "Income Inequality, Primary Care, and Health Indicators." *Journal of Family Practice* 48: 275–84.

Singh, Gopal K., and Michael D. Kogan. 2007a. "Widening Socioeconomic Disparities in U.S. Childhood Mortality, 1969–2000." *American Journal of Public Health* 97: 1658–65.

Singh, Gopal K., and Michael D. Kogan. 2007b. "Persistent Socioeconomic Disparities in Infant, Neonatal, and Postneonatal Mortality Rates in the United States, 1969–2001." *Pediatrics* 119.

Singh, Gopal K., and M. Siahpush. 2006. "Widening Socioeconomic Inequalities in U.S. Life Expectancy, 1980–2000." *International Journal of Epidemiology* 35: 969–79.

Skocpol, Theda, and Vanessa Williamson. 2012. *The Tea Party and the Remaking of Republican Conservatism*. New York: Oxford University Press.

Skrentny, John David. 1998. "The Effect of the Cold War on African-American Civil Rights: American and the World Audience, 1945–1968." *Theory and Society* 27: 237–85.

Stern, Philip M. 1992. *Still the Best Congress Money Can Buy*. Washington, DC: Regnery.

Stockman, David. 1986. *The Triumph of Politics: How the Reagan Revolution Failed*. New York: Harper and Row.

Stone, W. J., A. Abromowitz, and R. Rapoport. 1990. "Sex and the Caucus Participant: The Gender Gap in 1984 and 1988." *American Journal of Political Science* 34: 725–40.

Su, Tie-ting, Alan Neustadtl, and Dan Clawson. 1995. "Business and the Conservative Shift: Corporate PAC Contributions, 1976–1986." *Social Science Quarterly* 76: 20–40.

Sullivan, Sean, and Scott Clement. 2013. "Why the GOP's Youth Vote Problem = President Obama." *Washington Post*, December 10).

Susskind, Ron. 2004. *The Price of Loyalty: George W. Bush, the White House, and the Education of Paul O'Neill.* New York: Simon and Schuster.

Tarrow, Sidney. 2011[1994, 1998]. *Power in Movement* (3nd ed.). New York: Cambridge University Press.

Tesler, Michael, and David O. Sears. 2010. "President Obama and the Growing Polarization of Partisan Attachments by Racial Attitudes and Race." Paper Presented at the annual meeting of the American Political Science Association in Washington, DC, September 2010.

Thrasher, Sue. 2000. "Circle of Trust." Pp. 207–51 in Constance Curry et al., *Deep in Our Hearts: Nine White Women in the Freedom Movement.* Athens: University of Georgia Press.

Tomasky, Michael. 2013. "Can Obama Reverse the Republican Surge?" *The New York Review of Books*, December 5, pp. 8–12.

Tonry, Michael. 1995. *Malign Neglect: Race, Crime, and Punishment in America.* New York: Oxford University Press.

Toobin, Jeffrey. 2013. "Casting Votes." *The New Yorker*, January 14, pp. 17–18.

Tynes, Sheryl R. 1996. *Turning Points in Social Security: From "Crucial Hoax" to "Sacred Entitlement."* Palo, Alto, CA: Stanford University Press.

Uggen, Christopher, and Jeff Manza. 2002. "Democratic Contraction? Political Consequences of Felon Disenfranchisement in the United States." *American Sociological Review* 67: 777–803.

US Department of Health and Human Services. 2000. *Healthy People 2010.* Washington, DC: Gobernment Printing Office. GPO.

Visser, Jelle. 2006. "Union Membership Statistics in 24 Countries." *Monthly Labor Review*, January.

Walker, Jack. 1988. "The Primary Game." *Wilson Quarterly* 12: 64–77.

Watters, Pat. 1971. *Down to Now: Reflections on the Southern Civil Rights Movement.* New York: Pantheon Books.

Wattson, Peter S. "1990s Supreme Court Redistricting Decisions." Unpublished report presented to the Minnesota State Senate.

Weisman, Jonathon, and Ashley Parker. 2014. "House Approves Higher Debt Limit Without Condition." *New York Times*, February 12, p. 1.

Western, Bruce. 1997. *Between Class and Market: Postwar Unionization in the Capitalist Democracies.* Princeton, NJ: Princeton University Press.

White, Theodore H. 1965. *The Making of the President, 1964.* New York: Atheneum.

Wilcox, Clyde. 1992. *God's Warriors: The Christian Right in 20th Century America.* Baltimore, MD: Johns Hopkins University Press.

Williams, D. R., S. A. Mohammed, J. Leavell, and C. Collins. 2010. "Race, Socioeconomic Status, and Health: Complexities, Ongoing Challenges, and Research Opportunities." *Annals of the New York Academy Of Sciences*, 1186: 69–101.

Williams, Daniel K. 2010. *God's Own Party: The Making of the Christian Right.* New York: Oxford University Press.

Woodward, C. Vann. 1966. *The Strange Career of Jim Crow.* London: Oxford University Press.

Wright, Gerald C., and Brian F. Schaffner. 2002. "The Influence of Party: Evidence from the State Legislatures." *American Political Science Review* 96: 367–79.

Zinn, Howard, and Anthony Arnove. 2009. *Voices of a People's History of the United States* (2nd ed.). New York: Seven Stories Press.

INDEX